PENGUIN ENGLISH POETS

GENERAL EDITOR: CHRISTOPHER RICKS

William Wordsworth
The Prelude

EDITED BY J. C. MAXWELL

William Wordsworth
The Prelude
A Parallel Text

EDITED BY J. C. MAXWELL

PENGUIN BOOKS

Penguin Books Ltd, Harmondsworth,
Middlesex, England
Penguin Books, 625 Madison Avenue,
New York, New York 10022, U.S.A.
Penguin Books Australia Ltd,
Ringwood, Victoria, Australia
Penguin Books Canada Ltd, 2801 John Street,
Markham, Ontario, Canada L3R 1B4
Penguin Books (N.Z.) Ltd,
182–190 Wairau Road, Auckland 10,
New Zealand

First published in Penguin Education 1971
Reprinted with corrections 1972
Reprinted 1975, 1976, 1978

Made and printed in Great Britain by
Hazell Watson & Viney Ltd, Aylesbury, Bucks
Set in Monotype Ehrhardt

Contents

CONTENTS

Table of Dates

1770   *7 April* William Wordsworth born at Cockermouth, Cumberland, second son of John Wordsworth (1741–83), law-agent to Sir James Lowther, later Earl of Lonsdale.
16 August Mary Hutchinson (d. 1859), wife of Wordsworth, born at Penrith, Cumberland.

1771   *25 December* Dorothy Wordsworth (d. 1855), sister of Wordsworth, born at Cockermouth.

1773   From this year, Wordsworth and other members of the family spend long periods with his maternal grandparents, the Cooksons, at Penrith.

1776   *April–October* Attends school of the Reverend Joseph Gilbanks at Cockermouth.

1778   *c. 8 March* Ann Wordsworth, Wordsworth's mother, dies at Penrith.

1779   *May* Enters Hawkshead Grammar School.

1782   The Reverend William Taylor (1754–86) becomes headmaster of Hawkshead Grammar School.

1783   Hugh and Ann Tyson, with whom Wordsworth boards, move from Hawkshead village to Colthouse, half a mile east.
30 December John Wordsworth, Wordsworth's father, dies at Cockermouth.

1785   *June* Earliest surviving poem, *Lines Written as a School Exercise at Hawkshead*.

1786   *12 June* The Reverend William Taylor dies at Hawkshead.

1787   *March* Publication in *European Magazine*, signed 'Axiologus', of first published poem, *Sonnet: On Seeing Miss Helen Maria Williams Weep at a Tale of Distress*. First substantial poem, *The Vale of Esthwaite*, belongs principally to this year.

         5 July Admitted sizar at St John's College, Cambridge; takes up residence about 30 October.

         c. 15 December Maternal grandfather, William Cookson, dies at Penrith.

1788–9 Composes most of *An Evening Walk* (1793).

1790   *10 July–late October* Walking tour in France, Switzerland and Germany with Robert Jones, a Cambridge friend.

1791   *17 January* Examination for B.A. degree (conferred 21 January).

         January–late May Lives in London.

         May–early September Lives with Robert Jones at Plas-yn-Llan, Denbighshire, and tours North Wales.

         After short period in Cambridge and London, leaves for France on 26 November, reaching Paris on 30 November and Orleans on 6 December.

1792   Composes most of *Descriptive Sketches* (1793).

         Moves from Orleans to Blois about February.

         27 July Michel Beaupuy's regiment leaves Blois.

         September Wordsworth returns to Orleans.

         29 October Arrives in Paris.

         December Returns to London, where he lives till about June 1793.

         15 December His daughter, Anne-Caroline, by Marie-Anne (Annette) Vallon, born at Orleans.

1793   *29 January* *An Evening Walk* and *Descriptive Sketches* published.

         1 February France declares war on Britain. (Britain on France 11 February.)

         ? June Composes *A Letter to the Bishop of Llandaff* (published 1875). Spends about a month on the Isle of Wight.

August–late September Walking tour, from Salisbury to North Wales. Composes most of first version of *Salisbury Plain (Guilt and Sorrow)*.

Late September–early October Probably visits Paris, where he witnesses the execution of Gorsas (7 October), the first Girondist to be guillotined.

Mid-October–early 1794 In the north-west of England.

1794   *17 February* At Halifax, Yorkshire, with Dorothy. From then until January 1795 stays in the north-west, principally at Whitehaven, Keswick and Penrith, with Raisley Calvert.

1795   *? 9 January* Raisley Calvert dies at Penrith, leaving Wordsworth £900.

February–August Lives in London.

August Visits Bristol, where he stays until 26 September; meets Robert Southey, Samuel Taylor Coleridge and Joseph Cottle.

26 September Settles at Racedown, Dorset, with Dorothy, until 2 July 1797.

26 September–20 November Recasts *Salisbury Plain (Guilt and Sorrow)*.

1796   Probably begins *The Borderers* late this year.

1797   *? February* Completes *The Borderers*.

March–June First version of *The Ruined Cottage*.

June Coleridge (now at Nether Stowey) visits Racedown and hears *The Borderers* and *The Ruined Cottage* read.

c. 16 July Moves to Alfoxden House, where he stays until 25 June 1798.

November Plans for *Lyrical Ballads* laid.

November–December Visits London in the hope of getting *The Borderers* staged.

1798   *January–March* Writes much blank verse, some of it later incorporated in *The Prelude*, an expansion of *The Ruined Cottage*, and much of *Lyrical Ballads*.

April–May First version of *Peter Bell*.

1798 *10 July* Visits Tintern Abbey.
August Moves from Bristol to London.
September Publishes *Lyrical Ballads*, with Coleridge.
16 September Leaves for Germany with Dorothy and Coleridge.
6 October Arrives at Goslar where he stays until about 23 February 1799; begins *The Prelude*, Books I–II, completed 1799.

1799 *c. 1 May* Returns to England; at Sockburn-on-Tees till 17 December, with visit to Grasmere in November (preamble to *The Prelude*).
20 December Arrives with Dorothy at Dove Cottage, Grasmere.

1800 Composition of some poems in volume 2 of *Lyrical Ballads*.

1801 *c. 25 January* Publication of *Lyrical Ballads*, second edition of volume 1, first edition of volume 2, in two volumes (title-page 1800); reprinted 1802, 1805.

1802 Composes many of *Poems* (1807), including *Resolution and Independence*, and writes part of *Intimations of Immortality*.
August Visits Calais to see Annette Vallon and daughter Caroline.
4 October Marries Mary Hutchinson at Brompton, near Scarborough.
Lyrical Ballads, third edition.

1803 *18 June* Birth of first son, John.
15 August–25 September Tour in Scotland with Dorothy and (at first) Coleridge.

1804 *January* Resumes work on *The Prelude*.
February Composes *Ode to Duty*.
9 April Coleridge sails for Malta.
16 August Birth of daughter, Dora.

1805 *5 February* Brother, John Wordsworth, drowned in the wreck of the *Abergavenny*.

May   *The Prelude* completed.
Lyrical Ballads, fourth edition.

1806   *January*   Writes *The Waggoner*.
Late March–late May   Visits London.
15 June   Birth of second son, Thomas.
November–10 June 1807   Visits Coleorton, Leicestershire, staying at farm-house lent by Sir George Beaumont.

1807   *May*   *Poems in Two Volumes* published.
August   Return to Grasmere after visit to Halifax and Kirkstall (Leeds).
October–January 1808   Composes *The White Doe of Rylstone*.

1808   *February–April*   Visits London.
May   Moves to Allan Bank, Grasmere.
6 September   Birth of second daughter, Catherine.

1809   *May*   Publication of tract on *The Convention of Cintra*.
14 December (and 4 January 1810)   Publication of *A Reply to 'Mathetes'* in the *Friend*.

1810   *22 February*   *Essay on Epitaphs* published in the *Friend*.
April   *Description of the Scenery of the Lakes in the North of England* published as Introduction to Joseph Wilkinson's *Select Views in Cumberland, Westmorland and Lancashire*.
January–May   *The Excursion* continued.
11 May   Birth of third son, William.
Estrangement with Coleridge begins this autumn.

1811   *The Excursion* continued.

1812   *April–June*   Visit to London; reconciliation with Coleridge.
4 June   Death of daughter, Catherine.
1 December   Death of son, Thomas.
The Excursion continued.

1813   Appointed Distributor of Stamps for Westmorland in March.

1 May   Moves to Rydal Mount, near Ambleside.
The Excursion completed.

1814   *July–September*   Tour in Scotland.
August   The Excursion published.

1815   *March   Poems, including Lyrical Ballads* published in two
volumes.
May   The White Doe of Rylstone published.

1816   *May   Thanksgiving Ode* and *Letter to a Friend of Burns*
published.

1817   *November*   Visit to London, where he stays until 1818.

1818   Active in support of the Lonsdale interest at General
Election: *Two Addresses to the Freeholders of Westmorland*
published.

1819   *April   Peter Bell* published.
June   The Waggoner published.

1820   *May–December*   Tour with Dorothy to Oxford, Lambeth,
Switzerland, Italy, France, London, Cambridge, Cole-
orton.
*May   The River Duddon: A Series of Sonnets ; Vaudracour
and Julia, and Other Poems* published.
July   Publication of *Miscellaneous Poems*, in four volumes,
and the second edition of *The Excursion*.

1822   *March   Ecclesiastical Sketches* and *Memorials of a Tour on
the Continent, 1820* published.
*A Description of the Scenery of the Lakes in the North of
England* (see 1810), first published separately (new edition
1823).

1823   *February–June*   Visits to Coleorton Hall, London, Lee
Priory and Belgium.

1824   *April–May*   Visits to London, Cambridge and Coleorton
Hall.
August–October.   Tour of North Wales, including visit to
Robert Jones.

1825   *July*   Visit to Coleorton Hall.
        August   Visit to Lowther Castle.

1827   *May*   Publication of *Poetical Works* in five volumes, including *The Excursion*.

1828   *June*   Tour up the Rhine with Dora and Coleridge.
        Poetical Works in one volume published by Galignani in Paris.

1829   *August–September*   Tour in Ireland.

1830   *November*   Rides from Lancaster to Cambridge.
        December   Visit to London and Buxted, Sussex, where he stays until April 1831.

1831   *September–October*   Visit to Sir Walter Scott at Abbotsford, and to the Highlands.

1832   *June*   Visit to Moresby Rectory, near Whitehaven, where his son John is Rector.
        Poetical Works in four volumes published.
        Dorothy seriously ill throughout this year.

1833   *March*   Visit to Moresby Rectory (see 1832).
        July–August   Visit to Isle of Man, Staffa and Iona.

1834   *25 July*   Death of Coleridge.

1835   *January*   *Yarrow Revisited and Other Poems* published (reprinted 1836, 1839).
        February–April   Visit to London and Cambridge.
        A Description of the Scenery of the Lakes in the North of England (see 1810) enlarged and published as *A Guide through the District of the Lakes in the North of England* (reprinted 1842, 1843, 1846).
        23 June   Death of Sara Hutchinson, followed by complete mental collapse of Dorothy Wordsworth.

1836   *May–June*   Visit to London.
        Publication of volumes 1–2 of a six-volume *Poetical Works*.

1837   Publication of volumes 3–6 of a six-volume *Poetical Works* (reprinted 1839, 1840, 1841); in seven volumes with

13

Poems Chiefly of Early and Late Years as volume 7, 1842, 1843, 1845.
March–August Tour of France and Italy with Henry Crabb Robinson.
Poems published in one volume, Boston.

1838   *June* *Sonnets* published in one volume.
21 July D.C.L., University of Durham.

1839   *23 April* Open letter in *Morning Post* in support of Talfourd's Copyright Bill.
May–June Visit to London.
12 June D.C.L., University of Oxford.

1841   *April–July* Visit to Somerset (daughter Dora marries Edward Quillinan at Bath, 11 May), Wye Valley and London.

1842   *April* *Poems Chiefly of Early and Late Years* (including *The Borderers* and *Guilt and Sorrow*) published (also as volume 7 of *Poetical Works*).
July Resigns the post of Distributor of Stamps.
October Civil List pension of £300 conferred.

1843   *21 March* Death of Robert Southey.
April Succeeds Southey as Poet Laureate.

1845   *25 April* Attends Queen's Ball in London.
November *Poems* published in one volume (reprinted 1847, 1849).
September–October Visits Mrs Wordsworth's brother at Brinsop Court, Hereford, also York and Leeds.

1846   Publication of *Poetical Works* in seven volumes (reissued 1849).

1847   *April* Visits London.
9 July Death of daughter, Dora.
July *Ode on the Installation of . . . Prince Albert . . . As Chancellor . . . Cambridge* performed and published.

1849   Publication of volumes 1–2 of a six-volume *Poetical Works*.

1850   *23 April*   Dies at Rydal Mount.
        July   *The Prelude* published.
        Publication of volumes 3–6 of a six-volume *Poetical Works*
        (1849).

Introduction

Since the publication of Ernest de Selincourt's great edition in 1926, it has been customary to talk of the 1805 and the 1850 *Prelude*. These are, indeed, the first and the last version of the complete text of the poem, and it is these texts that are reproduced here. But if we are thinking in terms, not of revisions but of radically different forms of the whole poem, we must rather distinguish three versions; a two-book form completed by 1800, a proposed five-book version which Wordsworth had almost completed early in 1804, when he decided to expand it still further, and the full text as we have it both in 1805 and in 1850.

The Prelude was never so named by Wordsworth himself. The title-page of the final revision which he laid aside in 1839 for publication after his death still begins: 'Poem (Title not fixed upon)', and the 1850 title was suggested by the poet's widow. The title-page of MS B (1805–6) has 'Poem Title not yet fixed upon by William Wordsworth Addressed to S. T. Coleridge'. While he was at work on it, he and other members of his family referred to it in various ways: 'the poem to Coleridge', 'the poem on his own early life', and, in a letter to Sir George Beaumont, 25 December 1804, 'a Poem . . . on my earlier life or the growth of my own mind'. At the time of final revision, Wordsworth calls it in a letter to T. N. Talfourd, 11 April 1839, 'a long poem upon the formation of my own mind'.

All these descriptions belong to the time when the poem had already come to have a separate existence. But it was not originally so conceived, and before any of it was written in its present form we have references to the great unfinished poem of which both it and *The Excursion* were to be parts. This poem, *The Recluse*, is first referred to under that name in a letter of Wordsworth to James Losh, 11 March 1798, as 'a poem which I hope to make of

17

considerable utility', of which he has already written 1300 lines. A week earlier he had described it, without naming it, to another correspondent as 'a poem in which I contrive to convey most of the knowledge of which I am possessed. My object is to give pictures of Nature, Man, and Society.' Of the large body of blank verse he wrote about this time, some found its way into *The Prelude*, notably the episode of the Discharged Soldier (IV 363–504), the first form of which is found in a notebook (Alfoxden) of early 1798; much into Wordsworth's major completed work of this time, *The Ruined Cottage* (later called *The Pedlar*), which was published in Book I of *The Excursion*; some was never used. For the study of the origins of *The Prelude*, what is interesting is that a number of passages originally written about the Pedlar, the character who narrates the story of Margaret and the Ruined Cottage, were eventually transferred, as self-portraiture, to *The Prelude* (see, especially, notes on II 322–41, 416–34). This confirms both that the Pedlar is largely autobiographical, and that, at the time of writing, Wordsworth had no idea of composing a separate, overtly autobiographical poem.

The earliest piece of sustained composition that can reasonably be described as a version of *The Prelude* dates from the winter of 1798–9, spent in Germany. MS JJ contains a large part of Book I, and one important episode from a later book, 'There was a boy' (V 389–413). There is also, in a letter from Dorothy Wordsworth, a passage not in JJ, the skating scene of I 452–89. Moreover, JJ begins abruptly with the 'Was it for this' of I 271, and this formula is repeated several times later. Wordsworth must, therefore, already have had in mind a poem about his childhood, in which individual episodes were inserted in a framework.

The next stage comes with the decision to address the poem to Coleridge. This coincides with the beginning of work on a 'second part', opening, 'Friend of my heart and Genius', in a MS which cannot be exactly dated. However, in a letter of 12 October 1799, Coleridge enthusiastically greets the decision: 'O let it be the tail-piece of *The Recluse* for of nothing but *The Recluse* can I hear patiently. That it is to be addressed to me makes me more desirous that it should not be a poem of itself.' It sounds as if Coleridge had heard of this fairly recently, so the decision probably belongs to the summer of 1799. What can be described as the first version of *The Prelude*, containing the first two books (except for I 55–271, 'nothing back'), and a few passages from later books (V, VIII and XI), was probably complete by the end of 1799 and transcribed by October 1800.

At this point serious work on *The Prelude* seems to have halted for several years. There are a couple of references at the end of 1801 in Dorothy's *Journals*, one of them mentioning a 'third part', and one in January 1803. But substantially, the pause was as described by Wordsworth himself at VII 11.

Up to now, the poem had been relatively brief, about 960 lines, and could be regarded as no more than a 'tail-piece', in Coleridge's phrase, to the still-unwritten *Recluse*. When it was resumed in 1804, Wordsworth and his circle continued to use similar expressions – Dorothy in a letter of 13 February 1804 called it 'an appendix to *The Recluse*'; as late as 1814, Wordsworth in a rather misleading Preface to *The Excursion* described *The Prelude* as related to *The Recluse* in the same way as 'the Ante-chapel . . . to the body of a Gothic Church' – but it was now obvious that it was to be a substantial work on its own. Coleridge, it is true, still thought of it all as primarily part of *The Recluse*. On 14 October 1803, he wrote to Thomas Poole, rather prematurely, that Wordsworth had agreed to stop 'writing such a multitude of Small Poems', and would 'go on with *The Recluse* exclusively'. He did not in fact resume work until about January 1804, when he wrote to Francis Wrangham that he was 'engaged in a Poem on my own earlier life which will take five parts or books to complete, three of which are nearly finished'. This five-book *Prelude* was to consist of the first four books, the first three more or less as we have them, the fourth including parts of Books IV, V, XI and XIII, and a final book to begin (as the eventual Book XIII does) with the Snowdon episode.

The decision to expand the poem to what turned out to be more than twice its previous length was made quite suddenly in March 1804, between the 6th, when he described the five-book form, and the 29th, when Dorothy wrote to Coleridge that he had 'begun another part of the Poem addressed to you', including 'some very affecting lines' (VII 246–331). In Wordsworth's postscript to the same letter, he refers to a passage first found in the new (thirteen-book) version of Book V, and this is evidently what had been sent to Coleridge, to take with him to Malta, on 17 March. Since in this same postscript Wordsworth writes of starting again 'after a halt of near three weeks', the abandonment of the five-book plan must have followed close upon the letter of 6 March: indeed the intervening letter of 12 March, to William Sotheby, in which he writes of 'advancing rapidly in a Poetical Work', does not suggest one nearly completed, as the five-book *Prelude* would, by this time, have been.

Once this final version was embarked upon, its progress was rapid and smooth. On 29 April Wordsworth writes of being in the seventh book: he took a long rest during the summer (VII 18), but by 30 November had resumed it for long enough to have added 1600 to 1700 lines, and by 25 December, 'upwards of 2000'. At that time he expected to finish before next May. This estimate was not far out, in spite of the interruption caused by the tragic death of his brother John on 6 February 1805. He resumed work in April, and finished the poem late in May ('about a fortnight ago', he wrote to Sir George Beaumont on 3 June). The transcription by Dorothy Wordsworth and Sara Hutchinson of the MSS A and B was completed before 2 March 1806.

The subsequent revisions call for no more than brief mention. MS C in the hand of Wordsworth's assistant, John Carter, must be some time after 1813 (when Carter entered Wordsworth's service, at the age of 17) and probably not before 1816 (an insert sheet in A, used as copy for C in Book X, has an 1816 watermark), but before 1820, since it has pencil corrections to *Vaudracour and Julia* incorporated in the text of the poem published in that year. MS D was written in or after 1828, and corrected in 1832 and 1839. MS E was copied in 1839, and is marked 'reviewed July 1839'.

To the sketch of the history of composition may be added some more specific remarks on the manuscripts. The manuscript material for the early stages of the composition of *The Prelude* is plentiful and miscellaneous. For present purposes, it is enough to say that the earliest episode to be composed in something like its later form was the 'Discharged Soldier', in the early months of

1798. The earliest continuous version of a substantial part is the MS JJ written at Goslar during the winter of 1798-9, and containing, not always in the eventual order, a large portion of Book I, from line 271 to the end, as well as a few passages from later in the poem, notably 'There was a boy', V 389-413. A number of manuscripts of 1799-1800 bring Books I and II into substantially their present form except for I 1-271, and also include a number of passages that found their place in later books, notably V 450-72 and 345-89. When in 1845 Wordsworth published VI 553-72 as 'The Simplon Pass', he dated it 1799; but there is no manuscript before 1804, when the whole passage about the crossing of the Alps makes its appearance as a unity.

Numbers of manuscripts from 1804 attest the resumption of work in that year. MS W represents the five-book version, with what is now XIII 1-135 appearing as the opening of Book V. MS M is the first to contain I 1-271, and also the first to contain Books IV and V in the form they were to assume in the thirteen-book *Prelude*. In the other MSS before A and B, the most interesting single point is the use of the headings 'Book Twelfth' and 'Book Thirteenth' in accordance with the 1850, not the 1805, division, suggesting that the 1850 division of Book X was a reversion to the original plan.

This Edition

The purpose of this edition is to offer, in a form which will make comparison as easy as possible, the two main texts of *The Prelude*: that which Wordsworth completed in May 1805, and that which, after a final revision in 1839, he laid aside for publication after his death (1850). Apart from a few trifling errors, the earlier text can be accurately constructed from MSS A and B. The final text is more difficult. A number of errors of wording and, more particularly, of punctuation crept in during the process of revision, and several more unauthorized 'corrections' and omissions, as well as some misreadings of copy, occur in the 1850 edition. Many, but not all, of these errors were pointed out by de Selincourt: some had been conjecturally emended by earlier editors. It has been my aim to eliminate them: I discuss this more fully on pp. 27–8.

The accidentals of the text – spelling, punctuation, use of capitals – present a more difficult problem. Neither the A and B manuscripts (written, respectively, by Dorothy Wordsworth and Sara Hutchinson), nor the printed text of 1850, is sacrosanct in this respect. A sufficiently diligent modern editor could certainly improve on either of them. But 1850 has, I think, been unfairly decried by de Selincourt. It has a number of errors in punctuation which can be corrected by reference to earlier manuscripts. Its use of capitals is not entirely consistent. And it is overpunctuated, by modern standards. But, on the whole, it represents a fairly coherent house-style of its period, and is not too distracting for the modern reader. I have therefore departed from it only occasionally. I have recorded in the Textual Notes all places where I have altered its wording or punctuation. I have allowed myself a rather freer hand with spelling, normalizing, for instance, *-ise* forms to *-ize* (which sometimes occur in the manuscripts), and printing a number of compounds such as *birthplace*, *schoolboy* etc., without hyphens. On the other hand, I have retained the consistent *sate* for *sat* and, less confidently, *any thing* and *every thing*. Capitals are occasionally a problem, in words like *Man*, *Nature*, *Reason*. 1850 does not consistently follow an intelligible system of distinction, and I have normally introduced capitals where there seemed to be no differentiation from other passages where 1850 had them, especially if there was support from earlier manuscripts. Having fixed this text, I have adapted the punctuation, capitals and spelling of the 1805 text to agree with it, where they are close enough together in substance to make this possible. Where they diverge more widely, I have continued to adapt capitals and spelling to the 1850 norm, but have not altered the punctuation, except where it is clearly abnormal. De Selincourt, incidentally, does not by any means consistently follow his copy-text, A, for the 1805 text, and there are many disagreements between the two currently printed versions of that text: the 1959 revision of the Oxford English Texts edition, and the 1960 and 1970 revisions of the Oxford Standard Authors. In working through the two texts, I have been struck by the difficulty of generalizing about the punctuation. De Selincourt (p. xxv) describes 1850 as overpunctuated, which it certainly is, but he also claims that the punctuation of A and B 'errs, perhaps, on the side of lightness' (p. xxi), yet 'there is no doubt that these MSS represent [Wordsworth's] own intention in the matter far more accurately than either D or E' (p. xxii). Apart from definite errors in 1850, often originating in D or E, it is not clear to me that this is true. At least in some passages where the two versions are close enough to each other to make comparison possible, there is no consistent tendency in either direction. Thus in the first forty-seven lines of Book II, there are eight places where de Selincourt's own 1805 text has commas absent from 1850, and one where it has a colon which 1850 reduces to a comma, against two where 1850 adds a comma, four where it raises a comma to a colon or semi-colon, and two where it raises a colon or semi-colon to a full-stop. 1850 certainly has spasms of gross over-punctuation. But if I had been repunctuating the whole text to accord with modern practice, I doubt whether I should have departed from 1850 as often as from 1805. There are a few places where change of punctuation has itself been part of the revision. Thus, the 1850 text of VIII 323-5 has:

I had my face turned toward the truth, began
With an advantage furnished by that kind
Of prepossession, . . .

But this does not mean that the corresponding 1805 text (VIII 457-9) is wrong:

I had my face towards the truth, began
With an advantage; furnished with that kind
Of prepossession . . .

Whereas the final 'furnished by' goes with 'advantage', the original 'furnished with' goes with 'I'. And the reversion to the original verb 'furnished' is only a final choice after intervening experiments with 'rising from' and 'founded on'. This is an extreme, and clear, case. But I have also retained A's punctuation in the 1805 text where it seems superior, even if 1850 is not so bad as to need changing.

A correct text is the first object of an editor: then such notes as explain difficult or unintelligible passages or throw light upon them; and lastly, which is of much less importance, notes pointing out passages or authors to which the Poet has been indebted, not in the piddling way of phrase here and phrase there (which is detestable as a general practice) but where the Poet has really had essential obligations either as to matter or manner.

So Wordsworth wrote on 7 November 1805 to Walter Scott, then engaged on editing Dryden. (It is ironical, in the light of the first sentence, that Wordsworth's editors should have inserted, in square brackets, a piddling and unnecessary 'a' before 'phrase here'.) The principles on which this text has been established, I have already discussed. The notes would not, I hope, have been regarded with too much disfavour by Wordsworth, though I have been less sparing than he would have liked of the 'phrase here and phrase there' type of record of apparent echoes.

This is a relatively modest edition of a poem which has been elaborately edited and annotated by Ernest de Selincourt and Helen Darbishire, commented on, line by line, in a long book by R. D. Havens, and made the subject of several critical works and innumerable articles; and I have plundered all these without acknowledgement in detail. I have not, however, thought it my duty to supply a discussion of Wordsworth's ideas, or a critical analysis of his art, or a guide to the Lake District (but a map is included, and the topography of VIII 229–44 seemed to call for comment), or a potted history of the French Revolution; though some of these come into the notes incidentally. What I have attempted may be placed under the following heads:

1. Explanation of words and phrases that may be unfamiliar to many readers, or that have deceptively changed their meaning since Wordsworth's time, or that are just obscure. If there are not a great many notes of this kind, it is not because I think Wordsworth an easy writer, but because the difficulties he presents are seldom of a kind that can be cleared up by a brief glossarial note.

2. Brief notes on proper names – historical, mythological, geographical and literary – which will give the reader enough guidance to enable him to follow them up further in reference books, or in de Selincourt's edition.

3. Explanations of allusions to events mentioned in passing. Where Wordsworth's context itself gives sufficient guidance, I have refrained from comment.

4. Comments on inaccuracies in Wordsworth's statements which seem to have a sufficient degree of intrinsic interest or relevance to the poem.

5. References to passages in earlier authors to which Wordsworth is certainly or probably indebted, whether consciously or unconsciously. These cover a wide range: from straightforward quotations, signalized as such by inverted commas, through allusions clearly meant to be caught by the reader, and echoes that show Wordsworth steeped in a particular author, to less striking

phrases which do indeed occur in a favourite writer but may be coincidental, and even a few which are so infelicitous as echoes that Wordsworth must be supposed to have been unconscious of them. (Some were removed in revision.) I may sometimes have been seduced by the fact that this is a very easy way of writing notes, and one that earlier editors have followed extensively. But I think that it is worth while to include them fairly generously, by way of illustrating how 'literary' a writer Wordsworth often is. That Miltonic echoes so greatly outnumber those from all other poets may be partly due to the fact that, like earlier commentators (from whom I take the great majority of such notes), I am more likely to spot an echo from Milton than one from Thomson or Young or Akenside. But there is no doubt that Milton is the poet on whom Wordsworth draws most freely and most effectively; and I am encouraged by the fact that scholars (especially Abbie Potts) who have combed the eighteenth-century poets, have come up with so little that is either convincing or significant. I would emphasize that I am talking about phrasal echoes rather than general poetic texture, which is often markedly eighteenth-century. In notes of this type, I quote, and do not merely refer to, the passages believed to be echoed, except where the echo is verbatim, or nearly so.

Editorial work on the 1850 text was quite extensive and pains-taking. The final manuscript, E, was used as printer's copy, and presumably the first proofs, which do not survive, followed it closely. But the text as it eventually reached print shows signs of considerable editorial interference, often implying recourse to earlier manuscripts. Wordsworth's final text was deliberately altered for various reasons. Sometimes his grammar was judged faulty (VI 199; XI 107) or his choice of form obsolete (IX 144). The two lines on Calvert (XIV 358a–b) may have seemed too personal. There is evidence of metrical objections (II 297; IX 230, 248), or dislike of particular words (II 341–2). One particularly interesting example comes in the opening lines of the poem, where (at lines 2, 3 and 5), E has masculine, not neuter pronouns (so also D, but with *his* altered from *its* in line 5). Was this personification of the breeze thought objectionably animistic? All this is in addition to sheer misreadings, to places where the E text itself was already corrupt, and to a few where it appears that Wordsworth's final alterations, sometimes in pencil, were simply overlooked.

De Selincourt recorded in his commentary examples of all these types of error in the 1850 text, and some later editors have selectively restored the true text. But de Selincourt also missed a good deal. For example, of the two E readings altered on metrical grounds in Book IX, he noted that in line 230 but not that in line 248. And, most remarkable of all, he overlooked the E text of I 2, 3 and 5, mentioned in the last paragraph.

Stephen Gill's revision of the Oxford Standard Authors edition of the 1805 text has been available to me only at proof stage. I am indebted to it for the elimination of a number of de Selincourt errors which I had missed. My text still differs from his at a few points.

1. He has erroneous or questionable readings (some of them present in the 1960 Oxford Standard Authors, though not in the 1959 revision of de Selincourt) at III 152; V 423; VII 362; X 726; XIII 94, 257.

2. He has failed to correct errors of de Selincourt at I 100, 389, 565; II 61, 278; III 287; VI 211, 299, 654; VII 95, 216, 488, 596, 649; VIII 52; IX 70, 231, 878; X 1028; XII 360; XIII 260.

3. At IV 302, I read 'vile' (A², B) rather than 'wild' (A) and at VII 20, 'hindrance' (A², B) rather than 'indolence' (A), which both look like mere errors. At IX 76a the comma after 'merely', certainly present in A², seems to have been in the heavily deleted A, though Gill does not print it.

4. More important is the omission and addition of certain lines:
a. X 119 is not in the original text of A.
b. At XIII 114–16 the original text of A is hard to follow. Gill

excludes these lines, but they are in B, though over an erasure, and may reasonably stand as part of the 1805 text.

c. XIII 156 ('in') – 160 ('fill') is in B only.

5. My text of VII 275 is de Selincourt's conflated one, where Gill follows A exactly. I take this opportunity of recording a supra-lineal correction in A at X 847, 'apt' for 'out'. This reading (not recorded by de Selincourt) gives better sense, and, as it is graphic-ally similar, may be the correction of an error, not a revision.

With Gill, I follow de Selincourt's occasional use of square brackets for the insertion of words and phrases absent from A and B, but required by the sense, and supplied from later MSS.

Unless the 1850 text is specifically referred to, italic line num-bers have been used to differentiate it from the 1805 text. This occurs particularly in the poem itself and the notes.

A few passages were published during Wordsworth's lifetime. I have listed these on page 30, but have not commented on any textual variants between them and 1850.

For the second printing I have made a good many corrections. I am indebted to Stephen Gill for four new readings from A. These are at I 268; III 116; V 277; VII 251. The second is of particular interest, as Wordsworth is seen to have identified the 'Upholder' with 'the tranquil soul'. The first two corrections were com-municated to Dr Gill by W. J. B. Owen.

Lines of The Prelude *Published before 1850*

Line references are to the 1850 text.

Further Reading

The standard edition of *The Prelude* and the first to print the 1805 text, is that edited by Ernest de Selincourt (Oxford University Press, 1926) and revised by Helen Darbishire (1959). A less elaborate edition of the 1805 text alone was also edited by de Selincourt (1933) and revised by Miss Darbishire (1960), and by Stephen Gill (1970).

The fullest study of the poem is that by R. D. Havens, *The Mind of a Poet* (Johns Hopkins Press, 1941), which has a long Introduction, 'A Study of Wordsworth's Thought', followed by a Commentary. This is indispensable, though very long-winded and not always particularly penetrating. Another book-length study, by Abbie F. Potts, *Wordsworth's 'Prelude': A Study of its Literary Form* (Cornell University Press, 1953), has much less to offer and may be ignored except by those specially interested in conjectures, often implausible, about Wordsworth's eighteenth-century sources. Much more profitable is the 'series of related essays' (in the author's own words), Herbert Lindenberger's *On Wordsworth's 'Prelude'* (Princeton University Press, 1963). De Selincourt laid the foundation for study of the differences between the 1805 and 1850 versions. The fullest, but far from the best, discussion of this is Mary E. Burton's *The One Wordsworth* (University of North Carolina Press, 1942). There is a relevant chapter, 'Syntax in the Blank Verse of Wordsworth's *Prelude*', in Donald Davie's *Articulate Energy* (Routledge & Kegan Paul, 1955). The best short study of the poem's growth, and of the differences between the versions up to 1805, is the essay by J. R. MacGillivray, 'The Three Forms of *The Prelude*, 1798–1805', in *Essays in English Literature from the Renaissance to the Victorian Age. Presented to A. S. P. Woodhouse*, edited by M. MacLure and F. W. Watt (Toronto University Press, 1964). The best study of the opening of Book I is John Finch, 'Wordsworth's Two-Handed Engine', in *Bicentenary Wordsworth Studies in Memory of John Alban Finch,* edited by Jonathan Wordsworth (Cornell University Press, 1970). Useful for the Cambridge of Wordsworth's day, though less illuminating on Wordsworth himself, is B. R. Schneider's *Wordsworth's Cambridge Education* (Cambridge University Press, 1957). For Wordsworth and the French Revolution, F. M. Todd's *Politics and the Poet: A Study of Wordsworth* (Methuen, 1957) is useful.

From a very large number of separate articles, and chapters in books, I select, for the contrasting aspects they survey, W. B. Gallie, 'Is *The Prelude* a Philosophical Poem?' (*Philosophy*, vol. 22, 1947); William Empson, '"Sense" in *The Prelude*' (*Kenyon Review*, vol. 13, 1951) reprinted in *The Structure of Complex Words* (Chatto & Windus, 1951); Max Wildi, 'Wordsworth and the Simplon Pass' (*English Studies*, vol. 40, 1959; vol. 43, 1962); Karl Kroeber, 'Wordsworth: The Personal Epic', *Romantic Narrative Art* (University of Wisconsin Press, 1960).

All general books on Wordsworth pay attention to *The Prelude*. Specially valuable are John Jones, *The Egotistical Sublime* (Chatto & Windus, 1954) and Geoffrey Hartman, *Wordsworth's Poetry, 1787–1814* (Yale University Press, 1964), the latter often an unnecessarily difficult book, but full of ideas, and with good bibliographies.

The standard life of Wordsworth is Mary Moorman's two-volume *William Wordsworth* (Oxford University Press, 1957 and 1965). For the close student of the early Wordsworth, the indispensable guide is Mark Reed's *Wordsworth: The Chronology of the Early Years 1770–1799* (Harvard University Press, 1967).

T. W. Thompson's *Wordsworth's Hawkshead,* edited by Robert Woof (Oxford University Press, 1970), is a mine of information, which was unfortunately published too late for me to use. I have, however, included three of his identifications in the Notes.

Book First

INTRODUCTION
CHILDHOOD AND SCHOOL-TIME

O there is blessing in this gentle breeze
That blows from the green fields and from the clouds
And from the sky: it beats against my cheek,
And seems half-conscious of the joy it gives.
O welcome messenger! O welcome friend!
A captive greets thee, coming from a house
Of bondage, from yon city's walls set free,
A prison where he hath been long immured.
Now I am free, enfranchised and at large,
May fix my habitation where I will.
What dwelling shall receive me? in what vale
Shall be my harbour? underneath what grove
Shall I take up my home? and what sweet stream
Shall with its murmurs lull me to my rest?
The earth is all before me. With a heart
Joyous, nor scared at its own liberty,
I look about; and should the guide I choose
Be nothing better than a wandering cloud,
I cannot miss my way. I breathe again!
Trances of thought and mountings of the mind
Come fast upon me: it is shaken off,
As by miraculous gift 'tis shaken off,
That burden of my own unnatural self,
The heavy weight of many a weary day
Not mine, and such as were not made for me.
Long months of peace (if such bold word accord
With any promises of human life),
Long months of ease and undisturbed delight
Are mine in prospect; whither shall I turn,
By road or pathway, or through open field,

Book First

O there is blessing in this gentle breeze,
A visitant that while he fans my cheek
Doth seem half-conscious of the joy he brings
From the green fields, and from yon azure sky.
Whate'er his mission, the soft breeze can come
To none more grateful than to me; escaped
From the vast city, where I long had pined
A discontented sojourner: now free,
Free as a bird to settle where I will.
What dwelling shall receive me? in what vale
Shall be my harbour? underneath what grove
Shall I take up my home? and what clear stream
Shall with its murmur lull me into rest?
The earth is all before me. With a heart
Joyous, nor scared at its own liberty,
I look about; and should the chosen guide
Be nothing better than a wandering cloud,
I cannot miss my way. I breathe again!
Trances of thought and mountings of the mind
Come fast upon me: it is shaken off,
That burden of my own unnatural self,
The heavy weight of many a weary day
Not mine, and such as were not made for me.
Long months of peace (if such bold word accord
With any promises of human life),
Long months of ease and undisturbed delight
Are mine in prospect; whither shall I turn,
By road or pathway, or through trackless field,

35

Or shall a twig or any floating thing
Upon the river point me out my course?   *30*
   Enough that I am free; for months to come
May dedicate myself to chosen tasks;
May quit the tiresome sea and dwell on shore,
If not a settler on the soil, at least
To drink wild water, and to pluck green herbs,
And gather fruits fresh from their native tree.
Nay more, if I may trust myself, this hour
40 Hath brought a gift that consecrates my joy;
For I, methought, while the sweet breath of heaven
Was blowing on my body, felt within
A corresponding mild creative breeze,   *35*
A vital breeze which travelled gently on
O'er things which it had made, and is become
A tempest, a redundant energy,
Vexing its own creation. 'Tis a power
That does not come unrecognized, a storm,
Which, breaking up a long-continued frost,   *40*
50 Brings with it vernal promises, the hope
Of active days, of dignity and thought,
Of prowess in an honourable field,
Pure passions, virtue, knowledge, and delight,
The holy life of music and of verse.   *45*

   Thus, far, O Friend! did I, not used to make
A present joy the matter of my song,
Pour out that day my soul in measured strains
Even in the very words which I have here
Recorded: to the open fields I told   *50*
60 A prophecy: poetic numbers came
Spontaneously, and clothed in priestly robe
My spirit, thus singled out, as it might seem,
For holy services: great hopes were mine;
My own voice cheered me, and, far more, the mind's   *55*
Internal echo of the imperfect sound;
To both I listened, drawing from them both
A cheerful confidence in things to come.

Up hill or down, or shall some floating thing
30 Upon the river point me out my course?

Dear Liberty! Yet what would it avail
But for a gift that consecrates the joy?
For I, methought, while the sweet breath of heaven
Was blowing on my body, felt within
A correspondent breeze, that gently moved
With quickening virtue, but is now become
A tempest, a redundant energy,
Vexing its own creation. Thanks to both,
And their congenial powers, that, while they join
40 In breaking up a long-continued frost,
Bring with them vernal promises, the hope
Of active days urged on by flying hours, –
Days of sweet leisure, taxed with patient thought
Abstruse, nor wanting punctual service high,
Matins and vespers, of harmonious verse!

Thus far, O Friend! did I, not used to make
A present joy the matter of a song,
Pour forth that day my soul in measured strains
That would not be forgotten, and are here
50 Recorded: to the open fields I told
A prophecy: poetic numbers came
Spontaneously to clothe in priestly robe
A renovated spirit singled out,
Such hope was mine, for holy services.
My own voice cheered me, and, far more, the mind's
Internal echo of the imperfect sound;
To both I listened, drawing from them both
A cheerful confidence in things to come.

Whereat, being not unwilling now to give
A respite to this passion, I paced on   60
70 Gently, with careless steps; and came, ere long,
To a green shady place, where down I sate
Beneath a tree, slackening my thoughts by choice,
And settling into gentler happiness.
'Twas autumn, and a calm and placid day,   65
With warmth, as much as needed, from a sun
Two hours declined towards the west; a day
With silver clouds, and sunshine on the grass,
And in the sheltered grove where I was couched
A perfect stillness. On the ground I lay   70
80 Passing through many thoughts, yet mainly such
As to myself pertained. I made a choice
Of one sweet Vale, whither my steps should turn,
And saw, methought, the very house and fields
Present before my eyes: nor did I fail
To add, meanwhile, assurance of some work
Of glory there forthwith to be begun,
Perhaps too there performed. Thus long I lay   80
Cheered by the genial pillow of the earth
Beneath my head, soothed by a sense of touch
90 From the warm ground, that balanced me, else lost
Entirely, seeing nought, nought hearing, save
When here and there, about the grove of oaks
Where was my bed, an acorn from the trees
Fell audibly, and with a startling sound.   85

Thus occupied in mind, I lingered here
Contented, nor rose up until the sun
Had almost touched the horizon; bidding then
A farewell to the city left behind,
Even with the chance equipment of that hour
100 I journeyed towards the Vale which I had chosen.
It was a splendid evening, and my soul
Did once again make trial of the strength   95
Restored to her afresh; nor did she want
Aeolian visitations; but the harp

      Content and not unwilling now to give
60 A respite to this passion, I paced on
    With brisk and eager steps; and came, at length,
    To a green shady place, where down I sate
    Beneath a tree, slackening my thoughts by choice,
    And settling into gentler happiness.
    'Twas autumn, and a clear and placid day,
    With warmth, as much as needed, from a sun
    Two hours declined towards the west; a day
    With silver clouds, and sunshine on the grass,
    And in the sheltered and the sheltering grove
70 A perfect stillness. Many were the thoughts
    Encouraged and dismissed, till choice was made
    Of a known Vale, whither my feet should turn,
    Nor rest till they had reached the very door
    Of the one cottage which methought I saw.
    No picture of mere memory ever looked
    So fair; and while upon the fancied scene
    I gazed with growing love, a higher power
    Than Fancy gave assurance of some work
    Of glory there forthwith to be begun,
80 Perhaps too there performed. Thus long I mused,
    Nor e'er lost sight of what I mused upon,
    Save where, amid the stately grove of oaks,
    Now here, now there, an acorn, from its cup
    Dislodged, through sere leaves rustled, or at once
    To the bare earth dropped with a startling sound.
    From that soft couch I rose not, till the sun
    Had almost touched the horizon; casting then
    A backward glance upon the curling cloud
    Of city smoke, by distance ruralized;
90 Keen as a Truant or a Fugitive,
    But as a Pilgrim resolute, I took,
    Even with the chance equipment of that hour,
    The road that pointed toward the chosen Vale.
    It was a splendid evening, and my soul
    Once more made trial of her strength, nor lacked
    Aeolian visitations; but the harp

Was soon defrauded, and the banded host
Of harmony dispersed in straggling sounds,
And lastly utter silence! 'Be it so;
It is an injury,' said I, 'to this day
To think of any thing but present joy.'   *100*
110 So, like a peasant I pursued my road
Beneath the evening sun, nor had one wish
Again to bend the Sabbath of that time
To a servile yoke. What need of many words?   *105*
A pleasant loitering journey, through two days
Continued, brought me to my hermitage.

    I spare to speak, my Friend, of what ensued,
The admiration and the love, the life
In common things – the endless store of things,
Rare, or at least so seeming, every day   *110*
120 Found all about me in one neighbourhood –
The self-congratulation, the complete
Composure, and the happiness entire.
But speedily a longing in me rose
To brace myself to some determined aim,   *115*
Reading or thinking, either to lay up
New stores, or rescue from decay the old
By timely interference: I had hopes
Still higher, that with a frame of outward life
I might endue, might fix in a visible home
130 Some portion of those phantoms of conceit   *120*
That had been floating loose about so long,
And to such beings temperately deal forth
The many feelings that oppressed my heart.
But I have been discouraged; gleams of light
Flash often from the east, then disappear   *125*
And mock me with a sky that ripens not
Into a steady morning: if my mind,
Remembering the sweet promise of the past,
Would gladly grapple with some noble theme,
140 Vain is her wish; where'er she turns she finds   *130*
Impediments from day to day renewed.

40

Was soon defrauded, and the banded host
Of harmony dispersed in straggling sounds,
And lastly utter silence! 'Be it so;
100   Why think of anything but present good?'
So, like a home-bound labourer I pursued
My way beneath the mellowing sun, that shed
Mild influence; nor left in me one wish
Again to bend the Sabbath of that time
To a servile yoke. What need of many words?
A pleasant loitering journey, through three days
Continued, brought me to my hermitage.
I spare to tell of what ensued, the life
In common things – the endless store of things,
110   Rare, or at least so seeming, every day
Found all about me in one neighbourhood –
The self-congratulation, and, from morn
To night, unbroken cheerfulness serene.
But speedily an earnest longing rose
To brace myself to some determined aim,
Reading or thinking, either to lay up
New stores, or rescue from decay the old
By timely interference: and therewith
Came hopes still higher, that with outward life
120   I might endue some airy phantasies
That had been floating loose about for years,
And to such beings temperately deal forth
The many feelings that oppressed my heart.
That hope hath been discouraged; welcome light
Dawns from the east, but dawns to disappear
And mock me with a sky that ripens not
Into a steady morning: if my mind,
Remembering the bold promise of the past,
Would gladly grapple with some noble theme,
130   Vain is her wish; where'er she turns she finds
Impediments from day to day renewed.

And now it would content me to yield up
Those lofty hopes awhile, for present gifts
Of humbler industry. But, O dear Friend!
The Poet, gentle creature as he is,   *135*
Hath, like the Lover, his unruly times;
His fits when he is neither sick nor well,
Though no distress be near him but his own
Unmanageable thoughts: the mind itself,
150 The meditative mind, best pleased, perhaps,   *140*
While she as duteous as the mother dove
Sits brooding, lives not always to that end,
But hath less quiet instincts, goadings on
That drive her as in trouble through the groves;
With me is now such passion, which I blame
No otherwise than as it lasts too long.   *145*

When, as becomes a man who would prepare
For such a glorious work, I through myself
Make rigorous inquisition, the report
160 Is often cheering; for I neither seem
To lack that first great gift, the vital soul,   *150*
Nor general Truths, which are themselves a sort
Of Elements and Agents, Under-powers,
Subordinate helpers of the living mind:
Nor am I naked in external things,
Forms, images, nor numerous other aids   *155*
Of less regard, though won perhaps with toil
And needful to build up a Poet's praise.
Time, place, and manners, these I seek, and these
170 I find in plenteous store, but nowhere such
As may be singled out with steady choice;   *160*
No little band of yet remembered names
Whom I, in perfect confidence, might hope
To summon back from lonesome banishment,
And make them inmates in the hearts of men
Now living, or to live in times to come.   *165*
Sometimes, mistaking vainly, as I fear,
Proud spring-tide swellings for a regular sea,

And now it would content me to yield up
Those lofty hopes awhile, for present gifts
Of humbler industry. But, O dear Friend!
The Poet, gentle creature as he is,
Hath, like the Lover, his unruly times;
His fits when he is neither sick nor well,
Though no distress be near him but his own
Unmanageable thoughts: his mind, best pleased
140 While she as duteous as the mother dove
Sits brooding, lives not always to that end,
But like the innocent bird, hath goadings on
That drive her as in trouble through the groves;
With me is now such passion, to be blamed
No otherwise than as it lasts too long.

When, as becomes a man who would prepare
For such an arduous work, I through myself
Make rigorous inquisition, the report
Is often cheering; for I neither seem
150 To lack that first great gift, the vital soul,
Nor general Truths, which are themselves a sort
Of Elements and Agents, Under-powers,
Subordinate helpers of the living mind:
Nor am I naked of external things,
Forms, images, nor numerous other aids
Of less regard, though won perhaps with toil
And needful to build up a Poet's praise.
Time, place, and manners do I seek, and these
Are found in plenteous store, but nowhere such
160 As may be singled out with steady choice;
No little band of yet remembered names
Whom I, in perfect confidence, might hope
To summon back from lonesome banishment,
And make them dwellers in the hearts of men
Now living, or to live in future years.
Sometimes the ambitious Power of choice, mistaking
Proud spring-tide swellings for a regular sea,

I settle on some British theme, some old
180 Romantic tale by Milton left unsung;   *170*
More often resting at some gentle place
Within the groves of Chivalry, I pipe
Among the shepherds, with reposing knights
Sit by a fountain side, and hear their tales.
Sometimes, more sternly moved, I would relate
How vanquished Mithridates northward passed,
And, hidden in the cloud of years, became
That Odin, Father of a race by whom
Perished the Roman Empire: how the friends   *190*
190 And followers of Sertorius, out of Spain
Flying, found shelter in the Fortunate Isles,
And left their usages, their arts and laws,
To disappear by a slow gradual death,
To dwindle and to perish one by one,   *195*
Starved in those narrow bounds: but not the soul
Of Liberty, which fifteen hundred years
Survived, and, when the European came
With skill and power that could not be withstood,
Did, like a pestilence, maintain its hold   *200*
200 And wasted down by glorious death that race
Of natural heroes: or I would record
How, in tyrannic times, some unknown man,
Unheard of in the chronicles of kings,
Suffered in silence for the love of Truth;   *205*

Will settle on some British theme, some old
Romantic tale by Milton left unsung;
170   More often turning to some gentle place
Within the groves of Chivalry, I pipe
To shepherd swains, or seated harp in hand,
Amid reposing knights by a river side
Or fountain, listen to the grave reports
Of dire enchantments faced and overcome
By the strong mind, and tales of warlike feats,
Where spear encountered spear, and sword with sword
Fought, as if conscious of the blazonry
That the shield bore, so glorious was the strife;
180   Whence inspiration for a song that winds
Through ever-changing scenes of votive quest
Wrongs to redress, harmonious tribute paid
To patient courage and unblemished truth,
To firm devotion, zeal unquenchable,
And Christian meekness hallowing faithful loves.
Sometimes, more sternly moved, I would relate
How vanquished Mithridates northward passed,
And, hidden in the cloud of years, became
Odin, the Father of a race by whom
190   Perished the Roman Empire: how the friends
And followers of Sertorius, out of Spain
Flying, found shelter in the Fortunate Isles,
And left their usages, their arts and laws,
To disappear by a slow gradual death,
To dwindle and to perish one by one,
Starved in those narrow bounds: but not the soul
Of Liberty, which fifteen hundred years
Survived, and, when the European came
With skill and power that might not be withstood,
200   Did, like a pestilence, maintain its hold
And wasted down by glorious death that race
Of natural heroes: or I would record
How, in tyrannic times, some high-souled man,
Unnamed among the chronicles of kings,
Suffered in silence for Truth's sake: or tell,

How that one Frenchman, through continued force
Of meditation on the inhuman deeds
Of the first conquerors of the Indian Isles,
Went single in his ministry across
The Ocean; not to comfort the oppressed,   *210*
210 But, like a thirsty wind, to roam about
Withering the Oppressor: how Gustavus found
Help at his need in Dalecarlia's mines:
How Wallace fought for Scotland; left the name
Of Wallace to be found, like a wild flower,   *215*
All over his dear Country; left the deeds
Of Wallace, like a family of Ghosts,
To people the steep rocks and river banks,
Her natural sanctuaries, with a local soul
Of independence and stern liberty.   *220*
220 Sometimes it suits me better to shape out
Some tale from my own heart, more near akin
To my own passions and habitual thoughts;
Some variegated story, in the main
Lofty, with interchange of gentler things.   *225*
But deadening admonitions will succeed
And the whole beauteous fabric seems to lack
Foundation, and, withal, appears throughout
Shadowy and unsubstantial. Then, last wish,
My last and favourite aspiration, then
230 I yearn towards some philosophic song   *230*
Of Truth that cherishes our daily life;
With meditations passionate from deep
Recesses in man's heart, immortal verse
Thoughtfully fitted to the Orphean lyre;
But from this awful burden I full soon
Take refuge and beguile myself with trust   *235*
That mellower years will bring a riper mind
And clearer insight. Thus from day to day
I live, a mockery of the brotherhood
240 Of vice and virtue, with no skill to part
Vague longing that is bred by want of power
From paramount impulse not to be withstood,   *240*

How that one Frenchman, through continued force
Of meditation on the inhuman deeds
Of those who conquered first the Indian Isles,
Went single in his ministry across
210 The Ocean; not to comfort the oppressed,
But, like a thirsty wind, to roam about
Withering the Oppressor: how Gustavus sought
Help at his need in Dalecarlia's mines:
How Wallace fought for Scotland; left the name
Of Wallace to be found, like a wild flower,
All over his dear Country; left the deeds
Of Wallace, like a family of Ghosts,
To people the steep rocks and river banks,
Her natural sanctuaries, with a local soul
220 Of independence and stern liberty.
Sometimes it suits me better to invent
A tale from my own heart, more near akin
To my own passions and habitual thoughts;
Some variegated story, in the main
Lofty, but the unsubstantial structure melts
Before the very sun that brightens it,
Mist into air dissolving! Then a wish,
My best and favourite aspiration, mounts
With yearning toward some philosophic song
230 Of Truth that cherishes our daily life;
With meditations passionate from deep
Recesses in man's heart, immortal verse
Thoughtfully fitted to the Orphean lyre;
But from this awful burden I full soon
Take refuge and beguile myself with trust
That mellower years will bring a riper mind
And clearer insight. Thus my days are past
In contradiction; with no skill to part
Vague longing, haply bred by want of power,
240 From paramount impulse not to be withstood,

A timorous capacity from prudence,
From circumspection, infinite delay.
Humility and modest awe themselves
Betray me, serving often for a cloak
To a more subtle selfishness; that now   245
Doth lock my functions up in blank reserve,
Now dupes me by an over-anxious eye
250   That with a false activity beats off
Simplicity and self-presented truth.
Ah! better far than this, to stray about   250
Voluptuously through fields and rural walks,
And ask no record of the hours, given up
To vacant musing, unreproved neglect
Of all things, and deliberate holiday.
Far better never to have heard the name   255
Of zeal and just ambition, than to live
Thus baffled by a mind that every hour
260   Turns recreant to her task; takes heart again,
Then feels immediately some hollow thought
Hang like an interdict upon her hopes.   260
This is my lot; for either still I find
Some imperfection in the chosen theme,
Or see of absolute accomplishment
Much wanting, so much wanting, in myself,
That I recoil and droop, and seek repose   265
In indolence from vain perplexity,
Unprofitably travelling towards the grave,
270   Like a false steward who hath much received
And renders nothing back.
                                        Was it for this
That one, the fairest of all rivers, loved   270
To blend his murmurs with my nurse's song,
And, from his alder shades and rocky falls,
And from his fords and shallows, sent a voice
That flowed along my dreams? For this, didst thou,
O Derwent! travelling over the green plains   275
Near my 'sweet Birthplace', didst thou, beauteous stream,
Make ceaseless music through the night and day

A timorous capacity from prudence,
From circumspection, infinite delay.
Humility and modest awe themselves
Betray me, serving often for a cloak
To a more subtle selfishness; that now
Locks every function up in blank reserve,
Now dupes me, trusting to an anxious eye
That with intrusive restlessness beats off
Simplicity and self-presented truth.
250 Ah! better far than this, to stray about
Voluptuously through fields and rural walks,
And ask no record of the hours, resigned
To vacant musing, unreproved neglect
Of all things, and deliberate holiday.
Far better never to have heard the name
Of zeal and just ambition, than to live
Baffled and plagued by a mind that every hour
Turns recreant to her task; takes heart again,
Then feels immediately some hollow thought
260 Hang like an interdict upon her hopes.
This is my lot; for either still I find
Some imperfection in the chosen theme,
Or see of absolute accomplishment
Much wanting, so much wanting, in myself,
That I recoil and droop, and seek repose
In listlessness from vain perplexity,
Unprofitably travelling toward the grave,
Like a false steward who hath much received
And renders nothing back.
                                    Was it for this
270 That one, the fairest of all rivers, loved
To blend his murmurs with my nurse's song,
And, from his alder shades and rocky falls,
And from his fords and shallows, sent a voice
That flowed along my dreams? For this, didst thou,
O Derwent! winding among grassy holms
Where I was looking on, a babe in arms,
Make ceaseless music that composed my thoughts

280 Which with its steady cadence, tempering
Our human waywardness, composed my thoughts
To more than infant softness, giving me
Among the fretful dwellings of mankind
A knowledge, a dim earnest, of the calm
That Nature breathes among the hills and groves.   *281*
When, having left his mountains, to the towers
Of Cockermouth that beauteous river came,
Behind my father's house he passed, close by,
Along the margin of our terrace walk.   *286*
290 He was a playmate whom we dearly loved.
Oh, many a time have I, a five years' child,
A naked boy, in one delightful rill,
A little mill-race severed from his stream,
Made one long bathing of a summer's day;   *290*
Basked in the sun, and plunged and basked again
Alternate, all a summer's day, or coursed
Over the sandy fields, leaping through groves
Of yellow groundsel; or when crag and hill,
The woods, and distant Skiddaw's lofty height,   *295*
300 Were bronzed with a deep radiance, stood alone
Beneath the sky, as if I had been born
On Indian plains, and from my mother's hut
Had run abroad in wantonness, to sport
A naked savage, in the thunder shower.   *300*

Fair seed-time had my soul, and I grew up
Fostered alike by beauty and by fear:
Much favoured in my birthplace, and no less
In that belovèd Vale to which ere long
I was transplanted. Well I call to mind   *305*
310 ('Twas at an early age, ere I had seen
Nine summers) when upon the mountain slope
The frost, and breath of frosty wind, had snapped
The last autumnal crocus, 'twas my joy
To wander half the night among the cliffs
And the smooth hollows where the woodcocks ran
Along the open turf. In thought and wish

To more than infant softness, giving me
Amid the fretful dwellings of mankind
280 A foretaste, a dim earnest, of the calm
That Nature breathes among the hills and groves.
When he had left the mountains and received
On his smooth breast the shadow of those towers
That yet survive, a shattered monument
Of feudal sway, the bright blue river passed
Along the margin of our terrace walk;
A tempting playmate whom we dearly loved.
Oh, many a time have I, a five years' child,
In a small mill-race severed from his stream,
290 Made one long bathing of a summer's day;
Basked in the sun, and plunged and basked again
Alternate, all a summer's day, or scoured
The sandy fields, leaping through flowery groves
Of yellow ragwort; or when rock and hill,
The woods, and distant Skiddaw's lofty height,
Were bronzed with deepest radiance, stood alone
Beneath the sky, as if I had been born
On Indian plains, and from my mother's hut
Had run abroad in wantonness, to sport
300 A naked savage, in the thunder shower.

Fair seed-time had my soul, and I grew up
Fostered alike by beauty and by fear:
Much favoured in my birthplace, and no less
In that belovèd Vale to which ere long
We were transplanted – there were we let loose
For sports of wider range. Ere I had told
Ten birth-days, when among the mountain-slopes
Frost, and the breath of frosty wind, had snapped
The last autumnal crocus, 'twas my joy
310 With store of springes o'er my shoulder hung
To range the open heights where woodcocks ran
Among the smooth green turf. Through half the night,

That time, my shoulder all with springes hung,   *310*
I was a fell destroyer. On the heights
Scudding away from snare to snare, I plied
320 My anxious visitation, hurrying on,
Still hurrying, hurrying onward; – moon and stars
Were shining o'er my head. I was alone,
And seemed to be a trouble to the peace
That was among them. Sometimes it befell
In these night wanderings, that a strong desire
O'erpowered my better reason, and the bird
Which was the captive of another's toils   *320*
Became my prey; and when the deed was done
I heard among the solitary hills
330 Low breathings coming after me, and sounds
Of undistinguishable motion, steps
Almost as silent as the turf they trod.   *325*

     Nor less in springtime when on southern banks
The shining sun had from his knot of leaves
Decoyed the primrose flower, and when the Vales
And woods were warm, was I a plunderer then
In the high places, on the lonesome peaks
Where'er, among the mountains and the winds,
The mother-bird had built her lodge; though mean
340 My object and inglorious, yet the end
Was not ignoble. Oh! when I have hung   *330*
Above the raven's nest, by knots of grass
And half-inch fissures in the slippery rock
But ill sustained, and almost (as it seemed)
Suspended by the blast which blew amain,
Shouldering the naked crag, oh, at that time   *335*
While on the perilous ridge I hung alone,
With what strange utterance did the loud dry wind
Blow through my ears! the sky seemed not a sky
350 Of earth – and with what motion moved the clouds!

     The mind of man is framed even like the breath
And harmony of music; there is a dark   *341*

52

Scudding away from snare to snare, I plied
That anxious visitation; – moon and stars
Were shining o'er my head. I was alone,
And seemed to be a trouble to the peace
That dwelt among them. Sometimes it befell
In these night wanderings, that a strong desire
O'erpowered my better reason, and the bird
320 Which was the captive of another's toil
Became my prey; and when the deed was done
I heard among the solitary hills
Low breathings coming after me, and sounds
Of undistinguishable motion, steps
Almost as silent as the turf they trod.

Nor less when spring had warmed the cultured Vale,
Roved we as plunderers where the mother-bird
Had in high places built her lodge; though mean
Our object and inglorious, yet the end
330 Was not ignoble. Oh! when I have hung
Above the raven's nest, by knots of grass
And half-inch fissures in the slippery rock
But ill sustained, and almost (so it seemed)
Suspended by the blast that blew amain,
Shouldering the naked crag, oh, at that time
While on the perilous ridge I hung alone,
With what strange utterance did the loud dry wind
Blow through my ear! the sky seemed not a sky
Of earth – and with what motion moved the clouds!

340 Dust as we are, the immortal spirit grows
Like harmony in music; there is a dark

Invisible workmanship that reconciles
Discordant elements, and makes them move
In one society. Ah me! that all
The terrors, all the early miseries, *345*
Regrets, vexations, lassitudes, that all
The thoughts and feelings which have been infused
Into my mind, should ever have made up
360 The calm existence that is mine when I
Am worthy of myself! Praise to the end! *350*
Thanks likewise for the means! But I believe
That Nature, oftentimes, when she would frame
A favoured being, from his earliest dawn
Of infancy doth open out the clouds,
As at the touch of lightning, seeking him
With gentlest visitation; not the less,
Though haply aiming at the self-same end,
Does it delight her sometimes to employ
370 Severer interventions, ministry *355*
More palpable, and so she dealt with me.

One evening (surely I was led by her)
I went alone into a shepherd's boat,
A skiff that to a willow tree was tied
Within a rocky cave, its usual home.
'Twas by the shores of Patterdale, a vale
Wherein I was a stranger, thither come
A schoolboy traveller, at the holidays.
Forth rambled from the village inn alone,
380 No sooner had I sight of this small skiff,
Discovered thus by unexpected chance,
Than I unloosed her tether and embarked. *360*
The moon was up, the lake was shining clear
Among the hoary mountains; from the shore
I pushed, and struck the oars and struck again
In cadence, and my little boat moved on,
Even like a man who walks with stately step
Though bent on speed. It was an act of stealth *361*
And troubled pleasure, nor without the voice

54

Inscrutable workmanship that reconciles
Discordant elements, makes them cling together
In one society. How strange that all
The terrors, pains, and early miseries,
Regrets, vexations, lassitudes interfused
Within my mind, should e'er have borne a part,
And that a needful part, in making up
The calm existence that is mine when I
350 Am worthy of myself! Praise to the end!
Thanks to the means which Nature deigned to employ;
Whether her fearless visitings, or those
That came with soft alarm, like hurtless light
Opening the peaceful clouds; or she may use
Severer interventions, ministry
More palpable, as best might suit her aim.

One summer evening (led by her) I found
A little boat tied to a willow tree
Within a rocky cave, its usual home.
360 Straight I unloosed her chain, and stepping in
Pushed from the shore. It was an act of stealth
And troubled pleasure, nor without the voice

390 Of mountain-echoes did my boat move on;
Leaving behind her still, on either side,
Small circles glittering idly in the moon,   365
Until they melted all into one track
Of sparkling light. A rocky steep uprose
Above the cavern of the willow tree,
And now, as suited one who proudly rowed
With his best skill, I fixed a steady view
Upon the top of that same craggy ridge,   370
The bound of the horizon, for behind
400 Was nothing but the stars and the grey sky.
She was an elfin pinnace; lustily
I dipped my oars into the silent lake,
And, as I rose upon the stroke, my boat
Went heaving through the water like a swan;   375
When, from behind that craggy steep till then
The bound of the horizon, a huge cliff,
As if with voluntary power instinct,
Upreared its head. I struck and struck again,   380
And growing still in stature the huge cliff
410 Rose up between me and the stars, and still,
With measured motion, like a living thing,
Strode after me. With trembling hands I turned,   385
And through the silent water stole my way
Back to the cavern of the willow tree;
There in her mooring-place I left my bark, –
And through the meadows homeward went, with grave
And serious thoughts; and after I had seen   390
That spectacle, for many days, my brain
Worked with a dim and undetermined sense
420 Of unknown modes of being; in my thoughts
There was a darkness, call it solitude
Or blank desertion. No familiar shapes   395
Of hourly objects, images of trees,
Of sea or sky, no colours of green fields;
But huge and mighty forms, that do not live
Like living men, moved slowly through my mind
By day, and were the trouble of my dreams.   400

Of mountain-echoes did my boat move on;
Leaving behind her still, on either side,
Small circles glittering idly in the moon,
Until they melted all into one track
Of sparkling light. But now, like one who rows,
Proud of his skill, to reach a chosen point
With an unswerving line, I fixed my view
370 Upon the summit of a craggy ridge,
The horizon's utmost boundary, for above
Was nothing but the stars and the grey sky.
She was an elfin pinnace; lustily
I dipped my oars into the silent lake,
And, as I rose upon the stroke, my boat
Went heaving through the water like a swan;
When, from behind that craggy steep till then
The horizon's bound, a huge peak, black and huge,
As if with voluntary power instinct
380 Upreared its head. I struck and struck again,
And growing still in stature the grim shape
Towered up between me and the stars, and still,
For so it seemed, with purpose of its own
And measured motion like a living thing,
Strode after me. With trembling oars I turned,
And through the silent water stole my way
Back to the covert of the willow tree;
There in her mooring-place I left my bark, –
And through the meadows homeward went, in grave
390 And serious mood; but after I had seen
That spectacle, for many days, my brain
Worked with a dim and undetermined sense
Of unknown modes of being; o'er my thoughts
There hung a darkness, call it solitude
Or blank desertion. No familiar shapes
Remained, no pleasant images of trees,
Of sea or sky, no colours of green fields;
But huge and mighty forms, that do not live
Like living men, moved slowly through the mind
400 By day, and were a trouble to my dreams.

Wisdom and Spirit of the universe!
Thou Soul that art the eternity of thought,
430 That giv'st to forms and images a breath
And everlasting motion, not in vain
By day or star-light thus from my first dawn   405
Of childhood didst thou intertwine for me
The passions that build up our human soul;
Not with the mean and vulgar works of man,
But with high objects, with enduring things –
With life and Nature, purifying thus   410
The elements of feeling and of thought,
And sanctifying, by such discipline,
440 Both pain and fear, until we recognize
A grandeur in the beatings of the heart.
Nor was this fellowship vouchsafed to me   415
With stinted kindness. In November days,
When vapours rolling down the valleys made
A lonely scene more lonesome, among woods
At noon, and 'mid the calm of summer nights,
When, by the margin of the trembling lake,
Beneath the gloomy hills I homeward went   420
In solitude, such intercourse was mine;
450 'Twas mine among the fields both day and night,
And by the waters, all the summer long.

And in the frosty season, when the sun   425
Was set, and visible for many a mile
The cottage windows through the twilight blazed,
I heeded not the summons: happy time
It was indeed for all of us – to me
It was a time of rapture! Clear and loud   430
The village clock tolled six, – I wheeled about,
Proud and exulting like an untired horse
460 That cares not for its home. All shod with steel,
We hissed along the polished ice in games
Confederate, imitative of the chase   435
And woodland pleasures, – the resounding horn,
The pack loud bellowing, and the hunted hare.

Wisdom and Spirit of the universe!
Thou Soul that art the eternity of thought,
That giv'st to forms and images a breath
And everlasting motion, not in vain
By day or star-light thus from my first dawn
Of childhood didst thou intertwine for me
The passions that build up our human soul;
Not with the mean and vulgar works of man,
But with high objects, with enduring things –
410 With life and Nature, purifying thus
The elements of feeling and of thought,
And sanctifying, by such discipline,
Both pain and fear, until we recognize
A grandeur in the beatings of the heart.
Nor was this fellowship vouchsafed to me
With stinted kindness. In November days,
When vapours rolling down the valley made
A lonely scene more lonesome, among woods
At noon, and 'mid the calm of summer nights,
420 When, by the margin of the trembling lake,
Beneath the gloomy hills homeward I went
In solitude, such intercourse was mine;
Mine was it in the fields both day and night,
And by the waters, all the summer long.

And in the frosty season, when the sun
Was set, and visible for many a mile
The cottage windows blazed through twilight gloom,
I heeded not their summons: happy time
It was indeed for all of us – for me
430 It was a time of rapture! Clear and loud
The village clock tolled six, – I wheeled about,
Proud and exulting like an untired horse
That cares not for his home. All shod with steel,
We hissed along the polished ice in games
Confederate, imitative of the chase
And woodland pleasures, – the resounding horn,
The pack loud chiming, and the hunted hare.

59

So through the darkness and the cold we flew,
And not a voice was idle; with the din,
Meanwhile, the precipices rang aloud;   440
The leafless trees and every icy crag
Tinkled like iron; while the distant hills
470 Into the tumult sent an alien sound
Of melancholy not unnoticed, while the stars
Eastward were sparkling clear, and in the west   445
The orange sky of evening died away.
Not seldom from the uproar I retired
Into a silent bay, or sportively
Glanced sideway, leaving the tumultuous throng,
To cut across the image of a star   450
That gleamed upon the ice; and oftentimes,
When we had given our bodies to the wind,
480 And all the shadowy banks on either side
Came sweeping through the darkness, spinning still   455
The rapid line of motion, then at once
Have I, reclining back upon my heels,
Stopped short; yet still the solitary cliffs
Wheeled by me – even as if the earth had rolled
With visible motion her diurnal round!   460
Behind me did they stretch in solemn train,
Feebler and feebler, and I stood and watched
Till all was tranquil as a dreamless sleep.

490   Ye Presences of Nature in the sky
Or on the earth! Ye Visions of the hills!   465
And Souls of lonely places! can I think
A vulgar hope was yours when ye employed
Such ministry, when ye through many a year
Haunting me thus among my boyish sports,
On caves and trees, upon the woods and hills,   470
Impressed upon all forms the characters
Of danger or desire; and thus did make
The surface of the universal earth
500 With triumph and delight, and hope and fear,

So through the darkness and the cold we flew,
And not a voice was idle; with the din
440 Smitten, the precipices rang aloud;
The leafless trees and every icy crag
Tinkled like iron; while far distant hills
Into the tumult sent an alien sound
Of melancholy not unnoticed, while the stars
Eastward were sparkling clear, and in the west
The orange sky of evening died away.
Not seldom from the uproar I retired
Into a silent bay, or sportively
Glanced sideway, leaving the tumultuous throng,
450 To cut across the reflex of a star
That fled, and, flying still before me, gleamed
Upon the glassy plain; and oftentimes,
When we had given our bodies to the wind,
And all the shadowy banks on either side
Came sweeping through the darkness, spinning still
The rapid line of motion, then at once
Have I, reclining back upon my heels,
Stopped short; yet still the solitary cliffs
Wheeled by me – even as if the earth had rolled
460 With visible motion her diurnal round!
Behind me did they stretch in solemn train,
Feebler and feebler, and I stood and watched
Till all was tranquil as a dreamless sleep.

Ye Presences of Nature in the sky
And on the earth! Ye Visions of the hills!
And Souls of lonely places! can I think
A vulgar hope was yours when ye employed
Such ministry, when ye through many a year
Haunting me thus among my boyish sports,
470 On caves and trees, upon the woods and hills,
Impressed upon all forms the characters
Of danger or desire; and thus did make
The surface of the universal earth
With triumph and delight, with hope and fear,

Work like a sea? 475
        Not uselessly employed,
I might pursue this theme through every change
Of exercise and play, to which the year
Did summon us in its delightful round.

We were a noisy crew; the sun in heaven 480
Beheld not vales more beautiful than ours;
Nor saw a race in happiness and joy
More worthy of the fields where they were sown.
I would record with no reluctant voice
510 The woods of autumn, and their hazel bowers
With milk-white clusters hung; the rod and line, 485
True symbol of the foolishness of hope,
Which with its strong enchantment led us on
By rocks and pools shut out from every star,
All the green summer, to forlorn cascades
Among the windings of the mountain brooks. 490
– Unfading recollections! at this hour
The heart is almost mine with which I felt,
From some hill-top, on sunny afternoons
520 The kite high up among the fleecy clouds
Pull at its rein like an impatient courser; 495
Or, from the meadows sent on gusty days,
Beheld her breast the wind, then suddenly
Dashed headlong, and rejected by the storm.

Ye lowly cottages in which we dwelt,
A ministration of your own was yours, 500
A sanctity, a safeguard, and a love!
Can I forget you, being as ye were
So beautiful among the pleasant fields
530 In which ye stood? or can I here forget
The plain and seemly countenance with which
Ye dealt out your plain comforts? Yet had ye 505
Delights and exultations of your own.
Eager and never weary we pursued
Our home-amusements by the warm peat-fire

Work like a sea?
    Not uselessly employed,
Might I pursue this theme through every change
Of exercise and play, to which the year
Did summon us in his delightful round.

  We were a noisy crew; the sun in heaven
480 Beheld not vales more beautiful than ours;
Nor saw a band in happiness and joy
Richer, or worthier of the ground they trod.
I could record with no reluctant voice
The woods of autumn, and their hazel bowers
With milk-white clusters hung; the rod and line,
True symbol of hope's foolishness, whose strong
And unreproved enchantment led us on
By rocks and pools shut out from every star,
All the green summer, to forlorn cascades
490 Among the windings hid of mountain brooks.
– Unfading recollections! at this hour
The heart is almost mine with which I felt,
From some hill-top on sunny afternoons,
The paper kite high among fleecy clouds
Pull at her rein like an impetuous courser;
Or, from the meadows sent on gusty days,
Beheld her breast the wind, then suddenly
Dashed headlong, and rejected by the storm.

  Ye lowly cottages wherein we dwelt,
500 A ministration of your own was yours;
Can I forget you, being as you were
So beautiful among the pleasant fields
In which ye stood? or can I here forget
The plain and seemly countenance with which
Ye dealt out your plain comforts? Yet had ye
Delights and exaltations of your own.
Eager and never weary we pursued
Our home-amusements by the warm peat-fire

At evening, when with pencil and with slate
In square divisions parcelled out and all 510
With crosses and with cyphers scribbled o'er,
We schemed and puzzled, head opposed to head
540 In strife too humble to be named in verse:
Or round the naked table, snow-white deal,
Cherry or maple, sate in close array, 515
And to the combat, Loo or Whist, led on
A thick-ribbed army; not, as in the world,
Neglected and ungratefully thrown by
Even for the very service they had wrought,
But husbanded through many a long campaign. 520
Uncouth assemblage was it, where no few
Had changed their functions; some, plebeian cards
550 Which Fate, beyond the promise of their birth,
Had glorified, and called to represent
The persons of departed potentates. 525
Oh, with what echoes on the board they fell!
Ironic diamonds, – clubs, hearts, diamonds, spades,
A congregation piteously akin!
Cheap matter did they give to boyish wit,
Those sooty knaves, precipitated down 530
With scoffs and taunts, like Vulcan out of heaven:
The paramount ace, a moon in her eclipse,
560 Queens gleaming through their splendour's last decay,
And monarchs surly at the wrongs sustained
By royal visages. Meanwhile abroad 535
The heavy rain was falling, or the frost
Raged bitterly, with keen and silent tooth;
And, interrupting the impassioned game,
From Esthwaite's neighbouring lake the splitting ice,
While it sank down towards the water, sent,
Among the meadows and the hills, its long 541
And dismal yellings, like the noise of wolves
570 When they are howling round the Bothnic Main.

Nor, sedulous as I have been to trace
How Nature by extrinsic passion first 545
64

At evening, when with pencil, and smooth slate
510 In square divisions parcelled out and all
With crosses and with cyphers scribbled o'er,
We schemed and puzzled, head opposed to head
In strife too humble to be named in verse:
Or round the naked table, snow-white deal,
Cherry or maple, sate in close array,
And to the combat, Loo or Whist, led on
A thick-ribbed army; not, as in the world,
Neglected and ungratefully thrown by
Even for the very service they had wrought,
520 But husbanded through many a long campaign.
Uncouth assemblage was it, where no few
Had changed their functions; some, plebeian cards
Which Fate, beyond the promise of their birth,
Had dignified, and called to represent
The persons of departed potentates.
Oh, with what echoes on the board they fell!
Ironic diamonds, – clubs, hearts, diamonds, spades,
A congregation piteously akin!
Chief matter offered they to boyish wit,
530 Those sooty knaves, precipitated down
With scoffs and taunts, like Vulcan out of heaven:
The paramount ace, a moon in her eclipse,
Queens gleaming through their splendour's last decay,
And monarchs surly at the wrongs sustained
By royal visages. Meanwhile abroad
Incessant rain was falling, or the frost
Raged bitterly, with keen and silent tooth;
And, interrupting oft that eager game,
From under Esthwaite's splitting fields of ice
540 The pent-up air, struggling to free itself,
Gave out to meadow grounds and hills a loud
Protracted yelling, like the noise of wolves
Howling in troops along the Bothnic Main.

   Nor, sedulous as I have been to trace
How Nature by extrinsic passion first

Peopled my mind with beauteous forms or grand,
And made me love them, may I well forget
How other pleasures have been mine, and joys
Of subtler origin; how I have felt,
Not seldom even in that tempestuous time,   550
Those hallowed and pure motions of the sense
Which seem, in their simplicity, to own
580 An intellectual charm; that calm delight
Which, if I err not, surely must belong
To those first-born affinities that fit   555
Our new existence to existing things,
And, in our dawn of being, constitute
The bond of union betwixt life and joy.

Yes, I remember when the changeful earth,
And twice five seasons on my mind had stamped   560
The faces of the moving year, even then,
A child, I held unconscious intercourse
590 With the eternal beauty, drinking in
A pure organic pleasure from the lines
Of curling mist, or from the level plain   565
Of waters coloured by the steady clouds.

The sands of Westmoreland, the creeks and bays
Of Cumbria's rocky limits, they can tell
How, when the Sea threw off his evening shade,
And to the shepherd's huts beneath the crags   570
Did send sweet notice of the rising moon,
How I have stood, to fancies such as these,
600 Engrafted in the tenderness of thought,
A stranger, linking with the spectacle   575
No conscious memory of a kindred sight,
And bringing with me no peculiar sense
Of quietness or peace; yet I have stood,
Even while mine eye has moved o'er three long leagues
Of shining water, gathering as it seemed
Through every hair-breadth of that field of light
New pleasure like a bee among the flowers.   580

66

Peopled the mind with forms sublime or fair,
And made me love them, may I here omit
How other pleasures have been mine, and joys
Of subtler origin; how I have felt,
550   Not seldom even in that tempestuous time,
Those hallowed and pure motions of the sense
Which seem, in their simplicity, to own
An intellectual charm; that calm delight
Which, if I err not, surely must belong
To those first-born affinities that fit
Our new existence to existing things,
And, in our dawn of being, constitute
The bond of union between life and joy.

Yes, I remember when the changeful earth,
560   And twice five summers on my mind had stamped
The faces of the moving year, even then
I held unconscious intercourse with beauty
Old as creation, drinking in a pure
Organic pleasure from the silver wreaths
Of curling mist, or from the level plain
Of waters coloured by impending clouds.

The sands of Westmoreland, the creeks and bays
Of Cumbria's rocky limits, they can tell
How, when the Sea threw off his evening shade,
570   And to the shepherd's hut on distant hills
Sent welcome notice of the rising moon,
How I have stood, to fancies such as these
A stranger, linking with the spectacle
No conscious memory of a kindred sight,
And bringing with me no peculiar sense
Of quietness or peace; yet have I stood,
Even while mine eye hath moved o'er many a league
Of shining water, gathering as it seemed
Through every hair-breadth in that field of light
580   New pleasure like a bee among the flowers.

Thus often in those fits of vulgar joy
610 Which, through all seasons, on a child's pursuits
Are prompt attendants, 'mid that giddy bliss
Which, like a tempest, works along the blood
And is forgotten; even then I felt   585
Gleams like the flashing of a shield; – the earth
And common face of Nature spake to me
Rememberable things; sometimes, 'tis true,
By chance collisions and quaint accidents
(Like those ill-sorted unions, work supposed   590
Of evil-minded fairies), yet not vain
620 Nor profitless, if haply they impressed
Collateral objects and appearances,
Albeit lifeless then, and doomed to sleep   595
Until maturer seasons called them forth
To impregnate and to elevate the mind.
– And if the vulgar joy by its own weight
Wearied itself out of the memory,
The scenes which were a witness of that joy   600
Remained in their substantial lineaments
Depicted on the brain, and to the eye
630 Were visible, a daily sight; and thus
By the impressive discipline of fear,
By pleasure and repeated happiness,
So frequently repeated, and by force   605
Of obscure feelings representative
Of joys that were forgotten, these same scenes,
So beauteous and majestic in themselves,
Though yet the day was distant, did at length
Become habitually dear, and all   610
Their hues and forms were by invisible links
640 Allied to the affections.
                              I began
My story early – feeling, as I fear,
The weakness of a human love for days
Disowned by memory – ere the birth of spring   615
Planting my snowdrops among winter snows.

Thus oft amid those fits of vulgar joy
Which, through all seasons, on a child's pursuits
Are prompt attendants, 'mid that giddy bliss
Which, like a tempest, works along the blood
And is forgotten; even then I felt
Gleams like the flashing of a shield; – the earth
And common face of Nature spake to me
Rememberable things; sometimes, 'tis true,
By chance collisions and quaint accidents
590 (Like those ill-sorted unions, work supposed
Of evil-minded fairies), yet not vain
Nor profitless, if haply they impressed
Collateral objects and appearances,
Albeit lifeless then, and doomed to sleep
Until maturer seasons called them forth
To impregnate and to elevate the mind.
– And if the vulgar joy by its own weight
Wearied itself out of the memory,
The scenes which were a witness of that joy
600 Remained in their substantial lineaments
Depicted on the brain, and to the eye
Were visible, a daily sight; and thus
By the impressive discipline of fear,
By pleasure and repeated happiness,
So frequently repeated, and by force
Of obscure feelings representative
Of things forgotten, these same scenes so bright,
So beautiful, so majestic in themselves,
Though yet the day was distant, did become
610 Habitually dear, and all their forms
And changeful colours by invisible links
Were fastened to the affections.
                                        I began
My story early – not misled, I trust,
By an infirmity of love for days
Disowned by memory – fancying flowers where none
Not even the sweetest do or can survive
616a For him at least whose dawning day they cheered.

69

Nor will it seem to thee, my Friend! so prompt
In sympathy, that I have lengthened out
With fond and feeble tongue a tedious tale.
Meanwhile, my hope has been, that I might fetch   620
Invigorating thoughts from former years;
650 Might fix the wavering balance of my mind,
And haply meet reproaches too, whose power
May spur me on, in manhood now mature,
To honourable toil. Yet should these hopes   625
Be vain, and thus should neither I be taught
To understand myself, nor thou to know
With better knowledge how the heart was framed
Of him thou lovest; need I dread from thee
Harsh judgements, if I am so loth to quit   630
Those recollected hours that have the charm
660 Of visionary things, and lovely forms
And sweet sensations that throw back our life
And almost make our infancy itself
A visible scene, on which the sun is shining?   635

One end hereby at least hath been attained:
My mind hath been revived, and if this mood
Desert me not, I will forthwith bring down
Through later years the story of my life.
The road lies plain before me; – 'tis a theme   640
Single and of determined bounds; and hence
670 I choose it rather at this time, than work
Of ampler or more varied argument.

70

Nor will it seem to thee, O Friend! so prompt
In sympathy, that I have lengthened out
With fond and feeble tongue a tedious tale.
620 Meanwhile, my hope has been, that I might fetch
Invigorating thoughts from former years;
Might fix the wavering balance of my mind,
And haply meet reproaches too, whose power
May spur me on, in manhood now mature,
To honourable toil. Yet should these hopes
Prove vain, and thus should neither I be taught
To understand myself, nor thou to know
With better knowledge how the heart was framed
Of him thou lovest; need I dread from thee
630 Harsh judgements, if the song be loth to quit
Those recollected hours that have the charm
Of visionary things, those lovely forms
And sweet sensations that throw back our life,
And almost make remotest infancy
A visible scene, on which the sun is shining?

     One end at least hath been attained: my mind
Hath been revived, and if this genial mood
Desert me not, forthwith shall be brought down
Through later years the story of my life.
640 The road lies plain before me; – 'tis a theme
Single and of determined bounds; and hence
I choose it rather at this time, than work
Of ampler or more varied argument,
Where I might be discomfited and lost:
And certain hopes are with me, that to thee
This labour will be welcome, honoured Friend!

Thus far, O Friend! have we, though leaving much
Unvisited, endeavoured to retrace
My life through its first years, and measured back
The way I travelled when I first began
To love the woods and fields. The passion yet   5
Was in its birth, sustained as might befall
By nourishment that came unsought; for still
From week to week, from month to month, we lived
A round of tumult. Duly were our games
10 Prolonged in summer till the daylight failed: 10
No chair remained before the doors; the bench
And threshold steps were empty; fast asleep
The labourer, and the old man who had sate
A later lingerer; yet the revelry
Continued and the loud uproar: at last,   15
When all the ground was dark, and the huge clouds
Were edged with twinkling stars, to bed we went,
With weary joints and with a beating mind.
Ah! is there one who ever has been young,
20 And needs a monitory voice to tame   20
The pride of virtue and of intellect?
And is there one, the wisest and the best
Of all mankind, who does not sometimes wish
For things which cannot be; – who would not give,
If so he might, to duty and to truth   25
The eagerness of infantine desire?
A tranquillizing spirit presses now
On my corporeal frame, so wide appears
The vacancy between me and those days
30 Which yet have such self-presence in my mind,   30

SCHOOL-TIME (CONTINUED)

Thus far, O Friend! have we, though leaving much
Unvisited, endeavoured to retrace
The simple ways in which my childhood walked;
Those chiefly that first led me to the love
Of rivers, woods, and fields. The passion yet
Was in its birth, sustained as might befall
By nourishment that came unsought; for still
From week to weeek, from month to month, we lived
A round of tumult. Duly were our games
10 Prolonged in summer till the daylight failed:
No chair remained before the doors; the bench
And threshold steps were empty; fast asleep
The labourer, and the old man who had sate
A later lingerer; yet the revelry
Continued and the loud uproar: at last,
When all the ground was dark, and twinkling stars
Edged the black clouds, home and to bed we went,
Feverish with weary joints and beating minds.
Ah! is there one who ever has been young,
20 Nor needs a warning voice to tame the pride
Of intellect and virtue's self-esteem?
One is there, though the wisest and the best
Of all mankind, who covets not at times
Union that cannot be; – who would not give,
If so he might, to duty and to truth
The eagerness of infantine desire?
A tranquillizing spirit presses now
On my corporeal frame, so wide appears
The vacancy between me and those days
30 Which yet have such self-presence in my mind,

That, sometimes, when I think of it, I seem
Two consciousnesses, conscious of myself
And of some other Being. A grey stone
Of native rock, left midway in the square
Of our small market village, was the home
And centre of these joys; and when, returned   36
After long absence, thither I repaired,
I found that it was split, and gone to build
A smart Assembly-room that perked and flared
40   With wash and rough-cast elbowing the ground
Which had been ours. But let the fiddle scream,   40
And be ye happy! Yet, my Friends! I know
That more than one of you will think with me
Of those soft starry nights, and that old Dame
From whom the stone was named, who there had sate
And watched her table with its huckster's wares   45
Assiduous, through the length of sixty years.

     We ran a boisterous race; the year span round
With giddy motion. But the time approached
50   That brought with it a regular desire
For calmer pleasures, when the beauteous forms   50
Of Nature were collaterally attached
To every scheme of holiday delight
And every boyish sport, less grateful else
And languidly pursued.
                              When summer came,
It was the pastime of our afternoons   55
To beat along the plain of Windermere
With rival oars; and the selected bourne
Was now an Island musical with birds
60   That sang for ever; now a Sister Isle
Beneath the oak's umbrageous covert, sown   60
With lilies of the valley like a field;
And now a third small Island, where remained
An old stone table, and a mouldered cave,
A hermit's history. In such a race   65
So ended, disappointment could be none,

That, musing on them, often do I seem
Two consciousnesses, conscious of myself
And of some other Being. A rude mass
Of native rock, left midway in the square
Of our small market village, was the goal
Or centre of these sports; and when, returned
After long absence, thither I repaired,
Gone was the old grey stone, and in its place
A smart Assembly-room usurped the ground
40 That had been ours. There let the fiddle scream,
And be ye happy! Yet, my Friends! I know
That more than one of you will think with me
Of those soft starry nights, and that old Dame
From whom the stone was named, who there had sate,
And watched her table with its huckster's wares
Assiduous, through the length of sixty years.

    We ran a boisterous course; the year span round
With giddy motion. But the time approached
That brought with it a regular desire
50 For calmer pleasures, when the winning forms
Of Nature were collaterally attached
To every scheme of holiday delight
And every boyish sport, less grateful else
And languidly pursued.
               When summer came,
Our pastime was, on bright half-holidays,
To sweep along the plain of Windermere
With rival oars; and the selected bourne
Was now an Island musical with birds
That sang and ceased not; now a Sister Isle
60 Beneath the oak's umbrageous covert, sown
With lilies of the valley like a field;
And now a third small Island, where survived
In solitude the ruins of a shrine
Once to Our Lady dedicate, and served
Daily with chanted rites. In such a race
So ended, disappointment could be none,

Uneasiness, or pain, or jealousy:
We rested in the shade, all pleased alike,
Conquered and conqueror. Thus the pride of strength,
70 And the vain-glory of superior skill,   *70*
Were interfused with objects which subdued
And tempered them, and gradually produced
A quiet independence of the heart;
And to my Friend who knows me I may add,
Unapprehensive of reproof, that hence
Ensued a diffidence and modesty,   *75*
<u>And I was taught to feel, perhaps too much,</u>
<u>The self-sufficing power of Solitude.</u>

    No delicate viands sapped our bodily strength;
80 More than we wished we knew the blessing then
Of vigorous hunger, for our daily meals   *80*
Were frugal, Sabine fare! and then, exclude
A little weekly stipend, and we lived
Through three divisions of the quartered year
In penniless poverty. But now to school
Returned from the half-yearly holidays,   *85*
We came with purses more profusely filled,
Allowance which abundantly sufficed
To gratify the palate with repasts
90 More costly than the Dame of whom I spake,
That ancient woman, and her board supplied.
Hence inroads into distant vales, and long
Excursions far away among the hills,
Hence rustic dinners on the cool green ground,
Or in the woods, or near a river side,   *90*
Or by some shady fountain, while soft airs
Among the leaves were stirring, and the sun
Unfelt shone sweetly round us in our joy.
Nor is my aim neglected if I tell
100 How twice in the long length of those half-years   *95*
We from our funds, perhaps, with bolder hand
Drew largely, anxious for one day, at least,
To feel the motion of the galloping steed;

Uneasiness, or pain, or jealousy:
We rested in the shade, all pleased alike,
Conquered and conqueror. Thus the pride of strength,
70 And the vain-glory of superior skill,
Were tempered; thus was gradually produced
A quiet independence of the heart;
And to my Friend who knows me I may add,
Fearless of blame, that hence for future days
Ensued a diffidence and modesty,
And I was taught to feel, perhaps too much,
The self-sufficing power of Solitude.

    Our daily meals were frugal, Sabine fare!
More than we wished we knew the blessing then
80 Of vigorous hunger – hence corporeal strength
Unsapped by delicate viands; for, exclude
A little weekly stipend, and we lived
Through three divisions of the quartered year
In penniless poverty. But now to school
From the half-yearly holidays returned,
We came with weightier purses, that sufficed
To furnish treats more costly than the Dame
Of the old grey stone, from her scant board, supplied.
Hence rustic dinners on the cool green ground,
90 Or in the woods, or by a river side
Or shady fountain, while among the leaves
Soft airs were stirring, and the mid-day sun
Unfelt shone brightly round us in our joy.
Nor is my aim neglected if I tell
How sometimes, in the length of those half-years,
We from our funds drew largely; – proud to curb,
And eager to spur on, the galloping steed;

And with the good old inn-keeper, in truth,
On such occasion sometimes we employed
Sly subterfuge; for the intended bound   *100*
Of the day's journey was too distant far
For any cautious man, a structure famed
Beyond its neighbourhood, the antique walls
110 Of that large abbey which within the Vale
Of Nightshade, to St Mary's honour built,
Stands yet a mouldering pile with fractured arch,   *105*
Belfry, and images, and living trees,
A holy scene! Along the smooth green turf
Our horses grazed. To more than inland peace
Left by the sea wind passing overhead
(Though wind of roughest temper) trees and towers   *110*
May in that valley oftentimes be seen,
Both silent and both motionless alike;
120 Such is the shelter that is there, and such
The safeguard for repose and quietness.

       Our steeds remounted and the summons given,   *115*
With whip and spur we by the chantry flew
In uncouth race, and left the cross-legged knight,
And the stone-abbot, and that single wren
Which one day sang so sweetly in the nave
Of the old church, that – though from recent showers   *120*
The earth was comfortless, and, touched by faint
Internal breezes, sobbings of the place
130 And respirations, from the roofless walls
The shuddering ivy dripped large drops – yet still
So sweetly 'mid the gloom the invisible bird   *125*
Sang to itself, that there I could have made
My dwelling-place, and lived for ever there
To hear such music. Through the walls we flew
And down the valley, and, a circuit made
In wantonness of heart, through rough and smooth   *130*
We scampered homeward. Oh, ye rocks and streams,
And that still spirit of the evening air!
140 Even in this joyous time I sometimes felt

And with the cautious inn-keeper, whose stud
Supplied our want, we haply might employ
100 Sly subterfuges, if the adventure's bound
Were distant: some famed temple where of yore
The Druids worshipped, or the antique walls
Of that large abbey, where within the Vale
Of Nightshade, to St Mary's honour built,
Stands yet a mouldering pile with fractured arch,
Belfry, and images, and living trees,
A holy scene! Along the smooth green turf
Our horses grazed. To more than inland peace
Left by the west wind sweeping overhead
110 From a tumultuous ocean, trees and towers
In that sequestered valley may be seen,
Both silent and both motionless alike;
Such the deep shelter that is there, and such
The safeguard for repose and quietness.

Our steeds remounted and the summons given,
With whip and spur we through the chantry flew
In uncouth race, and left the cross-legged knight,
And the stone-abbot, and that single wren
Which one day sang so sweetly in the nave
120 Of the old church, that – though from recent showers
The earth was comfortless, and, touched by faint
Internal breezes, sobbings of the place
And respirations, from the roofless walls
The shuddering ivy dripped large drops – yet still
So sweetly 'mid the gloom the invisible bird
Sang to herself, that there I could have made
My dwelling-place, and lived for ever there
To hear such music. Through the walls we flew
And down the valley, and, a circuit made
130 In wantonness of heart, through rough and smooth
We scampered homewards. Oh, ye rocks and streams,
And that still spirit shed from evening air!
Even in this joyous time I sometimes felt

Your presence, when with slackened step we breathed   *135*
Along the sides of the steep hills, or when
Lighted by gleams of moonlight from the sea
We beat with thundering hoofs the level sand.

    Upon the eastern shore of <u>Windermere,</u>
Above the crescent of a pleasant bay,
There stood an inn; no homely-featured shed,
Brother of the surrounding cottages,   *140*
But 'twas a splendid place, the door beset
150 With chaises, grooms, and liveries, and within
Decanters, glasses, and the blood-red wine.
In ancient times, or ere the Hall was built   *145*
On the large island, had this dwelling been
More worthy of a poet's love, a hut,
Proud of its one bright fire and sycamore shade.
But – though the rhymes were gone which once inscribed
The threshold, and large golden characters   *150*
On the blue-frosted sign-board had usurped
The place of the old Lion, in contempt
160 And mockery of the rustic painter's hand –
Yet, to this hour, the spot to me is dear
With all its foolish pomp. The garden lay   *155*
Upon a slope surmounted by the plain
Of a small bowling-green; beneath us stood
A grove, with gleams of water through the trees
And over the tree-tops; nor did we want
Refreshment, strawberries and mellow cream.   *160*
And there, through half an afternoon, we played
On the smooth platform, and the shouts we sent
170 Made all the mountains ring. But, ere the fall
Of night, when in our pinnace we returned   *165*
Over the dusky lake, and to the beach
Of some small island steered our course with one,
The Minstrel of our Troop, and left him there,
And rowed off gently, while he blew his flute
Alone upon the rock – oh, then, the calm   *170*

Your presence, when with slackened step we breathed
Along the sides of the steep hills, or when
Lighted by gleams of moonlight from the sea
We beat with thundering hoofs the level sand.

Midway on long Winander's eastern shore,
Within the crescent of a pleasant bay,
140 A tavern stood; no homely-featured house,
Primeval like its neighbouring cottages,
But 'twas a splendid place, the door beset
With chaises, grooms, and liveries, and within
Decanters, glasses, and the blood-red wine.
In ancient times, or ere the Hall was built
On the large island, had this dwelling been
More worthy of a poet's love, a hut,
Proud of its one bright fire and sycamore shade.
But – though the rhymes were gone that once inscribed
150 The threshold, and large golden characters,
Spread o'er the spangled sign-board, had dislodged
The old Lion and usurped his place, in slight
And mockery of the rustic painter's hand –
Yet, to this hour, the spot to me is dear
With all its foolish pomp. The garden lay
Upon a slope surmounted by the plain
Of a small bowling-green; beneath us stood
A grove, with gleams of water through the trees
And over the tree-tops; nor did we want
160 Refreshment, strawberries and mellow cream.
There, while through half an afternoon we played
On the smooth platform, whether skill prevailed
Or happy blunder triumphed, bursts of glee
Made all the mountains ring. But, ere nightfall,
When in our pinnace we returned at leisure
Over the shadowy lake, and to the beach
Of some small island steered our course with one,
The Minstrel of the Troop, and left him there,
And rowed off gently, while he blew his flute
170 Alone upon the rock – oh, then, the calm

And dead still water lay upon my mind
Even with a weight of pleasure, and the sky,
Never before so beautiful, sank down
180 Into my heart, and held me like a dream.   *175*
Thus daily were my sympathies enlarged,
And thus the common range of visible things
Grew dear to me: already I began
To love the sun; a boy I loved the sun,
Not as I since have loved him, as a pledge
And surety of our earthly life, a light   *180*
Which while we view we feel we are alive;
But for this cause, that I had seen him lay
His beauty on the morning hills, had seen
190 The western mountain touch his setting orb,   *185*
In many a thoughtless hour, when, from excess
Of happiness, my blood appeared to flow
With its own pleasure, and I breathed with joy.
And, from like feelings, humble though intense,
To patriotic and domestic love   *190*
Analogous, the moon to me was dear;
For I would dream away my purposes,
Standing to look upon her while she hung
Midway between the hills, as if she knew
200 No other region, but belonged to thee,
Yea, appertained by a peculiar right
To thee and thy grey huts, my darling Vale!

Those incidental charms which first attached
My heart to rural objects, day by day
Grew weaker, and I hasten on to tell   *200*
How Nature, intervenient till this time,
And secondary, now at length was sought
For her own sake. But who shall parcel out
His intellect by geometric rules,
210 Split like a province into round and square?   *205*
Who knows the individual hour in which
His habits were first sown, even as a seed?

And dead still water lay upon my mind
Even with a weight of pleasure, and the sky,
Never before so beautiful, sank down
Into my heart, and held me like a dream!
Thus were my sympathies enlarged, and thus
Daily the common range of visible things
Grew dear to me: already I began
To love the sun; a boy I loved the sun,
Not as I since have loved him, as a pledge
180 And surety of our earthly life, a light
Which we behold and feel we are alive;
Nor for his bounty to so many worlds –
But for this cause, that I had seen him lay
His beauty on the morning hills, had seen
The western mountain touch his setting orb,
In many a thoughtless hour, when, from excess
Of happiness, my blood appeared to flow
For its own pleasure, and I breathed with joy.
And, from like feelings, humble though intense,
190 To patriotic and domestic love
Analogous, the moon to me was dear;
For I would dream away my purposes,
Standing to gaze upon her while she hung
Midway between the hills, as if she knew
No other region, but belonged to thee,
Yea, appertained by a peculiar right
To thee and thy grey huts, thou one dear Vale!

Those incidental charms which first attached
My heart to rural objects, day by day
200 Grew weaker, and I hasten on to tell
How Nature, intervenient till this time
And secondary, now at length was sought
For her own sake. But who shall parcel out
His intellect by geometric rules,
Split like a province into round and square?
Who knows the individual hour in which
His habits were first sown, even as a seed?

Who that shall point as with a wand and say
'This portion of the river of my mind
Came from yon fountain'? Thou, my Friend! art one
More deeply read in thy own thoughts; to thee
Science appears but what in truth she is,
Not as our glory and our absolute boast,
But as a succedaneum, and a prop
To our infirmity. Thou art no slave
Of that false secondary power by which,
In weakness, we create distinctions, then
Deem that our puny boundaries are things
Which we perceive, and not which we have made.
To thee, unblinded by these outward shows,
The unity of all has been revealed,
And thou wilt doubt, with me less aptly skilled
Than many are to class the cabinet
Of their sensations, and in voluble phrase
Run through the history and birth of each
As of a single independent thing.
Hard task to analyse a soul, in which,
Not only general habits and desires,
But each most obvious and particular thought,
Not in a mystical and idle sense,
But in the words of Reason deeply weighed,
Hath no beginning.
Blest the infant Babe,
(For with my best conjectures I would trace
The progress of our being,) blest the Babe,
Nursed in his Mother's arms, the Babe who sleeps
Upon his Mother's breast; who, when his soul
Claims manifest kindred with an earthly soul,
Doth gather passion from his Mother's eye!
Such feelings pass into his torpid life
Like an awakening breeze, and hence his mind
Even [in the first trial of its powers]
Is prompt and watchful, eager to combine
In one appearance, all the elements
And parts of the same object, else detached

Who that shall point as with a wand and say
'This portion of the river of my mind
210 Came from yon fountain'? Thou, my Friend! art one
More deeply read in thy own thoughts; to thee
Science appears but what in truth she is,
Not as our glory and our absolute boast,
But as a succedaneum, and a prop
To our infirmity. No officious slave
Art thou of that false secondary power
By which we multiply distinctions, then
Deem that our puny boundaries are things
That we perceive, and not that we have made.
220 To thee, unblinded by these formal arts,
The unity of all hath been revealed,
And thou wilt doubt, with me less aptly skilled
Than many are to range the faculties
In scale and order, class the cabinet
Of their sensations, and in voluble phrase
Run through the history and birth of each
As of a single independent thing.
Hard task, vain hope, to analyse the mind,
If each most obvious and particular thought,
230 Not in a mystical and idle sense,
But in the words of Reason deeply weighed,
Hath no beginning.
                    Blest the infant Babe,
(For with my best conjecture I would trace
Our Being's earthly progress,) blest the Babe,
Nursed in his Mother's arms, who sinks to sleep
Rocked on his Mother's breast; who with his soul
Drinks in the feelings of his Mother's eye!

250 And loth to coalesce. Thus, day by day,
Subjected to the discipline of love,
His organs and recipient faculties
Are quickened, are more vigorous, his mind spreads,
Tenacious of the forms which it receives.
In one beloved Presence, nay and more,
In that most apprehensive habitude
And those sensations which have been derived
From this beloved Presence, there exists
A virtue which irradiates and exalts
260 All objects through all intercourse of sense.   240
No outcast he, bewildered and depressed:
Along his infant veins are interfused
The gravitation and the filial bond
Of Nature that connect him with the world.   244
Emphatically such a Being lives,
An inmate of this *active* universe;
From nature largely he receives; nor so
Is satisfied, but largely gives again,
For feeling has to him imparted strength,   255
270 And powerful in all sentiments of grief,
Of exultation, fear, and joy, his mind,
Even as an agent of the one great Mind,
Creates, creator and receiver both,
Working but in alliance with the works
Which it beholds. – Such, verily, is the first   260
Poetic spirit of our human life,
By uniform control of after years,
In most, abated and suppressed; in some,
Through every change of growth or of decay,
280 Pre-eminent till death.   265
                          From early days,
Beginning not long after that first time
In which, a Babe, by intercourse of touch
I held mute dialogues with my Mother's heart,
I have endeavoured to display the means
Whereby the infant sensibility,   270
Great birthright of our being, was in me
86

For him, in one dear Presence, there exists
A virtue which irradiates and exalts
240   Objects through widest intercourse of sense.
No outcast he, bewildered and depressed:
Along his infant veins are interfused
The gravitation and the filial bond
Of Nature that connect him with the world.
Is there a flower, to which he points with hand
Too weak to gather it, already love
Drawn from love's purest earthly fount for him
Hath beautified that flower; already shades
Of pity cast from inward tenderness
250   Do fall around him upon aught that bears
Unsightly marks of violence or harm.
Emphatically such a Being lives,
Frail creature as he is, helpless as frail,
An inmate of this active universe:
For feeling has to him imparted power
That through the growing faculties of sense
Doth like an agent of the one great Mind
Create, creator and receiver both,
Working but in alliance with the works
260   Which it beholds. – Such, verily, is the first
Poetic spirit of our human life,
By uniform control of after years,
In most, abated or suppressed; in some,
Through every change of growth and of decay,
Pre-eminent till death.
                  From early days,
Beginning not long after that first time
In which, a Babe, by intercourse of touch
I held mute dialogues with my Mother's heart,
I have endeavoured to display the means
270   Whereby this infant sensibility,
Great birthright of our being, was in me

Augmented and sustained. Yet is a path
More difficult before me; and I fear
That in its broken windings we shall need
290   The chamois' sinews, and the eagle's wing: 275
For now a trouble came into my mind
From unknown causes. I was left alone
Seeking the visible world, nor knowing why.
The props of my affections were removed,
And yet the building stood, as if sustained   280
By its own spirit! All that I beheld
Was dear to me, and from this cause it came,
That now to Nature's finer influxes
My mind lay open, to that more exact
300   And intimate communion which our hearts
Maintain with the minuter properties
Of objects which already are beloved,
And of those only. Many are the joys
Of youth, but oh! what happiness to live   285
When every hour brings palpable access
Of knowledge, when all knowledge is delight,
And sorrow is not there! The seasons came,
And every season to my notice brought
A store of transitory qualities,   290
310   Which, but for this most watchful power of love,
Had been neglected; left a register
Of permanent relations, else unknown,
Hence life, and change, and beauty, solitude
More active even than 'best society' –   295
Society made sweet as solitude
By silent inobtrusive sympathies,
And gentle agitations of the mind
From manifold distinctions, difference
Perceived in things, where, to the common eye,   300
320   No difference is, and hence, from the same source,
Sublimer joy; for I would walk alone,
In storm and tempest, or in starlight nights
Beneath the quiet heavens, and at that time
Have felt whate'er there is of power in sound
88

Augmented and sustained. Yet is a path
More difficult before me; and I fear
That in its broken windings we shall need
The chamois' sinews, and the eagle's wing:
For now a trouble came into my mind
From unknown causes. I was left alone
Seeking the visible world, nor knowing why.
The props of my affections were removed,
280 And yet the building stood, as if sustained
By its own spirit! All that I beheld
Was dear, and hence to finer influxes
The mind lay open, to a more exact
And close communion. Many are our joys
In youth, but oh! what happiness to live
When every hour brings palpable access
Of knowledge, when all knowledge is delight,
And sorrow is not there! The seasons came,
And every season wheresoe'er I moved
290 Unfolded transitory qualities,
Which, but for this most watchful power of love,
Had been neglected; left a register
Of permanent relations, else unknown.
Hence life, and change, and beauty, solitude
More active even than 'best society' –
Society made sweet as solitude
By inward concords, silent, inobtrusive
And gentle agitations of the mind
From manifold distinctions, difference
300 Perceived in things, where, to the unwatchful eye,
No difference is, and hence, from the same source,
Sublimer joy; for I would walk alone,
Under the quiet stars, and at that time
Have felt whate'er there is of power in sound

To breathe an elevated mood, by form   *305*
Or image unprofaned; and I would stand,
Beneath some rock, listening to sounds that are
The ghostly language of the ancient earth,
Or make their dim abode in distant winds.   *310*
330 Thence did I drink the visionary power.
I deem not profitless those fleeting moods
Of shadowy exultation: not for this,
That they are kindred to our purer mind
And intellectual life; but that the soul,   *315*
Remembering how she felt, but what she felt
Remembering not, retains an obscure sense
Of possible sublimity, to which
With growing faculties she doth aspire,
With faculties still growing, feeling still   *320*
340 That whatsoever point they gain, they still
Have something to pursue.
                              And not alone
In grandeur and in tumult, but no less
In tranquil scenes, that universal power
And fitness in the latent qualities   *325*
And essences of things, by which the mind
Is moved by feelings of delight, to me
Came strengthened with a superadded soul,
A virtue not its own. My morning walks
Were early; – oft before the hours of school   *330*
350 I travelled round our little lake, five miles
Of pleasant wandering. Happy time! more dear
For this, that one was by my side, a Friend,
Then passionately loved; with heart how full
Will he peruse these lines, this page, perhaps
A blank to other men! For many years   *335*
Have since flowed in between us, and, our minds
Both silent to each other, at this time
We live as if those hours had never been.
Nor seldom did I lift our cottage latch
360 Far earlier, and before the vernal thrush

To breathe an elevated mood, by form
Or image unprofaned; and I would stand,
If the night blackened with a coming storm,
Beneath some rock, listening to notes that are
The ghostly language of the ancient earth,
310 Or make their dim abode in distant winds.
Thence did I drink the visionary power;
And deem not profitless those fleeting moods
Of shadowy exultation: not for this,
That they are kindred to our purer mind
And intellectual life; but that the soul,
Remembering how she felt, but what she felt
Remembering not, retains an obscure sense
Of possible sublimity, whereto
With growing faculties she doth aspire,
320 With faculties still growing, feeling still
That whatsoever point they gain, they yet
Have something to pursue.
                              And not alone
'Mid gloom and tumult, but no less 'mid fair
And tranquil scenes, that universal power
And fitness in the latent qualities
And essences of things, by which the mind
Is moved with feelings of delight, to me
Came strengthened with a superadded soul,
A virtue not its own. My morning walks
330 Were early; – oft before the hours of school
I travelled round our little lake, five miles
Of pleasant wandering. Happy time! more dear
For this, that one was by my side, a Friend,
Then passionately loved; with heart how full
Would he peruse these lines! For many years
Have since flowed in between us, and, our minds
Both silent to each other, at this time
We live as if those hours had never been.
Nor seldom did I lift our cottage latch
340 Far earlier, and ere one smoke-wreath had risen
From human dwelling, or the thrush, high-perched,

Was audible, among the hills I sate
Alone upon some jutting eminence,
At the first hour of morning, when the Vale
Lay quiet in an utter solitude.   *345*
How shall I trace the history? where seek
The origin of what I then have felt?
Oft in those moments such a holy calm
Did overspread my soul, that I forgot
That I had bodily eyes, and what I saw   *350*
370   Appeared like something in myself, a dream,
A prospect in my mind.
                              'Twere long to tell
What spring and autumn, what the winter snows,
And what the summer shade, what day and night,
The evening and the morning, what my dreams   *355*
And what my waking thoughts supplied, to nurse
That spirit of religious love in which
I walked with Nature. But let this at least
Be not forgotten, that I still retained
My first creative sensibility;   *360*
380   That by the regular action of the world
My soul was unsubdued. A plastic power
Abode with me; a forming hand, at times
Rebellious, acting in a devious mood;
A local spirit of its own, at war   *365*
With general tendency, but, for the most,
Subservient strictly to the external things
With which it communed. An auxiliar light
Came from my mind, which on the setting sun
Bestowed new splendour; the melodious birds,   *370*
390   The gentle breezes, fountains that ran on
Murmuring so sweetly in themselves, obeyed
A like dominion, and the midnight storm
Grew darker in the presence of my eye:
Hence my obeisance, my devotion hence,   *375*
And hence my transport.
                              Nor should this, perchance,
Pass unrecorded, that I still had loved

Piped to the woods his shrill reveillé, sate
Alone upon some jutting eminence,
At the first gleam of dawn-light, when the Vale,
Yet slumbering, lay in utter solitude.
How shall I seek the origin? where find
Faith in the marvellous things which then I felt?
Oft in these moments such a holy calm
Would overspread my soul, that bodily eyes
350 Were utterly forgotten, and what I saw
Appeared like something in myself, a dream,
A prospect in the mind.
                    'Twere long to tell
What spring and autumn, what the winter snows,
And what the summer shade, what day and night,
Evening and morning, sleep and waking thought
From sources inexhaustible, poured forth
To feed the spirit of religious love
In which I walked with Nature. But let this
Be not forgotten, that I still retained
360 My first creative sensibility;
That by the regular action of the world
My soul was unsubdued. A plastic power
Abode with me; a forming hand, at times
Rebellious, acting in a devious mood;
A local spirit of his own, at war
With general tendency, but, for the most,
Subservient strictly to external things
With which it communed. An auxiliar light
Came from my mind, which on the setting sun
370 Bestowed new splendour; the melodious birds,
The fluttering breezes, fountains that ran on
Murmuring so sweetly in themselves, obeyed
A like dominion, and the midnight storm
Grew darker in the presence of my eye:
Hence my obeisance, my devotion hence,
And hence my transport.
                    Nor should this, perchance,
Pass unrecorded, that I still had loved

The exercise and produce of a toil,
Than analytic industry to me
More pleasing, and whose character I deem   *380*
400 Is more poetic as resembling more
Creative agency. I mean to speak
Of that interminable building reared
By observation of affinities
In objects where no brotherhood exists   *385*
To common minds. My seventeenth year was come;
And, whether from this habit rooted now
So deeply in my mind, or from excess
Of the great social principle of life
Coercing all things into sympathy,   *390*
410 To unorganic natures I transferred
My own enjoyments; or the power of truth
Coming in revelation, I conversed
With things that really are; I, at this time,
Saw blessings spread around me like a sea.   *395*
Thus did my days pass on, and now at length
From Nature and her overflowing soul,
I had received so much, that all my thoughts
Were steeped in feeling; I was only then
Contented, when with bliss ineffable   *400*
420 I felt the sentiment of Being spread
O'er all that moves and all that seemeth still;
O'er all that, lost beyond the reach of thought
And human knowledge, to the human eye
Invisible, yet liveth to the heart;   *405*
O'er all that leaps and runs, and shouts and sings,
Or beats the gladsome air; o'er all that glides
Beneath the wave, yea, in the wave itself,
And mighty depth of waters. Wonder not
If such my transports were; for in all things   *410*
430 I saw one life, and felt that it was joy.
One song they sang, and it was audible,   *415*

The exercise and produce of a toil,
Than analytic industry to me
380 More pleasing, and whose character I deem
Is more poetic as resembling more
Creative agency. The song would speak
Of that interminable building reared
By observation of affinities
In objects where no brotherhood exists
To passive minds. My seventeenth year was come;
And, whether from this habit rooted now
So deeply in my mind, or from excess
In the great social principle of life
390 Coercing all things into sympathy,
To unorganic natures were transferred
My own enjoyments; or the power of truth
Coming in revelation, did converse
With things that really are; I, at this time,
Saw blessings spread around me like a sea.
Thus while the days flew by, and years passed on,
From Nature and her overflowing soul,
I had received so much, that all my thoughts
Were steeped in feeling; I was only then
400 Contented, when with bliss ineffable
I felt the sentiment of Being spread
O'er all that moves and all that seemeth still;
O'er all that, lost beyond the reach of thought
And human knowledge, to the human eye
Invisible, yet liveth to the heart;
O'er all that leaps and runs, and shouts and sings,
Or beats the gladsome air; o'er all that glides
Beneath the wave, yea, in the wave itself,
And mighty depth of waters. Wonder not
410 If high the transport, great the joy I felt,
Communing in this sort through earth and heaven
With every form of creature, as it looked
Towards the Uncreated with a countenance
Of adoration, with an eye of love.
One song they sang, and it was audible,

Most audible, then, when the fleshly ear,
O'ercome by grosser prelude of that strain,
Forgot its functions, and slept undisturbed.

If this be error, and another faith
Find easier access to the pious mind,   420
Yet were I grossly destitute of all
Those hùman sentiments which make this earth
So dear, if I should fail with grateful voice
To speak of you, ye mountains and ye lakes,
And sounding cataracts, ye mists and winds   425
That dwell among the hills where I was born.
If in my youth I have been pure in heart,
If, mingling with the world, I am content
With my own modest pleasures, and have lived
With God and Nature communing, removed   430
From little enmities and low desires,
The gift is yours; if in these times of fear,
This melancholy waste of hopes o'erthrown,
If, 'mid indifference and apathy
And wicked exultation, when good men   435
On every side fall off, we know not how,
To selfishness, disguised in gentle names
Of peace and quiet and domestic love,
Yet mingled not unwillingly with sneers
On visionary minds; if, in this time   440
Of dereliction and dismay, I yet
Despair not of our nature, but retain
A more than Roman confidence, a faith
That fails not, in all sorrow my support,
The blessing of my life; the gift is yours,   445
Ye mountains! thine, O Nature! Thou hast fed
My lofty speculations; and in thee,
For this uneasy heart of ours, I find
A never-failing principle of joy   450
And purest passion.
                    Thou, my Friend! wert reared

Most audible, then, when the fleshly ear,
O'ercome by humblest prelude of that strain,
Forgot her functions, and slept undisturbed.

      If this be error, and another faith
420 Find easier access to the pious mind,
Yet were I grossly destitute of all
Those human sentiments that make this earth
So dear, if I should fail with grateful voice
To speak of you, ye mountains, and ye lakes
And sounding cataracts, ye mists and winds
That dwell among the hills where I was born.
If in my youth I have been pure in heart,
If, mingling with the world, I am content
With my own modest pleasures, and have lived
430 With God and Nature communing, removed
From little enmities and low desires,
The gift is yours; if in these times of fear,
This melancholy waste of hopes o'erthrown,
If, 'mid indifference and apathy
And wicked exultation, when good men
On every side fall off, we know not how,
To selfishness, disguised in gentle names
Of peace and quiet and domestic love,
Yet mingled not unwillingly with sneers
440 On visionary minds; if, in this time
Of dereliction and dismay, I yet
Despair not of our nature, but retain
A more than Roman confidence, a faith
That fails not, in all sorrow my support,
The blessing of my life; the gift is yours,
Ye winds and sounding cataracts! 'tis yours,
Ye mountains! thine, O Nature! Thou hast fed
My lofty speculations; and in thee,
For this uneasy heart of ours, I find
450 A never-failing principle of joy
And purest passion.
                        Thou, my Friend! wert reared

In the great city, 'mid far other scenes;
But we, by different roads, at length have gained
The self-same bourne. And for this cause to thee
470　I speak, unapprehensive of contempt,　　　　　　　　　*455*
The insinuated scoff of coward tongues,
And all that silent language which so oft
In conversation betwixt man and man
Blots from the human countenance all trace
Of beauty and of love. For thou hast sought　　　　　*460*
The truth in solitude, and thou art one,
The most intense of Nature's worshippers;
In many things my brother, chiefly here　　　　　　　*465*
In this my deep devotion.
　　　　　　　　　　　Fare thee well!
480　Health and the quiet of a healthful mind
Attend thee! seeking oft the haunts of men,
And yet more often living with thyself,
And for thyself, so haply shall thy days　　　　　　　*470*
Be many, and a blessing to mankind.

In the great city, 'mid far other scenes;
But we, by different roads, at length have gained
The self-same bourne. And for this cause to thee
I speak, unapprehensive of contempt,
The insinuated scoff of coward tongues,
And all that silent language which so oft
In conversation between man and man
Blots from the human countenance all trace
460 Of beauty and of love. For thou hast sought
The truth in solitude, and, since the days
That gave thee liberty, full long desired,
To serve in Nature's temple, thou hast been
The most assiduous of her ministers;
In many things my brother, chiefly here
In this our deep devotion.
                                        Fare thee well!
Health and the quiet of a healthful mind
Attend thee! seeking oft the haunts of men,
And yet more often living with thyself,
470 And for thyself, so haply shall thy days
Be many, and a blessing to mankind.

Book Third

RESIDENCE AT CAMBRIDGE

It was a dreary morning when the chaise
Rolled over the flat plains of Huntingdon,
And, through the open windows, first I saw
The long-backed chapel of King's College rear
His pinnacles above the dusky groves.   5

Soon afterwards, we espied upon the road
A student clothed in gown and tasselled cap;
He passed – nor was I master of my eyes
Till he was left a hundred yards behind.
10 The place, as we approached, seemed more and more
To have an eddy's force, and sucked us in
More eagerly at every step we took.
Onward we drove beneath the Castle; down   15
By Magdalene Bridge we went and crossed the Cam;
And at the *Hoop* we landed, famous Inn.

My spirit was up, my thoughts were full of hope;
Some friends I had, acquaintances who there
Seemed friends, poor simple schoolboys, now hung round
With honour and importance: in a world
20 Of welcome faces up and down I roved;
Questions, directions, counsel and advice
Flowed in upon me, from all sides; fresh day
Of pride and pleasure! to myself I seemed   25
A man of business and expense, and went
From shop to shop about my own affairs,
To Tutors or to Tailors, as befell,

Book Third

RESIDENCE AT CAMBRIDGE

It was a dreary morning when the wheels
Rolled over a wide plain o'erhung with clouds,
And nothing cheered our way till first we saw
The long-roofed chapel of King's College lift
Turrets and pinnacles in answering files,
Extended high above a dusky grove.

    Advancing, we espied upon the road
A student clothed in gown and tasselled cap,
Striding along as if o'ertasked by Time,
10 Or covetous of exercise and air;
He passed – nor was I master of my eyes
Till he was left an arrow's flight behind.
As near and nearer to the spot we drew,
It seemed to suck us in with an eddy's force.
Onward we drove beneath the Castle; caught,
While crossing Magdalene Bridge, a glimpse of Cam;
And at the *Hoop* alighted, famous Inn.

    My spirit was up, my thoughts were full of hope;
Some friends I had, acquaintances who there
20 Seemed friends, poor simple schoolboys, now hung round
With honour and importance: in a world
Of welcome faces up and down I roved;
Questions, directions, warnings and advice,
Flowed in upon me, from all sides; fresh day
Of pride and pleasure! to myself I seemed
A man of business and expense, and went
From shop to shop about my own affairs,
To Tutor or to Tailor, as befell,

From street to street with loose and careless heart.

I was the Dreamer, they the Dream; I roamed 30
Delighted through the motley spectacle;
30 Gowns grave, or gaudy, doctors, students, streets,
Lamps, gateways, flocks of churches, courts and towers:
Strange transformation for a mountain youth,
A northern villager.
                As if by word 35
Of magic or some Fairy's power, at once
Behold me rich in moneys, and attired
In splendid clothes, with hose of silk, and hair
Glittering like rimy trees, when frost is keen.
My lordly dressing-gown, I pass it by, 40
With other signs of manhood which supplied
40 The lack of beard. – The weeks went roundly on,
With invitations, suppers, wine and fruit,
Smooth housekeeping within, and all without
Liberal, and suiting gentleman's array. 45

The Evangelist St John my patron was:
Three gloomy courts are his, and in the first
Was my abiding-place, a nook obscure;
Right underneath, the College kitchens made
A humming sound, less tuneable than bees, 50
But hardly less industrious; with shrill notes
50 Of sharp command and scolding intermixed.
Near me was Trinity's loquacious clock,
Who never let the quarters, night or day,
Slip by him unproclaimed, and told the hours 55
Twice over with a male and female voice.
Her pealing organ was my neighbour too;
And from my bedroom, I in moonlight nights
Could see, right opposite, a few yards off,
The antechapel, where the statue stood 60
Of Newton with his prism and silent face.

From street to street with loose and careless mind.

30   I was the Dreamer, they the Dream; I roamed
      Delighted through the motley spectacle;
      Gowns grave, or gaudy, doctors, students, streets,
      Courts, cloisters, flocks of churches, gateways, towers:
      Migration strange for a stripling of the hills,
      A northern villager.
                         As if the change
      Had waited on some Fairy's wand, at once
      Behold me rich in moneys, and attired
      In splendid garb, with hose of silk, and hair
      Powdered like rimy trees, when frost is keen.
40   My lordly dressing-gown, I pass it by,
      With other signs of manhood that supplied
      The lack of beard. – The weeks went roundly on,
      With invitations, suppers, wine and fruit,
      Smooth housekeeping within, and all without
      Liberal, and suiting gentleman's array.

      The Evangelist St John my patron was:
      Three Gothic courts are his, and in the first
      Was my abiding-place, a nook obscure;
      Right underneath, the College kitchens made
50   A humming sound, less tuneable than bees,
      But hardly less industrious; with shrill notes
      Of sharp command and scolding intermixed.
      Near me hung Trinity's loquacious clock,
      Who never let the quarters, night or day,
      Slip by him unproclaimed, and told the hours
      Twice over with a male and female voice.
      Her pealing organ was my neighbour too;
      And from my pillow, looking forth by light
      Of moon or favouring stars, I could behold
60   The antechapel where the statue stood
      Of Newton with his prism and silent face,
      The marble index of a mind for ever
      Voyaging through strange seas of Thought, alone.

60 Of College labours, of the Lecturer's room
    All studded round, as thick as chairs could stand,   65
    With loyal students faithful to their books,
    Half-and-half idlers, hardy recusants,
    And honest dunces – of important days,
    Examinations, when the man was weighed
    As in the balance! of excessive hopes,   70
    Tremblings withal and commendable fears,
    Small jealousies, and triumphs good or bad,
    I make short mention; things they were which then
70 I did not love, nor do I love them now.
    Such glory was but little sought by me,
    And little won. But it is right to say
    That even so early, from the first crude days   75
    Of settling time in this my new abode,
    Not seldom I had melancholy thoughts,
    From personal and family regards,
    Wishing to hope without a hope, some fears
    About my future worldly maintenance,
    And, more than all, a strangeness in my mind,   80
80 A feeling that I was not for that hour,
    Nor for that place. But wherefore be cast down?
    Why should I grieve? I was a chosen son.
    For hither I had come with holy powers
    And faculties, whether to work or feel: 89
    To apprehend all passions and all moods
    Which time and place and season do impress
    Upon the visible universe, and work
    Like changes there by force of my own mind.
    I was a Freeman; in the purest sense
90 Was free, and to majestic ends was strong.
    I do not speak of learning, moral truth,
    Or understanding; 'twas enough for me
    To know that I was otherwise endowed.
    When the first glitter of the show was passed,
    And the first dazzle of the taper light,
    As if with a rebound my mind returned
    Into its former self. Oft did I leave

Of College labours, of the Lecturer's room
All studded round, as thick as chairs could stand,
With loyal students faithful to their books,
Half-and-half idlers, hardy recusants,
And honest dunces – of important days,
70 Examinations, when the man was weighed
As in a balance! of excessive hopes,
Tremblings withal and commendable fears,
Small jealousies, and triumphs good or bad,
Let others that know more speak as they know.
Such glory was but little sought by me,
And little won. Yet from the first crude days
Of settling time in this untried abode,
I was disturbed at times by prudent thoughts,
Wishing to hope without a hope, some fears
About my future worldly maintenance,
80 And, more than all, a strangeness in the mind,
A feeling that I was not for that hour,
Nor for that place. But wherefore be cast down?
For (not to speak of Reason and her pure
Reflective acts to fix the moral law
Deep in the conscience, nor of Christian Hope,
Bowing her head before her sister Faith
As one far mightier), hither I had come,
Bear witness Truth, endowed with holy powers
And faculties, whether to work or feel.
90 Oft when the dazzling show no longer new
Had ceased to dazzle, ofttimes did I quit

My comrades, and the crowd, buildings and groves,   *92*
And walked along the fields, the level fields,
With heaven's blue concave reared above my head;
And now it was that, from such change entire
And this first absence from those shapes sublime
Wherewith I had been conversant, my mind   *95*
Seemed busier in itself than heretofore.
At least I more directly recognized
My powers and habits: let me dare to speak
A higher language, say that now I felt   *100*
The strength and consolation which were mine.
As if awakened, summoned, roused, constrained,
I looked for universal things; perused
The common countenance of earth and heaven;   *110*
And turning the mind in upon itself
Pored, watched, expected, listened, spread my thoughts
And spread them with a wider creeping; felt
Incumbences more awful, visitings
Of the Upholder, of the tranquil soul,   *120*
Which underneath all passion lives secure
A steadfast life. But peace! it is enough
To notice that I was ascending now   *125*
To such community with highest truth.

A track pursuing, not untrod before,
From deep analogies by thought supplied

My comrades, leave the crowd, buildings and groves,
And as I paced alone the level fields
Far from those lovely sights and sounds sublime
With which I had been conversant, the mind
Drooped not; but there into herself returning,
With prompt rebound seemed fresh as heretofore.
At least I more distinctly recognized
Her native instincts: let me dare to speak
100 A higher language, say that now I felt
What independent solaces were mine,
To mitigate the injurious sway of place
Or circumstance, how far soever changed
In youth, or *to* be changed in manhood's prime;
Or for the few who shall be called to look
On the long shadows in our evening years,
Ordained precursors to the night of death.
As if awakened, summoned, roused, constrained,
I looked for universal things; perused
110 The common countenance of earth and sky:
Earth, nowhere unembellished by some trace
Of that first Paradise whence man was driven;
And sky, whose beauty and bounty are expressed
By the proud name she bears – the name of Heaven.
I called on both to teach me what they might;
Or turning the mind in upon herself
Pored, watched, expected, listened, spread my thoughts
And spread them with a wider creeping; felt
Incumbencies more awful, visitings
120 Of the Upholder, of the tranquil soul,
That tolerates the indignities of Time,
And, from the centre of Eternity
All finite motions overruling, lives
In glory immutable. But peace! enough
Here to record I had ascended now
To such community with highest truth.

A track pursuing, not untrod before,
From strict analogies by thought supplied

Or consciousnesses not to be subdued,
To every natural form, rock, fruit or flower, *130*
Even the loose stones that cover the highway,
I gave a moral life: I saw them feel,
Or linked them to some feeling: the great mass
Lay bedded in a quickening soul, and all
That I beheld respired with inward meaning. *135*
130 Thus much for the one Presence, and the Life
Of the great whole; suffice it here to add
That whatsoe'er of Terror or of Love
Or Beauty, Nature's daily face put on
From transitory passion, unto this
I was as wakeful, even, as waters are
To the sky's motion: in a kindred sense *140*
Of passion, was obedient as a lute
That waits upon the touches of the wind.
So was it with me in my solitude;
140 So often among multitudes of men.
Unknown, unthought of, yet I was most rich –
I had a world about me – 'twas my own;
I made it, for it only lived to me, *145*
And to the God who looked into my mind.
Such sympathies would sometimes show themselves
By outward gestures and by visible looks:
Some called it madness – such indeed it was,
If child-like fruitfulness in passing joy, *150*
If steady moods of thoughtfulness matured
150 To inspiration, sort with such a name:
If prophecy be madness; if things viewed
By poets of old time, and higher up
By the first men, earth's first inhabitants, *155*
May in these tutored days no more be seen
With undisordered sight. But leaving this,
It was no madness, for I had an eye
Which in my strongest workings evermore
Was looking for the shades of difference *160*
As they lie hid in all exterior forms,
160 Near or remote, minute or vast, an eye

Or consciousnesses not to be subdued,
130 To every natural form, rock, fruit or flower,
Even the loose stones that cover the highway,
I gave a moral life: I saw them feel,
Or linked them to some feeling: the great mass
Lay bedded in a quickening soul, and all
That I beheld respired with inward meaning.
Add that whate'er of Terror or of Love
Or Beauty, Nature's daily face put on
From transitory passion, unto this
I was as sensitive as waters are
140 To the sky's influence: in a kindred mood
Of passion, was obedient as a lute
That waits upon the touches of the wind.
Unknown, unthought of, yet I was most rich –
I had a world about me – 'twas my own;
I made it, for it only lived to me,
And to the God who sees into the heart.
Such sympathies, though rarely, were betrayed
By outward gestures and by visible looks:
Some called it madness – so indeed it was,
150 If child-like fruitfulness in passing joy,
If steady moods of thoughtfulness matured
To inspiration, sort with such a name;
If prophecy be madness; if things viewed
By poets in old time, and higher up
By the first men, earth's first inhabitants,
May in these tutored days no more be seen
With undisordered sight. But leaving this,
It was no madness, for the bodily eye
Amid my strongest workings evermore
160 Was searching out the lines of difference
As they lie hid in all external forms,
Near or remote, minute or vast, an eye

Which from a stone, a tree, a withered leaf,
To the broad ocean and the azure heavens,
Spangled with kindred multitudes of stars,   *165*
Could find no surface where its power might sleep;
Which spake perpetual logic to my soul,
And by an unrelenting agency
Did bind my feelings even as in a chain.

    And here, O Friend! have I retraced my life   *170*
Up to an eminence, and told a tale
170 Of matters which not falsely I may call
The glory of my youth. Of genius, power,
Creation and divinity itself
I have been speaking, for my theme has been
What passed within me. Not of outward things
Done visibly for other minds, words, signs,
Symbols or actions, but of my own heart
Have I been speaking, and my youthful mind.
O Heavens! how awful is the might of souls,   *180*
And what they do within themselves while yet
180 The yoke of earth is new to them, the world
Nothing but a wild field where they were sown.
This is, in truth, heroic argument,
And genuine prowess, which I wished to touch   *185*
With hand however weak, but in the main
It lies far hidden from the reach of words.
Points have we all of us within our souls
Where all stand single; this I feel, and make
Breathings for incommunicable powers;   *190*
Yet each man is a memory to himself,
190 And, therefore, now that I must quit this theme,
I am not heartless, for there's not a man
That lives who hath not had his god-like hours,
And knows not what majestic sway we have   *195*
As natural beings in the strength of Nature.

    Enough: for now into a populous plain
We must descend. A Traveller I am,

Which from a tree, a stone, a withered leaf,
To the broad ocean and the azure heavens
Spangled with kindred multitudes of stars,
Could find no surface where its power might sleep;
Which spake perpetual logic to my soul,
And by an unrelenting agency
Did bind my feelings even as in a chain.

170   And here, O Friend! have I retraced my life
Up to an eminence, and told a tale
Of matters which not falsely may be called
The glory of my youth. Of genius, power,
Creation and divinity itself
I have been speaking, for my theme has been
What passed within me. Not of outward things
Done visibly for other minds, words, signs,
Symbols or actions, but of my own heart
Have I been speaking, and my youthful mind.
180 O Heavens! how awful is the might of souls,
And what they do within themselves while yet
The yoke of earth is new to them, the world
Nothing but a wild field where they were sown.
This is, in truth, heroic argument,
This genuine prowess, which I wished to touch
With hand however weak, but in the main
It lies far hidden from the reach of words.
Points have we all of us within our souls
Where all stand single; this I feel, and make
190 Breathings for incommunicable powers;
But is not each a memory to himself?
And, therefore, now that we must quit this theme,
I am not heartless, for there's not a man
That lives who hath not known his god-like hours,
And feels not what an empire we inherit
As natural beings in the strength of Nature.

    No more: for now into a populous plain
We must descend. A Traveller I am,

And all my tale is of myself; even so,
So be it, if the pure in heart delight   200
To follow me, and thou, O honoured Friend!
200   Who in my thoughts art ever at my side,
Uphold, as heretofore, my fainting steps.

It hath been told already, how my sight
Was dazzled by the novel show, and how,   205
Ere long, I did into myself return.
So did it seem, and so, in truth, it was.
Yet this was but short lived: thereafter came
Observance less devout. I had made a change
In climate, and my nature's outward coat
Changed also slowly and insensibly.
210   To the deep quiet and majestic thoughts   210
Of loneliness succeeded empty noise
And superficial pastimes; now and then
Forced labour, and more frequently forced hopes;
And, worse than all, a treasonable growth
Of indecisive judgements, that impaired   215
And shook the mind's simplicity. – And yet
This was a gladsome time. Could I behold –
Who, less insensible than sodden clay
On a sea-river's bed at ebb of tide,
220   Could have beheld – with undelighted heart,   220
So many happy youths, so wide and fair
A congregation in its budding-time
Of health, and hope, and beauty, all at once
So many divers samples of the growth
Of life's sweet season – could have seen unmoved   225
That miscellaneous garland of wild flowers
Upon the matron temples of a place
So famous through the world? To me, at least,
It was a goodly prospect: for, through youth,
230   Though I had been trained up to stand unpropped,   230
And independent musings pleased me so
That spells seemed on me when I was alone,
Yet could I only cleave to solitude

Whose tale is only of himself; even so,
200 So be it, if the pure of heart be prompt
To follow, and if thou, my honoured Friend!
Who in these thoughts art ever at my side,
Support, as heretofore, my fainting steps.

It hath been told, that when the first delight
That flashed upon me from this novel show
Had failed, the mind returned into herself;
Yet true it is, that I had made a change
In climate, and my nature's outward coat
Changed also slowly and insensibly.
210 Full oft the quiet and exalted thoughts
Of loneliness gave way to empty noise
And superficial pastimes; now and then
Forced labour, and more frequently forced hopes;
And, worst of all, a treasonable growth
Of indecisive judgements, that impaired
And shook the mind's simplicity. – And yet
This was a gladsome time. Could I behold –
Who, less insensible than sodden clay
In a sea-river's bed at ebb of tide,
220 Could have beheld, – with undelighted heart,
So many happy youths, so wide and fair
A congregation in its budding-time
Of health, and hope, and beauty, all at once
So many divers samples from the growth
Of life's sweet season – could have seen unmoved
That miscellaneous garland of wild flowers
Decking the matron temples of a place
So famous through the world? To me, at least,
It was a goodly prospect: for, in sooth,
230 Though I had learnt betimes to stand unpropped,
And independent musings pleased me so
That spells seemed on me when I was alone,
Yet could I only cleave to solitude

In lonesome places; if a throng was near
That way I leaned by nature; for my heart   235
Was social, and loved idleness and joy.

Not seeking those who might participate
My deeper pleasures (nay, I had not once,
Though not unused to mutter lonesome songs,
240 Even with myself divided such delight,   240
Or looked that way for aught that might be clothed
In human language), easily I passed
From the remembrances of better things,
And slipped into the weekday works of youth,
Unburdened, unalarmed, and unprofaned.   245
Caverns there were within my mind which sun
Could never penetrate, yet did there not
Want store of leafy arbours where the light
Might enter in at will. Companionships,
250 Friendships, acquaintances, were welcome all.   250
We sauntered, played, we rioted, we talked
Unprofitable talk at morning hours;
Drifted about along the streets and walks,
Read lazily in lazy books, went forth
To gallop through the country in blind zeal   255
Of senseless horsemanship, or on the breast
Of Cam sailed boisterously, and let the stars
Come out, perhaps without one quiet thought.

Such was the tenor of the opening act
260 In this new life. Imagination slept,   260
And yet not utterly. I could not print
Ground where the grass had yielded to the steps
Of generations of illustrious men,
Unmoved. I could not always lightly pass
Through the same gateways, sleep where they had slept,
Wake where they waked, range that enclosure old,
That garden of great intellects, undisturbed.
Place also by the side of this dark sense
Of nobler feeling, that those spiritual men,

In lonely places; if a throng was near
That way I leaned by nature; for my heart
Was social, and loved idleness and joy.

Not seeking those who might participate
My deeper pleasures (nay, I had not once,
Though not unused to mutter lonesome songs,
240 Even with myself divided such delight,
Or looked that way for aught that might be clothed
In human language), easily I passed
From the remembrances of better things,
And slipped into the ordinary works
Of careless youth, unburdened, unalarmed.
Caverns there were within my mind which sun
Could never penetrate, yet did there not
Want store of leafy *arbours* where the light
Might enter in at will. Companionships,
250 Friendships, acquaintances, were welcome all.
We sauntered, played, or rioted; we talked
Unprofitable talk at morning hours;
Drifted about along the streets and walks,
Read lazily in trivial books, went forth
To gallop through the country in blind zeal
Of senseless horsemanship, or on the breast
Of Cam sailed boisterously, and let the stars
Come forth, perhaps without one quiet thought.

Such was the tenor of the second act
260 In this new life. Imagination slept,
And yet not utterly. I could not print
Ground where the grass had yielded to the steps
Of generations of illustrious men,
Unmoved. I could not always lightly pass
Through the same gateways, sleep where they had slept,
Wake where they waked, range that enclosure old,
That garden of great intellects, undisturbed.
Place also by the side of this dark sense
Of nobler feeling, that those spiritual men,

270 Even the great Newton's own ethereal self,   *270*
Seemed humbled in these precincts, thence to be
The more beloved; invested here with tasks
Of life's plain business, as a daily garb;
Dictators at the plough, a change that left
All genuine admiration unimpaired.   *277*

Beside the pleasant Mills of Trompington
I laughed with Chaucer; in the hawthorn shade
Heard him, while birds were warbling, tell his tales   *280*
Of amorous passion. And that gentle Bard,
280 Chosen by the Muses for their Page of State –
Sweet Spenser, moving through his clouded heaven
With the moon's beauty and the moon's soft pace,
I called him Brother, Englishman, and Friend!   *285*
Yea, our blind Poet, who, in his later day,
Stood almost single; uttering odious truth –
Darkness before, and danger's voice behind,
Soul awful – if the earth hath ever lodged
An awful soul – I seemed to see him here   *290*
Familiarly, and in his scholar's dress
290 Bounding before me, yet a stripling youth –
A boy, no better, with his rosy cheeks
Angelical, keen eye, courageous look,
And conscious step of purity and pride.   *295*
Among the band of my compeers was one
My class-fellow at school, whose chance it was
To lodge in the apartments which had been,
Time out of mind, honoured by Milton's name;
The very shell reputed of the abode
Which he had tenanted. O temperate Bard!
300 One afternoon, the first time I set foot
In this thy innocent nest and oratory,   *300*
Seated with others in a festive ring
Of common-place convention, I to thee
Poured out libations, to thy memory drank,
Within my private thoughts, till my brain reeled
Never so clouded by the fumes of wine

270 Even the great Newton's own ethereal self,
Seemed humbled in these precincts, thence to be
The more endeared. Their several memories here
(Even like their persons in their portraits clothed
With the accustomed garb of daily life)
Put on a lowly and a touching grace
Of more distinct humanity, that left
All genuine admiration unimpaired.

Beside the pleasant Mill of Trompington
I laughed with Chaucer; in the hawthorn shade
280 Heard him, while birds were warbling, tell his tales
Of amorous passion. And that gentle Bard,
Chosen by the Muses for their Page of State –
Sweet Spenser, moving through his clouded heaven
With the moon's beauty and the moon's soft pace,
I called him Brother, Englishman, and Friend!
Yea, our blind Poet, who, in his later day,
Stood almost single; uttering odious truth –
Darkness before, and danger's voice behind,
Soul awful – if the earth has ever lodged
290 An awful soul – I seemed to see him here
Familiarly, and in his scholar's dress
Bounding before me, yet a stripling youth –
A boy, no better, with his rosy cheeks
Angelical, keen eye, courageous look,
And conscious step of purity and pride.
Among the band of my compeers was one
Whom chance had stationed in the very room
Honoured by Milton's name. O temperate Bard!
Be it confessed that, for the first time, seated
300 Within thy innocent lodge and oratory,
One of a festive circle, I poured out
Libations, to thy memory drank, till pride
And gratitude grew dizzy in a brain
Never excited by the fumes of wine

Before that hour, or since. Thence forth I ran 305
From that assembly; through a length of streets,
Ran, ostrich-like, to reach our chapel door
In not a desperate or opprobrious time,
Albeit long after the importunate bell
Had stopped, with wearisome Cassandra voice 310
No longer haunting the dark winter night.
Call back, O Friend! a moment to thy mind,
The place itself and fashion of the rites.
Upshouldering in a dislocated lump,
With shallow ostentatious carelessness,
My surplice, gloried in, and yet despised,
I clove in pride through the inferior throng 315
Of the plain Burghers, who in audience stood
On the last skirts of their permitted ground,
Beneath the pealing organ. Empty thoughts!
I am ashamed of them: and that great Bard,
And thou, O Friend! who in thy ample mind 320
Hast stationed me for reverence and love,
Ye will forgive the weakness of that hour,
In some of its unworthy vanities,
Brother of many more.

          In this mixed sort
The months passed on, remissly, not given up 325
To wilful alienation from the right,
Or walks of open scandal, but in vague
And loose indifference, easy likings, aims
Of a low pitch – duty and zeal dismissed,
Yet Nature, or a happy course of things 330
Not doing in their stead the needful work.
The memory languidly revolved, the heart
Reposed in noontide rest, the inner pulse
Of contemplation almost failed to beat.
Rotted as by a charm, my life became 334
A floating island, an amphibious thing,
Unsound, of spongy texture, yet withal
Not wanting a fair face of water weeds
And pleasant flowers. The thirst of living praise,

Before that hour, or since. Then, forth I ran
From the assembly; through a length of streets,
Ran, ostrich-like, to reach our chapel door
In not a desperate or opprobrious time,
Albeit long after the importunate bell
310 Had stopped, with wearisome Cassandra voice
No longer haunting the dark winter night.
Call back, O Friend! a moment to thy mind,
The place itself and fashion of the rites.
With careless ostentation shouldering up
My surplice, through the inferior throng I clove
Of the plain Burghers, who in audience stood
On the last skirts of their permitted ground,
Under the pealing organ. Empty thoughts!
I am ashamed of them: and that great Bard,
320 And thou, O Friend! who in thy ample mind
Hast placed me high above my best deserts,
Ye will forgive the weakness of that hour,
In some of its unworthy vanities,
Brother to many more.
                              In this mixed sort
The months passed on, remissly, not given up
To wilful alienation from the right,
Or walks of open scandal, but in vague
And loose indifference, easy likings, aims
Of a low pitch – duty and zeal dismissed,
330 Yet Nature, or a happy course of things
Not doing in their stead the needful work.
The memory languidly revolved, the heart
Reposed in noontide rest, the inner pulse
Of contemplation almost failed to beat.
Such life might not inaptly be compared
To a floating island, an amphibious spot
Unsound, of spongy texture, yet withal
Not wanting a fair face of water weeds
And pleasant flowers. The thirst of living praise,

A reverence for the glorious Dead, the sight   *340*
Of those long vistos, catacombs in which
Perennial minds lie visibly entombed,
Have often stirred the heart of youth, and bred
A fervent love of rigorous discipline. –
Alas! such high commotion touched not me.   *345*
350 No look was in these walls to put to shame
My easy spirits, and discountenance
Their light composure, far less to instil
A calm resolve of mind, firmly addressed
To puissant efforts. Nor was this the blame   *350*
Of others but my own; I should, in truth,
As far as doth concern my single self,
Misdeem most widely, lodging it elsewhere:
For I, bred up in Nature's lap, was even
As a spoiled child, and rambling like the wind,   *355*
360 As I had done in daily intercourse
With those delicious rivers, solemn heights,
And mountains; ranging like a fowl of the air,
I was ill-tutored for captivity,
To quit my pleasure, and, from month to month,   *360*
Take up a station calmly on the perch
Of sedentary peace. Those lovely forms
Had also left less space within my mind,
Which, wrought upon instinctively, had found
A freshness in those objects of its love,   *365*
370 A winning power, beyond all other power.
Not that I slighted books, – that were to lack
All sense, – but other passions had been mine,
More fervent, making me less prompt, perhaps,
To in-door study than was wise or well,   *370*
Or suited to my years. Yet I could shape
The image of a place which, soothed and lulled
As I had been, trained up in paradise
Among sweet garlands and delightful sounds,
Accustomed in my loneliness to walk
380 With Nature magisterially, yet I,
Methinks, could shape the image of a place

340 Fit reverence for the glorious Dead, the sight
  Of those long vistas, sacred catacombs,
  Where mighty *minds* lie visibly entombed,
  Have often stirred the heart of youth, and bred
  A fervent love of rigorous discipline. –
  Alas! such high emotion touched not me.
  Look was there none within these walls to shame
  My easy spirits, and discountenance
  Their light composure, far less to instil
  A calm resolve of mind, firmly addressed
350 To puissant efforts. Nor was this the blame
  Of others but my own; I should, in truth,
  As far as doth concern my single self,
  Misdeem most widely, lodging it elsewhere:
  For I, bred up 'mid Nature's luxuries,
  Was a spoiled child, and rambling like the wind,
  As I had done in daily intercourse
  With those crystalline rivers, solemn heights,
  And mountains; ranging like a fowl of the air,
  I was ill-tutored for captivity,
360 To quit my pleasure, and, from month to month,
  Take up a station calmly on the perch
  Of sedentary peace. Those lovely forms
  Had also left less space within my mind,
  Which, wrought upon instinctively, had found
  A freshness in those objects of her love,
  A winning power, beyond all other power.
  Not that I slighted books, – that were to lack
  All sense, – but other passions in me ruled,
  Passions more fervent, making me less prompt
370 To in-door study than was wise or well,
  Or suited to those years. Yet I, though used
  In magisterial liberty to rove,
  Culling such flowers of learning as might tempt
  A random choice, could shadow forth a place

Which with its aspect should have bent me down   376
To instantaneous service; should at once
Have made me pay to science and to arts
And written lore, acknowledged my liege lord,
A homage frankly offered up, like that   380
Which I had paid to Nature. Toil and pains
In this recess which I have bodied forth
Should spread from heart to heart; and stately groves,
390 Majestic edifices, should not want
A corresponding dignity within.   385
The congregating temper which pervades
Our unripe years, not wasted, should be made
To minister to works of high attempt,
Which the enthusiast would perform with love.
Youth should be awed, possessed, as with a sense   390
Religious, of what holy joy there is
In knowledge, if it be sincerely sought
For its own sake, in glory and in praise
400 If but by labour won, and to endure.
The passing day should learn to put aside   395
Her trappings here, should strip them off abashed
Before antiquity and steadfast truth
And strong book-mindedness; and over all
Should be a healthy sound simplicity,
A seemly plainness, name it as you will,   400
Republican or pious.
             If these thoughts
Be a gratuitous emblazonry
That does but mock this recreant age, at least
410 Let Folly and False-seeming, we might say,
Be free to affect whatever formal gait
Of moral or scholastic discipline   405
Shall raise them highest in their own esteem –
Let them parade among the Schools at will,
But spare the House of God. Was ever known
The witless shepherd who would drive his flock   409
With serious repetition to a pool
Of which 'tis plain to sight they never taste?

(If now I yield not to a flattering dream)
Whose studious aspect should have bent me down
To instantaneous service; should at once
Have made me pay to science and to arts
And written lore, acknowledged my liege lord,
380 A homage frankly offered up, like that
Which I had paid to Nature. Toil and pains
In this recess, by thoughtful Fancy built,
Should spread from heart to heart; and stately groves,
Majestic edifices, should not want
A corresponding dignity within.
The congregating temper that pervades
Our unripe years, not wasted, should be taught
To minister to works of high attempt –
Works which the enthusiast would perform with love.
390 Youth should be awed, religiously possessed
With a conviction of the power that waits
On knowledge, when sincerely sought and prized
For its own sake, on glory and on praise
If but by labour won, and fit to endure.
The passing day should learn to put aside
Her trappings here, should strip them off abashed
Before antiquity and steadfast truth
And strong book-mindedness; and over all
A healthy sound simplicity should reign,
400 A seemly plainness, name it what you will,
Republican or pious.
                              If these thoughts
Are a gratuitous emblazonry
That mocks the recreant age *we* live in, then
Be Folly and False-seeming free to affect
Whatever formal gait of discipline
Shall raise them highest in their own esteem –
Let them parade among the Schools at will,
But spare the House of God. Was ever known
The witless shepherd who persists to drive
410 A flock that thirsts not to a pool disliked?

A weight must surely hang on days begun
420 And ended with worst mockery. Be wise,
Ye Presidents and Deans, and to your bells
Give seasonable rest, for 'tis a sound   416
Hollow as ever vexed the tranquil air;
And your officious doings bring disgrace
On the plain steeples of our English Church,
Whose worship, 'mid remotest village trees,
Suffers for this. Even Science, too, at hand   420
In daily sight of such irreverence,
Is smitten thence with an unnatural taint,
430 Loses her just authority, falls beneath
Collateral suspicion, else unknown.   425
This obvious truth did not escape me then,
Unthinking as I was, and I confess,
That having in my native hills given loose
To a schoolboy's dreaming, I had raised a pile
Upon the basis of the coming time,
Which now before me melted fast away,
Which could not live, scarcely had life enough
To mock the builder. Oh, what joy it were   430
440 To see a sanctuary for our country's youth
With such a spirit in it as might be
Protection for itself, a virgin grove,
Primeval in its purity and depth;
Where, though the shades were filled with cheerfulness,
Nor indigent of songs warbled from crowds   435
In under-coverts, yet the countenance
Of the whole place should wear a stamp of awe;
A habitation sober and demure
For ruminating creatures; a domain
450 For quiet things to wander in; a haunt   440
In which the heron might delight to feed
By the shy rivers, and the pelican
Upon the cypress spire in lonely thought
Might sit and sun himself. – Alas! alas!
In vain for such solemnity we look;   445
Our eyes are crossed by butterflies, our ears

A weight must surely hang on days begun
And ended with such mockery. Be wise,
Ye Presidents and Deans, and, till the spirit
Of ancient times revive, and youth be trained
At home in pious service, to your bells
Give seasonable rest, for 'tis a sound
Hollow as ever vexed the tranquil air;
And your officious doings bring disgrace
On the plain steeples of our English Church,
420 Whose worship, 'mid remotest village trees,
Suffers for this. Even Science, too, at hand
In daily sight of this irreverence,
Is smitten thence with an unnatural taint,
Loses her just authority, falls beneath
Collateral suspicion, else unknown.
This truth escaped me not, and I confess,
That having 'mid my native hills given loose
To a schoolboy's vision, I had raised a pile
Upon the basis of the coming time,
430 That fell in ruins round me. Oh, what joy
To see a sanctuary for our country's youth
Informed with such a spirit as might be
Its own protection; a primeval grove,
Where, though the shades with cheerfulness were filled,
Nor indigent of songs warbled from crowds
In under-coverts, yet the countenance
Of the whole place should bear a stamp of awe;
A habitation sober and demure
For ruminating creatures; a domain
440 For quiet things to wander in; a haunt
In which the heron should delight to feed
By the shy rivers, and the pelican
Upon the cypress spire in lonely thought
Might sit and sun himself. – Alas! alas!
In vain for such solemnity I looked;
Mine eyes were crossed by butterflies, ears vexed

Hear chattering popinjays; the inner heart
Is trivial, and the impresses without
Are of a gaudy region.

460   Different sight   450
Those venerable Doctors saw of old,
When all who dwelt within these famous walls
Led in abstemiousness a studious life;
When, in forlorn and naked chambers cooped
And crowded, o'er their ponderous books they sate
Like caterpillars eating out their way   455
In silence, or with keen devouring noise
Not to be tracked or fathered. Princes then
At matins froze, and couched at curfew-time,
Trained up through piety and zeal to prize
470 Spare diet, patient labour, and plain weeds.   460
O seat of Arts! renowned throughout the world!
Far different service in those homely days
The nurslings of the Muses underwent
From their first childhood: in that glorious time
When Learning, like a stranger come from far,   465
Sounding through Christian lands her trumpet, roused
The peasant and the king; when boys and youths,
The growth of ragged villages and huts,
Forsook their homes, and, errant in the quest
480 Of Patron, famous school or friendly nook,   470
Where, pensioned, they in shelter might sit down,
From town to town and through wide scattered realms
Journeyed with their huge folios in their hands;
And often, starting from some covert place,
Saluted the chance comer on the road,   475
Crying, 'An obolus, a penny give
To a poor scholar!' – when illustrious men,
Lovers of truth, by penury constrained,
Bucer, Erasmus, or Melancthon, read
490 Before the doors or windows of their cells   480
By moonshine through mere lack of taper light.

But peace to vain regrets! We see but darkly

By chattering popinjays; the inner heart
Seemed trivial, and the impresses without
Of a too gaudy region.
                    Different sight
450 Those venerable Doctors saw of old,
When all who dwelt within these famous walls
Led in abstemiousness a studious life;
When, in forlorn and naked chambers cooped
And crowded, o'er the ponderous books they hung
Like caterpillars eating out their way
In silence, or with keen devouring noise
Not to be tracked or fathered. Princes then
At matins froze, and couched at curfew-time,
Trained up through piety and zeal to prize
460 Spare diet, patient labour, and plain weeds.
O seat of Arts! renowned throughout the world!
Far different service in those homely days
The Muses' modest nurslings underwent
From their first childhood: in that glorious time
When Learning, like a stranger come from far,
Sounding through Christian lands her trumpet, roused
Peasant and king; when boys and youths, the growth
Of ragged villages and crazy huts,
Forsook their homes, and, errant in the quest
470 Of Patron, famous school or friendly nook,
Where, pensioned, they in shelter might sit down,
From town to town and through wide scattered realms
Journeyed with ponderous folios in their hands;
And often, starting from some covert place,
Saluted the chance comer on the road,
Crying, 'An obolus, a penny give
To a poor scholar!' – when illustrious men,
Lovers of truth, by penury constrained,
Bucer, Erasmus, or Melancthon, read
480 Before the doors or windows of their cells
By moonshine through mere lack of taper light.

But peace to vain regrets! We see but darkly

Even when we look behind us, and best things
Are not so pure by nature that they needs
Must keep to all, as fondly all believe,   485
Their highest promise. If the mariner,
When at reluctant distance he hath passed
Some fair enticing island, did but know
What fate might have been his, could he have brought
His bark to land upon the wished-for spot,   490
Good cause full often would he have to bless
The belt of churlish surf that scared him thence,
Or haste of the inexorable wind.
For me, I grieve not; happy is the man,
Who only misses what I missed, who falls   495
No lower than I fell.
                  I did not love,
As hath been noticed heretofore, the guise
Of our scholastic studies; could have wished
The river to have had an ampler range
And freer pace; but this I tax not; far   500
Far more I grieved to see among the band
Of those who in the field of contest stood
As combatants, passions that did to me
Seem low and mean; from ignorance of mine,
In part, and want of just forbearance, yet
My wiser mind grieves now for what I saw.
Willingly did I part from these, and turn
Out of their track, to travel with the shoal   506
Of more unthinking natures, easy minds
And pillowy; and not wanting love that makes
The day pass lightly on, when foresight sleeps,
And wisdom and the pledges interchanged   510
With our own inner being are forgot.

    To books, our daily fare prescribed, I turned
With sickly appetite, and when I went,
At other times, in quest of my own food,
I chased not steadily the manly deer,
But laid me down to any casual feast

Even when we look behind us, and best things
Are not so pure by nature that they needs
Must keep to all, as fondly all believe,
Their highest promise. If the mariner,
When at reluctant distance he hath passed
Some tempting island, could but know the ills
That must have fallen upon him had he brought
490 His bark to land upon the wished-for shore,
Good cause would oft be his to thank the surf
Whose white belt scared him thence, or wind that blew
Inexorably adverse: for myself
I grieve not; happy is the gownèd youth,
Who only misses what I missed, who falls
No lower than I fell.
              I did not love,
Judging not ill perhaps, the timid course
Of our scholastic studies; could have wished
To see the river flow with ampler range
500 And freer pace; but more, far more, I grieved
To see displayed among an eager few,
Who in the field of contest persevered,
Passions unworthy of youth's generous heart
And mounting spirit, pitiably repaid,
When so disturbed, whatever palms are won.
From these I turned to travel with the shoal
Of more unthinking natures, easy minds
And pillowy; yet not wanting love that makes
The day pass lightly on, when foresight sleeps,
510 And wisdom and the pledges interchanged
With our own inner being are forgot.

Of wild wood-honey; or, with truant eyes
530 Unruly, peeped about for vagrant fruit.
And, as for what pertains to human life,
The deeper passions working round me here,
Whether of envy, jealousy, pride, shame,
Ambition, emulation, fear, or hope,
Or those of dissolute pleasure, were by me
Unshared; and only now and then observed,
So little was their hold upon my being,
As outward things that might administer
To knowledge or instruction. Hushed, meanwhile,
540 Was the under soul, locked up in such a calm,
That not a leaf of the great nature stirred.

    Yet was this deep vacation not given up
To utter waste. Hitherto I had stood
In my own mind remote from human life,
(At least from what we commonly so name,)   515
Even as a shepherd on a promontory
Who lacking occupation looks far forth
Into the endless sea, and rather makes
Than finds what he beholds. And sure it is,
550 That this first transit from the smooth delights   520
And wild outlandish walks of simple youth
To something that resembled an approach
Towards mortal business, to a privileged world
Within a world, a midway residence
With all its intervenient imagery,   525
Did better suit my visionary mind,
Far better, than to have been bolted forth,
Thrust out abruptly into Fortune's way
Among the conflicts of substantial life;
560 By a more just gradation did lead on   530
To higher things; more naturally matured,
For permanent possession, better fruits
Whether of truth or virtue, to ensue.

    In playful zest of fancy did we note   535

    Yet was this deep vacation not given up
To utter waste. Hitherto I had stood
In my own mind remote from social life,
(At least from what we commonly so name,)
Like a lone shepherd on a promontory
Who lacking occupation looks far forth
Into the boundless sea, and rather makes
Than finds what he beholds. And sure it is,
520 That this first transit from the smooth delights
And wild outlandish walks of simple youth
To something that resembled an approach
Towards human business, to a privileged world
Within a world, a midway residence
With all its intervenient imagery,
Did better suit my visionary mind,
Far better, than to have been bolted forth,
Thrust out abruptly into Fortune's way
Among the conflicts of substantial life;
530 By a more just gradation did lead on
To higher things; more naturally matured,
For permanent possession, better fruits,
Whether of truth or virtue, to ensue.
In serious mood, but oftener, I confess,
With playful zest of fancy, did we note

(How could we less?) the manners and the ways
Of those who in the livery were arrayed
Of good or evil fame; of those with whom
By frame of Academic discipline
Perforce we were connected, men whose sway   *540*
570 And whose authority of office served
To set our minds on edge, and did no more.
Nor wanted we rich pastime of this kind,
Found everywhere, but chiefly in the ring
Of the grave Elders, men unscoured, grotesque   *545*
In character, tricked out like aged trees
Which through the lapse of their infirmity
Give ready place to any random seed
That chooses to be reared upon their trunks.

    Here on my view, confronting as it were   *550*
580 Those shepherd swains whom I had lately left,
Did flash a different image of old age;
How different! yet both withal alike,
A book of rudiments for the unpractised sight,
Objects embossed! and which with sedulous care   *554*
Nature holds up before the eye of youth
In her great school; with further view, perhaps,
To enter early on her tender scheme
Of teaching comprehension with delight,   *560*
And mingling playful with pathetic thoughts.

590   The surfaces of artificial life
And manners finely spun, the delicate race
Of colours, lurking, gleaming up and down
Through that state arras woven with silk and gold; *565*
This wily interchange of snaky hues,
Willingly and unwillingly revealed,
I had not learned to watch; and at this time
Perhaps, had such been in my daily sight,
I might have been indifferent thereto
As hermits are to tales of distant things.
600 Hence for these rarities elaborate

(How could we less?) the manners and the ways
Of those who lived distinguished by the badge
Of good or ill report; or those with whom
By frame of Academic discipline
540 We were perforce connected, men whose sway
And known authority of office served
To set our minds on edge, and did no more.
Nor wanted we rich pastime of this kind,
Found everywhere, but chiefly in the ring
Of the grave Elders, men unscoured, grotesque
In character, tricked out like aged trees
Which through the lapse of their infirmity
Give ready place to any random seed
That chooses to be reared upon their trunks.

550   Here on my view, confronting vividly
Those shepherd swains whom I had lately left,
Appeared a different aspect of old age;
How different! yet both distinctly marked,
Objects embossed to catch the general eye,
Or portraitures for special use designed,
As some might seem, so aptly do they serve
To illustrate Nature's book of rudiments –
That book upheld as with maternal care
When she would enter on her tender scheme
560 Of teaching comprehension with delight,
And mingling playful with pathetic thoughts.

    The surfaces of artificial life
And manners finely wrought, the delicate race
Of colours, lurking, gleaming up and down
Through that state arras woven with silk and gold;
This wily interchange of snaky hues,
Willingly or unwillingly revealed,

Having no relish yet, I was content
With the more homely produce, rudely piled
In this our coarser warehouse. At this day   570
I smile in many a mountain solitude
At passages and fragments that remain
Of that inferior exhibition, played
By wooden images, a theatre
For wake or fair. And oftentimes do flit   576
Remembrances before me of old men –
610   Old humorists, who have been long in their graves,
And having almost in my mind put off
Their human names, have into phantoms passed   580
Of texture midway betwixt life and books.

      I play the loiterer: 'tis enough to note
That here in dwarf proportions were expressed
The limbs of the great world; its goings-on
Collaterally portrayed, as in mock fight,   585
A tournament of blows, some hardly dealt
Though short of mortal combat; and whate'er
620   Might of this pageant be supposed to hit
A simple rustic's notice, this way less,
More that way, was not wasted upon me.–   590
And yet this spectacle may well demand
A more substantial name, no mimic show,
Itself a living part of a live whole,
A creek of the vast sea; for, all degrees
And shapes of spurious fame and short-lived praise 595
Here sate in state, and fed with daily alms
Retainers won away from solid good;
630   And here was Labour, his own bond-slave; Hope,
That never set the pains against the prize;
Idleness halting with his weary clog,   600
And poor misguided Shame, and witless Fear,
And simple Pleasure foraging for Death;
Honour misplaced, and Dignity astray;
Feuds, factions, flatteries, enmity, and guile;

I neither knew nor cared for; and as such
Were wanting here, I took what might be found
570 Of less elaborate fabric. At this day
I smile, in many a mountain solitude
Conjuring up scenes as obsolete in freaks
Of character, in points of wit as broad,
As aught by wooden images performed
For entertainment of the gaping crowd
At wake or fair. And oftentimes do flit
Remembrances before me of old men –
Old humorists, who have been long in their graves,
And having almost in my mind put off
580 Their human names, have into phantoms passed
Of texture midway between life and books.

I play the loiterer: 'tis enough to note
That here in dwarf proportions were expressed
The limbs of the great world; its eager strifes
Collaterally portrayed, as in mock fight,
A tournament of blows, some hardly dealt
Though short of mortal combat; and whate'er
Might in this pageant be supposed to hit
An artless rustic's notice, this way less,
590 More that way, was not wasted upon me –
And yet the spectacle may well demand
A more substantial name, no mimic show,
Itself a living part of a live whole,
A creek in the vast sea; for, all degrees
And shapes of spurious fame and short-lived praise
Here sate in state, and fed with daily alms
Retainers won away from solid good;
And here was Labour, his own bondslave; Hope,
That never set the pains against the prize;
600 Idleness halting with his weary clog,
And poor misguided Shame, and witless Fear,
And simple Pleasure foraging for Death;
Honour misplaced, and Dignity astray;
Feuds, factions, flatteries, enmity, and guile;

Murmuring submission, and bald government,   605
(The idol weak as the idolator),
And Decency and Custom starving Truth,
640   And blind Authority beating with his staff
The child that might have led him; Emptiness
Followed as of good omen, and meek Worth   610
Left to itself unheard of and unknown.

Of these and other kindred notices
I cannot say what portion is in truth
The naked recollection of that time,
And what may rather have been called to life   615
By after-meditation. But delight
That, in an easy temper lulled asleep,
650   Is still with Innocence its own reward,
This surely was not wanting. Carelessly
I gazed, roving as through a cabinet   620
Or wide museum (thronged with fishes, gems,
Birds, crocodiles, shells) where little can be seen
Well understood, or naturally endeared,
Yet still does every step bring something forth
That quickens, pleases, stings; and here and there
A casual rarity is singled out,
And has its brief perusal, then gives way
660   To others, all supplanted in their turn.
Meanwhile, amid this gaudy congress, framed
Of things by nature most unneighbourly,   625
The head turns round and cannot right itself;
And though an aching and a barren sense
Of gay confusion still be uppermost,
With few wise longings and but little love,
Yet something to the memory sticks at last,   630
Whence profit may be drawn in times to come.

Thus in submissive idleness, my Friend!
670   The labouring time of autumn, winter, spring,
Nine months! rolled pleasingly away; the tenth   635
Returned me to my native hills again.

Murmuring submission, and bald government,
(The idol weak as the idolator),
And Decency and Custom starving Truth,
And blind Authority beating with his staff
The child that might have led him; Emptiness
610 Followed as of good omen, and meek Worth
Left to herself unheard of and unknown.

Of these and other kindred notices
I cannot say what portion is in truth
The naked recollection of that time,
And what may rather have been called to life
By after-meditation. But delight
That, in an easy temper lulled asleep,
Is still with Innocence its own reward,
This was not wanting. Carelessly I roamed
620 As through a wide museum from whose stores
A casual rarity is singled out
And has its brief perusal, then gives way
To others, all supplanted in their turn;
Till 'mid this crowded neighbourhood of things
That are by nature most unneighbourly,
The head turns round and cannot right itself;
And though an aching and a barren sense
Of gay confusion still be uppermost,
With few wise longings and but little love,
630 Yet to the memory something cleaves at last,
Whence profit may be drawn in times to come.

Thus in submissive idleness, my Friend!
The labouring time of autumn, winter, spring,
Eight months! rolled pleasingly away; the ninth
Came and returned me to my native hills.

Book Fourth

SUMMER VACATION

A pleasant sight it was when, having clomb
The Heights of Kendal, and that dreary moor
Was crossed, at length, as from a rampart's edge,
I overlooked the bed of Windermere.   5
I bounded down the hill, shouting amain
A lusty summons to the farther shore
For the old Ferryman; and when he came   13
I did not step into the well-known boat
Without a cordial welcome. Thence right forth
I took my way, now drawing towards home,
To that sweet Valley where I had been reared;
'Twas but a short hour's walk ere, veering round,   20
I saw the snow-white church upon its hill
Sit like a thronèd Lady, sending out
A gracious look all over its domain.
Glad greetings had I, and some tears, perhaps,   27
From my old Dame, so motherly and good,
While she perused me with a parent's pride.
The thoughts of gratitude shall fall like dew   30

Book Fourth

SUMMER VACATION

Bright was the summer's noon when quickening steps
Followed each other till a dreary moor
Was crossed, a bare ridge clomb, upon whose top
Standing alone, as from a rampart's edge,
I overlooked the bed of Windermere,
Like a vast river, stretching in the sun.
With exultation, at my feet I saw
Lake, islands, promontories, gleaming bays,
A universe of Nature's fairest forms
10 Proudly revealed with instantaneous burst,
Magnificent, and beautiful, and gay.
I bounded down the hill shouting amain
For the old Ferryman; to the shout the rocks
Replied, and when the Charon of the flood
Had staid his oars, and touched the jutting pier,
I did not step into the well-known boat
Without a cordial greeting. Thence with speed
Up the familiar hill I took my way
Towards that sweet Valley where I had been reared;
20 'Twas but a short hour's walk, ere veering round
I saw the snow-white church upon her hill
Sit like a thronèd Lady, sending out
A gracious look all over her domain.
Yon azure smoke betrays the lurking town;
With eager footsteps I advance and reach
The cottage threshold where my journey closed.
Glad welcome had I, with some tears, perhaps,
From my old Dame, so kind and motherly,
While she perused me with a parent's pride.
30 The thoughts of gratitude shall fall like dew

20 Upon thy grave, good creature! While my heart
    Can beat I never will forget thy name.
    Heaven's blessing be upon thee where thou liest
    After thy innocent and busy stir
    In narrow cares, thy little daily growth   *35*
    Of calm enjoyments, after eighty years,
    And more than eighty, of untroubled life,
    Childless, yet by the strangers to thy blood
    Honoured with little less than filial love.
    Great joy was mine to see thee once again,   *40*
30 Thee and thy dwelling, and a throng of things
    About its narrow precincts all beloved,
    And many of them seeming yet my own!
    Why should I speak of what a thousand hearts
    Have felt, and every man alive can guess?   *45*
    The rooms, the court, the garden were not left
    Long unsaluted, and the spreading pine
    And broad stone table underneath its boughs,
    Our summer seat in many a festive hour;
    And that unruly child of mountain birth,   *50*
40 The froward brook, which, soon as he was boxed
    Within our garden, found himself at once,
    As if by trick insidious and unkind,
    Stripped of his voice and left to dimple down
    (Without an effort and without a will)   *55*
    A channel pavèd by the hand of man.
    I looked at him and smiled, and smiled again,
    And in the press of twenty thousand thoughts,
    'Ha,' quoth I, 'pretty prisoner, are you there!'   *59*
    And now, reviewing soberly that hour,
50 I marvel that a fancy did not flash
    Upon me, and a strong desire, straightway,
    At sight of such an emblem that showed forth
    So aptly my late course of even days
    And all their smooth enthralment, to pen down
    A satire on myself. My aged Dame
    Was with me, at my side: she guided me;   *65*
    I willing, nay – nay, wishing to be led.

Upon thy grave, good creature! While my heart
Can beat never will I forget thy name.
Heaven's blessing be upon thee where thou liest
After thy innocent and busy stir
In narrow cares, thy little daily growth
Of calm enjoyments, after eighty years,
And more than eighty, of untroubled life,
Childless, yet by the strangers to thy blood
Honoured with little less than filial love.

40   What joy was mine to see thee once again,
Thee and thy dwelling, and a crowd of things
About its narrow precincts all beloved,
And many of them seeming yet my own!
Why should I speak of what a thousand hearts
Have felt, and every man alive can guess?
The rooms, the court, the garden were not left
Long unsaluted, nor the sunny seat
Round the stone table under the dark pine,
Friendly to studious or to festive hours;

50   Nor that unruly child of mountain birth,
The froward brook, who, soon as he was boxed
Within our garden, found himself at once,
As if by trick insidious and unkind,
Stripped of his voice and left to dimple down
(Without an effort and without a will)
A channel paved by man's officious care.
I looked at him and smiled, and smiled again,
And in the press of twenty thousand thoughts,
'Ha,' quoth I, 'pretty prisoner, are you there!'

60   Well might sarcastic Fancy then have whispered,
'An emblem here behold of thy own life;
In its late course of even days with all
Their smooth enthralment'; but the heart was full,
Too full for the reproach. My aged Dame
Walked proudly at my side: she guided me;
I willing, nay – nay, wishing to be led.

– The face of every neighbour whom I met
Was as a volume to me; some I hailed
60 Far off, upon the road, or at their work,   70
Unceremonious greetings interchanged
With half the length of a long field between.
Among my schoolfellows I scattered round
A salutation that was more constrained,
Though earnest, doubtless with a little pride,
But with more shame, for my habiliments,   75
The transformation, and the gay attire.

Delighted did I take my place again
At our domestic table: and, dear Friend!
70 Relating simply as my wish hath been
A Poet's history, can I leave untold   80
The joy with which I laid me down at night
In my accustomed bed, more welcome now
Perhaps than if it had been more desired
Or been more often thought of with regret?
That bed whence I had heard the roaring wind   85
And clamorous rain, that bed where I so oft
Had lain awake on breezy nights to watch
The moon in splendour couched among the leaves
80 Of a tall ash, that near our cottage stood;
Had watched her with fixed eyes while to and fro   90
In the dark summit of the moving tree
She rocked with every impulse of the wind.

Among the faces which it pleased me well
To see again, was one by ancient right
Our inmate, a rough terrier of the hills,   95
By birth and call of nature pre-ordained
To hunt the badger and unearth the fox
Among the impervious crags, but having been
90 From youth our own adopted, he had passed
Into a gentler service. And when first   100
The boyish spirit flagged, and day by day
Along my veins I kindled with the stir,

    – The face of every neighbour whom I met
    Was like a volume to me; some were hailed
    Upon the road, some busy at their work,
70 Unceremonious greetings interchanged
    With half the length of a long field between.
    Among my schoolfellows I scattered round
    Like recognitions, but with some constraint
    Attended, doubtless, with a little pride,
    But with more shame, for my habiliments,
    The transformation wrought by gay attire.
    Not less delighted did I take my place
    At our domestic table: and, dear Friend!
    In this endeavour simply to relate
80 A Poet's history, may I leave untold
    The thankfulness with which I laid me down
    In my accustomed bed, more welcome now
    Perhaps than if it had been more desired
    Or been more often thought of with regret?
    That lowly bed whence I had heard the wind
    Roar and the rain beat hard, where I so oft
    Had lain awake on summer nights to watch
    The moon in splendour couched among the leaves
    Of a tall ash, that near our cottage stood;
90 Had watched her with fixed eyes while to and fro
    In the dark summit of the waving tree
    She rocked with every impulse of the breeze.

      Among the favourites whom it pleased me well
    To see again, was one by ancient right
    Our inmate, a rough terrier of the hills;
    By birth and call of nature pre-ordained
    To hunt the badger and unearth the fox
    Among the impervious crags, but having been
    From youth our own adopted, he had passed
100 Into a gentler service. And when first
    The boyish spirit flagged, and day by day
    Along my veins I kindled with the stir,

The fermentation, and the vernal heat
Of poesy, affecting private shades
Like a sick Lover, then this dog was used   *105*
To watch me, an attendant and a friend,
Obsequious to my steps early and late,
Though often of such dilatory walk
100 Tired, and uneasy at the halts I made.
A hundred times when, in these wanderings,   *110*
I have been busy with the toil of verse,
Great pains and little progress, and at once
Some fair enchanting Image in my mind
Rose up full-formed, like Venus from the sea,
Have I sprung forth towards him, and let loose   *115*
My hand upon his back with stormy joy,
Caressing him again and yet again.
And when in the public roads at eventide
110 I sauntered, like a river murmuring
And talking to itself, at such a season   *120*
It was his custom to jog on before;
But, duly, whensoever he had met
A passenger approaching, would he turn
To give me timely notice, and straightway,
Punctual to such admonishment, I hushed   *125*
My voice, composed my gait, and shaped myself
To give and take a greeting that might save
My name from piteous rumours, such as wait
120 On men suspected to be crazed in brain.   *130*

    Those walks well worthy to be prized and loved –
Regretted! – that word, too, was on my tongue,
But they were richly laden with all good,
And cannot be remembered but with thanks
And gratitude, and perfect joy of heart –   *135*
Those walks did now like a returning Spring
Come back on me again. When first I made
Once more the circuit of our little lake,
If ever happiness hath lodged with man,

The fermentation, and the vernal heat
Of poesy, affecting private shades
Like a sick Lover, then this dog was used
To watch me, an attendant and a friend,
Obsequious to my steps early and late,
Though often of such dilatory walk
Tired, and uneasy at the halts I made.
110 A hundred times when, roving high and low,
I have been harassed with the toil of verse,
Much pains and little progress, and at once
Some lovely Image in the song rose up
Full-formed, like Venus rising from the sea;
Then have I darted forwards to let loose
My hand upon his back with stormy joy,
Caressing him again and yet again.
And when at evening on the public way
I sauntered, like a river murmuring
120 And talking to itself when all things else
Are still, the creature trotted on before;
Such was his custom; but whene'er he met
A passenger approaching, he would turn
To give me timely notice, and straightway,
Grateful for that admonishment, I hushed
My voice, composed my gait, and, with the air
And mien of one whose thoughts are free, advanced
To give and take a greeting that might save
My name from piteous rumours, such as wait
130 On men suspected to be crazed in brain.

Those walks well worthy to be prized and loved –
Regretted! – that word, too, was on my tongue,
But they were richly laden with all good,
And cannot be remembered but with thanks
And gratitude, and perfect joy of heart –
Those walks in all their freshness now came back
Like a returning Spring. When first I made
Once more the circuit of our little lake,
If ever happiness hath lodged with man,

130   That day consummate happiness was mine,   *140*
       Wide-spreading, steady, calm, contemplative.
       The sun was set, or setting, when I left
       Our cottage door, and evening soon brought on
       A sober hour, not winning or serene,
       For cold and raw the air was, and untuned;   *145*
       But as a face we love is sweetest then
       When sorrow damps it, or, whatever look
       It chance to wear is sweetest if the heart
       Have fulness in itself; even so with me
140   It fared that evening. Gently did my soul   *150*
       Put off her veil, and, self-transmuted, stood
       Naked, as in the presence of her God.
       As on I walked, a comfort seemed to touch
       A heart that had not been disconsolate:
       Strength came where weakness was not known to be,   *155*
       At least not felt; and restoration came
       Like an intruder knocking at the door
       Of unacknowledged weariness. I took
       The balance in my hand and weighed myself.
150   I saw but little, and thereat was pleased;   *161*
       Little did I remember, and even this
       Still pleased me more; but I had hopes and peace
       And swellings of the spirits, was rapt and soothed,
       Conversed with promises, had glimmering views
       How life pervades the undecaying mind;   *165*
       How the immortal soul with God-like power
       Informs, creates, and thaws the deepest sleep
       That time can lay upon her; how on earth,
       Man, if he do but live within the light
160   Of high endeavours, daily spreads abroad   *170*
       His being with a strength that cannot fail.
       Nor was there want of milder thoughts, of love,
       Of innocence, and holiday repose;
       And more than pastoral quiet, in the heart
       Of amplest projects, and a peaceful end   *175*
       At last, or glorious, by endurance won.
       Thus musing, in a wood I sate me down

140 That day consummate happiness was mine,
Wide-spreading, steady, calm, contemplative.
The sun was set, or setting, when I left
Our cottage door, and evening soon brought on
A sober hour, not winning or serene,
For cold and raw the air was, and untuned;
But as a face we love is sweetest then
When sorrow damps it, or, whatever look
It chance to wear is sweetest if the heart
Have fulness in herself; even so with me
150 It fared that evening. Gently did my soul
Put off her veil, and, self-transmuted, stood
Naked, as in the presence of her God.
While on I walked, a comfort seemed to touch
A heart that had not been disconsolate:
Strength came where weakness was not known to be,
At least not felt; and restoration came
Like an intruder knocking at the door
Of unacknowledged weariness. I took
The balance, and with firm hand weighed myself.
160 – Of that external scene which round me lay,
Little, in this abstraction, did I see;
Remembered less; but I had inward hopes
And swellings of the spirit, was rapt and soothed,
Conversed with promises, had glimmering views
How life pervades the undecaying mind;
How the immortal soul with God-like power
Informs, creates, and thaws the deepest sleep
That time can lay upon her; how on earth,
Man, if he do but live within the light
170 Of high endeavours, daily spreads abroad
His being armed with strength that cannot fail.
Nor was there want of milder thoughts, of love,
Of innocence, and holiday repose;
And more than pastoral quiet, 'mid the stir
Of boldest projects, and a peaceful end
At last, or glorious, by endurance won.
Thus musing, in a wood I sate me down

Alone, continuing there to muse: meanwhile
The mountain heights were slowly overspread
170 With darkness, and before a rippling breeze   *180*
The long lake lengthened out its hoary line,
And in the sheltered coppice where I sate,
Around me from among the hazel leaves,
Now here, now there, stirred by the straggling wind,
Came intermittingly a breath-like sound,   *185*
A respiration short and quick, which oft,
Yea, might I say, again and yet again,
Mistaking for the panting of my dog,
The off and on companion of my walk,
180 I turned my head, to look if he were there.   *189*

A freshness also found I at this time
In human Life, the life I mean of those
Whose occupations really I loved;
The prospect often touched me with surprise,
Crowded and full, and changed, as seemed to me,
Even as a garden in the heat of spring   *195*
After an eight-days' absence. For (to omit
The things which were the same and yet appeared
So different) amid this solitude,
190 The little Vale where was my chief abode,
'Twas not indifferent to a youthful mind   *200*
To note, perhaps, some sheltered seat in which
An old man had been used to sun himself,
Now empty; pale-faced babes whom I had left
In arms, known children of the neighbourhood,
Now rosy prattlers tottering up and down;   *205*
And growing girls whose beauty, filched away
With all its pleasant promises, was gone
To deck some slighted playmate's homely cheek.

200 Yes, I had something of another eye,
And often looking round was moved to smiles   *210*
Such as a delicate work of humour breeds;
I read, without design, the opinions, thoughts
148

Alone, continuing there to muse: the slopes
And heights meanwhile were slowly overspread
180 With darkness, and before a rippling breeze
The long lake lengthened out its hoary line,
And in the sheltered coppice where I sate,
Around me from among the hazel leaves,
Now here, now there, moved by the straggling wind,
Came ever and anon a breath-like sound,
Quick as the pantings of the faithful dog,
The off and on companion of my walk;
And such, at times, believing them to be,
I turned my head to look if he were there;
190 Then into solemn thought I passed once more.

A freshness also found I at this time
In human Life, the daily life of those
Whose occupations really I loved;
The peaceful scene oft filled me with surprise
Changed like a garden in the heat of spring
After an eight-days' absence. For (to omit
The things which were the same and yet appeared
Far otherwise) amid this rural solitude,
A narrow Vale where each was known to all,
200 'Twas not indifferent to a youthful mind
To mark some sheltering bower or sunny nook,
Where an old man had used to sit alone,
Now vacant; pale-faced babes whom I had left
In arms, now rosy prattlers at the feet
Of a pleased grandame tottering up and down;
And growing girls whose beauty, filched away
With all its pleasant promises, was gone
To deck some slighted playmate's homely cheek.

Yes, I had something of a subtler sense,
210 And often looking round was moved to smiles
Such as a delicate work of humour breeds;
I read, without design, the opinions, thoughts,

Of those plain-living people, in a sense
Of love and knowledge; with another eye
I saw the quiet woodman in the woods,   *215*
The shepherd on the hills. With new delight,
This chiefly, did I view my grey-haired Dame;
Saw her go forth to church or other work
210   Of state, equipped in monumental trim;
Short velvet cloak (her bonnet of the like)   *220*
A mantle such as Spanish Cavaliers
Wore in old time. Her smooth domestic life,
Affectionate without uneasiness,
Her talk, her business, pleased me; and no less
Her clear though shallow stream of piety   *225*
That ran on Sabbath days a fresher course;
With thoughts unfelt till now I saw her read
Her Bible on the Sunday afternoons,
220   And loved the book, when she had dropped asleep
And made of it a pillow for her head.   *230*

Nor less do I remember to have felt,
Distinctly manifested at this time,
A dawning, even as of another sense,
A human-heartedness about my love
For objects hitherto the gladsome air
Of my own private being and no more: *235*
Which I had loved, even as a blessèd spirit
Or Angel, if he were to dwell on earth,
230   Might love in individual happiness.
But now there opened on me other thoughts
Of change, congratulation and regret,   *240*
A new-born feeling! It spread far and wide;
The trees, the mountains shared it, and the brooks,
The stars of Heaven, now seen in their old haunts –
White Sirius glittering o'er the southern crags,
Orion with his belt, and those fair Seven,   *245*
Acquaintances of every little child,
And Jupiter, my own belovèd star!
240   Whatever shadings of mortality

Of those plain-living people now observed
With clearer knowledge; with another eye
I saw the quiet woodman in the woods,
The shepherd roam the hills. With new delight,
This chiefly, did I note my grey-haired Dame;
Saw her go forth to church or other work
Of state, equipped in monumental trim;
220   Short velvet cloak (her bonnet of the like),
A mantle such as Spanish Cavaliers
Wore in old time. Her smooth domestic life,
Affectionate without disquietude,
Her talk, her business, pleased me; and no less
Her clear though shallow stream of piety
That ran on Sabbath days a fresher course;
With thoughts unfelt till now I saw her read
Her Bible on hot Sunday afternoons,
And loved the book, when she had dropped asleep
230   And made of it a pillow for her head.

        Nor less do I remember to have felt,
Distinctly manifested at this time,
A human-heartedness about my love
For objects hitherto the absolute wealth
Of my own private being and no more:
Which I had loved, even as a blessèd spirit
Or Angel, if he were to dwell on earth,
Might love in individual happiness.
But now there opened on me other thoughts
240   Of change, congratulation or regret,
A pensive feeling! It spread far and wide;
The trees, the mountains shared it, and the brooks,
The stars of Heaven, now seen in their old haunts –
White Sirius glittering o'er the southern crags,
Orion with his belt, and those fair Seven,
Acquaintances of every little child,
And Jupiter, my own belovèd star!
Whatever shadings of mortality,

Had fallen upon these objects heretofore   250
Were different in kind; not tender: strong,
Deep, gloomy were they and severe; the scatterings
Of childhood; and, moreover, had given way
In later youth to beauty, and to love
Enthusiastic, to delight and joy.   255

  As one who hangs down-bending from the side
Of a slow-moving boat, upon the breast
Of a still water, solacing himself
250 With such discoveries as his eye can make
Beneath him in the bottom of the deeps,   260
Sees many beauteous sights – weeds, fishes, flowers,
Grots, pebbles, roots of trees, and fancies more,
Yet often is perplexed and cannot part
The shadow from the substance, rocks and sky,
Mountains and clouds, from that which is indeed   265
The region, and the things which there abide
In their true dwelling; now is crossed by gleam
Of his own image, by a sunbeam now,
260 And motions that are sent he knows not whence,
Impediments that make his task more sweet;   270
Such pleasant office have we long pursued
Incumbent o'er the surface of past time
With like success, nor have we often looked
On more alluring shows (to me, at least,)
More soft, or less ambiguously descried,
Than those which now we have been passing by,   275
And where we still are lingering. Yet in spite
Of all these new employments of the mind,
270 There was an inner falling off – I loved,
Loved deeply, all that I had loved before,
More deeply even than ever: but a swarm   280
Of heady thoughts jostling each other, gawds,
And feast and dance, and public revelry,
And sports and games (less pleasing in themselves,
Than as they were a badge glossy and fresh   285

Whatever imports from the world of death
250 Had come among these objects heretofore,
Were, in the main, of mood less tender: strong,
Deep, gloomy were they, and severe; the scatterings
Of awe or tremulous dread, that had given way
In later youth to yearnings of a love
Enthusiastic, to delight and hope.

As one who hangs down-bending from the side
Of a slow-moving boat, upon the breast
Of a still water, solacing himself
With such discoveries as his eye can make
260 Beneath him in the bottom of the deep,
Sees many beauteous sights – weeds, fishes, flowers,
Grots, pebbles, roots of trees, and fancies more,
Yet often is perplexed and cannot part
The shadow from the substance, rocks and sky,
Mountains and clouds, reflected in the depth
Of the clear flood, from things which there abide
In their true dwelling; now is crossed by gleam
Of his own image, by a sunbeam now,
And wavering motions sent he knows not whence,
270 Impediments that make his task more sweet;
Such pleasant office have we long pursued
Incumbent o'er the surface of past time
With like success, nor often have appeared
Shapes fairer or less doubtfully discerned
Than these to which the Tale, indulgent Friend!
Would now direct thy notice. Yet in spite
Of pleasure won, and knowledge not withheld,
There was an inner falling off – I loved,
Loved deeply all that had been loved before,
280 More deeply even than ever: but a swarm
Of heady schemes jostling each other, gawds,
And feast and dance, and public revelry,
And sports and games (too grateful in themselves,
Yet in themselves less grateful, I believe,
Than as they were a badge glossy and fresh

Of manliness and freedom) these did now
Seduce me from the firm habitual quest
Of feeding pleasures, from that eager zeal,
280   Those yearnings which had every day been mine –
A wild, unworldly-minded youth, given up   290
To Nature and to books, or, at the most,
From time to time, by inclination shipped,
One among many, in societies,
That were, or seemed, as simple as myself.
But now was come a change; it would demand
Some skill, and longer time than may be spared,
To paint, even to myself, these vanities,
And how they wrought. But, sure it is that now
290   Contagious air did oft environ me
Unknown among these haunts in former days.
The very garments that I wore appeared   295
To prey upon my strength, and stopped the course
And quiet stream of self-forgetfulness.
Something there was about me that perplexed
The authentic sight of reason, pressed too closely
On that religious dignity of mind
That is the very faculty of truth;
Which wanting, either, from the very first,
300   A function never lighted up, or else
Extinguished, man, a creature great and good,
Seems but a pageant plaything with vile claws,
And this great frame of breathing elements
A senseless idol.
                        That vague heartless chase
Of trivial pleasures was a poor exchange
For books and Nature at that early age.
'Tis true, some casual knowledge might be gained   300
Of character or life; but at that time,
Of manners put to school I took small note,
310   And all my deeper passions lay elsewhere.
Far better had it been to exalt the mind
By solitary study, to uphold   305
Intense desire by thought and quietness;

Of manliness and freedom) all conspired
To lure my mind from firm habitual quest
Of feeding pleasures, to depress the zeal
And damp those daily yearnings which had once been mine –
290   A wild, unworldly-minded youth, given up
To his own eager thoughts. It would demand
Some skill, and longer time than may be spared,
To paint these vanities, and how they wrought
In haunts where they, till now, had been unknown.
It seemed the very garments that I wore
Preyed on my strength, and stopped the quiet stream
Of self-forgetfulness.
                                    Yes, that heartless chase
Of trivial pleasures was a poor exchange
For books and Nature at that early age.
300   'Tis true, some casual knowledge might be gained
Of character or life; but at that time,
Of manners put to school I took small note,
And all my deeper passions lay elsewhere.
Far better had it been to exalt the mind
By solitary study, to uphold
Intense desire through meditative peace;

And yet, in chastisement of these regrets,
The memory of one particular hour
Doth here rise up against me. In a throng,
A festal company of maids and youths,
Old men, and matrons staid, promiscuous rout,   *310*
A medley of all tempers, I had passed
320 The night in dancing, gaiety, and mirth,
With din of instruments and shuffling feet,
And glancing forms, and tapers glittering,
And unaimed prattle flying up and down;
Spirits upon the stretch, and here and there   *316*
Slight shocks of young love-liking interspersed,
That mounted up like joy into the head,
And tingled through the veins. Ere we retired,
The cock had crowed, the sky was bright with day.   *320*
Two miles I had to walk along the fields
330 Before I reached my home. Magnificent
The morning was, a memorable pomp,
More glorious than I ever had beheld.   *325*
The sea was laughing at a distance; all
The solid mountains were as bright as clouds,
Grain-tinctured, drenched in empyrean light;
And in the meadows and the lower grounds
Was all the sweetness of a common dawn –   *330*
Dews, vapours, and the melody of birds,
And labourers going forth into the fields.
340   Ah! need I say, dear Friend! that to the brim
My heart was full; I made no vows, but vows
Were then made for me; bond unknown to me   *335*
Was given, that I should be, else sinning greatly,
A dedicated Spirit. On I walked
In blessedness, which even yet remains.

       Strange rendezvous my mind was at that time,
A parti-coloured show of grave and gay,   *340*
Solid and light, short-sighted and profound;
Of inconsiderate habits and sedate,
350 Consorting in one mansion unreproved.

And yet, for chastisement of these regrets,
The memory of one particular hour
Doth here rise up against me. 'Mid a throng
310 Of maids and youths, old men, and matrons staid,
A medley of all tempers, I had passed
The night in dancing, gaiety, and mirth,
With din of instruments and shuffling feet,
And glancing forms, and tapers glittering,
And unaimed prattle flying up and down;
Spirits upon the stretch, and here and there
Slight shocks of young love-liking interspersed,
Whose transient pleasure mounted to the head,
And tingled through the veins. Ere we retired,
320 The cock had crowed, and now the eastern sky
Was kindling, not unseen, from humble copse
And open field, through which the pathway wound,
And homeward led my steps. Magnificent
The morning rose, in memorable pomp,
Glorious as e'er I had beheld – in front,
The sea lay laughing at a distance; near,
The solid mountains shone, bright as the clouds,
Grain-tinctured, drenched in empyrean light;
And in the meadows and the lower grounds
330 Was all the sweetness of a common dawn –
Dews, vapours, and the melody of birds,
And labourers going forth to till the fields.
    Ah! need I say, dear Friend! that to the brim
My heart was full; I made no vows, but vows
Were then made for me; bond unknown to me
Was given, that I should be, else sinning greatly,
A dedicated Spirit. On I walked
In thankful blessedness, which yet survives.

    Strange rendezvous my mind was at that time,
340 A parti-coloured show of grave and gay,
Solid and light, short-sighted and profound;
Of inconsiderate habits and sedate,
Consorting in one mansion unreproved.

I knew the worth of that which I possessed,
Though slighted and misused. Besides, in truth,   *345*
That summer, swarming as it did with thoughts
Transient and loose, yet wanted not a store
Of primitive hours, when, by these hindrances
Unthwarted, I experienced in myself
Conformity as just as that of old   *350*
To the end and written spirit of God's works,
Whether held forth in Nature or in Man.

360   From many wanderings that have left behind
Remembrances not lifeless, I will here
Single out one, then pass to other themes.

A favourite pleasure hath it been with me,
From time of earliest youth, to walk alone
Along the public way, when, for the night
Deserted, in its silence it assumes
A character of deeper quietness
Than pathless solitudes. At such an hour
Once, ere these summer months were passed away,   *370*
370   I slowly mounted up a steep ascent

The worth I knew of powers that I possessed,
Though slighted and too oft misused. Besides,
That summer, swarming as it did with thoughts
Transient and idle, lacked not intervals
When Folly from the frown of fleeting Time
Shrunk, and the mind experienced in herself
350   Conformity as just as that of old
To the end and written spirit of God's works,
Whether held forth in Nature or in Man,
Through pregnant vision, separate or conjoined.

When from our better selves we have too long
Been parted by the hurrying world, and droop,
Sick of its business, of its pleasures tired,
How gracious, how benign, is Solitude;
How potent a mere image of her sway;
Most potent when impressed upon the mind
360   With an appropriate human centre – hermit,
Deep in the bosom of the wilderness;
Votary (in vast cathedral, where no foot
Is treading, where no other face is seen)
Kneeling at prayers; or watchman on the top
Of lighthouse, beaten by Atlantic waves;
Or as the soul of that great Power is met
Sometimes embodied on a public road,
When, for the night deserted, it assumes
A character of quiet more profound
370   Than pathless wastes.
                  Once, when those summer months
Were flown, and autumn brought its annual show
Of oars with oars contending, sails with sails,
Upon Winander's spacious breast, it chanced
That – after I had left a flower-decked room
(Whose in-door pastime, lighted up, survived
To a late hour), and spirits overwrought
Were making night do penance for a day
Spent in a round of strenuous idleness –
My homeward course led up a long ascent,

Where the road's watery surface, to the ridge   *380*
Of that sharp rising, glittered in the moon
And seemed before my eyes another stream
Creeping with silent lapse to join the brook
That murmured in the valley. On I went   *384*
Tranquil, receiving in my own despite
Amusement, as I slowly passed along,
From such near objects as from time to time
Perforce intruded on the listless sense
380   Quiescent, and disposed to sympathy,
With an exhausted mind, worn out by toil,
And all unworthy of the deeper joy
Which waits on distant prospect, cliff, or sea,
The dark blue vault, and universe of stars.
Thus did I steal along that silent road,
My body from the stillness drinking in
A restoration like the calm of sleep,
But sweeter far. Above, before, behind,
Around me, all was peace and solitude,
390   I looked not round, nor did the solitude
Speak to my eye; but it was heard and felt.
O happy state! what beauteous pictures now
Rose in harmonious imagery – they rose
As from some distant region of my soul
And came along like dreams; yet such as left
Obscurely mingled with their passing forms
A consciousness of animal delight,
A self-possession felt in every pause
And every gentle movement of my frame.

400   While thus I wandered, step by step led on,
It chanced a sudden turning of the road   *388*
Presented to my view an uncouth shape   *387*
So near that, slipping back into the shade
Of a thick hawthorn, I could mark him well,   *390*
Myself unseen. He was of stature tall,
A foot above man's common measure tall,
Stiff in his form, and upright, lank and lean;

380 Where the road's watery surface, to the top
Of that sharp rising, glittered to the moon
And bore the semblance of another stream
Stealing with silent lapse to join the brook
That murmured in the vale. All else was still;
No living thing appeared in earth or air,
And, save the flowing water's peaceful voice,
Sound there was none – but, lo! an uncouth shape,
Shown by a sudden turning of the road,
So near that, slipping back into the shade
390 Of a thick hawthorn, I could mark him well,
Myself unseen. He was of stature tall,
A span above man's common measure tall,
Stiff, lank, and upright; a more meagre man

A man more meagre, as it seemed to me,
Was never seen abroad by night or day.
410   His arms were long, and bare his hands; his mouth   *395*
Showed ghastly in the moonlight: from behind,
A milestone propped him, and his figure seemed
Half-sitting, and half-standing. I could mark
That he was clad in military garb,
Though faded, yet entire. He was alone,
Had no attendant, neither dog nor staff,   *400*
Nor knapsack; in his very dress appeared
A desolation, a simplicity
That seemed akin to solitude. Long time
420   Did I peruse him with a mingled sense
Of fear and sorrow. From his lips, meanwhile,
There issued murmuring sounds, as if of pain   *405*
Or of uneasy thought; yet still his form
Kept the same steadiness; and at his feet
His shadow lay, and moved not. In a glen
Hard by, a village stood, whose roofs and doors
Were visible among the scattered trees,
Scarce distant from the spot an arrow's flight;
I wished to see him move; but he remained
430   Fixed to his place, and still from time to time
Sent forth a murmuring voice of dead complaint,
Groans scarcely audible. Without self-blame
I had not thus prolonged my watch; and now,
Subduing my heart's specious cowardice,   *410*
I left the shady nook where I had stood
And hailed him. Slowly from his resting-place
He rose, and with a lean and wasted arm
In measured gesture lifted to his head
Returned my salutation; then resumed   *415*
440   His station as before; and when, ere long,
I asked his history, he in reply
Was neither slow nor eager; but, unmoved,
And with a quiet uncomplaining voice,
A stately air of mild indifference,   *420*
He told in simple words a soldier's tale –

Was never seen before by night or day.
Long were his arms, pallid his hands; his mouth
Looked ghastly in the moonlight: from behind,
A milestone propped him; I could also ken
That he was clothed in military garb,
Though faded, yet entire. Companionless,
400   No dog attending, by no staff sustained,
He stood, and in his very dress appeared
A desolation, a simplicity,
To which the trappings of a gaudy world
Make a strange background. From his lips, ere long,
Issued low muttered sounds, as if of pain
Or some uneasy thought; yet still his form
Kept the same awful steadiness – at his feet
His shadow lay, and moved not. From self-blame
Not wholly free, I watched him thus; at length
410   Subduing my heart's specious cowardice,
I left the shady nook where I had stood
And hailed him. Slowly from his resting-place
He rose, and with a lean and wasted arm
In measured gesture lifted to his head
Returned my salutation; then resumed
His station as before; and when I asked
His history, the veteran, in reply,
Was neither slow nor eager; but, unmoved,
And with a quiet uncomplaining voice,
420   A stately air of mild indifference,
He told in few plain words a soldier's tale –

That in the Tropic Islands he had served,
Whence he had landed scarcely ten days past;
That on his landing he had been dismissed,
And now was travelling to his native home.   *425*
450 At this, I turned and looked towards the village
But all were gone to rest; the fires all out;
And every silent window to the moon
Shone with a yellow glitter. 'No one there,'
Said I, 'is waking, we must measure back
The way which we have come: behind yon wood
A labourer dwells; and, take it on my word,
He will not murmur should we break his rest;
And with a ready heart will give you food
And lodging for the night.' At this he stooped,
460 And from the ground took up an oaken staff   *428*
By me yet unobserved – a traveller's staff
Which, I suppose, from his slack hand had dropped,
And lain till now neglected in the grass.   *430*
Towards the cottage without more delay
We shaped our course; as it appeared to me,
He travelled without pain, and I beheld   *432*
With ill-suppressed astonishment his tall
And ghastly figure moving at my side;
Nor, while we journeyed thus, could I forbear   *435*
470 To question him of what he had endured
From hardship, battle, or the pestilence.
He all the while was in demeanour calm,   *440*
Concise in answer; solemn and sublime
He might have seemed, but that in all he said
There was a strange half-absence, and a tone
Of weakness and indifference, as of one
Remembering the importance of his theme   *444*
But feeling it no longer. We advanced
Slowly, and ere we to the wood were come
480 Discourse had ceased. Together on we passed   *445–6*
In silence through the shades gloomy and dark.
Then, turning up along an open field,
We gained the cottage. At the door I knocked,   *449*

That in the Tropic Islands he had served,
Whence he had landed scarcely three weeks past;
That on his landing he had been dismissed,
And now was travelling towards his native home.
This heard, I said, in pity, 'Come with me.'
He stooped, and straightway from the ground took up
An oaken staff by me yet unobserved –
A staff which must have dropt from his slack hand
430   And lay till now neglected in the grass.
Though weak his step and cautious, he appeared
To travel without pain, and I beheld,
With an astonishment but ill suppressed,
His ghastly figure moving at my side;
Nor could I, while we journeyed thus, forbear
To turn from present hardships to the past,
And speak of war, battle, and pestilence,
Sprinkling this talk with questions, better spared,
On what he might himself have seen or felt.
440   He all the while was in demeanour calm,
Concise in answer; solemn and sublime
He might have seemed, but that in all he said
There was a strange half-absence, as of one
Knowing too well the importance of his theme,
But feeling it no longer. Our discourse
Soon ended, and together on we passed
In silence through a wood gloomy and still.
Up-turning, then, along an open field,
We reached a cottage. At the door I knocked,

Calling aloud 'My friend, here is a man
By sickness overcome; beneath your roof
This night let him find rest, and give him food,
If food he need, for he is faint and tired.'
Assured that now my comrade would repose
In comfort, I entreated that henceforth
490 He would not linger in the public ways,   455
But ask for timely furtherance and help
Such as his state required. At this reproof,
With the same ghastly mildness in his look
He said, 'My trust is in the God of Heaven,
And in the eye of him that passes me!'   460

The cottage door was speedily unlocked,
And now the soldier touched his hat again
With his lean hand, and in a voice that seemed
To speak with a reviving interest
500 Till then unfelt, he thanked me; I returned   465
The blessing of the poor unhappy man,
And so we parted. Back I cast a look,
And lingered near the door a little space,
Then sought with quiet heart my distant home.

450   And earnestly to charitable care
      Commended him as a poor friendless man,
      Belated and by sickness overcome.
      Assured that now the traveller would repose
      In comfort, I entreated that henceforth
      He would not linger in the public ways,
      But ask for timely furtherance and help
      Such as his state required. At this reproof,
      With the same ghastly mildness in his look,
      He said, 'My trust is in the God of Heaven,
460   And in the eye of him who passes me!'

         The cottage door was speedily unbarred,
      And now the soldier touched his hat once more
      With his lean hand, and in a faltering voice,
      Whose tone bespake reviving interests
      Till then unfelt, he thanked me; I returned
      The farewell blessing of the patient man,
      And so we parted. Back I cast a look,
      And lingered near the door a little space,
      Then sought with quiet heart my distant home.

Even in the steadiest mood of reason, when
All sorrow for thy transitory pains
Goes out, it grieves me for thy state, O Man,
Thou paramount Creature! and thy race, while ye
Shall sojourn on this planet; not for woes   5
Which thou endur'st; that weight, albeit huge,
I charm away; but for those palms achieved,
Through length of time, by study and hard thought,   10
The honours of thy high endowments; there
10   My sadness finds its fuel. Hitherto,
In progress through this verse, my mind hath looked
Upon the speaking face of earth and heaven
As her prime teacher, intercourse with man
Established by the sovereign Intellect,   15
Who through that bodily image hath diffused
A soul divine which we participate,
A deathless spirit. Thou also, man! hast wrought,
For commerce of thy nature with itself,
Things worthy of unconquerable life;   20
20   And yet we feel – we cannot choose but feel –
That these must perish. Tremblings of the heart
It gives, to think that the immortal being
No more shall need such garments; and yet man,
As long as he shall be the child of earth,   25
Might almost 'weep to have' what he may lose,
Nor be himself extinguished, but survive
Abject, depressed, forlorn, disconsolate.
A thought is with me sometimes, and I say, –
Should earth by inward throes be wrenched throughout,

When Contemplation, like the night-calm felt
Through earth and sky, spreads widely, and sends deep
Into the soul its tranquillizing power,
Even then I sometimes grieve for thee, O Man,
Earth's paramount Creature! not so much for woes
That thou endur'st; heavy though that weight be,
Cloud-like it mounts, or touched with light divine
Doth melt away; but for those palms achieved,
Through length of time, by patient exercise
10 Of study and hard thought; there, there, it is
That sadness finds its fuel. Hitherto,
In progress through this work, my mind hath looked
Upon the speaking face of earth and heaven
As her prime teacher, intercourse with man
Established by the sovereign Intellect,
Who through that bodily image hath diffused,
As might appear to the eye of fleeting time,
A deathless spirit. Thou also, man! hast wrought,
For commerce of thy nature with herself,
20 Things that aspire to unconquerable life;
And yet we feel – we cannot choose but feel –
That they must perish. Tremblings of the heart
It gives, to think that our immortal being
No more shall need such garments; and yet man,
As long as he shall be the child of earth,
Might almost 'weep to have' what he may lose,
Nor be himself extinguished, but survive,
Abject, depressed, forlorn, disconsolate.
A thought is with me sometimes, and I say, –
30 Should the whole frame of earth by inward throes

30 Or fire be sent from far to wither all
    Her pleasant habitations, and dry up
    Old Ocean, in his bed left singed and bare,
    Yet would the living Presence still subsist
    Victorious, and composure would ensue,   *35*
    And kindlings like the morning – presage sure,
    Though slow, perhaps, of a returning day.
    But all the meditations of mankind,
    Yea, all the adamantine holds of truth
    By reason built, or passion, which itself   *40*
40 Is highest reason in a soul sublime;
    The consecrated works of Bard and Sage,
    Sensuous or intellectual, wrought by men,
    Twin labourers and heirs of the same hopes;
    Where would they be? Oh! why hath not the Mind   *45*
    Some element to stamp her image on
    In nature somewhat nearer to her own?
    Why, gifted with such powers to send abroad
    Her spirit, must it lodge in shrines so frail?

       One day, when in the hearing of a friend,   *50*
50 I had given utterance to thoughts like these,
    He answered with a smile, that in plain truth
    'Twas going far to seek disquietude;
    But on the front of his reproof confessed
    That he, at sundry seasons, had himself   *55*
    Yielded to kindred hauntings. And forthwith
    Added, that once upon a summer's noon,
    While he was sitting in a rocky cave
    By the sea-side, perusing, as it chanced,
    The famous history of the errant knight   *60*
60 Recorded by Cervantes, these same thoughts
    Came to him, and to height unusual rose,
    While listlessly he sate, and, having closed
    The book, had turned his eyes towards the sea.
    On poetry and geometric truth,   *65*
    The knowledge that endures, upon these two,
    And their high privilege of lasting life,

Be wrenched, or fire come down from far to scorch
Her pleasant habitations, and dry up
Old Ocean, in his bed left singed and bare,
Yet would the living Presence still subsist
Victorious, and composure would ensue,
And kindlings like the morning – presage sure
Of day returning and of life revived.
But all the meditations of mankind,
Yea, all the adamantine holds of truth
40   By reason built, or passion, which itself
Is highest reason in a soul sublime;
The consecrated works of Bard and Sage,
Sensuous or intellectual, wrought by men,
Twin labourers and heirs of the same hopes;
Where would they be? Oh! why hath not the Mind
Some element to stamp her image on
In nature somewhat nearer to her own?
Why, gifted with such powers to send abroad
Her spirit, must it lodge in shrines so frail?

50   One day, when from my lips a like complaint
Had fallen in presence of a studious friend,
He with a smile made answer, that in truth
'Twas going far to seek disquietude;
But on the front of his reproof confessed
That he himself had oftentimes given way
To kindred hauntings. Whereupon I told,
That once in the stillness of a summer's noon,
While I was seated in a rocky cave
By the sea-side, perusing, so it chanced,
60   The famous history of the errant knight
Recorded by Cervantes, these same thoughts
Beset me, and to height unusual rose,
While listlessly I sate, and, having closed
The book, had turned my eyes toward the wide sea.
On poetry and geometric truth,
And their high privilege of lasting life,

Exempt from all internal injury,
He mused, upon these chiefly: and at length,
His senses yielding to the sultry air,
70   Sleep seized him, and he passed into a dream.   70
He saw before him an Arabian waste,
A desert, and he fancied that himself
Was sitting there in the wide wilderness,
Alone, upon the sands. Distress of mind
Was growing in him when, behold! at once
To his great joy a man was at his side,
Upon a dromedary, mounted high.   76
He seemed an Arab of the Bedouin tribes:
A lance he bore, and underneath one arm
80   A stone, and in the opposite hand, a shell
Of a surpassing brightness. Much rejoiced   80
The dreaming man that he should have a guide
To lead him through the desert; and he thought,
While questioning himself what this strange freight
Which the new-comer carried through the waste   85
Could mean, the Arab told him that the stone
(To give it in the language of the dream)
Was 'Euclid's Elements'; 'and this,' said he,
'This other,' pointing to the shell, 'this book
90   Is something of more worth'; and at the word
The stranger, said my friend continuing,
Stretched forth the shell towards me, with command   90
That I should hold it to my ear. I did so,
And heard that instant in an unknown tongue,
Which yet I understood, articulate sounds,
A loud prophetic blast of harmony;   95
An Ode, in passion uttered, which foretold
Destruction to the children of the earth
By deluge, now at hand. No sooner ceased
100   The song, but with calm look the Arab said
That all was true; that it was even so   100
As had been spoken; and that he himself
Was going then to bury those two books:
The one that held acquaintance with the stars,

From all internal injury exempt,
I mused, upon these chiefly: and at length,
My senses yielding to the sultry air,
70   Sleep seized me, and I passed into a dream.
I saw before me stretched a boundless plain
Of sandy wilderness, all black and void,
And as I looked around, distress and fear
Came creeping over me, when at my side,
Close at my side, an uncouth shape appeared
Upon a dromedary, mounted high.
He seemed an Arab of the Bedouin tribes:
A lance he bore, and underneath one arm
A stone, and in the opposite hand, a shell
80   Of a surpassing brightness. At the sight
Much I rejoiced, not doubting but a guide
Was present, one who with unerring skill
Would through the desert lead me; and while yet
I looked and looked, self-questioned what this freight
Which the new-comer carried through the waste
Could mean, the Arab told me that the stone
(To give it in the language of the dream)
Was 'Euclid's Elements'; and 'This,' said he,
'Is something of more worth'; and at the word
90   Stretched forth the shell, so beautiful in shape,
In colour so resplendent, with command
That I should hold it to my ear. I did so,
And heard that instant in an unknown tongue,
Which yet I understood, articulate sounds,
A loud prophetic blast of harmony;
An Ode, in passion uttered, which foretold
Destruction to the children of the earth
By deluge, now at hand. No sooner ceased
The song, than the Arab with calm look declared
100   That all would come to pass of which the voice
Had given forewarning, and that he himself
Was going then to bury those two books:
The one that held acquaintance with the stars,

And wedded man to man by purest bond
Of nature, undisturbed by space or time;   *105*
The other that was a god, yea many gods,
Had voices more than all the winds, and was
A joy, a consolation, and a hope.
110 My friend continued, 'strange as it may seem,   *110*
I wondered not, although I plainly saw
The one to be a stone, the other a shell;
Nor doubted once but that they both were books,
Having a perfect faith in all that passed.
A wish was now engendered in my fear
To cleave unto this man, and I begged leave   *115*
To share his errand with him. On he passed
Not heeding me: I followed, and took note
That he looked often backward with wild look,
120 Grasping his twofold treasure to his side. –
Upon a dromedary, lance in rest,   *120*
He rode, I keeping pace with him, and now
I fancied that he was the very knight
Whose tale Cervantes tells, yet not the knight,
But was an Arab of the desert too;
Of these was neither, and was both at once.   *125*
His countenance, meanwhile, grew more disturbed;
And, looking backwards when he looked, I saw
A glittering light, and asked him whence it came.
130 "It is," said he, "the waters of the deep   *130*
Gathering upon us"; quickening then his pace
He left me: I called after him aloud;
He heeded not; but with his twofold charge
Beneath his arm, before me, full in view,   *135*
I saw him riding o'er the desert sands,
With the fleet waters of the drowning world
In chase of him; whereat I waked in terror,
And saw the sea before me, and the book,
In which I had been reading, at my side.'   *140*

And wedded soul to soul in purest bond
Of reason, undisturbed by space or time;
The other that was a god, yea many gods,
Had voices more than all the winds, with power
To exhilarate the spirit, and to soothe,
Through every clime, the heart of human kind.
110 While this was uttering, strange as it may seem,
I wondered not, although I plainly saw
The one to be a stone, the other a shell;
Nor doubted once but that they both were books,
Having a perfect faith in all that passed.
Far stronger, now, grew the desire I felt
To cleave unto this man; but when I prayed
To share his enterprise, he hurried on
Reckless of me: I followed, not unseen,
For oftentimes he cast a backward look,
120 Grasping his twofold treasure. – Lance in rest,
He rode, I keeping pace with him; and now
He, to my fancy, had become the knight
Whose tale Cervantes tells; yet not the knight,
But was an Arab of the desert too;
Of these was neither, and was both at once.
His countenance, meanwhile, grew more disturbed;
And, looking backwards when he looked, mine eyes
Saw, over half the wilderness diffused,
A bed of glittering light: I asked the cause:
130 'It is,' said he, 'the waters of the deep
Gathering upon us'; quickening then the pace
Of the unwieldly creature he bestrode,
He left me: I called after him aloud;
He heeded not; but, with his twofold charge
Still in his grasp, before me, full in view,
Went hurrying o'er the illimitable waste,
With the fleet waters of a drowning world
In chase of him; whereat I waked in terror,
And saw the sea before me, and the book,
140 In which I had been reading, at my side.

140   Full often, taking from the world of sleep
       This Arab phantom, which my friend beheld,
       This semi-Quixote, I to him have given
       A substance, fancied him a living man,
       A gentle dweller in the desert, crazed   *145*
       By love and feeling, and internal thought
       Protracted among endless solitudes;
       Have shaped him, in the oppression of his brain,
       Wandering upon this quest, and thus equipped.
       And I have scarcely pitied him; have felt
150   A reverence for a being thus employed;   *150*
       And thought that, in the blind and awful lair
       Of such a madness, reason did lie couched.
       Enow there are on earth to take in charge
       Their wives, their children, and their virgin loves,
       Or whatsoever else the heart holds dear;   *155*
       Enow to think of these; yea, will I say,
       In sober contemplation of the approach
       Of such great overthrow, made manifest
       By certain evidence, that I, methinks,
160   Could share that maniac's anxiousness, could go   *160*
       Upon like errand. Oftentimes at least
       Me hath such deep entrancement half-possessed,
       When I have held a volume in my hand,
       Poor earthly casket of immortal verse,
       Shakespeare, or Milton, labourers divine!   *165*

           Mighty indeed, supreme must be the power
       Of living Nature, which could thus so long
       Detain me from the best of other thoughts.
       Even in the lisping time of infancy,   *170*
170   And later down, in prattling childhood, even
       While I was travelling back among those days,
       How could I ever play an ingrate's part?
       Once more should I have made those bowers resound,
       And intermingled strains of thankfulness   *175*
       With their own thoughtless melodies; at least,
       It might have well beseemed me to repeat

Full often, taking from the world of sleep
This Arab phantom, which I thus beheld,
This semi-Quixote, I to him have given
A substance, fancied him a living man,
A gentle dweller in the desert, crazed
By love and feeling, and internal thought
Protracted among endless solitudes;
Have shaped him wandering upon this quest!
Nor have I pitied him; but rather felt
150 Reverence was due to a being thus employed;
And thought that, in the blind and awful lair
Of such a madness, reason did lie couched.
Enow there are on earth to take in charge
Their wives, their children, and their virgin loves,
Or whatsoever else the heart holds dear;
Enow to stir for these; yea, will I say,
Contemplating in soberness the approach
Of an event so dire, by signs in earth
Or heaven made manifest, that I could share
160 That maniac's fond anxiety, and go
Upon like errand. Oftentimes at least
Me hath such strong entrancement overcome,
When I have held a volume in my hand,
Poor earthly casket of immortal verse,
Shakespeare, or Milton, labourers divine!

Great and benign, indeed, must be the power
Of living Nature, which could thus so long
Detain me from the best of other guides
And dearest helpers, left unthanked, unpraised.
170 Even in the time of lisping infancy,
And later down, in prattling childhood, even
While I was travelling back among those days,
How could I ever play an ingrate's part?
Once more should I have made those bowers resound,
By intermingling strains of thankfulness
With their own thoughtless melodies; at least
It might have well beseemed me to repeat

Some simply fashioned tale, to tell again,
In slender accents of sweet verse, some tale
That did bewitch me then, and soothes me now.   *180*
180 O Friend! O Poet! brother of my soul,
Think not that I could ever pass along
Untouched by these remembrances; no, no,
But I was hurried forward by a stream,
And could not stop. Yet wherefore should I speak?
Why call upon a few weak words to say
What is already written in the hearts   *185*
Of all that breathe? – what in the path of all
Drops daily from the tongue of every child,
Wherever man is found? The trickling tear
190 Upon the cheek of listening Infancy
Tells it, and the insuperable look   *190*
That drinks as if it never could be full.

    That portion of my story I shall leave
There registered: whatever else there be
Of power or pleasure, sown or fostered thus,
Peculiar to myself, let that remain   *195*
Where it lies hidden in its endless home
Among the depths of time. And yet it seems
That here, in memory of all books which lay
200 Their sure foundations in the heart of man,
Whether by native prose, or numerous verse,   *200*
That in the name of all inspirèd souls,
From Homer the great Thunderer, from the voice
Which roars along the bed of Jewish song,
And that more varied and elaborate,
Those trumpet-tones of harmony that shake   *205*
Our shores in England, – from those loftiest notes
Down to the low and wren-like warblings, made
For cottagers and spinners at the wheel,
210 And weary travellers when they rest themselves
By the highways and hedges, ballad tunes,   *210*
Food for the hungry ears of little ones,
And of old men who have survived their joy:

Some simply fashioned tale, to tell again,
In slender accents of sweet verse, some tale
180 That did bewitch me then, and soothes me now.
O Friend! O Poet! brother of my soul,
Think not that I could pass along untouched
By these remembrances. Yet wherefore speak?
Why call upon a few weak words to say
What is already written in the hearts
Of all that breathe? – what in the path of all
Drops daily from the tongue of every child,
Wherever man is found? The trickling tear
Upon the cheek of listening Infancy
190 Proclaims it, and the insuperable look
That drinks as if it never could be full.

    That portion of my story I shall leave
There registered: whatever else of power
Or pleasure, sown or fostered thus, may be
Peculiar to myself, let that remain
Where still it works, though hidden from all search
Among the depths of time. Yet is it just
That here, in memory of all books which lay
Their sure foundations in the heart of man,
200 Whether by native prose, or numerous verse,
That in the name of all inspirèd souls,
From Homer the great Thunderer, from the voice
That roars along the bed of Jewish song,
And that more varied and elaborate,
Those trumpet-tones of harmony that shake
Our shores in England, – from those loftiest notes
Down to the low and wren-like warblings, made
For cottagers and spinners at the wheel,
And sun-burnt travellers resting their tired limbs,
210 Stretched under wayside hedge-rows, ballad tunes,
Food for the hungry ears of little ones,
And of old men who have survived their joys:

It seemeth, in behalf of these, the works,
And of the men who framed them, whether known,
Or sleeping nameless in their scattered graves,   215
That I should here assert their rights, attest
Their honours, and should, once for all, pronounce
Their benediction; speak of them as Powers
For ever to be hallowed; only less,
For what we may become, and what we need,   220
Than Nature's self, which is the breath of God.

Rarely and with reluctance would I stoop
To transitory themes; yet I rejoice,
And, by these thoughts admonished, must speak out   225
Thanksgivings from my heart, that I was reared
Safe from an evil which these days have laid
Upon the children of the land, a pest
That might have dried me up, body and soul.
This verse is dedicate to Nature's self,   230
And things that teach as Nature teaches: then,
Oh! where had been the Man, the Poet where,
Where had we been, we two, belovèd Friend!
If we, in lieu of wandering, as we did,   235
Through heights and hollows, and bye-spots of tales
Rich with indigenous produce, open ground
Of Fancy, happy pastures ranged at will,
Had been attended, followed, watched, and noosed,
Each in his several melancholy walk
Stringed like a poor man's heifer at its feed,   240
Led through the lanes in forlorn servitude;
Or rather like a stallèd ox shut out
From touch of growing grass, that may not taste
A flower till it have yielded up its sweets
A prelibation to the mower's scythe.   245

Behold the parent hen amid her brood,
Though fledged and feathered, and well pleased to part
And straggle from her presence, still a brood,

'Tis just that in behalf of these, the works,
And of the men that framed them, whether known,
Or sleeping nameless in their scattered graves,
That I should here assert their rights, attest
Their honours, and should, once for all, pronounce
Their benediction; speak of them as Powers
For ever to be hallowed; only less,
220 For what we are and what we may become,
Than Nature's self, which is the breath of God,
Or His pure Word by miracle revealed.

Rarely and with reluctance would I stoop
To transitory themes; yet I rejoice,
And, by these thoughts admonished, will pour out
Thanks with uplifted heart, that I was reared
Safe from an evil which these days have laid
Upon the children of the land, a pest
That might have dried me up, body and soul.
230 This verse is dedicate to Nature's self,
And things that teach as Nature teaches: then,
Oh! where had been the Man, the Poet where,
Where had we been, we two, belovèd Friend!
If in the season of unperilous choice,
In lieu of wandering, as we did, through vales
Rich with indigenous produce, open ground
Of Fancy, happy pastures ranged at will,
We had been followed, hourly watched, and noosed,
Each in his several melancholy walk
240 Stringed like a poor man's heifer at its feed,
Led through the lanes in forlorn servitude;
Or rather like a stallèd ox debarred
From touch of growing grass, that may not taste
A flower till it have yielded up its sweets
A prelibation to the mower's scythe.

Behold the parent hen amid her brood,
Though fledged and feathered, and well pleased to part
And straggle from her presence, still a brood,

And she herself from the maternal bond
250 Still undischarged; yet doth she little more
Than move with them in tenderness and love,
A centre of the circle which they make;
And now and then, alike from need of theirs
And call of her own natural appetites,
255 She scratches, ransacks up the earth for food,
Which they partake at pleasure. Early died
My honoured Mother, she who was the heart
And hinge of all our learnings and our loves:
She left us destitute, and, as we might,
260 Trooping together. Little suits it me
To break upon the sabbath of her rest
With any thought that looks at others' blame;
Nor would I praise her but in perfect love.
Hence am I checked: but I will boldly say,
265 In gratitude, and for the sake of truth,
Unheard by her, that she, not falsely taught,
Fetching her goodness rather from times past,
Than shaping novelties for those to come,
Had no presumption, no such jealousy,
270 Nor did by habit of her thoughts mistrust
Our nature, but had virtual faith that He
Who fills the mother's breasts with innocent milk,
Doth also for our nobler part provide,
Under His great correction and control,
As innocent instincts, and as innocent food.
This was her creed, and therefore she was pure
From feverish dread of error and mishap,
And evil, overweeningly so called;
Was not puffed up by false unnatural hopes,
280 Nor selfish with unnecessary cares,
Nor with impatience from the season asked
More than its timely produce; rather loved
The hours for what they are, than from regards

And she herself from the maternal bond
250 Still undischarged; yet doth she little more
Than move with them in tenderness and love,
A centre to the circle which they make;
And now and then, alike from need of theirs
And call of her own natural appetites,
She scratches, ransacks up the earth for food,
Which they partake at pleasure. Early died
My honoured Mother, she who was the heart
And hinge of all our learnings and our loves:
She left us destitute, and, as we might,
260 Trooping together. Little suits it me
To break upon the sabbath of her rest
With any thought that looks at others' blame;
Nor would I praise her but in perfect love.
Hence am I checked: but let me boldly say,
In gratitude, and for the sake of truth,
Unheard by her, that she, not falsely taught,
Fetching her goodness rather from times past,
Than shaping novelties for times to come,
Had no presumption, no such jealousy,
270 Nor did by habit of her thoughts mistrust
Our nature, but had virtual faith that He
Who fills the mother's breast with innocent milk,
Doth also for our nobler part provide,
Under His great correction and control,
As innocent instincts, and as innocent food;
Or draws for minds that are left free to trust
In the simplicities of opening life
Sweet honey out of spurned or dreaded weeds.
This was her creed, and therefore she was pure
280 From anxious fear of error or mishap,
And evil, overweeningly so called;
Was not puffed up by false unnatural hopes,
Nor selfish with unnecessary cares,
Nor with impatience from the season asked
More than its timely produce; rather loved
The hours for what they are, than from regard

Glanced on their promises in restless pride.
Such was she – not from faculties more strong
Than others have, but from the times, perhaps,
And spot in which she lived, and through a grace   *290*
Of modest meekness, simple-mindedness,
A heart that found benignity and hope,
290   Being itself benign.
               My drift hath scarcely,
I fear, been obvious; for I have recoiled
From showing as it is the monster birth
Engendered by these too industrious times.
Let few words paint it: 'tis a child, no child,
But a dwarf man; in knowledge, virtue, skill;
In what he is not, and in what he is,
The noontide shadow of a man complete;
A worshipper of worldly seemliness,
Not quarrelsome; for that were far beneath   *300*
300   His dignity; with gifts he bubbles o'er
As generous as a fountain; selfishness
May not come near him, gluttony or pride;
The wandering beggars propagate his name,   *305*
Dumb creatures find him tender as a nun.
Yet deem him not for this a naked dish
Of goodness merely, he is garnished out.
Arch are his notices, and nice his sense
Of the ridiculous; deceit and guile,
Meanness and falsehood he detects, can treat
310   With apt and graceful laughter; nor is blind
To the broad follies of the licensed world;   *312*
Though shrewd, yet innocent himself withal
And can read lectures upon innocence.
He is fenced round, nay armed, for aught we know,
In panoply complete; and fear itself,
Natural or supernatural alike,   *307*
Unless it leap upon him in a dream,
Touches him not. Briefly, the moral part
Is perfect, and in learning and in books
320   He is a prodigy. His discourse moves slow,
184

Glanced on their promises in restless pride.
Such was she – not from faculties more strong
Than others have, but from the times, perhaps,
290 And spot in which she lived, and through a grace
Of modest meekness, simple-mindedness,
A heart that found benignity and hope,
Being itself benign.
                    My drift I fear
Is scarcely obvious; but, that common sense
May try this modern system by its fruits,
Leave let me take to place before her sight
A specimen portrayed with faithful hand.
Full early trained to worship seemliness,
This model of a child is never known
300 To mix in quarrels; that were far beneath
Its dignity; with gifts he bubbles o'er
As generous as a fountain; selfishness
May not come near him, nor the little throng
Of flitting pleasures tempt him from his path;
The wandering beggars propagate his name,
Dumb creatures find him tender as a nun,
And natural or supernatural fear,
Unless it leap upon him in a dream,
Touches him not. To enhance the wonder, see
310 How arch his notices, how nice his sense
Of the ridiculous; not blind is he
To the broad follies of the licensed world,
Yet innocent himself withal, though shrewd,
And can read lectures upon innocence;

Massy and ponderous as a prison door,
Tremendously embossed with terms of art;
Rank growth of propositions overruns
The stripling's brain; the path in which he treads
Is choked with grammars; cushion of divine
Was never such a type of thought profound
As is the pillow where he rests his head.
The ensigns of the empire which he holds,
The globe and sceptre of his royalties,
330 Are telescopes, and crucibles, and maps.
Ships he can guide across the pathless sea, *316*
And tell you all their cunning; he can read
The inside of the earth, and spell the stars;
He knows the policies of foreign lands;
Can string you names of districts, cities, towns, *320*
The whole world over, tight as beads of dew
Upon a gossamer thread; he sifts, he weighs;
Takes nothing upon trust: his teachers stare;
The country people pray for God's good grace,
340 And tremble at his deep experiments.
All things are put to question; he must live
Knowing that he grows wiser every day
Or else not live at all, and seeing too *325*
Each little drop of wisdom as it falls
Into the dimpling cistern of his heart: *327*
Meanwhile old grandame earth is grieved to find *337*
The playthings, which her love designed for him,
Unthought of: in their woodland beds the flowers
Weep, and the river sides are all forlorn. *340*

350   Now this is hollow, 'tis a life of lies
From the beginning, and in lies must end.
Forth bring him to the air of common sense,
And, fresh and showy as it is, the corpse
Slips from us into powder. Vanity,
That is his soul, there lives he, and there moves;
It is the soul of every thing he seeks;
That gone, nothing is left which he can love.

A miracle of scientific lore,
Ships he can guide across the pathless sea,
And tell you all their cunning; he can read
The inside of the earth, and spell the stars;
He knows the policies of foreign lands;
320 Can string you names of districts, cities, towns,
The whole world over, tight as beads of dew
Upon a gossamer thread; he sifts, he weighs;
All things are put to question; he must live
Knowing that he grows wiser every day
Or else not live at all, and seeing too
Each little drop of wisdom as it falls
Into the dimpling cistern of his heart:
For this unnatural growth the trainer blame,
Pity the tree. – Poor human vanity,
330 Wert thou extinguished, little would be left
Which he could truly love; but how escape?
For, ever as a thought of purer birth
Rises to lead him toward a better clime,
Some intermeddler still is on the watch
To drive him back, and pound him, like a stray,
Within the pinfold of his own conceit.
Meanwhile old grandame earth is grieved to find
The playthings, which her love designed for him,
Unthought of: in their woodland beds the flowers
340 Weep, and the river sides are all forlorn.

Nay, if a thought of purer birth should rise
To carry him towards a better clime,
360 Some busy helper still is on the watch
To drive him back, and pound him, like a stray,   *335*
Within the pinfold of his own conceit;
Which is his home, his natural dwelling place.
Oh! give us once again the wishing cap
Of Fortunatus, and the invisible coat
Of Jack the Giant-killer, Robin Hood,
And Sabra in the forest with St George!
The child, whose love is here, at least, doth reap   *345*
One precious gain, that he forgets himself.

370   These mighty workmen of our later age,
Who, with a broad highway, have overbridged
The froward chaos of futurity,
Tamed to their bidding; they who have the art   *350*
To manage books, and things, and make them work
Gently on infant minds, as does the sun
Upon a flower; the tutors of our youth,
The guides, the wardens of our faculties,
And stewards of our labour, watchful men
And skilful in the usury of time,
380 Sages who in their prescience would control   *355*
All accidents, and to the very road
Which they have fashioned would confine us down,
Like engines; when will they be taught
That in the unreasoning progress of the world
A wiser spirit is at work for us,   *360*
A better eye than theirs, most prodigal
Of blessings, and most studious of our good,
Even in what seem our most unfruitful hours?

     There was a Boy: ye knew him well, ye cliffs
390 And islands of Winander! – many a time   *365*
At evening, when the stars had just begun
To move along the edges of the hills,
Rising or setting, would he stand alone

Oh! give us once again the wishing cap
Of Fortunatus, and the invisible coat
Of Jack the Giant-killer, Robin Hood,
And Sabra in the forest with St George!
The child, whose love is here, at least, doth reap
One precious gain, that he forgets himself.

These mighty workmen of our later age,
Who, with a broad highway, have overbridged
The froward chaos of futurity,
350   Tamed to their bidding; they who have the skill
To manage books, and things, and make them act
On infant minds as surely as the sun
Deals with a flower; the keepers of our time,
The guides and wardens of our faculties,
Sages who in their prescience would control
All accidents, and to the very road
Which they have fashioned would confine us down,
Like engines; when will their presumption learn,
That in the unreasoning progress of the world
360   A wiser spirit is at work for us,
A better eye than theirs, most prodigal
Of blessings, and most studious of our good,
Even in what seem our most unfruitful hours?

There was a Boy: ye knew him well, ye cliffs
And islands of Winander! – many a time
At evening, when the earliest stars began
To move along the edges of the hills,
Rising or setting, would he stand alone

Beneath the trees or by the glimmering lake,
And there, with fingers interwoven, both hands   370
Pressed closely palm to palm, and to his mouth
Uplifted, he, as through an instrument,
Blew mimic hootings to the silent owls,
That they might answer him; and they would shout
400 Across the watery vale, and shout again,   375
Responsive to his call, with quivering peals,
And long halloos and screams, and echoes loud,
Redoubled and redoubled, concourse wild
Of mirth and jocund din; and when it chanced
That pauses of deep silence mocked his skill,   380
Then sometimes, in that silence while he hung
Listening, a gentle shock of mild surprise
Has carried far into his heart the voice
Of mountain torrents; or the visible scene
410 Would enter unawares into his mind,   385
With all its solemn imagery, its rocks,
Its woods, and that uncertain heaven, received
Into the bosom of the steady lake.

    This Boy was taken from his mates, and died
In childhood, ere he was full ten years old.   390
Fair are the woods, and beauteous is the spot,
The vale where he was born; the churchyard hangs
Upon a slope above the village school,
And there, along that bank, when I have passed
420 At evening, I believe that oftentimes   395
A full half hour together I have stood
Mute, looking at the grave in which he lies.
Even now, methinks, I have before my sight
That self-same village church; I see her sit
(The thronèd Lady spoken of erewhile)   400
On her green hill, forgetful of this Boy
Who slumbers at her feet, – forgetful, too,
Of all her silent neighbourhood of graves,
And listening only to the gladsome sounds
430 That, from the rural school ascending, play   405

Beneath the trees or by the glimmering lake,
370 And there, with fingers interwoven, both hands
Pressed closely palm to palm, and to his mouth
Uplifted, he, as through an instrument,
Blew mimic hootings to the silent owls,
That they might answer him; and they would shout
Across the watery vale, and shout again,
Responsive to his call, with quivering peals,
And long halloos and screams, and echoes loud,
Redoubled and redoubled, concourse wild
Of jocund din; and, when a lengthened pause
380 Of silence came and baffled his best skill,
Then sometimes, in that silence while he hung
Listening, a gentle shock of mild surprise
Has carried far into his heart the voice
Of mountain torrents; or the visible scene
Would enter unawares into his mind,
With all its solemn imagery, its rocks,
Its woods, and that uncertain heaven, received
Into the bosom of the steady lake.

This Boy was taken from his mates, and died
390 In childhood, ere he was full twelve years old.
Fair is the spot, most beautiful the vale
Where he was born; the grassy churchyard hangs
Upon a slope above the village school,
And through that churchyard when my way has led
On summer evenings, I believe that there
A long half hour together I have stood
Mute, looking at the grave in which he lies!
Even now appears before the mind's clear eye
That self-same village church; I see her sit
400 (The thronèd Lady whom erewhile we hailed)
On her green hill, forgetful of this Boy
Who slumbers at her feet, – forgetful, too,
Of all her silent neighbourhood of graves,
And listening only to the gladsome sounds
That, from the rural school ascending, play

Beneath her and about her. May she long
Behold a race of young ones like to those
With whom I herded! – (easily, indeed,
We might have fed upon a fatter soil
Of arts and letters – but be that forgiven) –   *410*
A race of real children; not too wise,
Too learned, or too good; but wanton, fresh,
And bandied up and down by love and hate;
Fierce, moody, patient, venturous, modest, shy;   *415*
440 Mad at their sports like withered leaves in winds;
Though doing wrong and suffering, and full oft
Bending beneath our life's mysterious weight
Of pain and fear, yet still in happiness
Not yielding to the happiest upon earth.   *420*
Simplicity in habit, truth in speech,
Be these the daily strengtheners of their minds;
May books and Nature be their early joy!
And knowledge, rightly honoured with that name –
Knowledge not purchased with the loss of power!   *425*

450   Well do I call to mind the very week
When I was first entrusted to the care
Of that sweet Valley; when its paths, its shores,
And brooks were like a dream of novelty
To my half-infant thoughts; that very week,   *430*
While I was roving up and down alone,
Seeking I knew not what, I chanced to cross
One of those open fields, which, shaped like ears,
Make green peninsulas on Esthwaite's Lake:
Twilight was coming on, yet through the gloom   *435*
460 I saw distinctly on the opposite shore
A heap of garments, left, as I supposed,
By one who there was bathing. Long I watched,
But no one owned them; meanwhile the calm lake
Grew dark with all the shadows on its breast,
And, now and then, a fish up-leaping snapped
The breathless stillness. The succeeding day,

Beneath her and about her. May she long
Behold a race of young ones like to those
With whom I herded! – (easily, indeed,
We might have fed upon a fatter soil
410 Of arts and letters – but be that forgiven) –
A race of real children; not too wise,
Too learned, or too good; but wanton, fresh,
And bandied up and down by love and hate;
Not unresentful where self-justified;
Fierce, moody, patient, venturous, modest, shy;
Mad at their sports like withered leaves in winds;
Though doing wrong and suffering, and full oft
Bending beneath our life's mysterious weight
Of pain, and doubt, and fear, yet yielding not
420 In happiness to the happiest upon earth.
Simplicity in habit, truth in speech,
Be these the daily strengtheners of their minds;
May books and Nature be their early joy!
And knowledge rightly honoured with that name –
Knowledge not purchased by the loss of power!

Well do I call to mind the very week
When I was first entrusted to the care
Of that sweet Valley; when its paths, its shores,
And brooks were like a dream of novelty
430 To my half-infant thoughts; that very week,
While I was roving up and down alone,
Seeking I knew not what, I chanced to cross
One of those open fields, which, shaped like ears,
Make green peninsulas on Esthwaite's Lake:
Twilight was coming on, yet through the gloom
Appeared distinctly on the opposite shore
A heap of garments, as if left by one
Who might have there been bathing. Long I watched,
But no one owned them; meanwhile the calm lake
440 Grew dark with all the shadows on its breast,
And, now and then, a fish up-leaping snapped
The breathless stillness. The succeeding day,

Those unclaimed garments telling a plain tale,   *443*
Went there a company, and in their boat
Sounded with grappling irons and long poles.   *447*
470 At length, the dead man, 'mid that beauteous scene
Of trees and hills and water, bolt upright
Rose, with his ghastly face, a spectre shape   *450*
Of terror even; and yet no vulgar fear,
Young as I was, a child not nine years old,
Possessed me, for my inner eye had seen
Such sights before, among the shining streams
Of faery land, the forests of romance.   *455*
Thence came a spirit hallowing what I saw
With decoration and ideal grace;
480 A dignity, a smoothness, like the works
Of Grecian art, and purest poesy.

    I had a precious treasure at that time,   *460*
A little yellow, canvas-covered book,
A slender abstract of the Arabian tales;
And when I learned, as now I first did learn,
From my companions in this new abode,
That this dear prize of mine was but a block
Hewn from a mighty quarry – in a word,   *465*
That there were four large volumes, laden all
490 With kindred matter, 'twas, in truth, to me
A promise scarcely earthly. Instantly
I made a league, a covenant with a friend
Of my own age, that we should lay aside   *470*
The money we possessed, and hoard up more,
Till our joint savings had amassed enough
To make this book our own. Through several months
Religiously did we preserve that vow,
And spite of all temptation, hoarded up
And hoarded up; but firmness failed at length,   *475*
500 Nor were we ever masters of our wish.

    And afterwards, when to my father's house
Returning at the holidays, I found

Those unclaimed garments telling a plain tale
Drew to the spot an anxious crowd; some looked
In passive expectation from the shore,
While from a boat others hung o'er the deep,
Sounding with grappling irons and long poles.
At last, the dead man, 'mid that beauteous scene
Of trees and hills and water, bolt upright
450 Rose, with his ghastly face, a spectre shape
Of terror; yet no soul-debasing fear,
Young as I was, a child not nine years old,
Possessed me, for my inner eye had seen
Such sights before, among the shining streams
Of faery land, the forest of romance.
Their spirit hallowed the sad spectacle
With decoration of ideal grace;
A dignity, a smoothness, like the words
Of Grecian art, and purest poesy.

460   A precious treasure had I long possessed,
A little yellow, canvas-covered book,
A slender abstract of the Arabian tales;
And, from companions in a new abode,
When first I learnt, that this dear prize of mine
Was but a block hewn from a mighty quarry –
That there were four large volumes, laden all
With kindred matter, 'twas to me, in truth,
A promise scarcely earthly. Instantly,
With one not richer than myself, I made
470 A covenant that each should lay aside
The moneys he possessed, and hoard up more,
Till our joint savings had amassed enough
To make this book our own. Through several months,
In spite of all temptation, we preserved
Religiously that vow; but firmness failed,
Nor were we ever masters of our wish.

    And when thereafter to my father's house
The holidays returned me, there to find

That golden store of books which I had left
Open to my enjoyment once again,
What heart was mine! Full often through the course   *480*
Of those glad respites in the summer-time
When, armed with rod and line we went abroad
For a whole day together, I have lain
Down by thy side, O Derwent! murmuring stream,
510 On the hot stones, and in the glaring sun,   *485*
And there have read, devouring as I read,
Defrauding the day's glory, desperate!
Till with a sudden bound of smart reproach,
Such as an idler deals with in his shame,
I to my sport betook myself again.   *490*

A gracious spirit o'er this earth presides,
And o'er the heart of man: invisibly
It comes, directing those to works of love
Who care not, know not, think not what they do.   *495*
520 The tales that charm away the wakeful night
In Araby, romances, legends, penned
For solace by the light of monkish lamps;
Fictions for ladies, of their love, devised
By youthful squires; adventures endless, spun   *500*
By the dismantled warrior in old age,
Out of the bowels of those very thoughts
In which his youth did first extravagate;
These spread like day, and something in the shape
Of these will live till man shall be no more.   *505*
530 Dumb yearnings, hidden appetites, are ours,
And they must have their food. Our childhood sits,
Our simple childhood, sits upon a throne
That hath more power than all the elements.
I guess not what this tells of Being past,   *510*
Nor what it augurs of the life to come;
But so it is, and, in that dubious hour,
That twilight when we first begin to see
This dawning earth, to recognize, expect,
And in the long probation that ensues,   *515*

196

That golden store of books which I had left,
480 What joy was mine! How often in the course
Of those glad respites, though a soft west wind
Ruffled the waters to the angler's wish,
For a whole day together, have I lain
Down by thy side, O Derwent! murmuring stream,
On the hot stones, and in the glaring sun,
And there have read, devouring as I read,
Defrauding the day's glory, desperate!
Till with a sudden bound of smart reproach,
Such as an idler deals with in his shame,
490 I to the sport betook myself again.

A gracious spirit o'er this earth presides,
And o'er the heart of man: invisibly
It comes, to works of unreproved delight,
And tendency benign, directing those
Who care not, know not, think not what they do.
The tales that charm away the wakeful night
In Araby, romances; legends penned
For solace by dim light of monkish lamps;
Fictions for ladies, of their love, devised
500 By youthful squires; adventures endless, spun
By the dismantled warrior in old age,
Out of the bowels of those very schemes
In which his youth did first extravagate;
These spread like day, and something in the shape
Of these will live till man shall be no more.
Dumb yearnings, hidden appetites, are ours,
And *they must* have their food. Our childhood sits,
Our simple childhood, sits upon a throne
That hath more power than all the elements.
510 I guess not what this tells of Being past,
Nor what it augurs of the life to come;
But so it is, and, in that dubious hour,
That twilight when we first begin to see
This dawning earth, to recognize, expect,
And, in the long probation that ensues,

540 The time of trial, ere we learn to live
In reconcilement with our stinted powers,
To endure this state of meagre vassalage;
Unwilling to forego, confess, submit,
Uneasy and unsettled, yoke-fellows   *520*
To custom, mettlesome, and not yet tamed
And humbled down; oh! then we feel, we feel,
We know when we have friends. Ye dreamers, then,
Forgers of lawless tales! we bless you then,
Impostors, drivellers, dotards, as the ape   *525*
550 Philosophy will call you: then we feel
With what, and how great might ye are in league,
Who make our wish, our power, our thought a deed,
An empire, a possession, – ye whom time
And seasons serve; all Faculties; to whom   *530*
Earth crouches, the elements are potter's clay,
Space like a heaven filled up with northern lights,
Here, nowhere, there, and everywhere at once.

    It might demand a more impassioned strain
To tell of later pleasures, linked to these,   *535*
560 A tract of the same isthmus which we cross
In progress from our native continent
To earth and human life; I mean to speak
Of that delightful time of growing youth,
When cravings for the marvellous relent,   *540*
And we begin to love what we have seen;
And sober truth, experience, sympathy,
Take stronger hold of us, and words themselves
Move us with conscious pleasure.   *545*
                            I am sad
At thought of raptures now for ever flown;
570 Even unto tears I sometimes could be sad
To think of, to read over, many a page,
Poems withal of name, which at that time
Did never fail to entrance me, and are now   *550*
Dead in my eyes as is a theatre

The time of trial, ere we learn to live
In reconcilement with our stinted powers,
To endure this state of meagre vassalage;
Unwilling to forego, confess, submit,
520 Uneasy and unsettled, yoke-fellows
To custom, mettlesome, and not yet tamed
And humbled down; oh! then we feel, we feel,
We know where we have friends. Ye dreamers, then,
Forgers of daring tales! we bless you then,
Impostors, drivellers, dotards, as the ape
Philosophy will call you: *then* we feel
With what, and how great might ye are in league,
Who make our wish, our power, our thought a deed,
An empire, a possession, – ye whom time
530 And seasons serve; all Faculties; to whom
Earth crouches, the elements are potter's clay,
Space like a heaven filled up with northern lights,
Here, nowhere, there, and everywhere at once.

   Relinquishing this lofty eminence
For ground, though humbler, not the less a tract
Of the same isthmus, which our spirits cross
In progress from their native continent
To earth and human life, the Song might dwell
On that delightful time of growing youth,
540 When craving for the marvellous gives way
To strengthening love for things that we have seen;
When sober truth and steady sympathies,
Offered to notice by less daring pens,
Take firmer hold of us, and words themselves
Move us with conscious pleasure.
                                                        I am sad
At thought of raptures now for ever flown;
Almost to tears I sometimes could be sad
To think of, to read over, many a page,
Poems withal of name, which at that time
550 Did never fail to entrance me, and are now
Dead in my eyes, dead as a theatre

Fresh emptied of spectators. Thirteen years
Or haply less I might have seen, when first
My ears began to open to the charm
Of words in tuneful order, found them sweet   555
For *their own sakes*, a passion and a power;
580   And phrases pleased me chosen for delight,
For pomp, or love. Oft, in the public roads
Yet unfrequented, while the morning light
Was yellowing the hill tops, with that dear friend   560
The same whom I have mentioned heretofore,
I went abroad, and for the better part
Of two delightful hours we strolled along
By the still borders of the misty lake,
Repeating favourite verses with one voice,
Or conning more, as happy as the birds   565
590   That round us chanted. Well might we be glad,
Lifted above the ground by airy fancies,
More bright than madness or the dreams of wine;
And, though full oft the objects of our love
Were false, and in their splendour overwrought,   570
Yet, surely, at such time no vulgar power
Was working in us, – nothing less, in truth,
Than that most noble attribute of man,
Though yet untutored and inordinate,
That wish for something loftier, more adorned,   575
600   Than is the common aspect, daily garb,
Of human life. What wonder then if sounds
Of exultation echoed through the groves!
For, images, and sentiments, and words,
And everything with which we had to do   580
In that delicious world of poesy,
Kept holiday, a never-ending show,
With music, incense, festival, and flowers!

Here must I pause: this only will I add,
From heart-experience, and in humblest sense   585
610   Of modesty, that he, who in his youth
A wanderer among the woods and fields

Fresh emptied of spectators. Twice five years
Or less I might have seen, when first my mind
With conscious pleasure opened to the charm
Of words in tuneful order, found them sweet
For their own *sakes*, a passion, and a power;
And phrases pleased me chosen for delight,
For pomp, or love. Oft, in the public roads
Yet unfrequented, while the morning light
560 Was yellowing the hill tops, I went abroad
With a dear friend, and for the better part
Of two delightful hours we strolled along
By the still borders of the misty lake,
Repeating favourite verses with one voice,
Or conning more, as happy as the birds
That round us chanted. Well might we be glad,
Lifted above the ground by airy fancies,
More bright than madness or the dreams of wine;
And, though full oft the objects of our love
570 Were false, and in their splendour overwrought,
Yet was there surely then no vulgar power
Working within us, – nothing less, in truth,
Than that most noble attribute of man,
Though yet untutored and inordinate,
That wish for something loftier, more adorned,
Than is the common aspect, daily garb,
Of human life. What wonder, then, if sounds
Of exultation echoed through the groves!
For, images, and sentiments, and words,
580 And everything encountered or pursued
In that delicious world of poesy,
Kept holiday, a never-ending show,
With music, incense, festival, and flowers!

　　Here must we pause: this only let me add,
From heart-experience, and in humblest sense
Of modesty, that he, who in his youth
A daily wanderer among woods and fields

With living Nature hath been intimate,
Not only in that raw unpractised time
Is stirred to ecstasy, as others are,   *590*
By glittering verse; but he doth furthermore,
In measure only dealt out to himself,
Receive enduring touches of deep joy
From the great Nature that exists in works
Of mighty Poets. Visionary power   *595*
620 Attends upon the motions of the winds,
Embodied in the mystery of words:
There, darkness makes abode, and all the host
Of shadowy things do work their changes there,
As in a mansion like their proper home.   *600*
Even forms and substances are circumfused
By that transparent veil with light divine,
And, through the turnings intricate of verse,
Present themselves as objects recognized,
In flashes, and with a glory scarce their own.   *605*

630   Thus far a scanty record is deduced
Of what I owed to books in early life;
Their later influence yet remains untold;
But as this work was taking in my thoughts
Proportions that seemed larger than had first
Been meditated, I was indisposed
To any further progress at a time
When these acknowledgements were left unpaid.

With living Nature hath been intimate,
Not only in that raw unpractised time
590 Is stirred to ecstasy, as others are,
By glittering verse; but further, doth receive,
In measure only dealt out to himself,
Knowledge and increase of enduring joy
From the great Nature that exists in works
Of mighty Poets. Visionary power
Attends the motions of the viewless winds,
Embodied in the mystery of words:
There, darkness makes abode, and all the host
Of shadowy things work endless changes there,
600 As in a mansion like their proper home.
Even forms and substances are circumfused
By that transparent veil with light divine,
And, through the turnings intricate of verse,
Present themselves as objects recognized,
In flashes, and with glory not their own.

Thus far a scanty record is deduced
Of what I owed to books in early life;
Their later influence yet remains untold;
But as this work was taking in my mind
610 Proportions that seemed larger than had first
Been meditated, I was indisposed
To any further progress at a time
When these acknowledgements were left unpaid.

The leaves were yellow when to Furness Fells,
The haunt of shepherds, and to cottage life
I bade adieu; and, one among the flock
Who by that season are convened, like birds
Trooping together at the fowler's lure,   5
Went back to Granta's cloisters, not so fond,
Or eager, though as gay and undepressed
In spirit, as when I thence had taken flight
A few short months before. I turned my face
10 Without repining from the mountain pomp   10
Of autumn, and its beauty entered in
With calmer lakes and louder streams; and you,
Frank-hearted maids of rocky Cumberland,
You and your not unwelcome days of mirth,   15
I quitted, and your nights of revelry,
And in my own unlovely cell sate down
In lightsome mood – such privilege has youth
That cannot take long leave of pleasant thoughts.

     We need not linger o'er the ensuing time,
20 But let me add at once that, now the bonds
Of indolent and vague society   20
Relaxing in their hold, I lived henceforth
More to myself, read more, reflected more,
Felt more, and settled daily into habits
More promising. Two winters may be passed
Without a separate notice; many books
Were read in process of this time, devoured,
Tasted or skimmed, or studiously perused,
Yet with no settled plan. I was detached   25

Book Sixth

CAMBRIDGE AND THE ALPS

The leaves were fading when to Esthwaite's banks
And the simplicities of cottage life
I bade farewell; and, one among the youth
Who, summoned by that season, reunite
As scattered birds troop to the fowler's lure,
Went back to Granta's cloisters, not so prompt
Or eager, though as gay and undepressed
In mind, as when I thence had taken flight
A few short months before. I turned my face
10 Without repining from the coves and heights
Clothed in the sunshine of the withering fern;
Quitted, not loth, the mild magnificence
Of calmer lakes and louder streams; and you,
Frank-hearted maids of rocky Cumberland,
You and your not unwelcome days of mirth,
Relinquished, and your nights of revelry,
And in my own unlovely cell sate down
In lightsome mood – such privilege has youth
That cannot take long leave of pleasant thoughts.

20   The bonds of indolent society
Relaxing in their hold, henceforth I lived
More to myself. Two winters may be passed
Without a separate notice: many books
Were skimmed, devoured, or studiously perused.
But with no settled plan. I was detached

30 Internally from academic cares,
From every hope of prowess and reward,
And wished to be a lodger in that house
Of letters, and no more: and should have been
Even such, but for some personal concerns
That hung about me in my own despite
Perpetually, no heavy weight, but still
A baffling and a hindrance, a control
Which made the thought of planning for myself
A course of independent study seem
40 An act of disobedience towards them
Who loved me, proud rebellion and unkind.
This bastard virtue, rather let it have   30
A name it more deserves, this cowardice,
Gave treacherous sanction to that over-love
Of freedom planted in me from the very first,
And indolence, by force of which I turned
From regulations even of my own
As from restraints and bonds. And who can tell –   35
Who knows what thus may have been gained, both then
50 And at a later season, or preserved;
What love of Nature, what original strength
Of contemplation, what intuitive truths,
The deepest and the best, and what research   40
Unbiassed, unbewildered, and unawed?

    The Poet's soul was with me at that time;
Sweet meditations, the still overflow
Of happiness and truth. A thousand hopes
Were mine, a thousand tender dreams, of which   45
No few have since been realized, and some
60 Do yet remain, hopes for my future life.
Four years and thirty, told this very week,
Have I been now a sojourner on earth,
And yet the morning gladness is not gone
Which then was in my mind. Those were the days
Which also first encouraged me to trust
With firmness, hitherto but lightly touched

Internally from academic cares;
Yet independent study seemed a course
Of hardy disobedience toward friends
And kindred, proud rebellion and unkind.
30 This spurious virtue, rather let it bear
A name it more deserves, this cowardice,
Gave treacherous sanctions to that over-love
Of freedom which encouraged me to turn
From regulations even of my own
As from restraints and bonds. Yet who can tell –
Who knows what thus may have been gained, both then
And at a later season, or preserved;
What love of Nature, what original strength
Of contemplation, what intuitive truths,
40 The deepest and the best, what keen research,
Unbiassed, unbewildered, and unawed?

The Poet's soul was with me at that time;
Sweet meditations, the still overflow
Of present happiness, while future years
Lacked not anticipations, tender dreams,
No few of which have since been realized;
And some remain, hopes for my future life.
Four years and thirty, told this very week,
Have I been now a sojourner on earth,
50 By sorrow not unsmitten; yet for me
Life's morning radiance hath not left the hills,
Her dew is on the flowers. Those were the days
Which also first emboldened me to trust
With firmness, hitherto but lightly touched

With such a daring thought, that I might leave   55
Some monument behind me which pure hearts
Should reverence. The instinctive humbleness,
70   Upheld even by the very name and thought
Of printed books and authorship, began
To melt away; and further, the dread awe   60
Of mighty names was softened down and seemed
Approachable, admitting fellowship
Of modest sympathy. Such aspect now,
Though not familiarly, my mind put on;
I loved, and I enjoyed, that was my chief
And ruling business, happy in the strength
And loveliness of imagery and thought.

80   All winter long, whenever free to take
My choice, did I at night frequent our groves
And tributary walks; the last, and oft
The only one, who had been lingering there
Through hours of silence, till the porter's bell,   70
A punctual follower on the stroke of nine,
Rang with its blunt unceremonious voice,
Inexorable summons! Lofty elms,
Inviting shades of opportune recess,
Did give composure to a neighbourhood   75
90   Unpeaceful in itself. A single tree
There was, no doubt yet standing there, an ash
With sinuous trunk, boughs exquisitely wreathed:
Up from the ground and almost to the top   80
The trunk and master branches everywhere
Were green with ivy, and the lightsome twigs
And outer spray profusely tipped with seeds
That hung in yellow tassels and festoons,
Moving or still, a favourite trimmed out
By winter for himself, as if in pride,
100 And with outlandish grace. Oft have I stood   85
Foot-bound uplooking at this lovely tree
Beneath a frosty moon. The hemisphere
Of magic fiction, verse of mine perhaps

By such a daring thought, that I might leave
Some monument behind me which pure hearts
Should reverence. The instinctive humbleness,
Maintained even by the very name and thought
Of printed books and authorship, began
60   To melt away; and further, the dread awe
Of mighty names was softened down and seemed
Approachable, admitting fellowship
Of modest sympathy. Such aspect now,
Though not familiarly, my mind put on,
Content to observe, to admire, and to enjoy.

    All winter long, whenever free to choose,
Did I by night frequent the College groves
And tributary walks; the last, and oft
The only one, who had been lingering there
70   Through hours of silence, till the porter's bell,
A punctual follower on the stroke of nine,
Rang with its blunt unceremonious voice,
Inexorable summons! Lofty elms,
Inviting shades of opportune recess,
Bestowed composure on a neighbourhood
Unpeaceful in itself. A single tree
With sinuous trunk, boughs exquisitely wreathed,
Grew there; an ash which Winter for himself
Decked as in pride, and with outlandish grace:
80   Up from the ground, and almost to the top,
The trunk and every master branch were green
With clustering ivy, and the lightsome twigs
And outer spray profusely tipped with seeds
That hung in yellow tassels, while the air
Stirred them, not voiceless. Often have I stood
Foot-bound uplooking at this lovely tree
Beneath a frosty moon. The hemisphere
Of magic fiction, verse of mine perchance

May never tread; but scarcely Spenser's self
Could have more tranquil visions in his youth,   90
More bright appearances could scarcely see
Of human forms and superhuman powers,
Than I beheld standing on winter nights
Alone, beneath this fairy work of earth.

110   'Twould be a waste of labour to detail
The rambling studies of a truant youth,   95
Which further may be easily divined,
What, and what kind they were. My inner knowledge,
(This barely will I note) was oft in depth
And delicacy like another mind
Sequestered from my outward taste in books,
And yet the books which then I loved the most
Are dearest to me now; for, being versed   100
In living Nature, I had there a guide
120   Which opened frequently my eyes, else shut,
A standard which was usefully applied,
Even when unconsciously, to other things
Which less I understood. – In general terms,
I was a better judge of thoughts than words,   106
Misled as to these latter, not alone
By common inexperience of youth,
But by the trade in classic niceties,
Delusion to young scholars incident
And old ones also, by that overprized
130   And dangerous craft of picking phrases out   110
From languages that want the living voice
To make of them a nature to the heart;
To tell us what is passion, what is truth,
What reason, what simplicity and sense.

Yet must I not entirely overlook   115
The pleasure gathered from the elements
Of geometric science. I had stepped
In these enquiries but a little way,
No farther than the threshold; with regret   119

May never tread; but scarcely Spenser's self
90   Could have more tranquil visions in his youth,
Or could more bright appearances create
Of human forms with superhuman powers,
Than I beheld loitering on calm clear nights
Alone, beneath this fairy work of earth.

On the vague reading of a truant youth
'Twere idle to descant. My inner judgement
Not seldom differed from my taste in books,
As if it appertained to another mind,
And yet the books which then I valued most
100   Are dearest to me *now*; for, having scanned,
Not heedlessly, the laws, and watched the forms
Of Nature, in that knowledge I possessed
A standard, often usefully applied,
Even when unconsciously, to things removed
From a familiar sympathy. – In fine,
I was a better judge of thoughts than words,
Misled in estimating words, not only
By common inexperience of youth,
But by the trade in classic niceties,
110   The dangerous craft of culling term and phrase
From languages that want the living voice
To carry meaning to the natural heart;
To tell us what is passion, what is truth,
What reason, what simplicity and sense.

Yet may we not entirely overlook
The pleasure gathered from the rudiments
Of geometric science. Though advanced
In these enquiries, with regret I speak,
No farther than the threshold, there I found

140   Sincere I mention this; but there I found
      Enough to exalt, to cheer me and compose:
      With Indian awe and wonder, ignorance
      Which even was cherished, did I meditate
      Upon the alliance of those simple, pure
      Proportions and relations with the frame
      And laws of Nature, how they could become   *126*
      Herein a leader to the human mind,
      And made endeavours frequent to detect
      The process by dark guesses of my own.
150   Yet from this source more frequently I drew
      A pleasure calm and deeper, a still sense   *130*
      Of permanent and universal sway
      And paramount endowment in the mind,
      An image not unworthy of the one
      Surpassing life which – out of space and time,   *135*
      Nor touched by welterings of passion – is,
      And hath the name of, God. Transcendent peace
      And silence did await upon these thoughts   *140*
      That were a frequent comfort to my youth.

160   And as I have read of one by shipwreck thrown,
      With fellow-sufferers whom the waves had spared,
      Upon a region uninhabited,
      An island of the deep, who having brought
      To land a single volume and no more,   *145*
      A treatise of Geometry, was used,
      Although of food and clothing destitute,
      And beyond common wretchedness depressed,
      To part from company and take this book
      (Then first a self-taught pupil in those truths)   *150*
170   To spots remote and corners of the isle
      By the sea side, and draw his diagrams
      With a long stick upon the sand, and thus
      Did oft beguile his sorrow, and almost
      Forget his feeling: even so (if things
      Producing like effect, from outward cause   *155*

120　Both elevation and composed delight:
　　　With Indian awe and wonder, ignorance pleased
　　　With its own struggles, did I meditate
　　　On the relation those abstractions bear
　　　To Nature's laws, and by what process led,
　　　Those immaterial agents bowed their heads
　　　Duly to serve the mind of earth-born man;
　　　From star to star, from kindred sphere to sphere,
　　　From system on to system without end.

　　　　More frequently from the same source I drew
130　A pleasure quiet and profound, a sense
　　　Of permanent and universal sway,
　　　And paramount belief; there, recognized
　　　A type, for finite natures, of the one
　　　Supreme Existence, the surpassing life
　　　Which – to the boundaries of space and time,
　　　Of melancholy space and doleful time,
　　　Superior, and incapable of change,
　　　Nor touched by welterings of passion – is,
　　　And hath the name of, God. Transcendent peace
140　And silence did await upon these thoughts
　　　That were a frequent comfort to my youth.

　　　　'Tis told by one whom stormy waters threw,
　　　With fellow-sufferers by the shipwreck spared,
　　　Upon a desert coast, that having brought
　　　To land a single volume, saved by chance,
　　　A treatise of Geometry, he wont,
　　　Although of food and clothing destitute,
　　　And beyond common wretchedness depressed,
　　　To part from company and take this book
150　(Then first a self-taught pupil in its truths)
　　　To spots remote, and draw his diagrams
　　　With a long staff upon the sand, and thus
　　　Did oft beguile his sorrow, and almost
　　　Forget his feeling: so (if like effect
　　　From the same cause produced, 'mid outward things

213

So different, may rightly be compared),
So was it with me then, and so will be
With Poets ever. Mighty is the charm
Of those abstractions to a mind beset
180 With images, and haunted by itself,   *160*
And specially delightful unto me
Was that clear synthesis built up aloft
So gracefully; even then when it appeared
No more than as a plaything, or a toy
Embodied to the sense: not what it is   *165*
In verity, an independent world,
Created out of pure intelligence.

     Such dispositions then were mine, almost
Through grace of heaven and inborn tenderness.   *170*
190 And not to leave the picture of that time
Imperfect, with these habits I must rank
A melancholy from humours of the blood
In part, and partly taken up, that loved
A pensive sky, sad days, and piping winds,
The twilight more than dawn, autumn than spring; *175*
A treasured and luxurious gloom of choice
And inclination mainly, and the mere
Redundancy of youth's contentedness.
– Add unto this a multitude of hours
200 Pilfered away by what the Bard who sang   *180*
Of the Enchanter Indolence hath called
'Good-natured lounging', and behold a map
Of my collegiate life – far less intense
Than duty called for, or without regard
To duty, might have sprung up of itself   *185*
By change of accidents, or even, to speak
Without unkindness, in another place.

     In summer among distant nooks I roved,
Dovedale, or Yorkshire dales, or through bye-tracts

So different, may rightly be compared),
So was it then with me, and so will be
With Poets ever. Mighty is the charm
Of those abstractions to a mind beset
160   With images, and haunted by herself,
And specially delightful unto me
Was that clear synthesis built up aloft
So gracefully; even then when it appeared
Not more than a mere plaything, or a toy
To sense embodied: not the thing it is
In verity, an independent world,
Created out of pure intelligence.

   Such dispositions then were mine unearned
By aught, I fear, of genuine desert –
170   Mine, through heaven's grace and inborn aptitudes.
And not to leave the story of that time
Imperfect, with these habits must be joined
Moods melancholy, fits of spleen, that loved
A pensive sky, sad days, and piping winds,
The twilight more than dawn, autumn than spring;
A treasured and luxurious gloom of choice
And inclination mainly, and the mere
Redundancy of youth's contentedness.
– To time thus spent, add multitudes of hours
180   Pilfered away, by what the Bard who sang
Of the Enchanter Indolence hath called
'Good-natured lounging', and behold a map
Of my collegiate life – far less intense
Than duty called for, or, without regard
To duty, *might* have sprung up of itself
By change of accidents, or even, to speak
Without unkindness, in another place.
Yet why take refuge in that plea? – the fault,
This I repeat, was mine; mine be the blame.

190   In summer, making quest for works of art,
Or scenes renowned for beauty, I explored

210 Of my own native region, and was blest   *195*
    Between those sundry wanderings with a joy
    Above all joys, that seemed another morn
    Risen on mid noon, the presence, Friend, I mean
    Of that sole Sister, she who hath been long
    Thy treasure also, thy true friend and mine,   *200*
    Now, after separation desolate,
    Restored to me – such absence that she seemed
    A gift then first bestowed. The gentle banks
    Of Emont, hitherto unnamed in song,
220 And that monastic castle, on a flat   *205*
    Low-standing by the margin of the stream,
    A mansion not unvisited of old
    By Sidney, where, in sight of our Helvellyn,
    Some snatches he might pen, for aught we know,
    Of his Arcadia, by fraternal love   *210*
    Inspired; – that river and that mouldering dome
    Have seen us sit in many a summer hour,
    My sister and myself, when, having climbed
    In danger through some window's open space,
230 We looked abroad, or on the turret's head
    Lay listening to the wild flowers and the grass,
    As they gave out their whispers to the wind.

    Another maid there was, who also breathed
    A gladness o'er that season, then to me,   *225*
    By her exulting outside look of youth
    And placid under-countenance, first endeared;
    That other spirit, Coleridge! who is now

That streamlet whose blue current works its way
Between romantic Dovedale's spiry rocks;
Pried into Yorkshire dales, or hidden tracts
Of my own native region, and was blest
Between these sundry wanderings with a joy
Above all joys, that seemed another morn
Risen on mid noon; blest with the presence, Friend!
Of that sole Sister, she who hath been long
200 Dear to thee also, thy true friend and mine,
Now, after separation desolate,
Restored to me – such absence that she seemed
A gift then first bestowed. The varied banks
Of Emont, hitherto unnamed in song,
And that monastic castle, 'mid tall trees,
Low-standing by the margin of the stream,
A mansion visited (as fame reports)
By Sidney, where, in sight of our Helvellyn,
Or stormy Cross-fell, snatches he might pen
210 Of his Arcadia, by fraternal love
Inspired; – that river and those mouldering towers
Have seen us side by side, when, having clomb
The darksome windings of a broken stair,
And crept along a ridge of fractured wall,
Not without trembling, we in safety looked
Forth, through some Gothic window's open space,
And gathered with one mind a rich reward
From the far-stretching landscape, by the light
Of morning beautified, or purple eve;
220 Or, not less pleased, lay on some turret's head,
Catching from tufts of grass and harebell flowers
Their faintest whisper to the passing breeze,
Given out while mid-day heat oppressed the plains.

Another maid there was, who also shed
A gladness o'er that season, then to me,
By her exulting outside look of youth
And placid under-countenance, first endeared;
That other spirit, Coleridge! who is now

So near to us, that meek confiding heart,
So reverenced by us both. O'er paths and fields　　*230*
240　In all that neighbourhood, through narrow lanes
Of eglantine, and through the shady woods,
And o'er the Border Beacon, and the waste
Of naked pools, and common crags that lay
Exposed on the bare fell, was scattered love,　　*235*
A spirit of pleasure, and youth's golden gleam.
O Friend! we had not seen thee at that time,
And yet a power is on me, and a strong
Confusion, and I seem to plant thee there.
Far art thou wandered now in search of health,　　*240*
250　And milder breezes, – melancholy lot!
But thou art with us, with us in the past,
The present, with us in the times to come.
There is no grief, no sorrow, no despair,
No languor, no dejection, no dismay,　　*245*
No absence scarcely can there be, for those
Who love as we do. Speed thee well! divide
Thy pleasure with us; thy returning strength,
Receive it daily as a joy of ours;
Share with us thy fresh spirits, whether gift　　*250*
260　Of gales Etesian or of loving thoughts.

　　I, too, have been a wanderer; but, alas!
How different is the fate of different men
Though twins almost in genius and in mind!
Unknown unto each other, yea, and breathing
As if in different elements, we were framed　　*255*
To bend at last to the same discipline,
Predestined, if two beings ever were,
To seek the same delights, and have one health,
One happiness. Throughout this narrative,
270　Else sooner ended, I have known full well　　*260*
For whom I thus record the birth and growth
Of gentleness, simplicity, and truth,
And joyous loves that hallow innocent days
Of peace and self-command. Of rivers, fields,

So near to us, that meek confiding heart,
230 So reverenced by us both. O'er paths and fields
In all that neighbourhood, through narrow lanes
Of eglantine, and through the shady woods,
And o'er the Border Beacon, and the waste
Of naked pools, and common crags that lay
Exposed on the bare fell, were scattered love,
The spirit of pleasure, and youth's golden gleam.
O Friend! we had not seen thee at that time,
And yet a power is on me, and a strong
Confusion, and I seem to plant thee there.
240 Far art thou wandered now in search of health
And milder breezes, – melancholy lot!
But thou art with us, with us in the past,
The present, with us in the times to come.
There is no grief, no sorrow, no despair,
No languor, no dejection, no dismay,
No absence scarcely can there be, for those
Who love as we do. Speed thee well! divide
With us thy pleasure; thy returning strength,
Receive it daily as a joy of ours;
250 Share with us thy fresh spirits, whether gift
Of gales Etesian or of tender thoughts.

    I, too, have been a wanderer; but, alas!
How different the fate of different men.
Though mutually unknown, yea, nursed and reared
As if in several elements, we were framed
To bend at last to the same discipline,
Predestined, if two beings ever were,
To seek the same delights, and have one health,
One happiness. Throughout this narrative,
260 Else sooner ended, I have borne in mind
For whom it registers the birth, and marks the growth,
Of gentleness, simplicity, and truth,
And joyous loves, that hallow innocent days
Of peace and self-command. Of rivers, fields,

And groves I speak to thee, my Friend! to thee,   *265*
Who, yet a liveried schoolboy, in the depths
Of the huge city, on the leaded roof
Of that wide edifice, thy home and school,
Wast used to lie and gaze upon the clouds
280 Moving in heaven; or haply, tired of this,   *270*
To shut thine eyes, and by internal light
See trees, and meadows, and thy native stream,
Far distant, thus beheld from year to year
Of thy long exile. Nor could I forget,
In this late portion of my argument,   *275*
That scarcely had I finally resigned
My rights among those academic bowers
When thou wert thither guided. From the heart
Of London, and from cloisters there, thou cam'st,
290 And didst sit down in temperance and peace,   *280*
A rigorous student. What a stormy course
Then followed. Oh! it is a pang that calls
For utterance, to think how small a change
Of circumstances might to thee have spared
A world of pain, ripened ten thousand hopes,   *285*
For ever withered. Through this retrospect
Of my own college life I still have had
Thy after-sojourn in the self-same place
Present before my eyes, have played with times,
300 (I speak of private business of the thought)
And accidents as children do with cards,   *290*
Or as a man, who, when his house is built,
A frame locked up in wood and stone, doth still,
In impotence of mind, by his fireside
Rebuild it to his liking. I have thought
Of thee, thy learning, gorgeous eloquence,   *295*
And all the strength and plumage of thy youth,
Thy subtle speculations, toils abstruse
Among the schoolmen, and Platonic forms
310 Of wild ideal pageantry, shaped out
From things well-matched or ill, and words for things,   *300*
The self-created sustenance of a mind

And groves I speak to thee, my Friend! to thee,
Who, yet a liveried schoolboy, in the depths
Of the huge city, on the leaded roof
Of that wide edifice, thy school and home,
Wert used to lie and gaze upon the clouds
270 Moving in heaven; or, of that pleasure tired,
To shut thine eyes, and by internal light
See trees, and meadows, and thy native stream,
Far distant, thus beheld from year to year
Of a long exile. Nor could I forget,
In this late portion of my argument,
That scarcely, as my term of pupilage
Ceased, had I left those academic bowers
When thou wert thither guided. From the heart
Of London, and from cloisters there, thou cam'st,
280 And didst sit down in temperance and peace,
A rigorous student. What a stormy course
Then followed. Oh! it is a pang that calls
For utterance, to think what easy change
Of circumstances might to thee have spared
A world of pain, ripened a thousand hopes,
For ever withered. Through this retrospect
Of my collegiate life I still have had
Thy after-sojourn in the self-same place
Present before my eyes, have played with times
290 And accidents as children do with cards,
Or as a man, who, when his house is built,
A frame locked up in wood and stone, doth still,
As impotent fancy prompts, by his fireside,
Rebuild it to his liking. I have thought
Of thee, thy learning, gorgeous eloquence,
And all the strength and plumage of thy youth,
Thy subtle speculations, toils abstruse
Among the schoolmen, and Platonic forms
Of wild ideal pageantry, shaped out
300 From things well-matched or ill, and words for things,
The self-created sustenance of a mind

Debarred from Nature's living images,
Compelled to be a life unto itself,
And unrelentingly possessed by thirst
Of greatness, love, and beauty. Not alone,   *305*
Ah! surely not in singleness of heart
Should I have seen the light of evening fade
Upon the silent Cam, if we had met,
320 Even at that early time; I needs must hope,
Must feel, must trust, that my maturer age,   *310*
And temperature less willing to be moved,
My calmer habits, and more steady voice,
Would with an influence benign have soothed,
Or chased away, the airy wretchedness
That battened on thy youth. But thou hast trod,
In watchful meditation thou hast trod,
A march of glory, which doth put to shame   *315*
These vain regrets; health suffers in thee, else
330 Such grief for thee would be the weakest thought
That ever harboured in the breast of man.

    A passing word erewhile did lightly touch
On wanderings of my own; and now to these   *320*
My poem leads me with an easier mind.
The employments of three winters when I wore
A student's gown have been already told,
Or shadowed forth, as far as there is need.
When the third summer brought its liberty,
A fellow student and myself, he too
340 A mountaineer, together sallied forth
And, staff in hand, on foot pursued our way   *325*
Towards the distant Alps. An open slight
Of college cares and study was the scheme,
Nor entertained without concern for those
To whom my worldly interests were dear.   *332*
But Nature then was sovereign in my heart,
And mighty forms, seizing a youthful fancy,
Had given a charter to irregular hopes.   *335*
In any age, without an impulse sent

Debarred from Nature's living images,
Compelled to be a life unto herself,
And unrelentingly possessed by thirst
Of greatness, love, and beauty. Not alone,
Ah! surely not in singleness of heart
Should I have seen the light of evening fade
From smooth Cam's silent waters: had we met,
Even at that early time, needs must I trust
310 In the belief, that my maturer age,
My calmer habits, and more steady voice,
Would with an influence benign have soothed,
Or chased away, the airy wretchedness
That battened on thy youth. But thou hast trod
A march of glory, which doth put to shame
These vain regrets; health suffers in thee, else
Such grief for thee would be the weakest thought
That ever harboured in the breast of man.

A passing word erewhile did lightly touch
320 On wanderings of my own, that now embraced
With livelier hope a region wider far.

When the third summer freed us from restraint,
A youthful friend, he too a mountaineer,
Not slow to share my wishes, took his staff,
And sallying forth, we journeyed side by side,
Bound to the distant Alps. A hardy slight
Did this unprecedented course imply
Of college studies and their set rewards;
Nor had, in truth, the scheme been formed by me
330 Without uneasy forethought of the pain,
The censures, and ill-omening of those
To whom my worldly interests were dear.
But Nature then was sovereign in my mind,
And mighty forms, seizing a youthful fancy,
Had given a charter to irregular hopes.
In any age of uneventful calm

350 From work of nations, and their goings-on,
     I should have been possessed by like desire;
     But 'twas a time when Europe was rejoiced,
     France standing on the top of golden hours,   *340*
     And human nature seeming born again.
     Bound, as I said, to the Alps, it was our lot
     To land at Calais on the very eve   *345*
     Of that great federal day; and there we saw,
     In a mean city, and among a few,
     How bright a face is worn when joy of one
360 Is joy of tens of millions. Southward thence
     We took our way, direct through hamlets, towns,   *350*
     Gaudy with reliques of that festival,
     Flowers left to wither on triumphal arcs,
     And window-garlands. On the public roads,
     And, once, three days successively, through paths
     By which our toilsome journey was abridged,   *355*
     Among sequestered villages we walked
     And found benevolence and blessedness
     Spread like a fragrance everywhere, like spring
370 That leaves no corner of the land untouched:
     Where elms for many and many a league in files,   *360*
     With their thin umbrage, on the stately roads
     Of that great kingdom, rustled o'er our heads,
     For ever near us as we paced along:
     'Twas sweet at such a time, with such delights
     On every side, in prime of youthful strength,   *365*
     To feed a Poet's tender melancholy
     And fond conceit of sadness, to the noise
     And gentle undulations which they made.
380 Unhoused, beneath the evening star we saw   *370*
     Dances of liberty, and, in late hours
     Of darkness, dances in the open air.
     Among the vine-clad hills of Burgundy,   *375*

Among the nations, surely would my heart
Have been possessed by similar desire;
But Europe at that time was thrilled with joy,
340 France standing on the top of golden hours,
And human nature seeming born again.

Lightly equipped, and but a few brief looks
Cast on the white cliffs of our native shore
From the receding vessel's deck, we chanced
To land at Calais on the very eve
Of that great federal day; and there we saw,
In a mean city, and among a few,
How bright a face is worn when joy of one
Is joy for tens of millions. Southward thence
350 We held our way, direct through hamlets, towns,
Gaudy with reliques of that festival,
Flowers left to wither on triumphal arcs,
And window-garlands. On the public roads,
And, once, three days successively, through paths
By which our toilsome journey was abridged,
Among sequestered villages we walked
And found benevolence and blessedness
Spread like a fragrance everywhere, when spring
Hath left no corner of the land untouched:
360 Where elms for many and many a league in files
With their thin umbrage, on the stately roads
Of that great kingdom, rustled o'er our heads,
For ever near us as we paced along:
How sweet at such a time, with such delight
On every side, in prime of youthful strength,
To feed a Poet's tender melancholy
And fond conceit of sadness, with the sound
Of undulations varying as might please
The wind that swayed them; once, and more than once,
370 Unhoused beneath the evening star we saw
Dances of liberty, and, in late hours
Of darkness, dances in the open air
Deftly prolonged, though grey-haired lookers on

Upon the bosom of the gentle Saone
We glided forward with the flowing stream.
Swift Rhone! thou wert the wings on which we cut
Between thy lofty rocks. Enchanting show   *380*
Those woods and farms and orchards did present,
And single cottages and lurking towns,
Reach after reach, procession without end
Of deep and stately vales! A lonely pair
Of Englishmen we were, and sailed along   *385*
Clustered together with a merry crowd
Of those emancipated, with a host
Of travellers, chiefly delegates returning
From the great spousals newly solemnized
At their chief city, in the sight of Heaven.   *390*
Like bees they swarmed, gaudy and gay as bees;
Some vapoured in the unruliness of joy,
And flourished with their swords as if to fight
The saucy air. In this blithe company
We landed – took with them our evening meal,   *395*
Guests welcome almost as the angels were
To Abraham of old. The supper done,
With flowing cups elate and happy thoughts
We rose at signal given, and formed a ring
And, hand in hand, danced round and round the board; *400*
All hearts were open, every tongue was loud
With amity and glee; we bore a name
Honoured in France, the name of Englishmen,
And hospitably did they give us hail,
As their forerunners in a glorious course;   *405*
And round and round the board they danced again.
With this same throng our voyage we pursued
At early dawn. The monastery bells
Made a sweet jingling in our youthful ears;
The rapid river flowing without noise,   *410*

Might waste their breath in chiding.
Under hills –
The vine-clad hills and slopes of Burgundy,
Upon the bosom of the gentle Saone
We glided forward with the flowing stream.
Swift Rhone! thou wert the *wings* on which we cut
A winding passage with majestic ease
380 Between thy lofty rocks. Enchanting show
Those woods and farms and orchards did present,
And single cottages and lurking towns,
Reach after reach, succession without end
Of deep and stately vales! A lonely pair
Of strangers, till day closed, we sailed along,
Clustered together with a merry crowd
Of those emancipated, a blithe host
Of travellers, chiefly delegates returning
From the great spousals newly solemnized
390 At their chief city, in the sight of Heaven.
Like bees they swarmed, gaudy and gay as bees;
Some vapoured in the unruliness of joy,
And with their swords flourished as if to fight
The saucy air. In this proud company
We landed – took with them our evening meal,
Guests welcome almost as the angels were
To Abraham of old. The supper done,
With flowing cups elate and happy thoughts
We rose at signal given, and formed a ring
400 And, hand in hand, danced round and round the board;
All hearts were open, every tongue was loud
With amity and glee; we bore a name
Honoured in France, the name of Englishmen,
And hospitably did they give us hail,
As their forerunners in a glorious course;
And round and round the board we danced again.
With these blithe friends our voyage we renewed
At early dawn. The monastery bells
Made a sweet jingling in our youthful ears;
410 The rapid river flowing without noise,

And every spire we saw among the rocks
Spake with a sense of peace, at intervals
420   Touching the heart amid the boisterous crew   *413*
With which we were environed. Having parted
From this glad rout, the Convent of Chartreuse
Received us two days afterwards, and there
We rested in an awful solitude;   *419*
Thence onward to the Country of the Swiss.

And each uprising or receding spire
Spake with a sense of peace, at intervals
Touching the heart amid the boisterous crew
By whom we were encompassed. Taking leave
Of this glad throng, foot-travellers side by side,
Measuring our steps in quiet, we pursued
Our journey, and ere twice the sun had set
Beheld the Convent of Chartreuse, and there
Rested within an awful *solitude*:
420   Yes, for even then no other than a place
Of soul-affecting *solitude* appeared
That far-famed region, though our eyes had seen,
As toward the sacred mansion we advanced,
Arms flashing, and a military glare
Of riotous men commissioned to expel
The blameless inmates, and belike subvert
That frame of social being, which so long
Had bodied forth the ghostliness of things
In silence visible and perpetual calm.
430   – 'Stay, stay your sacrilegious hands!' – The voice
Was Nature's, uttered from her Alpine throne;
I heard it then, and seem to hear it now –
'Your impious work forbear: perish what may,
Let this one temple last, be this one spot
Of earth devoted to eternity!'
She ceased to speak, but while St Bruno's pines
Waved their dark tops, not silent as they waved,
And while below, along their several beds,
Murmured the sister streams of Life and Death,
440   Thus by conflicting passions pressed, my heart
Responded; 'Honour to the patriot's zeal!
Glory and hope to new-born Liberty!
Hail to the mighty projects of the time!
Discerning sword that Justice wields, do thou
Go forth and prosper; and, ye purging fires,
Up to the loftiest towers of Pride ascend,
Fanned by the breath of angry Providence.
But oh! if Past and Future be the wings

On whose support harmoniously conjoined
450 Moves the great spirit of human knowledge, spare
These courts of mystery, where a step advanced
Between the portals of the shadowy rocks
Leaves far behind life's treacherous vanities,
For penitential tears and trembling hopes
Exchanged – to equalize in God's pure sight
Monarch and peasant: be the house redeemed
With its unworldly votaries, for the sake
Of conquest over sense, hourly achieved
Through faith and meditative reason, resting
460 Upon the word of heaven-imparted truth,
Calmly triumphant; and for humbler claim
Of that imaginative impulse sent
From these majestic floods, yon shining cliffs,
The untransmuted shapes of many worlds,
Cerulean ether's pure inhabitants,
These forests unapproachable by death,
That shall endure as long as man endures,
To think, to hope, to worship, and to feel,
To struggle, to be lost within himself
470 In trepidation, from the blank abyss
To look with bodily eyes, and be consoled.'
Not seldom since that moment have I wished
That thou, O Friend! the trouble or the calm
Hadst shared, when, from profane regards apart,
In sympathetic reverence we trod
The floors of those dim cloisters, till that hour,
From their foundation, strangers to the presence
Of unrestricted and unthinking man.
Abroad, how cheeringly the sunshine lay
480 Upon the open lawns! Vallombre's groves
Entering, we fed the soul with darkness; thence
Issued, and with uplifted eyes beheld,
In different quarters of the bending sky,
The cross of Jesus stand erect, as if
Hands of angelic powers had fixed it there,
Memorial reverenced by a thousand storms;

'Tis not my present purpose to retrace
That variegated journey step by step.   *490*
A march it was of military speed,
And Earth did change her images and forms
430 Before us, fast as clouds are changed in heaven.
Day after day, up early and down late,
From vale to vale, from hill to hill we went,   *495*
From province on to province did we pass,
Keen hunters in a chase of fourteen weeks,
Eager as birds of prey, or as a ship
Upon the stretch, when winds are blowing fair:
Sweet coverts did we cross of pastoral life,   *500*
Enticing valleys, greeted them and left
Too soon, while yet the very flash and gleam
440 Of salutation were not passed away.
Oh! sorrow for the youth who could have seen
Unchastened, unsubdued, unawed, unraised   *505*
To patriarchal dignity of mind,
And pure simplicity of wish and will,
Those sanctified abodes of peaceful man.
My heart leaped up when first I did look down
On that which was first seen of those deep haunts,
A green recess, an aboriginal vale,
Quiet and lorded over and possessed   *520*
450 By naked huts, wood-built, and sown like tents
Or Indian cabins over the fresh lawns

Yet then, from the undiscriminating sweep
And rage of one State-whirlwind, insecure.

'Tis not my present purpose to retrace
490 That variegated journey step by step.
A march it was of military speed,
And Earth did change her images and forms
Before us, fast as clouds are changed in heaven.
Day after day, up early and down late,
From hill to vale we dropped, from vale to hill
Mounted – from province on to province swept,
Keen hunters in a chase of fourteen weeks,
Eager as birds of prey, or as a ship
Upon the stretch, when winds are blowing fair:
500 Sweet coverts did we cross of pastoral life,
Enticing valleys, greeted them and left
Too soon, while yet the very flash and gleam
Of salutation were not passed away.
Oh! sorrow for the youth who could have seen
Unchastened, unsubdued, unawed, unraised
To patriarchal dignity of mind,
And pure simplicity of wish and will,
Those sanctified abodes of peaceful man,
Pleased (though to hardship born, and compassed round
510 With danger, varying as the seasons change),
Pleased with his daily task, or, if not pleased,
Contented, from the moment that the dawn
(Ah! surely not without attendant gleams
Of soul-illumination) calls him forth
To industry, by glistenings flung on rocks,
Whose evening shadows lead him to repose.

Well might a stranger look with bounding heart
Down on a green recess, the first I saw
Of those deep haunts, an aboriginal vale,
520 Quiet and lorded over and possessed
By naked huts, wood-built, and sown like tents
Or Indian cabins over the fresh lawns

And by the river side.

          That day we first
Beheld the summit of Mont Blanc, and grieved   *525*
To have a soulless image on the eye
Which had usurped upon a living thought
That never more could be. The wondrous Vale
Of Chamouny did, on the following dawn,
With its dumb cataracts and streams of ice,   *530*
A motionless array of mighty waves,
460 Five rivers broad and vast, make rich amends,
And reconciled us to realities;
There small birds warble from the leafy trees,
The eagle soareth in the element,   *535*
There doth the reaper bind the yellow sheaf,
The maiden spread the haycock in the sun,
While Winter like a tamèd lion walks,
Descending from the mountain to make sport
Among the cottages by beds of flowers.   *540*

     Whate'er in this wide circuit we beheld,
470 Or heard, was fitted to our unripe state
Of intellect and heart. By simple strains
Of feeling, the pure breath of real life,
We were not left untouched. With such a book
Before our eyes, we could not choose but read
A frequent lesson of sound tenderness,   *545*
The universal reason of mankind,
The truth of young and old. Nor, side by side
Pacing, two brother pilgrims, or alone
Each with his humour, could we fail to abound
480 (Craft this which hath been hinted at before)
In dreams and fictions pensively composed: *550*
Dejection taken up for pleasure's sake,
And gilded sympathies, the willow wreath,
Even among those solitudes sublime,
And sober posies of funereal flowers,
Culled from the gardens of the lady Sorrow,   *555*
Did sweeten many a meditative hour.

234

And by the river side.
               That very day,
From a bare ridge we also first beheld
Unveiled the summit of Mont Blanc, and grieved
To have a soulless image on the eye
That had usurped upon a living thought
That never more could be. The wondrous Vale
Of Chamouny stretched far below, and soon
530 With its dumb cataracts and streams of ice,
A motionless array of mighty waves,
Five rivers broad and vast, made rich amends,
And reconciled us to realities;
There small birds warble from the leafy trees,
The eagle soars high in the element,
There doth the reaper bind the yellow sheaf,
The maiden spread the haycock in the sun,
While Winter like a well-tamed lion walks,
Descending from the mountain to make sport
540 Among the cottages by beds of flowers.

Whate'er in this wide circuit we beheld,
Or heard, was fitted to our unripe state
Of intellect and heart. With such a book
Before our eyes, we could not choose but read
Lessons of genuine brotherhood, the plain
And universal reason of mankind,
The truths of young and old. Nor, side by side
Pacing, two social pilgrims, or alone
Each with his humour, could we fail to abound
550 In dreams and fictions, pensively composed:
Dejection taken up for pleasure's sake,
And gilded sympathies, the willow wreath,
And sober posies of funereal flowers,
Gathered among those solitudes sublime
From formal gardens of the lady Sorrow,
Did sweeten many a meditative hour.

    Yet still in me, mingling with these delights,
Was something of stern mood, an under-thirst
490 Of vigour, never utterly asleep.   *559*
Far different dejection once was mine,
A deep and genuine sadness then I felt;
The circumstances here I will relate
Even as they were. Upturning with a band
Of travellers, from the Vallais we had clomb
Along the road that leads to Italy;
A length of hours, making of these our guides
Did we advance, and having reached an inn
Among the mountains, we together ate
500 Our noon's repast, from which the travellers rose,
Leaving us at the board. Ere long we followed,
Descending by the beaten road that led
Right to a rivulet's edge, and there broke off.
The only track now visible was one   *570*
Upon the further side, right opposite,
And up a lofty mountain. This we took
After a little scruple, and short pause,
And climbed with eagerness, though not at length   *575*
Without surprise, and some anxiety
510 On finding that we did not overtake
Our comrades gone before. By fortunate chance,
While every moment now encreased our doubts,
A peasant met us, and from him we learned
That to the place which had perplexed us first   *580*
We must descend, and there should find the road,
Which in the stony channel of the stream,
Lay a few steps, and then along its banks;
And further, that thenceforward all our course
Was downwards, with the current of that stream.   *585*
520 Hard of belief, we questioned him again,
And all the answers which the man returned
To our inquiries, in their sense and substance,
Translated by the feelings which we had,   *590*
Ended in this, that we had crossed the Alps.

Yet still in me with those soft luxuries
Mixed something of stern mood, an under-thirst
Of vigour seldom utterly allayed.
560 And from that source how different a sadness
Would issue, let one incident make known.
When from the Vallais we had turned, and clomb
Along the Simplon's steep and rugged road,
Following a band of muleteers, we reached
A halting-place, where all together took
Their noon-tide meal. Hastily rose our guide,
Leaving us at the board; awhile we lingered,
Then paced the beaten downward way that led
Right to a rough stream's edge, and there broke off;
570 The only track now visible was one
That from the torrent's further brink held forth
Conspicuous invitation to ascend
A lofty mountain. After brief delay
Crossing the unbridged stream, that road we took,
And clomb with eagerness, till anxious fears
Intruded, for we failed to overtake
Our comrades gone before. By fortunate chance,
While every moment added doubt to doubt,
A peasant met us, from whose mouth we learned
580 That to the spot which had perplexed us first
We must descend, and there should find the road,
Which in the stony channel of the stream
Lay a few steps, and then along its banks;
And, that our future course, all plain to sight,
Was downwards, with the current of that stream.
Loth to believe what we so grieved to hear,
For still we had hopes that pointed to the clouds,
We questioned him again, and yet again;
But every word that from the peasant's lips
590 Came in reply, translated by our feelings,
Ended in this, – *that we had crossed the Alps.*

Imagination! lifting up itself
Before the eye and progress of my song
Like an unfathered vapour – here that Power,
In all the might of its endowments, came
Athwart me; I was lost as in a cloud,
530 Halted without a struggle to break through;   597
And now recovering, to my soul I say –
'I recognize thy glory': in such strength
Of usurpation, in such visitings
Of awful promise, when the light of sense   600
Goes out in flashes that have shown to us
The invisible world, doth greatness make abode,
There harbours, whether we be young or old.
Our destiny, our nature, and our home
Is with infinitude, and only there;   605
540 With hope it is, hope that can never die,
Effort, and expectation, and desire,
And something evermore about to be.
The mind beneath such banners militant
Thinks not of spoils or trophies, nor of aught   610
That may attest its prowess, blest in thoughts
That are their own perfection and reward,
Strong in itself, and in the access of joy
Which hides it like the overflowing Nile.

The dull and heavy slackening that ensued   617
550 Upon those tidings by the peasant given
Was soon dislodged. Downwards we hurried fast,
And entered with the road which we had missed   620
Into a narrow chasm. The brook and road
Were fellow-travellers in this gloomy pass,
And with them did we journey several hours
At a slow step. The immeasurable height
Of woods decaying, never to be decayed,   625
The stationary blasts of waterfalls,
And everywhere along the hollow rent
560 Winds thwarting winds, bewildered and forlorn,

Imagination – here the Power so called
Through sad incompetence of human speech,
That awful Power rose from the mind's abyss
Like an unfathered vapour that enwraps,
At once, some lonely traveller. I was lost;
Halted without an effort to break through;
But to my conscious soul I now can say –
'I recognize thy glory': in such strength
600 Of usurpation, when the light of sense
Goes out, but with a flash that has revealed
The invisible world, doth greatness make abode,
There harbours, whether we be young or old.
Our destiny, our being's heart and home,
Is with infinitude, and only there;
With hope it is, hope that can never die,
Effort, and expectation, and desire,
And something evermore about to be.
Under such banners militant, the soul
610 Seeks for no trophies, struggles for no spoils
That may attest her prowess, blest in thoughts
That are their own perfection and reward,
Strong in herself and in beatitude
That hides her, like the mighty flood of Nile
Poured from his fount of Abyssinian clouds
To fertilize the whole Egyptian plain.

The melancholy slackening that ensued
Upon those tidings by the peasant given
Was soon dislodged. Downwards we hurried fast,
620 And, with the half-shaped road which we had missed,
Entered a narrow chasm. The brook and road
Were fellow-travellers in this gloomy strait,
And with them did we journey several hours
At a slow pace. The immeasurable height
Of woods decaying, never to be decayed,
The stationary blasts of waterfalls,
And in the narrow rent at every turn
Winds thwarting winds, bewildered and forlorn,

The torrents shooting from the clear blue sky,
The rocks that muttered close upon our ears,   *630*
Black drizzling crags that spake by the wayside
As if a voice were in them, the sick sight
And giddy prospect of the raving stream,
The unfettered clouds and region of the Heavens,
Tumult and peace, the darkness and the light –   *635*
Were all like workings of one mind, the features
Of the same face, blossoms upon one tree;
570   Characters of the great Apocalypse,
The types and symbols of Eternity,
Of first, and last, and midst, and without end.   *640*

      That night our lodging was an Alpine house,
An inn, or hospital, as they are named,
Standing in that same valley by itself,
And close upon the confluence of two streams;
A dreary mansion, large beyond all need,   *645*
With high and spacious rooms, deafened and stunned
By noise of waters, making innocent sleep
580   Lie melancholy among weary bones.

      Uprisen betimes, our journey we renewed,
Led by the stream, ere noon-day magnified   *650*
Into a lordly river, broad and deep,
Dimpling along in silent majesty,
With mountains for its neighbours, and in view
Of distant mountains and their snowy tops,
And thus proceeding to Locarno's Lake,   *655*
Fit resting-place for such a visitant.
Locarno! spreading out in width like Heaven,
590   And Como! thou, a treasure by the earth   *660*
Kept to itself, a darling bosomed up
In Abyssinian privacy, I spake
Of thee, thy chestnut woods, and garden plots
Of Indian corn tended by dark-eyed maids;

The torrents shooting from the clear blue sky,
630   The rocks that muttered close upon our ears,
Black drizzling crags that spake by the wayside
As if a voice were in them, the sick sight
And giddy prospect of the raving stream,
The unfettered clouds and region of the Heavens,
Tumult and peace, the darkness and the light –
Were all like workings of one mind, the features
Of the same face, blossoms upon one tree;
Characters of the great Apocalypse,
The types and symbols of Eternity,
640   Of first, and last, and midst, and without end.

That night our lodging was a house that stood
Alone within the valley, at a point
Where, tumbling from aloft, a torrent swelled
The rapid stream whose margin we had trod;
A dreary mansion, large beyond all need,
With high and spacious rooms, deafened and stunned
By noise of waters, making innocent sleep
Lie melancholy among weary bones.

Uprisen betimes, our journey we renewed,
650   Led by the stream, ere noon-day magnified
Into a lordly river, broad and deep,
Dimpling along in silent majesty,
With mountains for its neighbours, and in view
Of distant mountains and their snowy tops,
And thus proceeding to Locarno's Lake,
Fit resting-place for such a visitant.
Locarno! spreading out in width like Heaven,
How dost thou cleave to the poetic heart,
Bask in the sunshine of the memory;
660   And Como! thou, a treasure whom the earth
Keeps to herself, confined as in a depth
Of Abyssinian privacy, I spake
Of thee, thy chestnut woods, and garden plots
Of Indian corn tended by dark-eyed maids;

Thy lofty steeps, and pathways roofed with vines,   665
Winding from house to house, from town to town,
Sole link that binds them to each other; walks,
League after league, and cloistral avenues,
Where silence is if music be not there:
While yet a youth undisciplined in verse,   670
Through fond ambition of my heart, I told
Your praises; nor can I approach you now
Ungreeted by a more melodious Song,
Where tones of learned Art and Nature mixed
May frame enduring language. Like a breeze   675
Or sunbeam over your domain I passed
In motion without pause; but ye have left
Your beauty with me, an impassioned sight
Of colours and of forms, whose power is sweet   680
And gracious, almost might I dare to say,
As virtue is, or goodness; sweet as love,
Or the remembrance of a noble deed,
Or gentlest visitations of pure thought
When God, the giver of all joy, is thanked
Religiously, in silent blessedness;   686
Sweet as this last herself, for such it is.

Through those delightful pathways we advanced,
Two days, and still in presence of the Lake,
Which winding up among the Alps, now changed   690
Slowly its lovely countenance, and put on
A sterner character. The second night,
In eagerness, and by report misled
Of those Italian clocks that speak the time
In fashion different from ours, we rose
By moonshine, doubting not that day was near,   695
And that meanwhile, coasting the water's edge
As hitherto, and with as plain a track
To be our guide, we might behold the scene
In its most deep repose. We left the town
Of Gravedona with this hope; but soon   700
Were lost, bewildered among woods immense,

600

610

620

630

Thy lofty steeps, and pathways roofed with vines,
Winding from house to house, from town to town,
Sole link that binds them to each other; walks,
League after league, and cloistral avenues,
Where silence dwells if music be not there:
670 While yet a youth undisciplined in verse,
Through fond ambition of that hour, I strove
To chant your praise; nor can approach you now
Ungreeted by a more melodious Song,
Where tones of Nature smoothed by learned Art
May flow in lasting current. Like a breeze
Or sunbeam over your domain I passed
In motion without pause; but ye have left
Your beauty with me, a serene accord
Of forms and colours, passive, yet endowed
680 In their submissiveness with power as sweet
And gracious, almost might I dare to say,
As virtue is, or goodness; sweet as love,
Or the remembrance of a generous deed,
Or mildest visitations of pure thought,
When God, the giver of all joy, is thanked
Religiously, in silent blessedness;
Sweet as this last herself, for such it is.

With those delightful pathways we advanced,
For two days' space, in presence of the Lake,
690 That, stretching far among the Alps, assumed
A character more stern. The second night,
From sleep awakened, and misled by sound
Of the church clock telling the hours with strokes
Whose import then we had not learned, we rose
By moonlight, doubting not that day was nigh,
And that meanwhile, by no uncertain path,
Along the winding margin of the lake,
Led, as before, we should behold the scene,
Hushed in profound repose. We left the town
700 Of Gravedona with this hope; but soon
Were lost, bewildered among woods immense,

Where, having wandered for a while, we stopped
And on a rock sate down, to wait for day.
An open place it was, and overlooked,
From high, the sullen water underneath,
On which a dull red image of the moon   705
Lay bedded, changing oftentimes its form
Like an uneasy snake. Long time we sate,
For scarcely more than one hour of the night,
640 Such was our error, had been done, when we
Renewed our journey. On the rock we lay
And wished to sleep but could not, for the stings   711
Of insects, which, with noise like that of noon,
Filled all the woods. The cry of unknown birds;
The mountains more by darkness visible
And their own size, than any outward light;   715
The breathless wilderness of clouds; the clock
That told, with unintelligible voice,
The widely parted hours; the noise of streams,
650 And sometimes rustling motions nigh at hand,
Which did not leave us free from personal fear;   720
And, lastly, the withdrawing moon, that set
Before us, while she still was high in heaven; –
These were our food; and such a summer night
Did to that pair of golden days succeed,
With now and then a doze and snatch of sleep,
On Como's banks, the same delicious Lake.   725

     But here I must break off, and quit at once,   727
   Though loth, the record of these wanderings,
660 A theme which may seduce me else beyond
All reasonable bounds. Let this alone
Be mentioned as a parting word, that not
In hollow exultation, dealing forth
Hyperboles of praise comparative;
Not rich one moment to be poor for ever;   735
Not prostrate, overborne, as if the mind
Itself were nothing, a mean pensioner
On outward forms – did we in presence stand

And on a rock sate down, to wait for day.
An open place it was, and overlooked,
From high, the sullen water far beneath,
On which a dull red image of the moon
Lay bedded, changing oftentimes its form
Like an uneasy snake. From hour to hour
We sate and sate, wondering, as if the night
Had been ensnared by witchcraft. On the rock
710 At last we stretched our weary limbs for sleep,
But *could not* sleep, tormented by the stings
Of insects, which, with noise like that of noon
Filled all the woods. The cry of unknown birds;
The mountains more by blackness visible
And their own size, than any outward light;
The breathless wilderness of clouds; the clock
That told, with unintelligible voice,
The widely parted hours; the noise of streams,
And sometimes rustling motions nigh at hand,
720 That did not leave us free from personal fear;
And, lastly, the withdrawing moon, that set
Before us, while she still was high in heaven; –
These were our food; and such a summer's night
Followed that pair of golden days that shed
On Como's Lake, and all that round it lay,
Their fairest, softest, happiest influence.

But here I must break off, and bid farewell
To days, each offering some new sight, or fraught
With some untried adventure, in a course
730 Prolonged till sprinklings of autumnal snow
Checked our unwearied steps. Let this alone
Be mentioned as a parting word, that not
In hollow exultation, dealing out
Hyperboles of praise comparative;
Not rich one moment to be poor for ever;
Not prostrate, overborne, as if the mind
Herself were nothing, a mean pensioner
On outward forms – did we in presence stand

Of that magnificent region. On the front
670 Of this whole Song is written that my heart   *740*
Must, in such Temple, needs have offered up
A different worship. Finally, whate'er
I saw, or heard, or felt, was but a stream
That flowed into a kindred stream; a gale   *744*
That helped me forwards, did administer
To grandeur and to tenderness, – to the one
Directly, but to tender thoughts by means
Less often instantaneous in effect;   *750*
Conducted me to these along a path
680 Which, in the main, was more circuitous.

    Oh, most belovèd Friend! a glorious time,
A happy time that was; triumphant looks   *755*
Were then the common language of all eyes;
As if awaked from sleep, the Nations hailed
Their great expectancy: the fife of war
Was then a spirit-stirring sound indeed,
A blackbird's whistle in a vernal grove.   *760*
We left the Swiss exulting in the fate
Of their near neighbours; and, when shortening fast
690 Our pilgrimage, nor distant far from home,
We crossed the Brabant armies on the fret
For battle in the cause of Liberty.   *765*
A stripling, scarcely of the household then
Of social life, I looked upon these things
As from a distance; heard, and saw, and felt,
Was touched, but with no intimate concern;
I seemed to move among them, as a bird   *770*
Moves through the air, or as a fish pursues
Its business, in its proper element;
700 I needed not that joy, I did not need
Such help; the ever-living universe,   *774*
And independent spirit of pure youth

Of that magnificent region. On the front
740 Of this whole Song is written that my heart
Must, in such Temple, needs have offered up
A different worship. Finally, whate'er
I saw, or heard, or felt, was but a stream
That flowed into a kindred stream; a gale,
Confederate with the current of the soul,
To speed my voyage; every sound or sight,
In its degree of power, administered
To grandeur or to tenderness, – to the one
Directly, but to tender thoughts by means
750 Less often instantaneous in effect;
Led me to these by paths that, in the main,
Were more circuitous, but not less sure
Duly to reach the point marked out by Heaven.

Oh, most belovèd Friend! a glorious time,
A happy time that was; triumphant looks
Were then the common language of all eyes;
As if awaked from sleep, the Nations hailed
Their great expectancy: the fife of war
Was then a spirit-stirring sound indeed,
760 A blackbird's whistle in a budding grove.
We left the Swiss exulting in the fate
Of their near neighbours; and, when shortening fast
Our pilgrimage, nor distant far from home,
We crossed the Brabant armies on the fret
For battle in the cause of Liberty.
A stripling, scarcely of the household then
Of social life, I looked upon these things
As from a distance; heard, and saw, and felt,
Was touched, but with no intimate concern;
770 I seemed to move along them, as a bird
Moves through the air, or as a fish pursues
Its sport, or feeds in its proper element;
I wanted not that joy, I did not need
Such help; the ever-living universe,
Turn where I might, was opening out its glories,

Were with me at that season, and delight
Was in all places spread around my steps
As constant as the grass upon the fields.

And the independent spirit of pure youth
Called forth, at every season, new delights
Spread round my steps like sunshine o'er green fields.

Book Seventh

RESIDENCE IN LONDON

Five years are vanished since I first poured out
(Saluted by that animating breeze
Which met me issuing from the City's walls)
A glad preamble to this Verse: I sang
Aloud, in dithyrambic fervour, deep   5
But short-lived uproar, like a torrent sent
Out of the bowels of a bursting cloud
Down Scafell, or Blencathra's rugged sides,
A waterspout from heaven. But 'twas not long
Ere the interrupted stream broke forth once more,
And flowed awhile in strength, then stopped for years;   10
Not heard again until a little space
Before last primrose-time. Belovèd Friend!
The assurances then given unto myself
Which did beguile me of some heavy thoughts
At thy departure to a foreign land
Have failed; for slowly doth this work advance.   15
Through the whole summer have I been at rest,
Partly from voluntary holiday,
And part through outward hindrance. But I heard,
After the hour of sunset yester-even,
Sitting within doors betwixt light and dark,   20
A voice that stirred me. 'Twas a little band,
A choir of redbreasts gathered somewhere near
My threshold, – minstrels from the distant woods
And dells, sent in by Winter to bespeak
For the old man a welcome, to announce,
With preparation artful and benign,
Yea the most gentle music of the year,
That their rough lord had left the surly North   25

Book Seventh

Six changeful years have vanished since I first
Poured out (saluted by that quickening breeze
Which met me issuing from the City's walls)
A glad preamble to this Verse: I sang
Aloud, with fervour irresistible
Of short-lived transport, like a torrent bursting,
From a black thunder-cloud, down Scafell's side
To rush and disappear. But soon broke forth
(So willed the Muse) a less impetuous stream,
That flowed awhile with unabating strength,
Then stopped for years; not audible again
Before last primrose-time. Belovèd Friend!
The assurance which then cheered some heavy thoughts
On thy departure to a foreign land
Has failed; too slowly moves the promised work.
Through the whole summer have I been at rest,
Partly from voluntary holiday,
And part through outward hindrance. But I heard,
After the hour of sunset yester-even,
Sitting within doors between light and dark,
A choir of redbreasts gathered somewhere near
My threshold, – minstrels from the distant woods
Sent in on Winter's service to announce,
With preparation artful and benign,
That the rough lord had left the surly North

And hath begun his journey. A delight,
At this unthought of greeting, unawares
Smote me, a sweetness of the coming time,
And listening, I half whispered, 'We will be
Ye heartsome Choristers, ye and I will be
Brethren, and in the hearing of bleak winds   30
Will chant together.' And, thereafter, walking
By later twilight on the hills, I saw
A glow-worm from beneath a dusky shade
Or canopy of the yet unwithered fern,
Clear-shining, like a hermit's taper seen   35
Through a thick forest. Silence touched me here
No less than sound had done before; the child
Of Summer, lingering, shining by itself,
The voiceless worm on the unfrequented hills,
Seemed sent on the same errand with the choir   40
Of Winter that had warbled at my door,
And the whole year seemed tenderness and love.

    The last night's genial feeling overflowed
Upon this morning, and my favourite grove,
Now tossing its dark boughs in sun and wind,   45
Spreads through me a commotion like its own,
Something that fits me for the Poet's task,
Which we will now resume with cheerful hope,
Nor checked by aught of tamer argument   50
That lies before us, needful to be told.

    Returned from that excursion, soon I bade
Farewell for ever to the private bowers
Of gownèd students, quitted these, no more   54
To enter them, and pitched my vagrant tent,
A casual dweller and at large, among
The unfenced regions of society.

    Yet undetermined to what plan of life
I should adhere, and seeming thence to have
A little space of intermediate time   60

252

On his accustomed journey. The delight,
Due to this timely notice, unawares
Smote me, and, listening, I in whispers said,
'Ye heartsome Choristers, ye and I will be
30   Associates, and, unscared by blustering winds,
Will chant together.' Thereafter, as the shades
Of twilight deepened, going forth, I spied
A glow-worm underneath a dusky plume
Or canopy of yet unwithered fern,
Clear-shining, like a hermit's taper seen
Through a thick forest. Silence touched me here
No less than sound had done before; the child
Of Summer, lingering, shining by herself,
The voiceless worm on the unfrequented hills,
40   Seemed sent on the same errand with the choir
Of Winter that had warbled at my door,
And the whole year breathed tenderness and love.

The last night's genial feeling overflowed
Upon this morning, and my favourite grove,
Tossing in sunshine its dark boughs aloft,
As if to make the strong wind visible,
Wakes in me agitations like its own,
A spirit friendly to the Poet's task,
Which we will now resume with lively hope,
50   Nor checked by aught of tamer argument,
That lies before us, needful to be told.

Returned from that excursion, soon I bade
Farewell for ever to the sheltered seats
Of gownèd students, quitted hall and bower,
And every comfort of that privileged ground,
Well pleased to pitch a vagrant tent among
The unfenced regions of society.

Yet undetermined to what course of life
I should adhere, and seeming to possess
60   A little space of intermediate time

253

Loose and at full command, to London first
I turned, if not in calmness, nevertheless
In no disturbance of excessive hope,
At ease from all ambition personal,
70 Frugal as there was need, and, though self-willed,   *64*
Yet temperate and reserved, and wholly free
From dangerous passions. 'Twas at least two years
Before this season when I first beheld
That mighty place, a transient visitant:
And now it pleased me my abode to fix   *69*
Single in the wide waste, to have a house
It was enough (what matter for a home?)
That owned me; living cheerfully abroad
With fancy on the stir from day to day,   *75*
80 And all my young affections out of doors.

    There was a time when whatsoe'er is feigned
Of airy palaces, and gardens built
By Genii of romance; or hath in grave
Authentic history been set forth of Rome,   *80*
Alcairo, Babylon, or Persepolis;
Or given upon report by pilgrim friars
Of golden cities ten months' journey deep
Among Tartarian wilds – fell short, far short,
Of that which I in simpleness believed   *85*
90 And thought of London – held me by a chain
Less strong of wonder and obscure delight.
I know not that herein I shot beyond
The common mark of childhood; but I well
Remember that among our flock of boys   *90*
Was One, a cripple from the birth, whom chance
Summoned from school to London; fortunate
And envied traveller! And when he returned,
After short absence, and I first set eyes
Upon his person, verily though strange
100 The thing may seem, I was not wholly free   *95*
From disappointment to behold the same
Appearance, the same body, not to find

At full command, to London first I turned,
In no disturbance of excessive hope,
By personal ambition unenslaved,
Frugal as there was need, and, though self-willed,
From dangerous passions free. Three years had flown
Since I had felt in heart and soul the shock
Of the huge town's first presence, and had paced
Her endless streets, a transient visitant:
Now, fixed amid that concourse of mankind
70 Where Pleasure whirls about incessantly,
And life and labour seem but one, I filled
An idler's place; an idler well content
To have a house (what matter for a home?)
That owned him; living cheerfully abroad
With unchecked fancy ever on the stir,
And all my young affections out of doors.

There was a time when whatsoe'er is feigned
Of airy palaces, and gardens built
By Genii of romance; or hath in grave
80 Authentic history been set forth of Rome,
Alcairo, Babylon, or Persepolis;
Or given upon report by pilgrim friars,
Of golden cities ten months' journey deep
Among Tartarian wilds – fell short, far short,
Of what my fond simplicity believed
And thought of London – held me by a chain
Less strong of wonder and obscure delight.
Whether the bolt of childhood's Fancy shot
For me beyond its ordinary mark,
90 'Twere vain to ask; but in our flock of boys
Was One, a cripple from his birth, whom chance
Summoned from school to London; fortunate
And envied traveller! When the Boy returned,
After short absence, curiously I scanned
His mien and person, nor was free, in sooth,
From disappointment, not to find some change

Some change, some beams of glory brought away
From that new region. Much I questioned him;
And every word he uttered, on my ears
Fell flatter than a cagèd parrot's note,   *100*
That answers unexpectedly awry,
And mocks the prompter's listening. Marvellous things
My fancy had shaped forth, of sights and shows,
110 Processions, equipages, Lords and Dukes,
The King, and the King's Palace, and, not last,
Or least, Heaven bless him! the renowned Lord Mayor:
Dreams hardly less intense than those which wrought
A change of purpose in young Whittington,
When he in friendlessness, a drooping boy,
Sate on a stone, and heard the bells speak out
Articulate music. Above all, one thought   *115*
Baffled my understanding, how men lived
Even next-door neighbours, as we say, yet still
120 Strangers, and knowing not each other's names.

O, wond'rous power of words, how sweet they are
According to the meaning which they bring!   *120*
Vauxhall and Ranelagh! I then had heard
Of your green groves, and wilderness of lamps,
Your gorgeous ladies, fairy cataracts,   *124*
And pageant fireworks; nor must we forget
Those other wonders different in kind,
Though scarcely less illustrious in degree,
The River proudly bridged; the giddy top
130 And Whispering Gallery of St Paul's; the tombs   *130*
Of Westminster; the Giants of Guildhall;
Bedlam, and the two maniacs at its gates,
Streets without end, and churches numberless,

In look and air, from that new region brought,
As if from Fairy-land. Much I questioned him;
And every word he uttered, on my ears
100 Fell flatter than a cagèd parrot's note,
That answers unexpectedly awry,
And mocks the prompter's listening. Marvellous things
Had vanity (quick Spirit that appears
Almost as deeply seated and as strong
In a Child's heart as fear itself) conceived
For my enjoyment. Would that I could now
Recall what then I pictured to myself,
Of mitred Prelates, Lords in ermine clad,
The King, and the King's Palace, and, not last,
110 Nor least, Heaven bless him! the renowned Lord Mayor:
Dreams not unlike to those which once begat
A change of purpose in young Whittington,
When he, a friendless and a drooping boy,
Sate on a stone, and heard the bells speak out
Articulate music. Above all, one thought
Baffled my understanding: how men lived
Even next-door neighbours, as we say, yet still
Strangers, nor knowing each the other's name.

O, wond'rous power of words, by simple faith
120 Licensed to take the meaning that we love!
Vauxhall and Ranelagh! I then had heard
Of your green groves, and wilderness of lamps
Dimming the stars, and fireworks magical,
And gorgeous ladies, under splendid domes,
Floating in dance, or warbling high in air
The songs of spirits! Nor had Fancy fed
With less delight upon that other class
Of marvels, broad-day wonders permanent:
The River proudly bridged; the dizzy top
130 And Whispering Gallery of St Paul's; the tombs
Of Westminster; the Giants of Guildhall;
Bedlam, and those carved maniacs at the gates,
Perpetually recumbent; Statues – man,

Statues, with flowery gardens in vast squares,   *135*
The Monument and armoury of the Tower.
These fond imaginations of themselves   *142*
Had long before given way in season due,
Leaving a throng of others in their stead:
And now I looked upon the real scene;
140 Familiarly perused it day by day   *145*
With keen and lively pleasure even there
Where disappointment was the strongest, pleased
Through courteous self-submission, as a tax
Paid to the object by prescriptive right,   *148*
A thing that ought to be. Shall I give way,
Copying the impression of the memory,
Though things remembered idly do half seem
The work of fancy, shall I, as the mood
Inclines me, here describe, for pastime's sake
150 Some portion of that motley imagery,
A vivid pleasure of my youth, and now
Among the lonely places that I love
A frequent day-dream for my riper mind?
– And first the look and aspect of the place,
The broad highway appearance, as it strikes
On strangers, of all ages; the quick dance
Of colours, lights, and forms; the Babel din;   *155*
The endless stream of men, and moving things,
From hour to hour the illimitable walk
160 Still among streets with clouds and sky above,
The wealth, the bustle and the eagerness,
The glittering chariots with their pampered steeds,
Stalls, barrows, porters; midway in the street
The scavenger, who begs with hat in hand,
The labouring hackney coaches, the rash speed
Of coaches travelling far, whirled on with horn
Loud blowing, and the sturdy drayman's team,
Ascending from some alley of the Thames
And striking right across the crowded Strand
170 Till the fore horse veer round with punctual skill:
Here there and everywhere a weary throng,

And the horse under him – in gilded pomp
Adorning flowery gardens, 'mid vast squares;
The Monument, and that Chamber of the Tower
Where England's sovereigns sit in long array,
Their steeds bestriding, – every mimic shape
Cased in the gleaming mail the monarch wore,
140   Whether for gorgeous tournament addressed,
Or life or death upon the battle-field.
Those bold imaginations in due time
Had vanished, leaving others in their stead:
And now I looked upon the living scene;
Familiarly perused it; oftentimes,
In spite of strongest disappointment, pleased
Through courteous self-submission, as a tax
Paid to the object by prescriptive right.

Rise up, thou monstrous ant-hill on the plain
150   Of a too busy world! Before me flow,
Thou endless stream of men and moving things!
Thy every-day appearance, as it strikes –
With wonder heightened, or sublimed by awe –
On strangers, of all ages; the quick dance
Of colours, lights, and forms; the deafening din;

The comers and the goers face to face,   *156*
Face after face; the string of dazzling wares,
Shop after shop, with symbols, blazoned names,
And all the tradesman's honours overhead:
Here, fronts of houses, like a title-page   *160*
With letters huge inscribed from top to toe;
Stationed above the door, like guardian saints,
There, allegoric shapes, female or male,
180 Or physiognomies of real men,
Land-warriors, kings, or admirals of the sea,   *165*
Boyle, Shakespeare, Newton, or the attractive head
Of some Scotch doctor, famous in his day.

Meanwhile the roar continues, till at length,
Escaped as from an enemy, we turn
Abruptly into some sequestered nook,   *170*
Still as a sheltered place when winds blow loud!
At leisure, thence, through tracts of thin resort,
And sights and sounds that come at intervals,
190 We take our way. A raree-show is here,
With children gathered round; another street   *175*
Presents a company of dancing dogs,
Or dromedary, with an antic pair
Of monkeys on his back; a minstrel band
Of Savoyards; or, single and alone,
An English ballad-singer. Private courts,   *180*
Gloomy as coffins, and unsightly lanes
Thrilled by some female vendor's scream, belike
The very shrillest of all London cries,
200 May then entangle us awhile;
Conducted through those labyrinths, unawares,   *185*
To privileged regions and inviolate,
Where from their airy lodges studious lawyers
Look out on waters, walks, and gardens green.

Thence back into the throng, until we reach,
Following the tide that slackens by degrees,   *190*
Some half-frequented scene, where wider streets

The comers and the goers face to face,
Face after face; the string of dazzling wares,
Shop after shop, with symbols, blazoned names,
And all the tradesman's honours overhead:
160 Here, fronts of houses, like a title-page
With letters huge inscribed from top to toe;
Stationed above the door, like guardian saints,
There, allegoric shapes, female or male,
Or physiognomies of real men,
Land-warriors, kings, or admirals of the sea,
Boyle, Shakespeare, Newton, or the attractive head
Of some quack-doctor, famous in his day.

Meanwhile the roar continues, till at length,
Escaped as from an enemy, we turn
170 Abruptly into some sequestered nook,
Still as a sheltered place when winds blow loud!
At leisure, thence, through tracts of thin resort,
And sights and sounds that come at intervals,
We take our way. A raree-show is here,
With children gathered round; another street
Presents a company of dancing dogs,
Or dromedary, with an antic pair
Of monkeys on his back; a minstrel band
Of Savoyards; or, single and alone,
180 An English ballad-singer. Private courts,
Gloomy as coffins, and unsightly lanes
Thrilled by some female vendor's scream, belike
The very shrillest of all London cries,
May then entangle our impatient steps;
Conducted through those labyrinths, unawares,
To privileged regions and inviolate,
Where from their airy lodges studious lawyers
Look out on waters, walks, and gardens green.

Thence back into the throng, until we reach,
190 Following the tide that slackens by degrees,
Some half-frequented scene, where wider streets

Bring straggling breezes of suburban air.
Here files of ballads dangle from dead walls;
210 Advertisements, of giant-size, from high
Press forward, in all colours, on the sight;   *195*
These, bold in conscious merit, lower down
That, fronted with a most imposing word,
Is, peradventure, one in masquerade.
As on the broadening causeway we advance,
Behold a face turned up towards us, strong   *200*
In lineaments, and red with over-toil.
'Tis one perhaps already met elsewhere,
A travelling cripple, by the trunk cut short,
220 And stumping with his arms. In sailor's garb
Another lies at length, beside a range   *205*
Of written characters, with chalk inscribed
Upon the smooth flat stones: the Nurse is here,
The Bachelor, that loves to sun himself,
The military Idler, and the Dame,
That field-ward takes her walk in decency.   *210*

Now homeward through the thickening hubbub, where
See, among less distinguishable shapes,
The Italian, with his frame of images   *215*
230 Upon his head; with basket at his waist
The Jew; the stately and slow-moving Turk,
With freight of slippers piled beneath his arm!

Briefly, we find, if tired of random sights
And haply to that search our thoughts should turn,
Among the crowd, conspicuous less or more,   *221*
As we proceed, all specimens of man
Through all the colours which the sun bestows,
And every character of form and face:
The Swede, the Russian; from the genial south,
240 The Frenchman and the Spaniard; from remote   *225*
America, the Hunter-Indian; Moors,
Malays, Lascars, the Tartar and Chinese,

Bring straggling breezes of suburban air.
Here files of ballads dangle from dead walls;
Advertisements, of giant-size, from high
Press forward, in all colours, on the sight;
These, bold in conscious merit, lower down
That, fronted with a most imposing word,
Is, peradventure, one in masquerade.
As on the broadening causeway we advance,
200 Behold, turned upwards, a face hard and strong
In lineaments, and red with over-toil.
'Tis one encountered here and everywhere;
A travelling cripple, by the trunk cut short,
And stumping on his arms. In sailor's garb
Another lies at length, beside a range
Of well-formed characters, with chalk inscribed
Upon the smooth flat stones; the Nurse is here,
The Bachelor, that loves to sun himself,
The military Idler, and the Dame,
210 That field-ward takes her walk with decent steps.

Now homeward through the thickening hubbub, where
See, among less distinguishable shapes,
The begging scavenger, with hat in hand;
The Italian, as he thrids his way with care,
Steadying, far-seen, a frame of images
Upon his head; with basket at his breast
The Jew; the stately and slow-moving Turk,
With freight of slippers piled beneath his arm!

Enough; – the mighty concourse I surveyed
220 With no unthinking mind, well pleased to note
Among the crowd all specimens of man,
Through all the colours which the sun bestows,
And every character of form and face:
The Swede, the Russian; from the genial south,
The Frenchman and the Spaniard; from remote
America, the Hunter-Indian; Moors,
Malays, Lascars, the Tartar, the Chinese,

And Negro Ladies in white muslin gowns.

    At leisure let us view, from day to day,
As they present themselves, the spectacles
Within doors, troops of wild beasts, birds and beasts   *230*
Of every nature, from all climes convened;
And, next to these, those mimic sights that ape
The absolute presence of reality,
250 Expressing, as in mirror, sea and land,
And what earth is, and what she hath to show.   *235*
I do not here allude to subtlest craft,
By means refined attaining purest ends,
But imitations, fondly made in plain
Confession of man's weakness and his loves.
Whether the Painter, fashioning a work   *240*
To Nature's circumambient scenery,
And with his greedy pencil taking in
A whole horizon on all sides, with power,
260 Like that of angels or commissioned spirits,
Plant us upon some lofty pinnacle,
Or in a ship on waters, with a world   *245*
Of life, and life-like mockery, to east,
To west, beneath, behind us, and before;
Or more mechanic artist represent
By scale exact, in model, wood or clay,
From shading colours also borrowing help,   *250*
Some miniature of famous spots and things, –
Domestic or the boast of foreign realms;
270 The Firth of Forth, and Edinburgh throned
On crags, fit empress of that mountain land;
St Peter's Church; or, more aspiring aim,
In microscopic vision, Rome itself;
Or else, perhaps, some rural haunt, – the Falls
Of Tivoli; and, high upon that steep,   *255*
The Temple of the Sibyl! every tree
Through all the landscape, tuft, stone, scratch minute,
And every cottage, lurking in the rocks –
All that the traveller sees when he is there.

And Negro Ladies in white muslin gowns.

At leisure, then, I viewed, from day to day,
230   The spectacles within doors, – birds and beasts
Of every nature, and strange plants convened
From every clime; and, next, those sights that ape
The absolute presence of reality,
Expressing, as in mirror, sea and land,
And what earth is, and what she has to show.
I do not here allude to subtlest craft,
By means refined attaining purest ends,
But imitations, fondly made in plain
Confession of man's weakness and his loves.
240   Whether the Painter, whose ambitious skill
Submits to nothing less than taking in
A whole horizon's circuit, do with power,
Like that of angels or commissioned spirits,
Fix us upon some lofty pinnacle,
Or in a ship on waters, with a world
Of life, and life-like mockery beneath,
Above, behind, far stretching and before;
Or more mechanic artist represent
By scale exact, in model, wood or clay,
250   From blended colours also borrowing help,
Some miniature of famous spots or things, –
St Peter's Church; or, more aspiring aim,
In microscopic vision, Rome herself;
Or, haply, some choice rural haunt, – the Falls
Of Tivoli; and, high upon that steep,
The Sibyl's mouldering Temple! every tree,
Villa, or cottage, lurking among rocks
Throughout the landscape; tuft, stone, scratch minute –
All that the traveller sees when he is there.

280	Add to these exhibitions, mute and still,	*260*
	Others of wider scope, where living men,	
	Music, and shifting pantomimic scenes,	
	Together joined their multifarious aid	
	To heighten the allurement. Need I fear	
	To mention by its name, as in degree	
	Lowest of these and humblest in attempt,	*265*
	Though richly graced with honours of its own,	
	Half-rural Sadler's Wells? Though at that time	
	Intolerant, as is the way of youth	
290	Unless itself be pleased, I more than once	
	Here took my seat, and maugre frequent fits	*270*
	Of irksomeness, with ample recompense	
	Saw singers, rope-dancers, giants and dwarfs,	
	Clowns, conjurors, posture-masters, harlequins,	
	Amid the uproar of the rabblement,	
	Perform their feats. Nor was it mean delight	
	To watch crude Nature work in untaught minds;	*275*
	To note the laws and progress of belief;	
	Though obstinate on this way, yet on that	
300	How willingly we travel, and how far!	
	To have, for instance, brought upon the scene	
	The champion, Jack the Giant-killer: Lo!	
	He dons his coat of darkness; on the stage	*281*
	Walks, and achieves his wonders, from the eyes	
	Of living mortal safe as is the moon	
	'Hid in her vacant interlunar cave'.	
	Delusion bold! and faith must needs be coy;	*285*
	How is it wrought? His garb is black, the word	
	'*Invisible*' flames forth upon his chest.	
310	Nor was it unamusing here to view	
	Those samples as of ancient comedy	
	And Thespian times, dramas of living men,	
	And recent things yet warm with life; a sea-fight,	
	Shipwreck, or some domestic incident	
	The fame of which is scattered through the land;	
	Such as this daring brotherhood of late	

260   Add to these exhibitions, mute and still,
       Others of wider scope, where living men,
       Music, and shifting pantomimic scenes,
       Diversified the allurement. Need I fear
       To mention by its name, as in degree
       Lowest of these and humblest in attempt,
       Yet richly graced with honours of her own,
       Half-rural Sadler's Wells? Though at that time
       Intolerant, as is the way of youth
       Unless itself be pleased, here more than once
270   Taking my seat, I saw (nor blush to add,
       With ample recompense) giants and dwarfs,
       Clowns, conjurors, posture-masters, harlequins,
       Amid the uproar of the rabblement,
       Perform their feats. Nor was it mean delight
       To watch crude Nature work in untaught minds;
       To note the laws and progress of belief;
       Though obstinate on this way, yet on that
       How willingly we travel, and how far!
       To have, for instance, brought upon the scene
280   The champion, Jack the Giant-killer: Lo!
       He dons his coat of darkness; on the stage
       Walks, and achieves his wonders, from the eye
       Of living Mortal covert, 'as the moon
       Hid in her vacant interlunar cave'.
       Delusion bold! and how can it be wrought?
       The garb he wears is black as death, the word
       'Invisible' flames forth upon his chest.

       Here, too, were 'forms and pressures of the time',
       Rough, bold, as Grecian comedy displayed
290   When Art was young; dramas of living men,
       And recent things yet warm with life; a sea-fight,
       Shipwreck, or some domestic incident
       Divulged by Truth and magnified by Fame,
       Such as the daring brotherhood of late

267

Set forth, too holy theme for such a place,   *295*
And doubtless treated with irreverence
Albeit with their very best of skill,
320 I mean, O distant Friend! a story drawn
From our own ground, – the Maid of Buttermere, –
And how the spoiler came, 'a bold bad Man'
To God unfaithful, children, wife, and home,
And wooed the artless daughter of the hills,   *300*
And wedded her, in cruel mockery
Of love and marriage bonds. O Friend! I speak
With tender recollection of that time
When first we saw the maiden, then a name
By us unheard of; in her cottage inn   *305*
330 Were welcomed, and attended on by her,
Both stricken with one feeling of delight,
An admiration of her modest mien
And carriage, marked by unexampled grace.
Not unfamiliarly we since that time
Have seen her, – her discretion have observed,   *310*
Her just opinions, female modesty,
Her patience, and retiredness of mind
Unsoiled by commendation and the excess
Of public notice. This memorial verse
340 Comes from the Poet's heart, and is her due.
For we were nursed, as almost might be said,
On the same mountains; children at one time
Must haply often on the self-same day
Have from our several dwellings gone abroad
To gather daffodils on Coker's Stream.

These last words uttered, to my argument
I was returning, when, with sundry forms
Mingled, that in the way which I must tread
Before me stand, thy image rose again,
350 Mary of Buttermere! She lives in peace   *320*
Upon the ground where she was born and reared;
Without contamination does she live
In quietness, without anxiety:

Set forth, too serious theme for that light place –
I mean, O distant Friend! a story drawn
From our own ground, – the Maid of Buttermere, –
And how, unfaithful to a virtuous wife
Deserted and deceived, the spoiler came
300 And wooed the artless daughter of the hills,
And wedded her, in cruel mockery
Of love and marriage bonds. These words to thee
Must needs bring back the moment when we first,
Ere the broad world rang with the maiden's name,
Beheld her serving at the cottage inn,
Both stricken, as she entered or withdrew,
With admiration of her modest mien
And carriage, marked by unexampled grace.
Not unfamiliarly we since that time
310 Have seen her, – her discretion have observed,
Her just opinions, delicate reserve,
Her patience, and humility of mind
Unspoiled by commendation and the excess
Of public notice – an offensive light
To a meek spirit suffering inwardly.

From this memorial tribute to my theme
I was returning, when, with sundry forms
Commingled – shapes which met me in the way
That we must tread – thy image rose again,
320 Maiden of Buttermere! She lives in peace
Upon the spot where she was born and reared;
Without contamination doth she live
In quietness, without anxiety:

Beside the mountain chapel, sleeps in earth
Her new-born infant, fearless as a lamb   *325*
That thither comes, from some unsheltered place,
To rest beneath the little rock-like pile
When storms are blowing. Happy are they both –
Mother and child! – These feelings, in themselves
360 Trite, do yet scarcely seem so when I think   *330*
Of those ingenuous moments of our youth
Ere yet by use we have learnt to slight the crimes
And sorrows of the world. Those days are now
My theme; and, mid the numerous scenes which they   *334*
Have left behind them, foremost I am crossed
Here by remembrance of two figures, one
A rosy babe, who, for a twelvemonth's space
Perhaps, had been of age to deal about
Articulate prattle – Child as beautiful
370 As ever sate upon a mother's knee;
The other was the parent of that babe;
But on the mother's cheek the tints were false,
A painted bloom. 'Twas at a theatre
That I beheld this pair; the Boy had been
The pride and pleasure of all lookers-on
In whatsoever place, but seemed in this
A sort of alien scattered from the clouds.   *350*
Of lusty vigour, more than infantine,
He was in limbs, in face a cottage rose
380 Just three parts blown – a cottage-child – but ne'er
Saw I, by cottage or elsewhere, a babe   *355*
By Nature's gifts so honoured. Upon a board
Whence an attendant of the theatre
Served out refreshments, had this child been placed,
And there he sate, environed with a ring
Of chance spectators, chiefly dissolute men   *360*
And shameless women; treated and caressed,

Beside the mountain chapel, sleeps in earth
Her new-born infant, fearless as a lamb
That, thither driven from some unsheltered place,
Rests underneath the little rock-like pile
When storms are raging. Happy are they both –
Mother and child! – These feelings, in themselves
330   Trite, do yet scarcely seem so when I think
On those ingenuous moments of our youth
Ere we have learnt by use to slight the crimes
And sorrows of the world. Those simple days
Are now my theme; and, foremost of the scenes,
Which yet survive in memory, appears
One, at whose centre sate a lovely Boy,
A sportive infant, who, for six months' space,
Not more, had been of age to deal about
Articulate prattle – Child as beautiful
340   As ever clung around a mother's neck,
Or father fondly gazed upon with pride.
There, too, conspicuous for stature tall
And large dark eyes, beside her infant stood
The mother; but, upon her cheeks diffused,
False tints too well accorded with the glare
From play-house lustres thrown without reserve
On every object near. The Boy had been
The pride and pleasure of all lookers-on
In whatsoever place, but seemed in this
350   A sort of alien scattered from the clouds.
Of lusty vigour, more than infantine,
He was in limb, in cheek a summer rose
Just three parts blown – a cottage-child – if e'er,
By cottage-door on breezy mountain-side,
Or in some sheltering vale, was seen a babe
By Nature's gift so favoured. Upon a board
Decked with refreshments had this child been placed,
His little stage in the vast theatre,
And there he sate surrounded with a throng
360   Of chance spectators, chiefly dissolute men
And shameless women; treated and caressed,

Ate, drank, and with the fruit and glasses played,
While oaths, indecent speech, and ribaldry
390 Were rife about him as are songs of birds
In spring-time after showers. The mother, too,   365
Was present! but of her I know no more
Than hath been said, and scarcely at this time
Do I remember her. But I behold
The lovely Boy as I beheld him then
Among the wretched and the falsely gay,
Like one of those who walked with hair unsinged
Amid the fiery furnace. He hath since   370
Appeared to me oft times as if embalmed
400 By Nature; through some special privilege,   375
Stopped at the growth he had; destined to live,
To be, to have been, come and go, a child
And nothing more, no partner in the years
That bear us forward to distress and guilt,
Pain and abasement, beauty in such excess
Adorned him in that miserable place.
So have I thought of him a thousand times,
And seldom otherwise. But he perhaps,
Mary! may now have lived till he could look
410 With envy on thy nameless babe that sleeps,   380
Beside the mountain chapel, undisturbed.

It was but little more than three short years
Before the season which I speak of now
When first, a traveller from our pastoral hills,
Southward two hundred miles I had advanced,
And for the first time in my life did hear
The voice of woman utter blasphemy –   385
Saw woman as she is to open shame
Abandoned, and the pride of public vice.
420 Full surely from the bottom of my heart
I shuddered; but the pain was almost lost,
Absorbed and buried in the immensity
Of the effect: a barrier seemed at once
Thrown in, that from humanity divorced

Ate, drank, and with the fruit and glasses played,
While oaths and laughter and indecent speech
Were rife about him as the songs of birds
Contending after showers. The mother now
Is fading out of memory, but I see
The lovely Boy as I beheld him then
Among the wretched and the falsely gay,
Like one of those who walked with hair unsinged
370   Amid the fiery furnace. Charms and spells
Muttered on black and spiteful instigation
Have stopped, as some believe, the kindliest growths.
Ah, with how different spirit might a prayer
Have been preferred, that this fair creature, checked
By special privilege of Nature's love,
Should in his childhood be detained for ever!
But with its universal freight the tide
Hath rolled along, and this bright innocent,
Mary! may now have lived till he could look
380   With envy on thy nameless babe that sleeps,
Beside the mountain chapel, undisturbed.

Four rapid years had scarcely then been told
Since, travelling southward from our pastoral hills,
I heard, and for the first time in my life,
The voice of woman utter blasphemy –
Saw woman as she is to open shame
Abandoned, and the pride of public vice;
I shuddered, for a barrier seemed at once
Thrown in, that from humanity divorced

The human form, splitting the race of man   *390*
In twain, yet leaving the same outward shape.
Distress of mind ensued upon this sight
And ardent meditation. Afterwards
A milder sadness on such spectacles
430 Attended; thought, commiseration, grief   *395*
For the individual and the overthrow
Of her soul's beauty; farther at that time
Than this I was but seldom led; in truth
The sorrow of the passion stopped me here.

    I quit this painful theme; enough is said   *400*
To show what thoughts must often have been mine
At theatres, which then were my delight,
A yearning made more strong by obstacles
Which slender funds imposed. Life then was new,
440 The senses easily pleased; the lustres, lights,
The carving and the gilding, paint and glare,
And all the mean upholstery of the place,
Wanted not animation in my sight: *410*
Far less the living figures on the stage,
Solemn or gay: whether some beauteous dame
Advanced in radiance through a deep recess
Of thick entangled forest, like the moon   *415*
Opening the clouds; or sovereign king, announced
With flourishing trumpets, came in full-blown state
450 Of the world's greatness, winding round with train
Of courtiers, banners, and a length of guards;
Or captive led in abject weeds, and jingling   *420*
His slender manacles; or romping girl
Bounced, leapt, and pawed the air; or mumbling sire,
A scare-crow pattern of old age patched up
Of all the tatters of infirmity
All loosely put together, hobbled in,   *425*
Stumping upon a cane with which he smites,

390 Humanity, splitting the race of man
In twain, yet leaving the same outward form.
Distress of mind ensued upon the sight
And ardent meditation. Later years
Brought to such spectacle a milder sadness,
Feelings of pure commiseration, grief
For the individual and the overthrow
Of her soul's beauty; farther I was then
But seldom led, or wished to go; in truth
The sorrow of the passion stopped me there.

400 But let me now, less moved, in order take
Our argument. Enough is said to show
How casual incidents of real life,
Observed where pastime only had been sought,
Outweighed, or put to flight, the set events
And measured passions of the stage, albeit
By Siddons trod in the fulness of her power.
Yet was the theatre my dear delight;
The very gilding, lamps and painted scrolls,
And all the mean upholstery of the place,
410 Wanted not animation, when the tide
Of pleasure ebbed but to return as fast
With the ever-shifting figures of the scene,
Solemn or gay: whether some beauteous dame
Advanced in radiance through a deep recess
Of thick entangled forest, like the moon
Opening the clouds; or sovereign king, announced
With flourishing trumpet, came in full-blown state
Of the world's greatness, winding round with train
Of courtiers, banners, and a length of guards;
420 Or captive led in abject weeds, and jingling
His slender manacles; or romping girl
Bounced, leapt, and pawed the air; or mumbling sire,
A scare-crow pattern of old age dressed up
In all the tatters of infirmity
All loosely put together, hobbled in,
Stumping upon a cane with which he smites,

From time to time, the solid boards, and makes them
460 Prate somewhat loudly of the whereabout
Of one so overloaded with his years.
But what of this! the laugh, the grin, grimace, *430*
And all the antics and buffoonery,
The least of them not lost, were all received
With charitable pleasure. Through the night,
Between the show, and many-headed mass
Of the spectators, and each little nook *435*
That had its fray or brawl, how eagerly
And with what flashes, as it were, the mind
470 Turned this way – that way! sportive and alert
And watchful, as a kitten when at play,
While winds are blowing round her, among grass *440*
And rustling leaves. Enchanting age and sweet!
Romantic almost, looked at through a space,
How small, of intervening years! For then,
Though surely no mean progress had been made
In meditations holy and sublime, *445*
Yet something of a girlish child-like gloss
Of novelty survived for scenes like these;
480 Pleasure that had been handed down from times
When at a country-playhouse, having caught, *449*
In summer, through the fractured wall, a glimpse
Of daylight, at the thought of where I was
I gladdened more than if I had beheld
Before me some bright cavern of romance, *455*
Or than we do, when on our beds we lie
At night, in warmth, when rains are beating hard.

The matter which detains me now will seem,
To many, neither dignified enough
490 Nor arduous; and is, doubtless, in itself *460*
Humble and low; yet not to be despised
By those who have observed the curious props
By which the perishable hours of life
Rest on each other, and the world of thought

From time to time, the solid boards, and makes them
Prate somewhat loudly of the whereabout
Of one so overloaded with his years.
430   But what of this! the laugh, the grin, grimace,
The antics striving to outstrip each other,
Were all received, the least of them not lost,
With an unmeasured welcome. Through the night,
Between the show, and many-headed mass
Of the spectators, and each several nook
Filled with its fray or brawl, how eagerly
And with what flashes, as it were, the mind
Turned this way – that way! sportive and alert
And watchful, as a kitten when at play,
440   While winds are eddying round her, among straws
And rustling leaves. Enchanting age and sweet!
Romantic almost, looked at through a space,
How small, of intervening years! For then,
Though surely no mean progress had been made
In meditations holy and sublime,
Yet something of a girlish child-like gloss
Of novelty survived for scenes like these;
Enjoyment haply handed down from times
When at a country-playhouse, some rude barn
450   Tricked out for that proud use, if I perchance
Caught, on a summer evening through a chink
In the old wall, an unexpected glimpse
Of daylight, the bare thought of where I was
Gladdened me more than if I had been led
Into a dazzling cavern of romance,
Crowded with Genii busy among works
Not to be looked at by the common sun.

The matter that detains us now may seem,
To many, neither dignified enough
460   Nor arduous, yet will not be scorned by them,
Who, looking inward, have observed the ties
That bind the perishable hours of life
Each to the other, and the curious props

Exists and is sustained. More lofty themes,　　　*465*
Such as at least do wear a prouder face,
Might here be spoken of; but when I think
Of these, I feel the imaginative power
Languish within me; even then it slept,
500　When, wrought upon by tragic sufferings,　　　*470*
The heart was full; amid my sobs and tears
It slept, even in the season of my youth.
For though I was most passionately moved
And yielded to the changes of the scene
With most obsequious feeling, yet all this　　　*475*
Passed not beyond the suburbs of the mind;
If aught there were of real grandeur here
'Twas only then when gross realities,
The incarnation of the spirits that moved
510　Amid the Poet's beauteous world, called forth　　　*480*
With that distinctness which a contrast gives
Or opposition, made me recognize
As by a glimpse, the things which I had shaped,
And yet not shaped, had seen and scarcely seen,
Had felt, and thought of in my solitude.　　　*485*

　　Pass we from entertainments, that are such
Professedly, to others titled higher,
Yet, in the estimate of youth at least,
More near akin to those than names imply, –
520　I mean the brawls of lawyers in their courts　　　*490*
Before the ermined judge, or that great stage
Where senators, tongue-favoured Men, perform,
Admired and envied. Oh! the beating heart,
When one among the prime of these rose up,
One, of whose name from childhood we had heard　　　*495*
Familiarly, a household term, like those,
The Bedfords, Glosters, Salisburys of old
Which the fifth Harry talks of. Silence! hush!
This is no trifler, no short-flighted wit,
530　No stammerer of a minute, painfully　　　*500*

By which the world of memory and thought
Exists and is sustained. More lofty themes,
Such as at least do wear a prouder face,
Solicit our regard; but when I think
Of these, I feel the imaginative power
Languish within me; even then it slept,
470 When, pressed by tragic sufferings, the heart
Was more than full; amid my sobs and tears
It slept, even in the pregnant season of youth.
For though I was most passionately moved
And yielded to all changes of the scene
With an obsequious promptness, yet the storm
Passed not beyond the suburbs of the mind;
Save when realities of act and mien,
The incarnation of the spirits that move
In harmony amid the Poet's world,
480 Rose to ideal grandeur, or, called forth
By power of contrast, made me recognize,
As at a glance, the things which I had shaped,
And yet not shaped, had seen and scarcely seen,
When, having closed the mighty Shakspeare's page,
I mused, and thought, and felt, in solitude.

    Pass we from entertainments, that are such
Professedly, to others titled higher,
Yet, in the estimate of youth at least,
More near akin to those than names imply, –
490 I mean the brawls of lawyers in their courts
Before the ermined judge, or that great stage
Where senators, tongue-favoured men, perform,
Admired and envied. Oh! the beating heart,
When one among the prime of these rose up, –
One, of whose name from childhood we had heard
Familiarly, a household term, like those,
The Bedfords, Glosters, Salisburys, of old
Whom the fifth Harry talks of. Silence! hush!
This is no trifler, no short-flighted wit,
500 No stammerer of a minute, painfully

Delivered. No! the Orator hath yoked
The Hours, like young Aurora, to his car:
O Presence of delight, can patience e'er
Grow weary of attending on a track
That kindles with such glory! Marvellous!   505
The enchantment spreads and rises; all are rapt,
Astonished; like a hero in romance,
He winds away his never-ending horn;
Words follow words, sense seems to follow sense:
540 What memory and what logic! till the strain
Transcendent, superhuman as it is,   510
Grows tedious even in a young man's ear.

  These are grave follies: other public shows

Delivered. No! the Orátor hath yoked
The Hours, like young Aurora, to his car:
Thrice welcome Presence! how can patience e'er
Grow weary of attending on a track
That kindles with such glory! All are charmed,
Astonished; like a hero in romance,
He winds away his never-ending horn;
Words follow words, sense seems to follow sense:
What memory and what logic! till the strain
510   Transcendent, superhuman as it seemed,
Grows tedious even in a young man's ear.

Genius of Burke! forgive the pen seduced
By specious wonders, and too slow to tell
Of what the ingenuous, what bewildered men,
Beginning to mistrust their boastful guides,
And wise men, willing to grow wiser, caught,
Rapt auditors! from thy most eloquent tongue –
Now mute, for ever mute in the cold grave.
I see him, – old, but vigorous in age, –
520   Stand like an oak whose stag-horn branches start
Out of its leafy brow, the more to awe
The younger brethren of the grove. But some –
While he forewarns, denounces, launches forth,
Against all systems built on abstract rights,
Keen ridicule; the majesty proclaims
Of Institutes and Laws, hallowed by time;
Declares the vital power of social ties
Endeared by Custom; and with high disdain,
Exploding upstart Theory, insists
530   Upon the allegiance to which men are born –
Some – say at once a froward multitude –
Murmur (for truth is hated, where not loved)
As the winds fret within the Aeolian cave,
Galled by their monarch's chain. The times were big
With ominous change, which, night by night, provoked
Keen struggles, and black clouds of passion raised;
But memorable moments intervened,

The capital city teems with, of a kind
More light, and where but in the holy church?
There have I seen a comely bachelor,   *551*
Fresh from a toilette of two hours, ascend
The pulpit, with seraphic glance look up,
And, in a tone elaborately low
550 Beginning, lead his voice through many a maze   *555*
A minuet course; and, winding up his mouth,
From time to time, into an orifice
Most delicate, a lurking eyelet, small
And only not invisible, again
Open it out, diffusing thence a smile   *560*
Of rapt irradiation, exquisite.
Meanwhile the Evangelists, Isaiah, Job,
Moses, and he who penned, the other day,
The Death of Abel, Shakespeare, Doctor Young,
560 And Ossian (doubt not – 'tis the naked truth)
Summoned from streamy Morven – each and all
Must in their turn lend ornament and flowers
To entwine the crook of eloquence with which   *570*
This pretty Shepherd, pride of all the plains,
Leads up and down his captivated flock.

    I glance but at a few conspicuous marks,

When Wisdom, like the Goddess from Jove's brain,
Broke forth in armour of resplendent words,
540 Startling the Synod. Could a youth, and one
In ancient story versed, whose breast had heaved
Under the weight of classic eloquence,
Sit, see, and hear, unthankful, uninspired?

    Nor did the Pulpit's oratory fail
To achieve its higher triumph. Not unfelt
Were its admonishments, nor lightly heard
The awful truths delivered thence by tongues
Endowed with various power to search the soul;
Yet ostentation, domineering, oft
550 Poured forth harangues, how sadly out of place! –
There have I seen a comely bachelor,
Fresh from a toilette of two hours, ascend
His rostrum, with seraphic glance look up,
And, in a tone elaborately low
Beginning, lead his voice through many a maze
A minuet course; and, winding up his mouth,
From time to time, into an orifice
Most delicate, a lurking eyelet, small,
And only not invisible, again
560 Open it out, diffusing thence a smile
Of rapt irradiation, exquisite.
Meanwhile the Evangelists, Isaiah, Job,
Moses, and he who penned, the other day,
The Death of Abel, Shakespeare, and the Bard
Whose genius spangled o'er a gloomy theme
With fancies thick as his inspiring stars,
And Ossian (doubt not – 'tis the naked truth)
Summoned from streamy Morven – each and all
Would, in their turns, lend ornaments and flowers
570 To entwine the crook of eloquence that helped
This pretty Shepherd, pride of all the plains,
To rule and guide his captivated flock.

    I glance but at a few conspicuous marks,

Leaving ten thousand others, that do each,
In hall or court, conventicle, or shop,   575
In public room or private, park or street,
570   With fondness reared on his own pedestal,
Look out for admiration. Folly, vice,
Extravagance in gesture, mien, and dress,
And all the strife of singularity,   580
Lies to the ear, and lies to every sense –
Of these, and of the living shapes they wear,
There is no end. Such candidates for regard,
Although well pleased to be where they were found,
I did not hunt after, or greatly prize,   585
Nor made unto myself a secret boast
580   Of reading them with quick and curious eye;
But, as a common produce, things that are
To-day, to-morrow will be, took of them
Such willing note, as, on some errand bound   590
Of pleasure or of love, some traveller might,
Among a thousand other images,
Of sea-shells that bestud the sandy beach,
Or daisies swarming through the fields in June.

But foolishness and madness in parade,
Though most at home in this their dear domain,   595
590   Are scattered everywhere, no rarities,
Even to the rudest novice of the Schools.   597

Leaving a thousand others, that, in hall,
Court, theatre, conventicle, or shop,
In public room or private, park or street,
Each fondly reared on his own pedestal,
Looked out for admiration. Folly, vice,
Extravagance in gesture, mien, and dress,
580 And all the strife of singularity,
Lies to the ear, and lies to every sense –
Of these, and of the living shapes they wear,
There is no end. Such candidates for regard,
Although well pleased to be where they were found,
I did not hunt after, nor greatly prize,
Nor made unto myself a secret boast
Of reading them with quick and curious eye;
But, as a common produce, things that are
To-day, to-morrow will be, took of them
590 Such willing note, as, on some errand bound
That asks not speed, a traveller might bestow
On sea-shells that bestrew the sandy beach,
Or daisies swarming through the fields of June.

    But foolishness and madness in parade,
Though most at home in this their dear domain,
Are scattered everywhere, no rarities,
Even to the rudest novice of the Schools.
Me, rather, it employed, to note, and keep
In memory, those individual sights
600 Of courage, or integrity, or truth,
Or tenderness, which there, set off by foil,
Appeared more touching. One will I select;
A Father – for he bore that sacred name –
Him saw I, sitting in an open square,
Upon a corner-stone of that low wall,
Wherein were fixed the iron pales that fenced
A spacious grass-plot; there, in silence, sate
This One Man, with a sickly babe outstretched
Upon his knee, whom he had thither brought
610 For sunshine, and to breathe the fresher air.

O Friend! one feeling was there which belonged
To this great city, by exclusive right;
How often, in the overflowing streets,   *626*
Have I gone forwards with the crowd, and said
Unto myself, 'The face of every one
That passes by me is a mystery!'
Thus have I looked, nor ceased to look, oppressed   *630*
By thoughts of what and whither, when and how,
600   Until the shapes before my eyes became
A second-sight procession, such as glides
Over still mountains, or appears in dreams;
And all the ballast of familiar life,
The present, and the past; hope, fear; all stays,
All laws of acting, thinking, speaking man
Went from me, neither knowing me, nor known.
And once, far-travelled in such mood, beyond   *635*
The reach of common indications, lost
Amid the moving pageant, 'twas my chance
610   Abruptly to be smitten with the view
Of a blind Beggar, who, with upright face,
Stood, propped against a wall, upon his chest   *640*
Wearing a written paper, to explain
The story of the man, and who he was.
My mind did at this spectacle turn round
As with the might of waters, and it seemed
To me that in this label was a type,
Or emblem, of the utmost that we know,   *645*
Both of ourselves and of the universe;
620   And, on the shape of the unmoving man,

Of those who passed, and me who looked at him,
He took no heed; but in his brawny arms
(The Artificer was to the elbow bare,
And from his work this moment had been stolen)
He held the child, and, bending over it,
As if he were afraid both of the sun
And of the air, which he had come to seek,
Eyed the poor babe with love unutterable.

As the black storm upon the mountain top
620   Sets off the sunbeam in the valley, so
That huge fermenting mass of humankind
Serves as a solemn background, or relief,
To single forms and objects, whence they draw,
For feeling and contemplative regard,
More than inherent liveliness and power.
How oft, amid those overflowing streets,
Have I gone forward with the crowd, and said
Unto myself, 'The face of every one
That passes by me is a mystery!'
630   Thus have I looked, nor ceased to look, oppressed
By thoughts of what and whither, when and how,
Until the shapes before my eyes became
A second-sight procession, such as glides
Over still mountains, or appears in dreams;
And once, far-travelled in such mood, beyond
The reach of common indication, lost
Amid the moving pageant, I was smitten
Abruptly, with the view (a sight not rare)
Of a blind Beggar, who, with upright face,
640   Stood, propped against a wall, upon his chest
Wearing a written paper, to explain
His story, whence he came, and who he was.
Caught by the spectacle my mind turned round
As with the might of waters; an apt type
This label seemed of the utmost we can know,
Both of ourselves and of the universe;
And, on the shape of that unmoving man,

His fixèd face and sightless eyes, I looked,
As if admonished from another world.

    Though reared upon the base of outward things,   *650*
These, chiefly, are such structures as the mind
Builds for itself; scenes different there are,
Full-formed, which take, with small internal help,
Possession of the faculties, – the peace
Of night, for instance, the solemnity   *655*
Of nature's intermediate hours of rest,
When the great tide of human life stands still;
The business of the day to come, unborn,
Of that gone by, locked up, as in the grave;
The calmness, beauty, of the spectacle,   *660*
Sky, stillness, moonshine, empty streets, and sounds
Unfrequent as in deserts; at late hours
Of winter evenings, when unwholesome rains
Are falling hard, with people yet astir,
The feeble salutation from the voice   *665*
Of some unhappy woman, now and then
Heard as we pass, when no one looks about,
Nothing is listened to. But these, I fear,
Are falsely catalogued; things that are, are not,
Even as we give them welcome, or assist,   *670*
Are prompt, or are remiss. What say you, then,
To times, when half the city shall break out
Full of one passion, vengeance, rage, or fear?
To executions, to a street on fire,
Mobs, riots, or rejoicings? From those sights   *675*
Take one, – an annual festival, the Fair
Holden where martyrs suffered in past time,
And named of St Bartholomew; there, see
A work that's finished to our hands, that lays,
If any spectacle on earth can do,   *680*
The whole creative powers of man asleep! –
For once, the Muse's help will we implore,
And she shall lodge us, wafted on her wings,
Above the press and danger of the crowd,

His steadfast face and sightless eyes, I gazed,
As if admonished from another world.

650   Though reared upon the base of outward things,
Structures like these the excited spirit mainly
Builds for herself; scenes different there are,
Full-formed, that take, with small internal help,
Possession of the faculties, – the peace
That comes with night; the deep solemnity
Of nature's intermediate hours of rest,
When the great tide of human life stands still;
The business of the day to come, unborn,
Of that gone by, locked up, as in the grave;
660 The blended calmness of the heavens and earth,
Moonlight and stars, and empty streets, and sounds
Unfrequent as in deserts; at late hours
Of winter evenings, when unwholesome rains
Are falling hard, with people yet astir,
The feeble salutation from the voice
Of some unhappy woman, now and then
Heard as we pass, when no one looks about,
Nothing is listened to. But these, I fear,
Are falsely catalogued; things that are, are not,
670 As the mind answers to them, or the heart
Is prompt, or slow, to feel. What say you, then,
To times, when half the city shall break out
Full of one passion, vengeance, rage or fear?
To executions, to a street on fire,
Mobs, riots, or rejoicings! From those sights
Take one, – that ancient festival, the Fair,
Holden where martyrs suffered in past time,
And named of St Bartholomew; there, see
A work completed to our hands, that lays,
680 If any spectacle on earth can do,
The whole creative powers of man asleep! –
For once, the Muse's help will we implore,
And she shall lodge us, wafted on her wings,
Above the press and danger of the crowd,

Upon some showman's platform. What a hell   685
For eyes and ears! what anarchy and din
660 Barbarian and infernal, – 'tis a dream,
Monstrous in colour, motion, shape, sight, sound!
Below, the open space, through every nook
Of the wide area, twinkles, is alive   690
With heads; the midway region, and above,
Is thronged with staring pictures and huge scrolls,
Dumb proclamations of the Prodigies;
And chattering monkeys dangling from their poles,
And children whirling in their roundabouts;   695
With those that stretch the neck and strain the eyes,
670 And crack the voice in rivalship, the crowd
Inviting; with buffoons against buffoons
Grimacing, writhing, screaming, – him who grinds
The hurdy-gurdy, at the fiddle weaves,   700
Rattles the salt-box, thumps the kettle-drum,
And him who at the trumpet puffs his cheeks,
The silver-collared Negro with his timbrel,
Equestrians, tumblers, women, girls, and boys,
Blue-breeched, pink-vested, and with towering plumes. –
All moveables of wonder, from all parts,   706
680 Are here – Albinos, painted Indians, Dwarfs,
The Horse of knowledge, and the learned Pig,
The Stone-eater, the man that swallows fire,
Giants, Ventriloquists, the Invisible Girl,   710
The Bust that speaks and moves its goggling eyes,
The Wax-work, Clock-work, all the marvellous craft
Of modern Merlins, Wild Beasts, Puppet-shows,
All out-o'-the-way, far-fetched, perverted things,
All freaks of nature, all Promethean thoughts   715
Of man, his dulness, madness, and their feats
690 All jumbled up together to make up
This Parliament of Monsters. Tents and Booths
Meanwhile, as if the whole were one vast mill,
Are vomiting, receiving, on all sides,   720
Men, Women, three-years' Children, Babes in arms.

Upon some showman's platform. What a shock
For eyes and ears! what anarchy and din,
Barbarian and infernal, – a phantasma,
Monstrous in colour, motion, shape, sight, sound!
Below, the open space, through every nook
690 Of the wide area, twinkles, is alive
With heads; the midway region, and above,
Is thronged with staring pictures and huge scrolls,
Dumb proclamations of the Prodigies;
With chattering monkeys dangling from their poles,
And children whirling in their roundabouts;
With those that stretch the neck and strain the eyes,
And crack the voice in rivalship, the crowd
Inviting; with buffoons against buffoons
Grimacing, writhing, screaming, – him who grinds
700 The hurdy-gurdy, at the fiddle weaves,
Rattles the salt-box, thumps the kettle-drum,
And him who at the trumpet puffs his cheeks,
The silver-collared Negro with his timbrel,
Equestrians, tumblers, women, girls, and boys,
Blue-breeched, pink-vested, with high-towering plumes. –
All moveables of wonder, from all parts,
Are here – Albinos, painted Indians, Dwarfs,
The Horse of knowledge, and the learned Pig,
The Stone-eater, the man that swallows fire,
710 Giants, Ventriloquists, the Invisible Girl,
The Bust that speaks and moves its goggling eyes,
The Wax-work, Clock-work, all the marvellous craft
Of modern Merlins, Wild Beasts, Puppet-shows,
All out-o'-the-way, far-fetched, perverted things,
All freaks of nature, all Promethean thoughts
Of man, his dulness, madness, and their feats
All jumbled up together, to compose
A Parliament of Monsters. Tents and Booths
Meanwhile, as if the whole were one vast mill,
720 Are vomiting, receiving, on all sides,
Men, Women, three-years' Children, Babes in arms.

     Oh, blank confusion! and a type not false
Of what the mighty City is itself
To all except a straggler here and there,
To the whole swarm of its inhabitants;
An undistinguishable world to men,
700 The slaves unrespited of low pursuits,
Living amid the same perpetual flow   725
Of trivial objects, melted and reduced
To one identity, by differences
That have no law, no meaning, and no end –
Oppression, under which even highest minds
Must labour, whence the strongest are not free. 730
But though the picture weary out the eye,
By nature an unmanageable sight,
It is not wholly so to him who looks
710 In steadiness, who hath among least things
An under-sense of greatest; sees the parts   735
As parts, but with a feeling of the whole.
This, of all acquisitions first, awaits
On sundry and most widely different modes
Of education, nor with least delight
On that through which I passed. Attention comes, 740
And comprehensiveness and memory,
From early converse with the works of God
Among all regions; chiefly where appear
720 Most obviously simplicity and power.   744
By influence habitual to the mind
The mountain's outline and its steady form
Gives a pure grandeur, and its presence shapes
The measure and the prospect of the soul   755
To majesty. Such virtue have the forms
Perennial of the ancient hills; nor less
The changeful language of their countenances
Gives movement to the thoughts, and multitude,

Oh, blank confusion! true epitome
Of what the mighty City is herself
To thousands upon thousands of her sons,
Living amid the same perpetual whirl
Of trivial objects, melted and reduced
To one identity, by differences
That have no law, no meaning, and no end –
Oppression, under which even highest minds
730   Must labour, whence the strongest are not free.
But though the picture weary out the eye,
By nature an unmanageable sight,
It is not wholly so to him who looks
In steadiness, who hath among least things
An under-sense of greatest; sees the parts
As parts, but with a feeling of the whole.
This, of all acquisitions first, awaits
On sundry and most widely different modes
Of education, nor with least delight
740   On that through which I passed. Attention springs,
And comprehensiveness and memory flow,
From early converse with the works of God
Among all regions; chiefly where appear
Most obviously simplicity and power.
Think, how the everlasting streams and woods,
Stretched and still stretching far and wide, exalt
The roving Indian. On his desert sands
What grandeur not unfelt, what pregnant show
Of beauty, meets the sun-burnt Arab's eye:
750   And, as the sea propels, from zone to zone,
Its currents; magnifies its shoals of life
Beyond all compass; spreads, and sends aloft
Armies of clouds, – even so, its powers and aspects
Shape for mankind, by principles as fixed,
The views and aspirations of the soul
To majesty. Like virtue have the forms
Perennial of the ancient hills; nor less
The changeful language of their countenances
Quickens the slumbering mind, and aids the thoughts,

With order and relation. This, if still,   *761*
730 As hitherto, with freedom I may speak,
And the same perfect openness of mind,
Not violating any just restraint,
As I would hope, of real modesty, –
This did I feel, in that vast receptacle.   *765*
The Spirit of Nature was upon me here;
The soul of Beauty and enduring Life
Was present as a habit, and diffused,
Through meagre lines and colours, and the press
Of self-destroying, transitory things,   *770*
740 Composure, and ennobling Harmony.

760   However multitudinous, to move
      With order and relation. This, if still,
      As hitherto, in freedom I may speak,
      Not violating any just restraint,
      As may be hoped, of real modesty, –
      This did I feel, in London's vast domain.
      The Spirit of Nature was upon me there;
      The soul of Beauty and enduring Life
      Vouchsafed her inspiration, and diffused,
      Through meagre lines and colours, and the press
770   Of self-destroying, transitory things,
      Composure, and ennobling Harmony.

Book Eighth

RETROSPECT LOVE OF NATURE LEADING TO
LOVE OF MANKIND

What sounds are those, Helvellyn, which are heard
Up to thy summit, through the depth of air
Ascending, as if distance had the power
To make the sounds more audible? What crowd
Is yon, assembled in the gay green field?   5
Crowd seems it, solitary hill! to thee,
Though but a little family of men,
Twice twenty, with their children and their wives,
And here and there a stranger interspersed.   10
10   It is a summer festival – a fair,
Such as, on this side now, and now on that,
Repeated through his tributary vales,
Helvellyn, in the silence of his rest,
Sees annually, if storms be not abroad,   15
And mists have left him an unshrouded head.
Delightful day it is for all who dwell
In this secluded glen, and eagerly
They give it welcome. Long ere heat of noon,   20
Behold the cattle are driven down; the sheep
20   That have for traffic been culled out are penned
In cotes that stand together on the plain
Ranged side by side; the chaffering is begun.
The heifer lows, uneasy at the voice
Of a new master; bleat the flocks aloud.
Booths are there none; a stall or two is here;   25
A lame man or a blind, the one to beg,
The other to make music; hither, too,
From far, with basket, slung upon her arm,
Of hawker's wares – books, pictures, combs, and pins –
30   Some aged woman finds her way again,   30

Book Eighth

RETROSPECT LOVE OF NATURE LEADING TO
LOVE OF MANKIND

What sounds are those, Helvellyn, that are heard
Up to thy summit, through the depth of air
Ascending, as if distance had the power
To make the sounds more audible? What crowd
Covers, or sprinkles o'er, yon village green?
Crowd seems it, solitary hill! to thee,
Though but a little family of men,
Shepherds and tillers of the ground – betimes
Assembled with their children and their wives,
10 And here and there a stranger interspersed.
They hold a rustic fair – a festival,
Such as, on this side now, and now on that,
Repeated through his tributary vales,
Helvellyn, in the silence of his rest,
Sees annually, if clouds towards either ocean
Blown from their favourite resting-place, or mists
Dissolved, have left him an unshrouded head.
Delightful day it is for all who dwell
In this secluded glen, and eagerly
20 They give it welcome. Long ere heat of noon,
From byre or field the kine were brought; the sheep
Are penned in cotes; the chaffering is begun.
The heifer lows, uneasy at the voice
Of a new master; bleat the flocks aloud.
Booths are there none; a stall or two is here;
A lame man or a blind, the one to beg,
The other to make music; hither, too,
From far, with basket, slung upon her arm,
Of hawker's wares – books, pictures, combs, and pins –
30 Some aged woman finds her way again,

297

Year after year a punctual visitant!
The showman with his freight upon his back,
And once, perchance, in lapse of many years
Prouder itinerant, mountebank, or he   35
Whose wonders in a covered wain lie hid.
But one is here, the loveliest of them all,
Some sweet lass of the valley, looking out
For gains, and who that sees her would not buy?
Fruits of her father's orchard, apples, pears,   40
(On that day only to such office stooping)
She carries in her basket, and walks round
Among the crowd, half pleased with, half ashamed
Of her new calling, blushing restlessly.
The children now are rich, the old man now
Is generous; so gaiety prevails   45
Which all partake of, young and old. – Immense   55
Is the recess, the circumambient world
Magnificent, by which they are embraced:
They move about upon the soft green field:
How little they, they and their doings, seem,
Their herds and flocks about them, they themselves,
And all which they can further or obstruct!   60
Through utter weakness pitiably dear
As tender infants are: and yet how great!
For all things serve them: them the morning light
Loves, as it glistens on the silent rocks;
And them the silent rocks, which now from high   65
Look down upon them; the reposing clouds,
The lurking brooks from their invisible haunts;
And old Helvellyn, conscious of the stir,

Year after year a punctual visitant!
There also stands a speech-maker by rote,
Pulling the strings of his boxed raree-show;
And in the lapse of many years may come
Prouder itinerant, mountebank, or he
Whose wonders in a covered wain lie hid.
But one there is, the loveliest of them all,
Some sweet lass of the valley, looking out
For gains, and who that sees her would not buy?
40   Fruits of her father's orchard, are her wares,
And with the ruddy produce, she walks round
Among the crowd, half pleased with, half ashamed
Of her new office, blushing restlessly.
The children now are rich, for the old to-day
Are generous as the young; and if content
With looking on, some ancient wedded pair
Sit in the shade together, while they gaze,
'A cheerful smile unbends the wrinkled brow,
The days departed start again to life,
50   And all the scenes of childhood reappear,
Faint, but more tranquil, like the changing sun
To him who slept at noon and wakes at eve.'
Thus gaiety and cheerfulness prevail,
Spreading from young to old, from old to young,
And no one seems to want his share. – Immense
Is the recess, the circumambient world
Magnificent, by which they are embraced:
They move about upon the soft green turf:
How little they, they and their doings, seem,
60   And all that they can further or obstruct!
Through utter weakness pitiably dear,
As tender infants are: and yet how great!
For all things serve them: them the morning light
Loves, as it glistens on the silent rocks;
And them the silent rocks, which now from high
Look down upon them; the reposing clouds;
The wild brooks prattling from invisible haunts;
And old Helvellyn, conscious of the stir

And the blue sky that roofs their calm abode.

With deep devotion, Nature, did I feel,   *70*
In that great City, what I owed to thee,
High thoughts of God and Man, and love of Man,
Triumphant over all those loathsome sights
Of wretchedness and vice; a watchful eye,
Which with the outside of our human life
Not satisfied, must read the inner mind;
For I already had been taught to love
70   My fellow-beings, to such habits trained
Among the woods and mountains, where I found
In thee a gracious guide, to lead me forth
Beyond the bosom of my family,
My friends and youthful playmates. 'Twas thy power
That raised the first complacency in me,
And noticeable kindliness of heart,   *124*
Love human to the creature in himself
As he appeared, a stranger in my path,
Before my eyes a brother of this world;
80   Thou first didst with those motions of delight
Inspire me. – I remember, far from home
Once having strayed, while yet a very child,
I saw a sight, and with what joy and love!
It was a day of exhalations, spread
Upon the mountains, mists and steam-like fogs
Redounding everywhere, not vehement,
But calm and mild, gentle and beautiful,
With gleams of sunshine on the eyelet spots
And loop-holes of the hills, wherever seen,
90   Hidden by quiet process, and as soon
Unfolded, to be huddled up again:
Along a narrow valley and profound
I journeyed, when, aloft above my head,
Emerging from the silvery vapours, lo!
A shepherd and his dog! in open day:
Girt round with mists they stood and looked about
From that enclosure small, inhabitants

Which animates this day their calm abode.

70   With deep devotion, Nature, did I feel,
In that enormous City's turbulent world
Of men and things, what benefit I owed
To thee, and those domains of rural peace,

Of an aerial island floating on,
As seemed, with that abode in which they were,
100 A little pendant area of grey rocks,
By the soft wind breathed forward. With delight
As bland almost, one evening I beheld,
And at as early age (the spectacle
Is common, but by me was then first seen)
A shepherd in the bottom of a vale
Towards the centre standing, who with voice,
And hand waved to and fro as need required,
Gave signal to his dog, thus teaching him
To chase along the mazes of steep crags
110 The flock he could not see: and so the brute,
Dear creature! with a man's intelligence
Advancing, or retreating on his steps,
Through every pervious strait, to right or left,
Thridded a way unbaffled; while the flock
Fled upwards from the terror of his bark
Through rocks and seams of turf with liquid gold
Irradiate, that deep farewell light by which
The setting sun proclaims the love he bears
To mountain regions.
                              Beauteous the domain
120 Where to the sense of beauty first my heart   75
Was opened, tract more exquisitely fair
Than is that paradise of ten thousand trees,
Or Gehol's famous gardens, in a clime
Chosen from widest empire, for delight
Of the Tartarian dynasty composed
(Beyond that mighty wall, not fabulous,
China's stupendous mound) by patient skill   80
Of myriads and boon Nature's lavish help;
Scene linked to scene, and evergrowing change,
130 Soft, grand, or gay! with palaces and domes
Of pleasure spangled over, shady dells   85
For eastern monasteries, sunny mounds
With temples crested, bridges, gondolas,
Rocks, dens, and groves of foliage taught to melt

Where to the sense of beauty first my heart
Was opened; tract more exquisitely fair
Than that famed paradise of ten thousand trees,
Or Gehol's matchless gardens, for delight
Of the Tartarian dynasty composed
(Beyond that mighty wall, not fabulous,
80 China's stupendous mound) by patient toil
Of myriads and boon Nature's lavish help;
There, in a clime from widest empire chosen,
Fulfilling (could enchantment have done more?)
A sumptuous dream of flowery lawns, with domes
Of pleasure sprinkled over, shady dells
For eastern monasteries, sunny mounts
With temples crested, bridges, gondolas,
Rocks, dens, and groves of foliage taught to melt

Into each other their obsequious hues,
Going and gone again, in subtle chase,   90
Too fine to be pursued; or standing forth
In no discordant opposition, strong
And gorgeous as the colours side by side
140 Bedded among rich plumes of tropic birds;
And mountains over all, embracing all;   95
And all the landscape endlessly enriched
With waters running, falling, or asleep.

But lovelier far than this, the paradise
Where I was reared; in Nature's primitive gifts
Favoured no less, and more to every sense   100
Delicious, seeing that the sun and sky,
The elements, and seasons in their change,
Do find their dearest fellow-labourer there –
150 The heart of man, a district on all sides
The fragrance breathing of humanity,
Man free, man working for himself, with choice
Of time, and place, and object; by his wants,   105
His comforts, native occupations, cares,
Conducted on to individual ends
Or social, and still followed by a train
Unwooed, unthought-of even – simplicity,
And beauty, and inevitable grace.   110

Yea, doubtless, at an age when but a glimpse
160 Of those resplendent gardens, with their frame
Imperial, and elaborate ornaments,
Would to a child be transport over-great,
When but a half-hour's roam through such a place
Would leave behind a dance of images,
That shall break in upon his sleep for weeks;   115
Even then the common haunts of the green earth,
With the ordinary human interests
Which they embosom, all without regard
As both may seem, are fastening on the heart
170 Insensibly, each with the other's help,   120

Into each other their obsequious hues,
90 Vanished and vanishing in subtle chase,
Too fine to be pursued; or standing forth
In no discordant opposition, strong
And gorgeous as the colours side by side
Bedded among rich plumes of tropic birds;
And mountains over all, embracing all;
And all the landscape endlessly enriched
With waters running, falling, or asleep.

But lovelier far than this, the paradise
Where I was reared; in Nature's primitive gifts
100 Favoured no less, and more to every sense
Delicious, seeing that the sun and sky,
The elements, and seasons as they change,
Do find a worthy fellow-labourer there –
Man free, man working for himself, with choice
Of time, and place, and object; by his wants,
His comforts, native occupations, cares,
Cheerfully led to individual ends
Or social, and still followed by a train
Unwooed, unthought-of even – simplicity,
110 And beauty, and inevitable grace.

Yea, when a glimpse of those imperial bowers
Would to a child be transport over-great,
When but a half-hour's roam through such a place
Would leave behind a dance of images,
That shall break in upon his sleep for weeks;
Even then the common haunts of the green earth,
And ordinary interests of man,
Which they embosom, all without regard
As both may seem, are fastening on the heart
120 Insensibly, each with the other's help.

So that we love, not knowing that we love,
And feel, not knowing whence our feeling comes.

    Such league have these two principles of joy
In our affections. I have singled out
Some moments, the earliest that I could, in which
Their several currents blended into one,
Weak yet, and gathering imperceptibly,
Flowed in by gushes. My first human love,
As hath been mentioned, did incline to those
180 Whose occupations and concerns were most
Illustrated by Nature and adorned,   *127*
And Shepherds were the men who pleased me first;
Not such as in Arcadian fastnesses
Sequestered, handed down among themselves,
So ancient poets sing, the golden age;
Nor such, a second race, allied to these,
As Shakespeare in the wood of Arden placed
Where Phoebe sighed for the false Ganymede,   *141*
Or there where Florizel and Perdita
190 Together danced, Queen of the feast, and King;
Nor such as Spenser fabled. True it is,
That I had heard (what he perhaps had seen)   *145*
Of maids at sunrise bringing in from far
Their May-bush, and along the streets in flocks
Parading with a song of taunting rhymes,
Aimed at the laggards slumbering within doors;
Had also heard, from those who yet remembered,   *150*
Tales of the May-pole dance, and flowers that decked
The posts and the kirk-pillars; and of youths,
200 That each one with his maid, at break of day,
By annual custom issued forth in troops,
To drink the waters of some favourite well,
And hang it round with garlands. This, alas!
Was but a dream; the times had scattered all

For me, when my affections first were led
From kindred, friends, and playmates, to partake
Love for the human creature's absolute self,
That noticeable kindliness of heart
Sprang out of fountains, there abounding most
Where sovereign Nature dictated the tasks
And occupations which her beauty adorned,
And Shepherds were the men that pleased me first;
Not such as Saturn ruled 'mid Latian wilds,
130 With arts and laws so tempered, that their lives
Left, even to us toiling in this late day,
A bright tradition of the golden age;
Not such as, 'mid Arcadian fastnesses
Sequestered, handed down among themselves
Felicity, in Grecian song renowned;
Nor such as, when an adverse fate had driven,
From house and home, the courtly band whose fortunes
Entered, with Shakespeare's genius, the wild woods
Of Arden, amid sunshine or in shade
140 Culled the best fruits of Time's uncounted hours,
Ere Phoebe sighed for the false Ganymede;
Or there where Perdita and Florizel
Together danced, Queen of the feast, and King;
Nor such as Spenser fabled. True it is,
That I had heard (what he perhaps had seen)
Of maids at sunrise bringing in from far
Their May-bush, and along the street in flocks
Parading with a song of taunting rhymes,
Aimed at the laggards slumbering within doors;
150 Had also heard, from those who yet remembered,
Tales of the May-pole dance, and wreaths that decked
Porch, door-way, or kirk-pillar; and of youths,
Each with his maid, before the sun was up,
By annual custom, issuing forth in troops,
To drink the waters of some sainted well,
And hang it round with garlands. Love survives;
But for such purpose, flowers no longer grow:
The times, too sage, perhaps too proud, have dropped

These lighter graces, and the rural custom
And manners which it was my chance to see   160
In childhood were severe and unadorned,
The unluxuriant produce of a life
Intent on little but substantial needs,
210 Yet beautiful, and beauty that was felt.
But images of danger and distress,
And suffering, these took deepest hold of me,
Man suffering among awful Powers and Forms;   165
Of this I heard, and saw enough to make
The imagination restless; nor was free
Myself from frequent perils; nor were tales
Wanting, – the tragedies of former times,
Or hazards and escapes, which in my walks   170
I carried with me among crags and woods
220 And mountains; and of these may here be told
One, as recorded by my household Dame.

     At the first falling of autumnal snow
A shepherd and his son one day went forth
(Thus did the Matron's tale begin) to seek
A straggler of their flock. They both had ranged
Upon this service the preceding day
All over their own pastures and beyond,
And now at sunrise sallying out again
Renewed their search begun where from Dove Crag,
230 Ill home for bird so gentle, they looked down
On Deep-dale Head, and Brothers-water, named
From those two brothers that were drowned therein.
Thence, northward, having passed by Arthur's Seat,
To Fairfield's highest summit; on the right
Leaving St Sunday's Pike, to Grisedale Tarn
They shot, and over that cloud-loving hill,
Seat Sandal, a fond lover of the clouds;
Thence up Helvellyn, a superior mount
With prospect underneath of Striding-Edge,
240 And Grisedale's houseless vale, along the brink
Of Russet Cove, and those two other coves,

These lighter graces; and the rural ways
160 And manners which my childhood looked upon
Were the unluxuriant produce of a life
Intent on little but substantial needs,
Yet rich in beauty, beauty that was felt.
But images of danger and distress,
Man suffering among awful Powers and Forms;
Of this I heard, and saw enough to make
Imagination restless; nor was free
Myself from frequent perils; nor were tales
Wanting, – the tragedies of former times,
170 Hazards and strange escapes, of which the rocks
Immutable, and everflowing streams,
Where'er I roamed, were speaking monuments.

Huge skeletons of crags, which from the trunk
Of old Helvellyn spread their arms abroad,
And make a stormy harbour for the winds.
Far went those shepherds in their devious quest,
From mountain ridges peeping as they passed
Down into every glen: at length the boy
Said, 'Father, with your leave I will go back,
And range the ground which we have searched before.'
250 So speaking, southward down the hill the lad
Sprang like a gust of wind, crying aloud
'I know where I shall find him.' 'For take note,'
Said here my grey-haired Dame, 'that though the storm
Drive one of these poor creatures miles and miles,
If he can crawl he will return again
To his own hills, the spots where, when a lamb,
He learnt to pasture at his mother's side.'
After so long a labour, suddenly
Bethinking him of this, the boy
260 Pursued his way towards a brook whose course
Was through that unfenced tract of mountain-ground
Which to his father's little farm belonged,
The home and ancient birth-right of their flock.
Down the deep channel of the stream he went,
Prying through every nook; meanwhile the rain
Began to fall upon the mountain tops,
Thick storm and heavy which for three hours' space
Abated not; and all that time the boy
Was busy in his search until at length
270 He spied the sheep upon a plot of grass,
An island in the brook. It was a place
Remote and deep, piled round with rocks where foot
Of man or beast was seldom used to tread;
But now, when everywhere the summer grass
Had failed, this one adventurer, hunger-pressed,
Had left his fellows, and made his way alone
To the green plot of pasture in the brook.
Before the boy knew well what he had seen
He leapt upon the island with proud heart

280 And with a prophet's joy. Immediately
     The sheep sprang forward to the further shore
     And was borne headlong by the roaring flood.
     At this the boy looked round him, and his heart
     Fainted with fear; thrice did he turn his face
     To either brink; nor could he summon up
     The courage that was needful to leap back
     Cross the tempestuous torrent; so he stood,
     A prisoner on the island, not without
     More than one thought of death and his last hour.
290 Meanwhile the father had returned alone
     To his own house; and now at the approach
     Of evening he went forth to meet his son,
     Conjecturing vainly for what cause the boy
     Had stayed so long. The shepherd took his way
     Up his own mountain grounds, where, as he walked
     Along the steep that overhung the brook,
     He seemed to hear a voice, which was again
     Repeated, like the whistling of a kite.
     At this, not knowing why, as oftentimes
300 Long afterwards he has been heard to say,
     Down to the brook he went, and tracked its course
     Upwards among the o'erhanging rocks; nor thus
     Had he gone far, ere he espied the boy
     Where on that little plot of ground he stood
     Right in the middle of the roaring stream,
     Now stronger every moment and more fierce.
     The sight was such as no one could have seen
     Without distress and fear. The shepherd heard
     The outcry of his son, he stretched his staff
310 Towards him, bade him leap, which word scarce said,
     The boy was safe within his father's arms.

     Smooth life had flock and shepherd in old time,
     Long springs and tepid winters, on the banks
     Of delicate Galesus; and no less   175
     Those scattered along Adria's myrtle shores:
     Smooth life the herdsman, and his snow-white herd

312

Smooth life had flock and shepherd in old time,
Long springs and tepid winters, on the banks
Of delicate Galesus; and no less
Those scattered along Adria's myrtle shores:
Smooth life had herdsman, and his snow-white herd

To triumphs and to sacrificial rites
Devoted, on the inviolable stream
Of rich Clitumnus; and the goat-herd lived   *180*
320 As sweetly, underneath the pleasant brows
Of cool Lucretilis, where the pipe was heard
Of Pan, the invisible God, thrilling the rocks
With tutelary music, from all harm
The fold protecting. I myself, mature   *185*
In manhood then, have seen a pastoral tract
Like one of these, where Fancy might run wild,
Though under skies less generous and serene:
Yet there, as for herself, had Nature framed
A pleasure-ground, diffused a fair expanse   *190*
330 Of level pasture, islanded with groves
And banked with woody risings; but the Plain
Endless, here opening widely out, and there
Shut up in lesser lakes or beds of lawn
And intricate recesses, creek or bay   *195*
Sheltered within a shelter, where at large
The shepherd strays, a rolling hut his home.
Thither he comes with spring-time, there abides
All summer, and at sunrise ye may hear
His flute or flageolet resounding far.
340 There's not a nook or hold of that vast space,
Nor strait where passage is, but it shall have
In turn its visitant, telling there his hours
In unlaborious pleasure, with no task   *205*
More toilsome than to carve a beechen bowl
For spring or fountain, which the traveller finds,
When through the region he pursues at will
His devious course. A glimpse of such sweet life
I saw when, from the melancholy walls   *210*
Of Goslar, once imperial, I renewed
350 My daily walk along that cheerful plain,
Which, reaching to her gates, spreads east and west
And northwards, from beneath the mountainous verge
Of the Hercynian forest. Yet, hail to you,   *215*

To triumphs and to sacrificial rites
Devoted, on the inviolable stream
180 Of rich Clitumnus; and the goat-herd lived
As calmly, underneath the pleasant brows
Of cool Lucretilis, where the pipe was heard
Of Pan, invisible God, thrilling the rocks
With tutelary music, from all harm
The fold protecting. I myself, mature
In manhood then, have seen a pastoral tract
Like one of these, where Fancy might run wild,
Though under skies less generous, less serene:
There, for her own delight had Nature framed
190 A pleasure-ground, diffused a fair expanse
Of level pasture, islanded with groves
And banked with woody risings; but the Plain
Endless, here opening widely out, and there
Shut up in lesser lakes or beds of lawn
And intricate recesses, creek or bay
Sheltered within a shelter, where at large
The shepherd strays, a rolling hut his home.
Thither he comes with spring-time, there abides
All summer, and at sunrise ye may hear
200 His flageolet to liquid notes of love
Attuned, or sprightly fife resounding far.
Nook is there none, nor tract of that vast space
Where passage opens, but the same shall have
In turn its visitant, telling there his hours
In unlaborious pleasure, with no task
More toilsome than to carve a beechen bowl
For spring or fountain, which the traveller finds,
When through the region he pursues at will
His devious course. A glimpse of such sweet life
210 I saw when, from the melancholy walls
Of Goslar, once imperial, I renewed
My daily walk along that wide champaign,
That, reaching to her gates, spreads east and west,
And northwards, from beneath the mountainous verge
Of the Hercynian forest. Yet, hail to you

Your rocks and precipices! Ye that seize
The heart with firmer grasp! Your snows and streams
Ungovernable, and your terrifying winds,   220
That howled so dismally when I have been
Companionless among your solitudes!
There, 'tis the shepherd's task the winter long
360 To wait upon the storms: of their approach   225
Sagacious, from the height he drives his flock
Down into sheltering coves, and feeds them there
Through the hard time, long as the storm is locked,
(So do they phrase it) bearing from the stalls
A toilsome burden up the craggy ways,
To strew it on the snow. And when the spring
Looks out, and all the mountains dance with lambs,   230
He through the enclosures won from the steep waste,
And through the lower heights hath gone his rounds;
370 And when the flock, with warmer weather, climbs
Higher and higher, him his office leads
To range among them, through the hills dispersed,
And watch their goings, whatsoever track
Each wanderer chooses for itself; a work
That lasts the summer through. He quits his home
At day-spring, and no sooner doth the sun   235
Begin to strike him with a fire-like heat,
Than he lies down upon some shining place,
And breakfasts with his dog. When he hath stayed,
380 As for the most he doth, beyond his time,   239
He springs up with a bound, and then away!
Ascending fast with his long pole in hand,
Or winding in and out among the crags.
What need to follow him through what he does   250
Or sees in his day's march? He feels himself,
In those vast regions where his service is,
A freeman, wedded to his life of hope

Moors, mountains, headlands, and ye hollow vales,
Ye long deep channels for the Atlantic's voice,
Powers of my native region! Ye that seize
The heart with firmer grasp! Your snows and streams
220 Ungovernable, and your terrifying winds,
That howl so dismally for him who treads
Companionless your awful solitudes!
There, 'tis the shepherd's task the winter long
To wait upon the storms: of their approach
Sagacious, into sheltering coves he drives
His flock, and thither from the homestead bears
A toilsome burden up the craggy ways,
And deals it out, their regular nourishment
Strewn on the frozen snow. And when the spring
230 Looks out, and all the pastures dance with lambs,
And when the flock, with warmer weather, climbs
Higher and higher, him his office leads
To watch their goings, whatsoever track
The wanderers choose. For this he quits his home
At day-spring, and no sooner doth the sun
Begin to strike him with a fire-like heat,
Than he lies down upon some shining rock,
And breakfasts with his dog. When they have stolen,
As is their wont, a pittance from strict time,
240 For rest not needed or exchange of love,
Then from his couch he starts; and now his feet
Crush out a livelier fragrance from the flowers
Of lowly thyme, by Nature's skill enwrought
In the wild turf: the lingering dews of morn
Smoke round him, as from hill to hill he hies,
His staff portending like a hunter's spear,
Or by its aid leaping from crag to crag,
And o'er the brawling beds of unbridged streams.
Philosophy, methinks, at Fancy's call,
250 Might deign to follow him through what he does
Or sees in his day's march; himself he feels,
In those vast regions where his service lies,
A freeman, wedded to his life of hope

And hazard, and hard labour interchanged
With that majestic indolence so dear   255
390 To native man. A rambling schoolboy, thus
Have I beheld him, without knowing why
Having felt his presence in his own domain,
As of a lord and master, or a power,
Or genius, under Nature, under God,
Presiding; and severest solitude   260
Seemed more commanding oft when he was there.
Seeking the raven's nest, and suddenly
Surprised with vapours, or on rainy days
When I have angled up the lonely brooks,
400 Mine eyes have glanced upon him few steps off,   265
In size a giant, stalking through the fog,
His sheep like Greenland bears; at other times
When round some shady promontory turning,
His form hath flashed upon me, glorified
By the deep radiance of the setting sun: 270
Or him have I descried in distant sky,
A solitary object and sublime,
Above all height! like an aerial cross,
As it is stationed on some spiry rock
410 Of the Chartreuse, for worship. Thus was man   275
Ennobled outwardly before mine eyes,
And thus my heart at first was introduced
To an unconscious love and reverence
Of human nature; hence the human form
To me was like an index of delight,   280
Of grace and honour, power and worthiness.
Meanwhile this creature – spiritual almost
As those of books, but more exalted far;
Far more of an imaginative form,
420 Was not a Corin of the groves, who lives   285
For his own fancies, or to dance by the hour,
In coronal, with Phyllis in the midst,
But, for the purposes of kind, a man
With the most common; husband, father; learned,
Could teach, admonish; suffered with the rest   290

And hazard, and hard labour interchanged
With that majestic indolence so dear
To native man. A rambling schoolboy, thus
I felt his presence in his own domain,
As of a lord and master, or a power,
Or genius, under Nature, under God,
260 Presiding; and severest solitude
Had more commanding looks when he was there.
When up the lonely brooks on rainy days
Angling I went, or trod the trackless hills
By mists bewildered, suddenly mine eyes
Have glanced upon him distant a few steps,
In size a giant, stalking through thick fog,
His sheep like Greenland bears; or, as he stepped
Beyond the boundary line of some hill-shadow,
His form hath flashed upon me, glorified
270 By the deep radiance of the setting sun:
Or him have I descried in distant sky,
A solitary object and sublime,
Above all height! like an aerial cross
Stationed alone upon a spiry rock
Of the Chartreuse, for worship. Thus was man
Ennobled outwardly before my sight,
And thus my heart was early introduced
To an unconscious love and reverence
Of human nature; hence the human form
280 To me became an index of delight,
Of grace and honour, power and worthiness.
Meanwhile this creature – spiritual almost
As those of books, but more exalted far;
Far more of an imaginative form
Than the gay Corin of the groves, who lives
For his own fancies, or to dance by the hour,
In coronal, with Phyllis in the midst –
Was, for the purposes of kind, a man
With the most common; husband, father; learned,
290 Could teach, admonish; suffered with the rest

From vice and folly, wretchedness and fear;
Of this I little saw, cared less for it,
But something must have felt.
                              Call ye these appearances –
Which I beheld of shepherds in my youth,
This sanctity of Nature given to man –   *295*
A shadow, a delusion, ye who are fed
By the dead letter, not the spirit of things;
Whose truth is not a motion or a shape
Instinct with vital functions, but a block
Or waxen image which yourselves have made,   *300*
And ye adore. But blessèd be the God
Of Nature and of Man that this was so;
That men did at the first present themselves
Before my untaught eyes thus purified,
Removed, and at a distance that was fit: *305*
And so we all of us in some degree
Are led to knowledge, whencesoever led,
And howsoever; were it otherwise,
And we found evil fast as we find good
In our first years, or think that it is found,   *310*
How could the innocent heart bear up and live!
But doubly fortunate my lot; not here
Alone, that something of a better life
Perhaps was round me than it is the privilege
Of most to move in, but that first I looked   *315*
At Man through objects that were great and fair;
First communed with him by their help. And thus
Was founded a sure safeguard and defence
Against the weight of meanness, selfish cares,
Coarse manners, vulgar passions, that beat in   *320*
On all sides from the ordinary world
In which we traffic. Starting from this point,
I had my face towards the truth, began
With an advantage; furnished with that kind
Of prepossession without which the soul   *325*
Receives no knowledge that can bring forth good,
No genuine insight ever comes to her.

From vice and folly, wretchedness and fear;
Of this I little saw, cared less for it,
But something must have felt.
                                    Call ye these appearances –
Which I beheld of shepherds in my youth,
This sanctity of Nature given to man –
A shadow, a delusion, ye who pore
On the dead letter, miss the spirit of things;
Whose truth is not a motion or a shape
Instinct with vital functions, but a block
300   Or waxen image which yourselves have made,
And ye adore! But blessèd be the God
Of Nature and of Man that this was so;
That men before my inexperienced eyes
Did first present themselves thus purified,
Removed, and to a distance that was fit:
And so we all of us in some degree
Are led to knowledge, whencesoever led,
And howsoever; were it otherwise,
And we found evil fast as we find good
310   In our first years, or think that it is found,
How could the innocent heart bear up and live!
But doubly fortunate my lot; not here
Alone, that something of a better life
Perhaps was round me than it is the privilege
Of most to move in, but that first I looked
At Man through objects that were great or fair;
First communed with him by their help. And thus
Was founded a sure safeguard and defence
Against the weight of meanness, selfish cares,
320   Coarse manners, vulgar passions, that beat in
On all sides from the ordinary world
In which we traffic. Starting from this point
I had my face turned toward the truth, began
With an advantage furnished by that kind
Of prepossession, without which the soul
Receives no knowledge that can bring forth good,
No genuine insight ever comes to her.

Happy in this, that I with nature walked,   330
Not having a too early intercourse
With the deformities of crowded life,
And those ensuing laughters and contempts,
Self-pleasing, which, if we would wish to think
With admiration and respect of man,   335
Will not permit us; but pursue the mind,
470   That to devotion willingly would be raised,
Into the temple and the temple's heart.

    Yet do not deem, my Friend! though thus I speak
Of Man as having taken in my mind   340
A place thus early which might almost seem
Pre-eminent, that it was really so.
Nature herself was, at this unripe time,
But secondary to my own pursuits
And animal activities, and all
Their trivial pleasures; and long afterwards   345
480   When these had died away, and Nature did
For her own sake become my joy, even then –
And upwards through late youth, until not less
Than three-and-twenty summers had been told –
Was Man in my affections and regards   350
Subordinate to her, her awful forms
And viewless agencies: a passion, she,
A rapture often, and immediate joy
Ever at hand; he distant, but a grace
Occasional, an accidental thought,   355
490   His hour being not yet come. Far less had then
The inferior creatures, beast or bird, attuned
My spirit to that gentleness of love,
Won from me those minute obeisances   360
Of tenderness, which I may number now
With my first blessings. Nevertheless, on these
The light of beauty did not fall in vain,
Or grandeur circumfuse them to no end.   364

From the restraint of over-watchful eyes
Preserved, I moved about, year after year,
330 Happy, and now most thankful that my walk
Was guarded from too early intercourse
With the deformities of crowded life,
And those ensuing laughters and contempts,
Self-pleasing, which, if we would wish to think
With a due reverence on earth's rightful lord,
Here placed to be the inheritor of heaven,
Will not permit us; but pursue the mind,
That to devotion willingly would rise,
Into the temple and the temple's heart.

340   Yet deem not, Friend! that human kind with me
Thus early took a place pre-eminent;
Nature herself was, at this unripe time,
But secondary to my own pursuits
And animal activities, and all
Their trivial pleasures; and when these had drooped
And gradually expired, and Nature, prized
For her own sake, became my joy, even then –
And upwards through late youth, until not less
Than two-and-twenty summers had been told –
350 Was Man in my affections and regards
Subordinate to her, her visible forms
And viewless agencies: a passion, she,
A rapture often, and immediate love
Ever at hand; he, only a delight
Occasional, an accidental grace,
His hour being not yet come. Far less had then
The inferior creatures, beast or bird, attuned
My spirit to that gentleness of love
(Though they had long been carefully observed),
360 Won from me those minute obeisances
Of tenderness, which I may number now
With my first blessings. Nevertheless, on these
The light of beauty did not fall in vain,
Or grandeur circumfuse them to no end.

Why should I speak of tillers of the soil?
The ploughman and his team; or men and boys
500 In festive summer busy with the rake,
Old men and ruddy maids, and little ones
All out together, and in sun and shade
Dispersed among the hay-grounds alder-fringed,
The quarry-man, far heard! that blasts the rock,
The fishermen in pairs, the one to row,
And one to drop the net, plying their trade
''Mid tossing lakes and tumbling boats' and winds
Whistling; the miner, melancholy man!
That works by taper light, while all the hills
510 Are shining with the glory of the day.

But when that first poetic faculty   365
Of plain Imagination and severe,
No longer a mute influence of the soul,
An element of the nature's inner self,
Began to have some promptings to put on
A visible shape, and to the works of art,
The notions and the images of books,   370
Did knowingly conform itself, by these
Enflamed, and proud of that her new delight,
520 There came among those shapes of human life
A wilfulness of fancy and conceit
Which gave them new importance to the mind:
And Nature and her objects beautified
These fictions, as in some sort, in their turn,   375
They burnished her. From touch of this new power
Nothing was safe: the elder-tree that grew
Beside the well-known charnel-house had then
A dismal look: the yew-tree had its ghost,
That took its station there for ornament: 380
530 Then common death was none, common mishap,
But matter for this humour everywhere,
The tragic super-tragic, else left short.
Then, if a widow, staggering with the blow
Of her distress, was known to have made her way   385

But when that first poetic faculty
Of plain Imagination and severe,
No longer a mute influence of the soul,
Ventured, at some rash Muse's earnest call,
To try her strength among harmonious words;
370 And to book-notions and the rules of art
Did knowingly conform itself; there came
Among the simple shapes of human life
A wilfulness of fancy and conceit:
And Nature and her objects beautified
These fictions, as in some sort, in their turn,
They burnished her. From touch of this new power
Nothing was safe: the elder-tree that grew
Beside the well-known charnel-house had then
A dismal look: the yew-tree had its ghost,
380 That took his station there for ornament:
The dignities of plain occurrence then
Were tasteless, and truth's golden mean, a point
Where no sufficient pleasure could be found.
Then, if a widow, staggering with the blow
Of her distress, was known to have turned her steps

To the cold grave in which her husband slept,
One night, or haply more than one, through pain
Or half-insensate impotence of mind,
The fact was caught at greedily, and there
She was a visitant the whole year through,   *390*
540 Wetting the turf with never-ending tears,
And all the storms of heaven must beat on her.

   Through wild obliquities could I pursue
Among all objects of the fields and groves
These cravings; when the foxglove, one by one,
Upwards through every stage of its tall stem,
Had shed its bells, and stood by the wayside   *395*
Dismantled, with a single one, perhaps,
Left at the ladder's top, with which the plant
Appeared to stoop, as slender blades of grass   *398*
550 Tipped with a bead of rain or dew, behold!
If such a sight were seen, would Fancy bring
Some vagrant thither with her babes, and seat her
Upon the turf beneath the stately flower
Drooping in sympathy, and making so
A melancholy crest above the head
Of the lorn creature, while her little ones,
All unconcerned with her unhappy plight,
Were sporting with the purple cups that lay   *405*
Scattered upon the ground.
                              There was a copse,
560 An upright bank of wood and woody rock,
That opposite our rural dwelling stood,
In which a sparkling patch of diamond light
Was in bright weather duly to be seen
On summer afternoons, within the wood
At the same place. 'Twas doubtless nothing more
Than a black rock, which, wet with constant springs,
Glistered far seen from out its lurking-place
As soon as ever the declining sun
Had smitten it. Beside our cottage hearth   *410*
570 Sitting, with open door, a hundred times

To the cold grave in which her husband slept,
One night, or haply more than one, through pain
Or half-insensate impotence of mind,
The fact was caught at greedily, and there
390 She must be visitant the whole year through,
Wetting the turf with never-ending tears.

Through quaint obliquities I might pursue
These cravings; when the foxglove, one by one,
Upwards through every stage of the tall stem,
Had shed beside the public way its bells,
And stood of all dismantled, save the last
Left at the tapering ladder's top, that seemed
To bend as doth a slender blade of grass
Tipped with a rain-drop, Fancy loved to seat,
400 Beneath the plant despoiled, but crested still
With this last relic, soon itself to fall,
Some vagrant mother, whose arch little ones,
All unconcerned by her dejected plight,
Laughed as with rival eagerness their hands
Gathered the purple cups that round them lay,
Strewing the turf's green slope.
                                          A diamond light
(Whene'er the summer sun, declining, smote
A smooth rock wet with constant springs) was seen
Sparkling from out a copse-clad bank that rose
410 Fronting our cottage. Oft beside the hearth
Seated, with open door, often and long

Upon this lustre have I gazed, that seemed
To have some meaning which I could not find;
And now it was a burnished shield, I fancied,
Suspended over a knight's tomb, who lay   *415*
Inglorious, buried in the dusky wood:
An entrance now into some magic cave
Or palace for a fairy of the rock;
Nor would I, though not certain whence the cause
Of the effulgence, thither have repaired
580   Without a precious bribe, and day by day
And month by month I saw the spectacle,
Nor ever once have visited the spot   *420*
Unto this hour. Thus sometimes were the shapes
Of wilful Fancy grafted upon feelings
Of the Imagination, and they rose
In worth accordingly. My present theme
Is to retrace the way that led me on
Through Nature to the love of human kind;
Nor could I with such object overlook
590   The influence of this Power which turned itself
Instinctively to human passions, things   *425*
Least understood; of this adulterate Power,
For so it may be called, and without wrong,
When with that first compared. Yet in the midst
Of these vagaries, with an eye so rich
As mine was through the chance on me not wasted
Of having been brought up in such a grand
And lovely region, I had forms distinct
To steady me: these thoughts did oft revolve   *430*
600   About some centre palpable, which at once
Incited them to motion, and controlled,
And whatsoever shape the fit might take,
And whencesoever it might come, I still
At all times had a real solid world
Of images about me; did not pine
As one in cities bred might do; as thou,
Belovèd Friend! hast told me that thou didst,
Great Spirit as thou art, in endless dreams   *435*

Upon this restless lustre have I gazed,
That made my fancy restless as itself.
'Twas now for me a burnished silver shield
Suspended over a knight's tomb, who lay
Inglorious, buried in the dusky wood:
An entrance now into some magic cave
Or palace built by fairies of the rock;
Nor could I have been bribed to disenchant
420   The spectacle, by visiting the spot.
Thus wilful Fancy, in no hurtful mood,
Engrafted far-fetched shapes on feelings bred
By pure Imagination: busy Power
She was, and with her ready pupil turned
Instinctively to human passions, then
Least understood. Yet, 'mid the fervent swarm
Of these vagaries, with an eye so rich
As mine was through the bounty of a grand
And lovely region, I had forms distinct
430   To steady me: each airy thought revolved
Round a substantial centre, which at once
Incited it to motion, and controlled.
I did not pine like one in cities bred,
As was thy melancholy lot, dear Friend!
Great Spirit as thou art, in endless dreams

Of sickliness, disjoining, joining, things
610 Without the light of knowledge. Where the harm,
If, when the woodman languished with disease
From sleeping night by night among the woods
Within his sod-built cabin, Indian-wise,   440
I called the pangs of disappointed love
And all the long etcetera of such thought,
To help him to his grave? Meanwhile the man,
If not already from the woods retired
To die at home, was haply, as I knew,   445
Pining alone among the gentle airs,
620 Birds, running streams, and hills so beautiful
On golden evenings, while the charcoal pile
Breathed up its smoke, an image of his ghost
Or spirit that was soon to take its flight.   450

Of sickliness, disjoining, joining, things
Without the light of knowledge. Where the harm,
If, when the woodman languished with disease
Induced by sleeping nightly on the ground
440 Within his sod-built cabin, Indian-wise,
I called the pangs of disappointed love,
And all the sad etcetera of the wrong,
To help him to his grave? Meanwhile the man,
If not already from the woods retired
To die at home, was haply, as I knew,
Withering by slow degrees, 'mid gentle airs,
Birds, running streams, and hills so beautiful
On golden evenings, while the charcoal pile
Breathed up its smoke, an image of his ghost
450 Or spirit that full soon must take her flight.
Nor shall we not be tending towards that point
Of sound humanity to which our Tale
Leads, though by sinuous ways, if here I show
How Fancy, in a season when she wove
Those slender cords, to guide the unconscious Boy
For the Man's sake, could feed at Nature's call
Some pensive musings which might well beseem
Maturer years.
                              A grove there is whose boughs
Stretch from the western marge of Thurston-mere,
460 With length of shade so thick, that whoso glides
Along the line of low-roofed water, moves
As in a cloister. Once – while, in that shade
Loitering, I watched the golden beams of light
Flung from the setting sun, as they reposed
In silent beauty on the naked ridge
Of a high eastern hill – thus flowed my thoughts
In a pure stream of words fresh from the heart;
Dear native Region, wheresoe'er shall close
My mortal course, there will I think on you;
470 Dying, will cast on you a backward look;
Even as this setting sun (albeit the Vale
Is no where touched by one memorial gleam)

    There came a time of greater dignity
Which had been gradually prepared, and now
Rushed in as if on wings, the time in which
The pulse of Being everywhere was felt,   *480*
When all the several frames of things, like stars,
Through every magnitude distinguishable,
630 Were half confounded in each other's blaze,
One galaxy of life and joy. Then rose   *485*
Man, inwardly contemplated, and present
In my own being, to a loftier height,
As, of all visible natures, crown; and first
In capability of feeling what
Was to be felt; in being rapt away   *490*
By the divine effect of power and love;
As, more than anything we know, instinct
With godhead, and, by reason and by will,
640 Acknowledging dependency sublime.

    Ere long transported hence as in a dream   *495*
I found myself begirt with temporal shapes
Of vice and folly thrust upon my view,
Objects of sport, and ridicule, and scorn,
Manners and characters discriminate,
And little busy passions that eclipsed,   *500*
As well they might, the impersonated thought,
The idea, or abstraction of the kind.
An idler among academic bowers,
650 Such was my new condition, as at large
Hath been set forth; yet here the vulgar light   *505*
Of present, actual, superficial life,
Gleaming through colouring of other times,

Doth with the fond remains of his last power
Still linger, and a farewell lustre sheds
On the dear mountain-tops where first he rose.

Enough of humble arguments; recall,
My Song! those high emotions which thy voice
Has heretofore made known; that bursting forth
Of sympathy, inspiring and inspired,
480   When everywhere a vital pulse was felt,
And all the several frames of things, like stars,
Through every magnitude distinguishable,
Shone mutually indebted, or half lost
Each in the other's blaze, a galaxy
Of life and glory. In the midst stood Man,
Outwardly, inwardly contemplated,
As, of all visible natures, crown, though born
Of dust, and kindred to the worm; a Being,
Both in perception and discernment, first
490   In every capability of rapture,
Through the divine effect of power and love;
As, more than anything we know, instinct
With godhead, and, by reason and by will,
Acknowledging dependency sublime.

Ere long, the lonely mountains left, I moved,
Begirt, from day to day, with temporal shapes
Of vice and folly thrust upon my view,
Objects of sport, and ridicule, and scorn,
Manners and characters discriminate,
500   And little bustling passions that eclipsed,
As well they might, the impersonated thought,
The idea, or abstraction of the kind.

An idler among academic bowers,
Such was my new condition, as at large
Has been set forth; yet here the vulgar light
Of present, actual, superficial life,
Gleaming through colouring of other times,

Old usages and local privilege,
Thereby was softened, almost solemnized,
And rendered apt and pleasing to the view.
This notwithstanding, being brought more near,   510
As I was now, to guilt and wretchedness,
I trembled, – thought of human life, at times,
660 With an indefinite terror and dismay,
Such as the storms and angry elements
Had bred in me; but gloomier far, a dim   515
Analogy to uproar and misrule,
Disquiet, danger, and obscurity.

   It might be told (but wherefore speak of things
Common to all?) that, seeing, I essayed
To give relief, began to deem myself
A moral agent – judging between good   520
And evil, not as for the mind's delight
670 But for her safety – one who was to *act*,
As sometimes, to the best of my weak means,
I did, by human sympathy impelled:
And, through dislike and most offensive pain,   525
Was to the truth conducted; of this faith
Never forsaken, that, by acting well,
And understanding, I should learn to love
The end of life, and every thing we know.

   Preceptress stern, that didst instruct me next,   530
London! to thee I willingly return.
680 Erewhile my verse played only with the flowers
Enwrought upon thy mantle; satisfied
With this amusement, and a simple look   535
Of child-like inquisition now and then
Cast upwards on thine eye, to puzzle out
Some inner meanings which might harbour there.
Yet did I not give way to this light mood   539
Wholly beguiled, as one incapable
Of higher things, and ignorant that high things
Were round me. Never shall I forget the hour,

Old usages and local privilege,
Was welcome, softened, if not solemnized.
510 This notwithstanding, being brought more near
To vice and guilt, forerunning wretchedness,
I trembled, – thought, at times, of human life
With an indefinite terror and dismay,
Such as the storms and angry elements
Had bred in me; but gloomier far, a dim
Analogy to uproar and misrule,
Disquiet, danger, and obscurity.

It might be told (but wherefore speak of things
Common to all?) that, seeing, I was led
520 Gravely to ponder – judging between good
And evil, not as for the mind's delight
But for her guidance – one who was to *act*,
As sometimes to the best of feeble means
I did, by human sympathy impelled:
And, through dislike and most offensive pain,
Was to the truth conducted; of this faith
Never forsaken, that, by acting well,
And understanding, I should learn to love
The end of life, and every thing we know.

530 Grave Teacher, stern Preceptress! for at times
Thou canst put on an aspect most severe;
London, to thee I willingly return.
Erewhile my verse played idly with the flowers
Enwrought upon thy mantle; satisfied
With that amusement, and a simple look
Of child-like inquisition now and then
Cast upwards on thy countenance, to detect
Some inner meanings which might harbour there.
But how could I in mood so light indulge,
540 Keeping such fresh remembrance of the day,

690 The moment rather say, when, having thridded
     The labyrinth of suburban villages,
     At length I did unto myself first seem
     To enter the great city. On the roof
     Of an itinerant vehicle I sate,
     With vulgar men about me, vulgar forms   545
     Of houses, pavements, streets, of men and things, –
     Mean shapes on every side: but, at the time,
     When to myself it fairly might be said,
     The very moment that I seemed to know,
700 The threshold now is overpast, great God!
     That aught *external* to the living mind   550
     Should have such mighty sway! yet so it was
     A weight of ages did at once descend
     Upon my heart; no thought embodied, no
     Distinct remembrances, but weight and power, –
     Power growing with the weight: alas! I feel   555
     That I am trifling: 'twas a moment's pause, –
     All that took place within me came and went
     As in a moment, and I only now
710 Remember that it was a thing divine.

         As when a traveller hath from open day   560
     With torches passed into some vault of earth,
     The Grotto of Antiparos, or the Den
     Of Yordas among Craven's mountain tracts;
     He looks and sees the cavern spread and grow,
     Widening itself on all sides; sees, or thinks   565
     He sees, ere long, the roof above his head,
     Which instantly unsettles and recedes, –
     Substance and shadow, light and darkness, all
720 Commingled, making up a canopy
     Of shapes and forms and tendencies to shape   570
     That shift and vanish, change and interchange
     Like spectres, – ferment quiet and sublime!
     Which after a short space works less and less,
     Till, every effort, every motion gone,
     The scene before him lies in perfect view   575

When, having thridded the long labyrinth
Of the suburban villages, I first
Entered thy vast dominion? On the roof
Of an itinerant vehicle I sate,
With vulgar men about me, trivial forms
Of houses, pavements, streets, of men and things, –
Mean shapes on every side: but, at the instant,
When to myself it fairly might be said,
The threshold now is overpast, (how strange
550 That aught external to the living mind
Should have such mighty sway! yet so it was),
A weight of ages did at once descend
Upon my heart; no thought embodied, no
Distinct remembrances, but weight and power, –
Power growing under weight: alas! I feel
That I am trifling: 'twas a moment's pause, –
All that took place within me came and went
As in a moment; yet with Time it dwells,
And grateful memory, as a thing divine.

560   The curious traveller, who, from open day,
Hath passed with torches into some huge cave,
The Grotto of Antiparos, or the Den
In old time haunted by that Danish Witch,
Yordas; he looks around and sees the vault
Widening on all sides; sees, or thinks he sees,
Ere long, the massy roof above his head,
That instantly unsettles and recedes, –
Substance and shadow, light and darkness, all
Commingled, making up a canopy
570 Of shapes and forms and tendencies to shape
That shift and vanish, change and interchange
Like spectres, – ferment silent and sublime!
That after a short space works less and less,
Till, every effort, every motion gone,
The scene before him stands in perfect view

337

Exposed, and lifeless as a written book!
But let him pause awhile, and look again,
And a new quickening shall succeed, at first
730 Beginning timidly, then creeping fast
Through all which he beholds; the senseless mass,   *580*
In its projections, wrinkles, cavities,
Through all its surface, with all colours streaming,
Like a magician's airy pageant, parts,
Unites, embodying everywhere some pressure
Or image, recognized or new, some type
Or picture of the world; forests and lakes,
Ships, rivers, towers, the warrior clad in mail,   *585*
The prancing steed, the pilgrim with his staff,
740 The mitred bishop and the thronèd king,
A spectacle to which there is no end.

    No otherwise had I at first been moved   *590*
With such a swell of feeling, followed soon
By a blank sense of greatness passed away,
And afterwards continued to be moved
In presence of that vast metropolis,
The fountain of my country's destiny
And of the destiny of earth itself;
That great emporium, chronicle at once
750 And burial-place of passions, and their home   *595*
Imperial, and chief living residence.

    With strong sensations teeming as it did
Of past and present, such a place must needs
Have pleased me, in those times; I sought not then
Knowledge; but craved for power, and power I found   *600*
In all things; nothing had a circumscribed
And narrow influence; but all objects, being
Themselves capacious, also found in me   *605*
Capaciousness and amplitude of mind;
760 Such is the strength and glory of our youth!
The human nature unto which I felt
That I belonged, and which I loved and reverenced,

Exposed, and lifeless as a written book! –
But let him pause awhile, and look again,
And a new quickening shall succeed, at first
Beginning timidly, then creeping fast,
580 Till the whole cave, so late a senseless mass,
Busies the eye with images and forms
Boldly assembled, – here is shadowed forth
From the projections, wrinkles, cavities,
A variegated landscape, – there the shape
Of some gigantic warrior clad in mail,
The ghostly semblance of a hooded monk,
Veiled nun, or pilgrim resting on his staff:
Strange congregation! yet not slow to meet
Eyes that perceive through minds that can inspire.

590 Even in such sort had I at first been moved,
Nor otherwise continued to be moved,
As I explored the vast metropolis,
Fount of my country's destiny and the world's;
That great emporium, chronicle at once
And burial-place of passions, and their home
Imperial, their chief living residence.

With strong sensations teeming as it did
Of past and present, such a place must needs
Have pleased me, seeking knowledge at that time
600 Far less than craving power; yet knowledge came,
Sought or unsought, and influxes of power
Came, of themselves, or at her call derived
In fits of kindliest apprehensiveness,
From all sides, when whate'er was in itself
Capacious found, or seemed to find, in me
A correspondent amplitude of mind;
Such is the strength and glory of our youth!
The human nature unto which I felt
That I belonged, and reverenced with love,

Was not a punctual presence, but a spirit   610
Living in time and space, and far diffused.
In this my joy, in this my dignity
Consisted; the external universe,
By striking upon what is found within,
Had given me this conception, with the help
Of books and what they picture and record.   616

770   'Tis true, the history of my native land,
With those of Greece compared and popular Rome,
Events not lovely nor magnanimous,
But harsh and unaffecting in themselves
And in our high-wrought modern narratives
Stript of their harmonizing soul, the life
Of manners and familiar incidents,   621
Had never much delighted me. And less
Than other minds I had been used to owe
The pleasure which I found in place or thing
780   To extrinsic transitory accidents,
To records or traditions; but a sense   625
Of what had been here done, and suffered here
Through ages, and was doing, suffering, still,
Weighed with me, could support the test of thought,
Was like the enduring majesty and power   631
Of independent nature; and not seldom
Even individual remembrances,
By working on the shapes before my eyes,
Became like vital functions of the soul;
790   And out of what had been, what was, the place
Was thronged with impregnations, like those Wilds
In which my early feelings had been nursed,
And naked valleys, full of caverns, rocks,   635
And audible seclusions, dashing lakes,
Echoes and waterfalls, and pointed crags
That into music touch the passing wind.
Thus here imagination also found
An element that pleased her, tried her strength,   640
Among new objects simplified, arranged,

610 Was not a punctual presence, but a spirit
Diffused through time and space, with aid derived
Of evidence from monuments, erect,
Prostrate, or leaning towards their common rest
In earth, the widely scattered wreck sublime
Of vanished nations, or more clearly drawn
From books and what they picture and record.

'Tis true, the history of our native land,
With those of Greece compared and popular Rome,
And in our high-wrought modern narratives
620 Stript of their harmonizing soul, the life
Of manners and familiar incidents,
Had never much delighted me. And less
Than other intellects had mine been used
To lean upon extrinsic circumstance
Of record or tradition; but a sense
Of what in the Great City had been done
And suffered, and was doing, suffering, still,
Weighed with me, could support the test of thought;
And, in despite of all that had gone by,
630 Or was departing never to return,
There I conversed with majesty and power
Like independent natures. Hence the place
Was thronged with impregnations like the Wilds
In which my early feelings had been nursed –
Bare hills and valleys, full of caverns, rocks,
And audible seclusions, dashing lakes,
Echoes and waterfalls, and pointed crags
That into music touch the passing wind.
Here then my young imagination found
640 No uncongenial element; could here
Among new objects serve or give command,

800   Impregnated my knowledge, made it live,
       And the result was elevating thoughts
       Of human nature. Neither guilt nor vice,   645
       Debasement of the body or the mind,
       Nor all the misery forced upon my sight,
       Which was not lightly passed, but often scanned
       Most feelingly, could overthrow my trust
       In what we may become; induce belief   650
       That I was ignorant, had been falsely taught,
       A solitary, who with vain conceits
810   Had been inspired, and walked about in dreams.
       When from that awful prospect overcast
       And in eclipse my meditations turned,
       Lo! every thing that was indeed divine   655
       Retained its purity inviolate
       And unencroached upon, nay, seemed brighter far
       For this deep shade in counterview, that gloom
       Of opposition, such as showed itself
       To the eyes of Adam, yet in Paradise
       Though fallen from bliss, when in the East he saw   660
820   Darkness ere day's mid course, and morning light
       More orient in the western cloud, that drew
       O'er the blue firmament a radiant white,
       Descending slow with something heavenly fraught.

       Add also, that among the multitudes   665
       Of that great city, oftentimes was seen
       Affectingly set forth, more than elsewhere
       Is possible, the unity of man,
       One spirit over ignorance and vice
       Predominant, in good and evil hearts   670
830   One sense for moral judgements, as one eye
       For the sun's light. When strongly breathed upon
       By this sensation, whencesoe'er it comes,
       Of union or communion, doth the soul
       Rejoice as in her highest joy: for there,
       There chiefly, hath she feeling whence she is,
       And passing through all Nature rests with God.

Even as the heart's occasions might require,
To forward reason's else too scrupulous march.
The effect was, still more elevated views
Of human nature. Neither vice nor guilt,
Debasement undergone by body or mind,
Nor all the misery forced upon my sight,
Misery not lightly passed, but sometimes scanned
Most feelingly, could overthrow my trust
650 In what we *may* become; induce belief
That I was ignorant, had been falsely taught,
A solitary, who with vain conceits
Had been inspired, and walked about in dreams.
From those sad scenes when meditation turned,
Lo! every thing that was indeed divine
Retained its purity inviolate,
Nay brighter shone, by this portentous gloom
Set off; such opposition as aroused
The mind of Adam, yet in Paradise
660 Though fallen from bliss, when in the East he saw
Darkness ere day's mid course, and morning light
More orient in the western cloud, that drew
O'er the blue firmament a radiant white,
Descending slow with something heavenly fraught.

    Add also, that among the multitudes
Of that huge city, oftentimes was seen
Affectingly set forth, more than elsewhere
Is possible, the unity of man,
One spirit over ignorance and vice
670 Predominant, in good and evil hearts
One sense for moral judgements, as one eye
For the sun's light. The soul when smitten thus
By a sublime *idea*, whencesoe'er
Vouchsafed for union or communion, feeds
On the pure bliss, and takes her rest with God.

And is not, too, that vast abiding-place
Of human creatures, turn where'er we may,
Profusely sown with individual sights
840 Of courage, and integrity, and truth   VII 600
And tenderness, which, here set off by foil,
Appears more touching. In the tender scenes   VII 600
Chiefly was my delight, and one of these
Never will be forgotten. 'Twas a man,
Whom I saw sitting in an open square
Close to an iron paling that fenced in   VII 605
The spacious grass-plot; on the corner-stone
Of the low wall in which the pales were fixed
Sate this One Man, and with a sickly babe
850 Upon his knee, whom he had thither brought
For sunshine, and to breathe the fresher air.   VII 610
Of those who passed, and me who looked at him,
He took no note; but in his brawny arms
(The Artificer was to the elbow bare,
And from his work this moment had been stolen)
He held the child, and, bending over it,   VII 615
As if he were afraid both of the sun
And of the air, which he had come to seek,
He eyed it with unutterable love.

860   Thus were my thoughts attracted more and more   676
By slow gradations towards human-kind,
And to the good and ill of human life;
Nature had led me on, and now I seemed
To travel independent of her help,   681
As if I had forgotten her; but no,
My fellow beings still were unto me
Far less than she was; though the scale of love
Were filling fast, 'twas light, as yet, compared   685
With that in which her mighty objects lay.

Thus from a very early age, O Friend!
My thoughts by slow gradations had been drawn
To human-kind, and to the good and ill
Of human life: Nature had led me on;
680 And oft amid the 'busy hum' I seemed
To travel independent of her help,
As if I had forgotten her; but no,
The world of human-kind outweighed not hers
In my habitual thoughts; the scale of love,
Though filling daily, still was light, compared
With that in which *her* mighty objects lay.

As oftentimes a river, it might seem,
Yielding in part to old remembrances,
Part swayed by fear to tread an onward road
That leads direct to the devouring sea
Turns, and will measure back his course, far back,   5
Towards the very regions which he crossed
In his first outset; so have we long time
Made motions retrograde, in like pursuit
Detained. But now we start afresh; I feel
10   An impulse to precipitate my verse.
Fair greetings to this shapeless eagerness,
Whene'er it comes! needful in work so long,   20
Thrice needful to the argument which now
Awaits us! Oh, how much unlike the past!
One which though bright the promise, will be found
Ere far we shall advance, ungenial, hard
To treat of, and forbidding in itself.

    Free as a colt at pasture on the hill,
I ranged at large, through the Metropolis,
20   Month after month. Obscurely did I live,   25
Not courting the society of men,
By literature, or elegance, or rank,
Distinguished; in the midst of things, it seemed,
Looking as from a distance on the world
That moved about me; yet insensibly
False preconceptions were corrected thus
And errors of the fancy rectified,
Alike with reference to men and things,
And sometimes from each quarter were poured in

Book Ninth

RESIDENCE IN FRANCE

Even as a river, – partly (it might seem)
Yielding to old remembrances, and swayed
In part by fear to shape a way direct,
That would engulph him soon in the ravenous sea –
Turns, and will measure back his course, far back,
Seeking the very regions which he crossed
In his first outset; so have we, my Friend!
Turned and returned with intricate delay.
Or as a traveller, who has gained the brow
10   Of some aerial Down, while there he halts
For breathing-time, is tempted to review
The region left behind him; and, if aught
Deserving notice have escaped regard,
Or been regarded with too careless eye,
Strives, from that height, with one and yet one more
Last look, to make the best amends he may:
So have we lingered. Now we start afresh
With courage, and new hope risen on our toil.
Fair greetings to this shapeless eagerness,
20   Whene'er it comes! needful in work so long,
Thrice needful to the argument which now
Awaits us! Oh, how much unlike the past!

      Free as a colt at pasture on the hill,
I ranged at large, through London's wide domain,
Month after month. Obscurely did I live,
Not seeking frequent intercourse with men,
By literature, or elegance, or rank,

30 Novel imaginations and profound.
A year thus spent, this field (with small regret
Save only for the book-stalls in the streets,   *32*
Wild produce, hedge-row fruit, on all sides hung
To tempt the sauntering traveller from his track)
I quitted, and betook myself to France,
Led thither chiefly by a personal wish
To speak the language more familiarly,
With which intent I chose for my abode
A city on the borders of the Loire.   *41*

40   Through Paris lay my readiest path, and there
I sojourned a few days, and visited
In haste each spot of old and recent fame,
The latter chiefly; from the field of Mars   *45*
Down to the suburbs of St Antony,
And from Mont Martyr southward to the Dome
Of Geneviève. In both her clamorous Halls,
The National Synod and the Jacobins,
I saw the Revolutionary Power   *50*
Toss like a ship at anchor, rocked by storms;
50 The Arcades I traversed, in the Palace huge
Of Orleans; coasted round and round the line
Of Tavern, Brothel, Gaming-house, and Shop,
Great rendezvous of worst and best, the walk   *55*
Of all who had a purpose, or had not;
I stared and listened, with a stranger's ears,
To Hawkers and Haranguers, hubbub wild!
And hissing Factionists with ardent eyes,
In knots, or pairs, or single, ant-like swarms   *60*
Of builders and subverters, every face
60 That hope or apprehension could put on,

Distinguished. Scarcely was a year thus spent
Ere I forsook the crowded solitude.
30 With less regret for its luxurious pomp,
And all the nicely-guarded shows of art,
Than for the humble book-stalls in the streets,
Exposed to eye and hand where'er I turned.

France lured me forth; the realm that I had crossed
So lately, journeying toward the snow-clad Alps.
But now, relinquishing the scrip and staff,
And all enjoyment which the summer sun
Sheds round the steps of those who meet the day
With motion constant as his own, I went
40 Prepared to sojourn in a pleasant town,
Washed by the current of the stately Loire.

Through Paris lay my readiest course, and there
Sojourning a few days, I visited
In haste, each spot of old or recent fame,
The latter chiefly; from the field of Mars
Down to the suburbs of St Antony,
And from Mont Martyr southward to the Dome
Of Geneviève. In both her clamorous Halls,
The National Synod and the Jacobins,
50 I saw the Revolutionary Power
Toss like a ship at anchor, rocked by storms;
The Arcades I traversed, in the Palace huge
Of Orleans; coasted round and round the line
Of Tavern, Brothel, Gaming-house and Shop,
Great rendezvous of worst and best, the walk
Of all who had a purpose, or had not;
I stared and listened, with a stranger's ears,
To Hawkers and Haranguers, hubbub wild!
And hissing Factionists with ardent eyes,
60 In knots, or pairs, or single. Not a look
Hope takes, or Doubt or Fear are forced to wear,
But seemed there present; and I scanned them all,
Watched every gesture uncontrollable,

349

Joy, anger, and vexation in the midst
Of gaiety and dissolute idleness.   66

  Where silent zephyrs sported with the dust
Of the Bastille, I sate in the open sun,
And from the rubbish gathered up a stone
And pocketed the relic, in the guise   70
Of an enthusiast; yet, in honest truth,
Though not without some strong incumbences,
And glad (could living man be otherwise),
70 I looked for something which I could not find,
Affecting more emotion than I felt;
For 'tis most certain, that the utmost force   74
Of all these various objects which may show
The temper of my mind as then it was
Seemed less to recompense the traveller's pains,
Less moved me, gave me less delight than did
76a A single picture merely, hunted out
Among other sights, the Magdalene of Le Brun,
A beauty exquisitely wrought, fair face
And rueful, with its everflowing tears.   80

80 But hence to my more permanent residence
I hasten; there, by novelties in speech,
Domestic manners, customs, gestures, looks,
And all the attire of ordinary life,
Attention was at first engrossed; and thus,   85
Amused and satisfied, I scarcely felt
The shock of these concussions, unconcerned,
Tranquil almost, and careless as a flower
Glassed in a greenhouse, or a parlour shrub
When every bush and tree, the country through,   90
90 Is shaking to the roots: indifference this
Which may seem strange: but I was unprepared
With needful knowledge, had abruptly passed
Into a theatre, of which the stage
Was busy with an action far advanced.   95
Like others, I had read, and eagerly

Of anger, and vexation, and despite,
All side by side, and struggling face to face,
With gaiety and dissolute idleness.

   Where silent zephyrs sported with the dust
Of the Bastille, I sate in the open sun,
And from the rubbish gathered up a stone,
70 And pocketed the relic, in the guise
Of an enthusiast; yet, in honest truth,
I looked for something that I could not find,
Affecting more emotion than I felt;
For 'tis most certain, that these various sights,
However potent their first shock, with me
Appeared to recompense the traveller's pains
Less than the painted Magdalene of Le Brun,
A beauty exquisitely wrought, with hair
Dishevelled, gleaming eyes, and rueful cheek
80 Pale and bedropped with everflowing tears.

   But hence to my more permanent abode
I hasten; there, by novelties in speech,
Domestic manners, customs, gestures, looks,
And all the attire of ordinary life,
Attention was engrossed; and, thus amused,
I stood, 'mid those concussions, unconcerned,
Tranquil almost, and careless as a flower
Glassed in a greenhouse, or a parlour shrub
That spreads its leaves in unmolested peace,
90 While every bush and tree, the country through,
Is shaking to the roots: indifference this
Which may seem strange: but I was unprepared
With needful knowledge, had abruptly passed
Into a theatre, whose stage was filled
And busy with an action far advanced.
Like others, I had skimmed, and sometimes read

Sometimes, the master pamphlets of the day;
Nor wanted such half-insight as grew wild
Upon that meagre soil, helped out by talk
And public news; but having never chanced   *100*
100   To see a regular chronicle which might show,
(If any such indeed existed then)
Whence the main organs of the public power
Had sprung, their transmigrations, when and how
Accomplished, giving thus unto events
A form and body; all things were to me   *105*
Loose and disjointed, and the affections left
Without a vital interest. At that time,
Moreover, the first storm was overblown,
And the strong hand of outward violence
110   Locked up in quiet. For myself, I fear   *110*
Now in connection with so great a theme
To speak (as I must be compelled to do)
Of one so unimportant; a short time
I loitered, and frequented night by night
Routs, card-tables, the formal haunts of men,
Whom, in the city, privilege of birth   *115*
Sequestered from the rest, societies
Where, through punctilios of elegance
And deeper causes, all discourse alike
120   Of good and evil of the time was shunned
With studious care; but 'twas not long ere this   *120*
Proved tedious, and I gradually withdrew
Into a noisier world, and thus did soon
Become a patriot; and my heart was all
Given to the people, and my love was theirs.

A knot of military Officers,   *125*
That to a regiment appertained which then
Was stationed in the city, were the chief
Of my associates: some of these wore swords
130   Which had been seasoned in the wars, and all
Were men well-born, at least laid claim to such
Distinction, as the chivalry of France.

With care, the master pamphlets of the day;
Nor wanted such half-insight as grew wild
Upon that meagre soil, helped out by talk
100   And public news; but having never seen
A chronicle that might suffice to show
Whence the main organs of the public power
Had sprung, their transmigrations, when and how
Accomplished, giving thus unto events
A form and body; all things were to me
Loose and disjointed, and the affections left
Without a vital interest. At that time,
Moreover, the first storm was overblown,
And the strong hand of outward violence
110   Locked up in quiet. For myself, I fear
Now in connection with so great a theme
To speak (as I must be compelled to do)
Of one so unimportant; night by night
Did I frequent the formal haunts of men,
Whom, in the city, privilege of birth
Sequestered from the rest, societies
Polished in arts, and in punctilio versed;
Whence, and from deeper causes, all discourse
Of good and evil of the time was shunned
120   With scrupulous care; but these restrictions soon
Proved tedious, and I gradually withdrew
Into a noisier world, and thus ere long
Became a patriot; and my heart was all
Given to the people, and my love was theirs.

    A band of military Officers,
Then stationed in the city, were the chief
Of my associates: some of these wore swords
That had been seasoned in the wars, and all
Were men well-born; the chivalry of France.

In age and temper differing, they had yet   *130*
One spirit ruling in them all; alike
(Save only one, hereafter to be named)
Were bent upon undoing what was done:
This was their rest and only hope; therewith
No fear had they of bad becoming worse,   *135*
For worst to them was come; nor would have stirred,
140 Or deemed it worth a moment's while to stir,
In any thing, save only as the act
Looked thitherward. One, reckoning by years,
Was in the prime of manhood, and erewhile   *140*
He had sate lord in many tender hearts;
Though heedless of such honours now, and changed:
His temper was quite mastered by the times,
And they had blighted him, had eat away
The beauty of his person, doing wrong   *145*
Alike to body and to mind: his port,
150 Which once had been erect and open, now
Was stooping and contracted, and a face,
By nature lovely in itself, expressed   *150*
As much as any that was ever seen,
A ravage out of season, made by thoughts
Unhealthy and vexatious. At the hour,
The most important of each day, in which
The public news was read, the fever came,   *155*
A punctual visitant, to shake this man,
Disarmed his voice and fanned his yellow cheek
160 Into a thousand colours; while he read,
Or mused, his sword was haunted by his touch
Continually, like an uneasy place   *160*
In his own body. 'Twas in truth an hour
Of universal ferment; mildest men
Were agitated; and commotions, strife
Of passion and opinion, filled the walls
Of peaceful houses with unquiet sounds.   *165*
The soil of common life, was, at that time,
Too hot to tread upon. Oft said I then,

130   In age and temper differing, they had yet
       One spirit ruling in each heart; alike
       (Save only one, hereafter to be named)
       Were bent upon undoing what was done:
       This was their rest and only hope; therewith
       No fear had they of bad becoming worse,
       For worst to them was come; nor would have stirred,
       Or deemed it worth a moment's thought to stir,
       In any thing, save only as the act
       Looked thitherward. One, reckoning by years,
140   Was in the prime of manhood, and erewhile
       He had sate lord in many tender hearts;
       Though heedless of such honours now, and changed:
       His temper was quite mastered by the times,
       And they had blighted him, had eat away
       The beauty of his person, doing wrong
       Alike to body and to mind: his port,
       Which once had been erect and open, now
       Was stooping and contracted, and a face,
       Endowed by Nature with her fairest gifts
150   Of symmetry and light and bloom, expressed,
       As much as any that was ever seen,
       A ravage out of season, made by thoughts
       Unhealthy and vexatious. With the hour,
       That from the press of Paris duly brought
       Its freight of public news, the fever came,
       A punctual visitant, to shake this man,
       Disarmed his voice and fanned his yellow cheek
       Into a thousand colours; while he read,
       Or mused, his sword was haunted by his touch
160   Continually, like an uneasy place
       In his own body. 'Twas in truth an hour
       Of universal ferment; mildest men
       Were agitated; and commotions, strife
       Of passions and opinions, filled the walls
       Of peaceful houses with unquiet sounds.
       The soil of common life, was, at that time,
       Too hot to tread upon. Oft said I then,

170   And not then only, 'What a mockery this
      Of history, the past and that to come!
      Now do I feel how I have been deceived,   *170*
      Reading of nations and their works, in faith,
      Faith given to vanity and emptiness;
      Oh! laughter for the page that would reflect
      To future times the face of what now is!'
      The land all swarmed with passion, like a plain   *175*
      Devoured by locusts, – Carra, Gorsas, – add
      A hundred other names, forgotten now,
180   Nor to be heard of more; yet were they powers,
      Like earthquakes, shocks repeated day by day,
      And felt through every nook of town and field.   *180*

      The men already spoken of as chief
      Of my associates were prepared for flight
      To augment the band of emigrants in arms
      Upon the borders of the Rhine, and leagued
      With foreign foes mustered for instant war.   *185*
      This was their undisguised intent, and they
      Were waiting with the whole of their desires
190   The moment to depart.
                            An Englishman,
      Born in a land the name of which appeared
      To license some unruliness of mind;   *190*
      A stranger, with youth's further privilege,
      And that indulgence which a half-learnt speech
      Wins from the courteous; I, who had been else
      Shunned and not tolerated, freely lived
      With these defenders of the Crown, and talked,   *195*
      And heard their notions; nor did they disdain
      The wish to bring me over to their cause.

200   But though untaught by thinking or by books
      To reason well of polity or law,
      And nice distinctions, then on every tongue,   *200*
      Of natural rights and civil; and to acts
      Of nations and their passing interests,

And not then only, 'What a mockery this
Of history, the past and that to come!
170 Now do I feel how all men are deceived,
Reading of nations and their works, in faith,
Faith given to vanity and emptiness;
Oh! laughter for the page that would reflect
To future times the face of what now is!'
The land all swarmed with passion, like a plain
Devoured by locusts, – Carra, Gorsas, – add
A hundred other names, forgotten now,
Nor to be heard of more; yet, they were powers,
Like earthquakes, shocks repeated day by day,
180 And felt through every nook of town and field.

Such was the state of things. Meanwhile the chief
Of my associates stood prepared for flight
To augment the band of emigrants in arms
Upon the borders of the Rhine, and leagued
With foreign foes mustered for instant war.
This was their undisguised intent, and they
Were waiting with the whole of their desires
The moment to depart.
                              An Englishman,
Born in a land whose very name appeared
190 To license some unruliness of mind;
A stranger, with youth's further privilege,
And the indulgence that a half-learnt speech
Wins from the courteous; I, who had been else
Shunned and not tolerated, freely lived
With these defenders of the Crown, and talked,
And heard their notions; nor did they disdain
The wish to bring me over to their cause.

But though untaught by thinking or by books
To reason well of polity or law,
200 And nice distinctions, then on every tongue,
Of natural rights and civil; and to acts
Of nations and their passing interests,

(I speak comparing these with other things)
Almost indifferent, even the historian's tale
Prizing but little otherwise than I prized 205
Tales of the poets, as it made my heart
Beat high and filled my fancy with fair forms,
Old heroes and their sufferings and their deeds;
Yet in the regal sceptre, and the pomp
Of orders and degrees, I nothing found 210
Then, or had ever, even in crudest youth,
That dazzled me, but rather what my soul
Mourned for, or loathed, beholding that the best
Ruled not, and feeling that they ought to rule.

For, born in a poor district, and which yet 215
Retaineth more of ancient homeliness,
Manners erect, and frank simplicity,
Than any other nook of English land,
It was my fortune scarcely to have seen
Through the whole tenor of my school-day time
The face of one, who, whether boy or man, 220
Was vested with attention or respect
Through claims of wealth or blood; nor was it least
Of many debts which afterwards I owed
To Cambridge and an academic life
That something there was holden up to view 225
Of a Republic, where all stood thus far
Upon equal ground; that they were brothers all
In honour, as of one community,
Scholars and gentlemen; where, furthermore,
Distinction lay open to all that came, 230
And wealth and titles were in less esteem
Than talents and successful industry.
Add unto this, subservience from the first
To God and Nature's single sovereignty, 235
Familiar presences of awful power,
And fellowship with venerable books,
To sanction the proud workings of the soul,
And mountain liberty. It could not be

(If with unworldly ends and aims compared)
Almost indifferent, even the historian's tale
Prizing but little otherwise than I prized
Tales of the poets, as it made the heart
Beat high, and filled the fancy with fair forms,
Old heroes and their sufferings and their deeds;
Yet in the regal sceptre, and the pomp
210 Of orders and degrees, I nothing found
Then, or had ever, even in crudest youth,
That dazzled me, but rather what I mourned
And ill could brook, beholding that the best
Ruled not, and feeling that they ought to rule.

For, born in a poor district, and which yet
Retaineth more of ancient homeliness,
Than any other nook of English ground,
It was my fortune scarcely to have seen,
Through the whole tenor of my school-day time,
220 The face of one, who, whether boy or man,
Was vested with attention or respect
Through claims of wealth or blood; nor was it least
Of many benefits, in later years
Derived from academic institutes
And rules, that they held something up to view
Of a Republic, where all stood thus far
Upon equal ground; that we were brothers all
In honour, as in one community,
Scholars and gentlemen; where, furthermore,
230 Distinction lay open to all that came,
And wealth and titles were in less esteem
Than talents, worth, and prosperous industry.
Add unto this, subservience from the first
To presences of God's mysterious power
Made manifest in Nature's sovereignty,
And fellowship with venerable books,
To sanction the proud workings of the soul,
And mountain liberty. It could not be

He existed on a republic

But that one tutored thus, who had been formed
To thought and moral feeling in the way
This story hath described, should look with awe
Upon the faculties of man, receive   240
Gladly the highest promises, and hail,
As best, the government of equal rights
And individual worth. And hence, O Friend!
If at the first great outbreak I rejoiced
250   Less than might well befit my youth, the cause   245
In part lay here, that unto me the events
Seemed nothing out of nature's certain course,
A gift that rather was come late than soon.

The created not sympathy

No wonder, then, if advocates like these   249
Whom I have mentioned, at this riper day,
Were impotent to make my hopes put on
The shape of theirs, my understanding bend
In honour to their honour: zeal, which yet

by his French friends they were

Had slumbered, now in opposition burst   255
260   Forth like a Polar summer: every word
They uttered was a dart, by counter-winds
Blown back upon themselves; their reason seemed
Confusion-stricken by a higher power

for the crown

Than human understanding, their discourse   260
Maimed, spiritless; and, in their weakness strong,
I triumphed.
                Meantime, day by day, the roads
(While I consorted with these royalists)
Were crowded with the bravest youth of France,
And all the promptest of her spirits, linked
270   In gallant soldiership, and posting on   265
To meet the war upon her frontier bounds.
Yet at this very moment do tears start
Into mine eyes: I do not say I weep –
I wept not then, – but tears have dimmed my sight,
In memory of the farewells of that time,   270
Domestic severings, female fortitude
At dearest separation, patriot love
And self-devotion, and terrestrial hope,

But that one tutored thus should look with awe
240 Upon the faculties of man, receive
Gladly the highest promises, and hail,
As best, the government of equal rights
And individual worth. And hence, O Friend!
If at the first great outbreak I rejoiced
Less than might well befit my youth, the cause
In part lay here, that unto me the events
Seemed nothing out of nature's certain course,
A gift that was rather come late than soon.
No wonder, then, if advocates like these,
250 Inflamed by passion, blind with prejudice,
And stung with injury, at this riper day,
Were impotent to make my hopes put on
The shape of theirs, my understanding bend
In honour to their honour: zeal, which yet
Had slumbered, now in opposition burst
Forth like a Polar summer: every word
They uttered was a dart, by counter-winds
Blown back upon themselves; their reason seemed
Confusion-stricken by a higher power
260 Than human understanding, their discourse
Maimed, spiritless; and, in their weakness strong,
I triumphed.
           Meantime, day by day, the roads
Were crowded with the bravest youth of France,
And all the promptest of her spirits, linked
In gallant soldiership, and posting on
To meet the war upon her frontier bounds.
Yet at this very moment do tears start
Into mine eyes: I do not say I weep –
I wept not then, – but tears have dimmed my sight,
270 In memory of the farewells of that time,
Domestic severings, female fortitude
At dearest separation, patriot love
And self-devotion, and terrestrial hope,

Encouraged with a martyr's confidence;
280 Even files of strangers merely, seen but once,   275
And for a moment, men from far with sound
Of music, martial tunes, and banners spread,
Entering the city, here and there a face,
Or person singled out among the rest,
Yet still a stranger and beloved as such;   280
Even by these passing spectacles my heart
Was oftentimes uplifted, and they seemed
Like arguments from Heaven, that 'twas a cause
Good, and which no one could stand up against,
290 Who was not lost, abandoned, selfish, proud,   285
Mean, miserable, wilfully depraved,
Hater perverse of equity and truth.

   Among that band of Officers was one,
Already hinted at, of other mould –
A patriot, thence rejected by the rest,
And with an oriental loathing spurned,   290
As of a different caste. A meeker man
Than this lived never, or a more benign,
Meek though enthusiastic to the height
300 Of highest expectation. Injuries
Made *him* more gracious, and his nature then   295
Did breathe its sweetness out most sensibly,
As aromatic flowers on Alpine turf,
When foot hath crushed them. He through the events
Of that great change wandered in perfect faith,
As through a book, an old romance, or tale   300
Of Fairy, or some dream of actions wrought
Behind the summer clouds. By birth he ranked
With the most noble, but unto the poor
310 Among mankind he was in service bound,
As by some tie invisible, oaths professed   305
To a religious order. Man he loved
As man; and, to the mean and the obscure,
And all the homely in their homely works,
Transferred a courtesy which had no air

362

Encouraged with a martyr's confidence;
Even files of strangers merely, seen but once,
And for a moment, men from far with sound
Of music, martial tunes, and banners spread,
Entering the city, here and there a face,
Or person singled out among the rest,
280 Yet still a stranger and beloved as such;
Even by these passing spectacles my heart
Was oftentimes uplifted, and they seemed
Arguments sent from Heaven to prove the cause
Good, pure, which no one could stand up against,
Who was not lost, abandoned, selfish, proud,
Mean, miserable, wilfully depraved,
Hater perverse of equity and truth.

Among that band of Officers was one,
Already hinted at, of other mould –
290 A patriot, thence rejected by the rest,
And with an oriental loathing spurned,
As of a different caste. A meeker man
Than this lived never, nor a more benign,
Meek though enthusiastic. Injuries
Made *him* more gracious, and his nature then
Did breathe its sweetness out most sensibly,
As aromatic flowers on Alpine turf,
When foot hath crushed them. He through the events
Of that great change wandered in perfect faith,
300 As through a book, an old romance, or tale
Of Fairy, or some dream of actions wrought
Behind the summer clouds. By birth he ranked
With the most noble, but unto the poor
Among mankind he was in service bound,
As by some tie invisible, oaths professed
To a religious order. Man he loved
As man; and, to the mean and the obscure,
And all the homely in their homely works,
Transferred a courtesy which had no air

Of condescension; but did rather seem   *310*
A passion and a gallantry, like that
Which he, a soldier, in his idler day
Had paid to woman: somewhat vain he was,
320   Or seemed so, yet it was not vanity,
But fondness, and a kind of radiant joy   *315*
That covered him about, when he was bent
On works of love or freedom, or revolved
Complacently the progress of a cause
Whereof he was a part: yet this was meek
And placid, and took nothing from the man   *320*
That was delightful. Oft in solitude
With him did I discourse about the end
Of civil government, and its wisest forms;
330   Of ancient prejudice, and chartered rights,
Allegiance, faith, and law by time matured,
Custom and habit, novelty and change;   *325*
Of self-respect, and virtue in the few
For patrimonial honour set apart,
And ignorance in the labouring multitude.
For he, an upright man and tolerant,
Balanced these contemplations in his mind;   *330*
And I, who at that time was scarcely dipped
Into the turmoil, had a sounder judgement
340   Than afterwards, carried about me yet,
With less alloy to its integrity,
The experience of past ages, as, through help   *335*
Of books and common life, it finds its way
To youthful minds, by objects over near
Not pressed upon, nor dazzled or misled
By struggling with the crowd for present ends.

But though not deaf and obstinate to find   *340*
Error without apology on the side
Of those who were against us, more delight
350   We took, and let this freely be confessed,
In painting to ourselves the miseries
Of royal courts, and that voluptuous life   *345*

310 Of condescension; but did rather seem
A passion and a gallantry, like that
Which he, a soldier, in his idler day
Had paid to woman: somewhat vain he was,
Or seemed so, yet it was not vanity,
But fondness, and a kind of radiant joy
Diffused around him, while he was intent
On works of love or freedom, or revolved
Complacently the progress of a cause,
Whereof he was a part: yet this was meek
320 And placid, and took nothing from the man
That was delightful. Oft in solitude
With him did I discourse about the end
Of civil government, and its wisest forms;
Of ancient loyalty, and chartered rights,
Custom and habit, novelty and change;
Of self-respect, and virtue in the few
For patrimonial honour set apart,
And ignorance in the labouring multitude.
For he, to all intolerance indisposed,
330 Balanced these contemplations in his mind;
And I, who at that time was scarcely dipped
Into the turmoil, bore a sounder judgement
Than later days allowed; carried about me,
With less alloy to its integrity,
The experience of past ages, as, through help
Of books and common life, it makes sure way
To youthful minds, by objects over near
Not pressed upon, nor dazzled or misled
By struggling with the crowd for present ends.

340   But though not deaf, nor obstinate to find
Error without excuse upon the side
Of them who strove against us, more delight
We took, and let this freely be confessed,
In painting to ourselves the miseries
Of royal courts, and that voluptuous life

Unfeeling, where the man who is of soul
The meanest thrives the most; where dignity,
True personal dignity, abideth not;
A light and cruel world, cut off from all
The natural inlets of just sentiment,   *350*
From lowly sympathy and chastening truth;
Where good and evil never have that name,
360 That which they ought to have, but wrong prevails,
And vice at home. We added dearest themes –
Man and his noble nature, as it is   *355*
The gift of God and lies in his own power,
His blind desires and steady faculties
Capable of clear truth, the one to break
Bondage, the other to build liberty
On firm foundations, making social life,   *360*
Through knowledge spreading and imperishable,
As just in regulation, and as pure
370 As individual in the wise and good.

     We summoned up the honourable deeds
Of ancient Story, thought of each bright spot,   *365*
That could be found in all recorded time,
Of truth preserved and error passed away;
Of single spirits that catch the flame from Heaven,
And how the multitude of men will feed
And fan each other; thought of sects, how keen   *370*
They are to put the appropriate nature on,
Triumphant over every obstacle
380 Of custom, language, country, love and hate,
And what they do and suffer for their creed;
How far they travel, and how long endure;   *375*
How quickly mighty Nations have been formed
From least beginnings; how, together locked
By new opinions, scattered tribes have made
One body, spreading wide as clouds in heaven.
To aspirations then of our own minds   *380*
Did we appeal; and finally beheld
A living confirmation of the whole

Unfeeling, where the man who is of soul
The meanest thrives the most; where dignity,
True personal dignity, abideth not;
A light, a cruel, and vain world cut off
350 From the natural inlets of just sentiment,
From lowly sympathy and chastening truth;
Where good and evil interchange their names,
And thirst for bloody spoils abroad is paired
With vice at home. We added dearest themes –
Man and his noble nature, as it is
The gift which God has placed within his power,
His blind desires and steady faculties
Capable of clear truth, the one to break
Bondage, the other to build liberty
360 On firm foundations, making social life,
Through knowledge spreading and imperishable,
As just in regulation, and as pure
As individual in the wise and good.

We summoned up the honourable deeds
Of ancient Story, thought of each bright spot,
That could be found in all recorded time,
Of truth preserved and error passed away;
Of single spirits that catch the flame from Heaven,
And how the multitudes of men will feed
370 And fan each other; thought of sects, how keen
They are to put the appropriate nature on,
Triumphant over every obstacle
Of custom, language, country, love, or hate,
And what they do and suffer for their creed;
How far they travel, and how long endure;
How quickly mighty Nations have been formed,
From least beginnings; how, together locked
By new opinions, scattered tribes have made
One body, spreading wide as clouds in heaven.
380 To aspirations then of our own minds
Did we appeal; and, finally, beheld
A living confirmation of the whole

390   Before us, in a people risen up
     Fresh as the morning star. Elate we looked   *385*
     Upon their virtues; saw, in rudest men,
     Self-sacrifice the firmest; generous love,
     And continence of mind, and sense of right,
     Uppermost in the midst of fiercest strife.

       Oh, sweet it is, in academic groves,   *390*
     Or such retirement, Friend! as we have known
     Among the mountains, by our Rotha's stream,
     Greta, or Derwent, or some nameless rill,
400   To ruminate, with interchange of talk,
     On rational liberty, and hope in man,   *395*
     Justice and peace. But far more sweet such toil –
     Toil, say I, for it leads to thoughts abstruse –
     If nature then be standing on the brink
     Of some great trial, and we hear the voice
     Of one devoted, – one whom circumstance   *400*
     Hath called upon to embody his deep sense
     In action, give it outwardly a shape,
     And that of benediction to the world.
410   Then doubt is not, and truth is more than truth, –
     A hope it is, and a desire; a creed   *405*
     Of zeal, by an authority Divine
     Sanctioned, of danger, difficulty, or death.
     Such conversation, under Attic shades,
     Did Dion hold with Plato, ripened thus
     For a Deliverer's glorious task, – and such   *410*
     He, on that ministry already bound,
     Held with Eudemus and Timonides,
     Surrounded by adventurers in arms,
420   When those two vessels with their daring freight,
     For the Sicilian Tyrant's overthrow,   *415*
     Sailed from Zacynthus, – philosophic war,
     Led by Philosophers. With harder fate,
     Though like ambition, such was he, O Friend!
     Of whom I speak. So Beaupuis (let the name

Before us, in a people from the depth
Of shameful imbecility uprisen,
Fresh as the morning star. Elate we looked
Upon their virtues; saw, in rudest men,
Self-sacrifice the firmest; generous love,
And continence of mind, and sense of right,
Uppermost in the midst of fiercest strife.

390   Oh, sweet it is, in academic groves,
Or such retirement, Friend! as we have known
In the green dales beside our Rotha's stream,
Greta, or Derwent, or some nameless rill,
To ruminate, with interchange of talk,
On rational liberty, and hope in man,
Justice and peace. But far more sweet such toil –
Toil, say I, for it leads to thoughts abstruse –
If nature then be standing on the brink
Of some great trial, and we hear the voice
400 Of one devoted, – one whom circumstance
Hath called upon to embody his deep sense
In action, give it outwardly a shape,
And that of benediction to the world.
Then doubt is not, and truth is more than truth, –
A hope it is, and a desire; a creed
Of zeal, by an authority Divine
Sanctioned, of danger, difficulty, or death.
Such conversation, under Attic shades,
Did Dion hold with Plato; ripened thus
410 For a Deliverer's glorious task, – and such
He, on that ministry already bound,
Held with Eudemus and Timonides,
Surrounded by adventurers in arms,
When those two vessels with their daring freight,
For the Sicilian Tyrant's overthrow,
Sailed from Zacynthus, – philosophic war,
Led by Philosophers. With harder fate,
Though like ambition, such was he, O Friend!
Of whom I speak. So Beaupuis (let the name

Stand near the worthiest of Antiquity)   420
Fashioned his life; and many a long discourse,
With like persuasion honoured, we maintained:
He, on his part, accoutred for the worst.
430   He perished fighting, in supreme command,
Upon the borders of the unhappy Loire,   425
For liberty, against deluded men,
His fellow country-men, and yet most blessed
In this, that he the fate of later times
Lived not to see, nor what we now behold
Who have as ardent hearts as he had then.   430

    Along that very Loire, with festivals
Resounding at all hours, and innocent yet
Of civil slaughter, was our frequent walk;
440   Or in wide forests of the neighbourhood,
High woods and over-arched, with open space   435
On every side, and footing many a mile –
Inwoven roots and moss smooth as the sea,
A solemn region. Often in such place,
From earnest dialogues I slipped in thought,
And let remembrance steal to other times,   439
When Hermits, from their sheds and caves forth-strayed,
Walked by themselves, so met in shades like these,
And if a devious traveller was heard   447
450   Approaching from a distance, as might chance,
With speed and echoes loud of trampling hoofs
From the hard floor reverberated, then   450
It was Angelica thundering through the woods
Upon her palfrey, or that gentler maid
Erminia, fugitive as fair as she.
Sometimes I saw, methought, a pair of knights
Joust underneath the trees, that as in storm   455
Did rock above their heads; anon, the din

420 Stand near the worthiest of Antiquity)
Fashioned his life; and many a long discourse,
With like persuasion honoured, we maintained:
He, on his part, accoutred for the worst.
He perished fighting, in supreme command,
Upon the borders of the unhappy Loire,
For liberty, against deluded men,
His fellow country-men; and yet most blessed
In this, that he the fate of later times
Lived not to see, nor what we now behold,
430 Who have as ardent hearts as he had then.

Along that very Loire, with festal mirth
Resounding at all hours, and innocent yet
Of civil slaughter, was our frequent walk;
Or in wide forests of continuous shade,
Lofty and over-arched, with open space
Beneath the trees, clear footing many a mile –
A solemn region. Oft amid those haunts,
From earnest dialogues I slipped in thought,
And let remembrance steal to other times,
440 When o'er those interwoven roots, moss-clad,
And smooth as marble or a waveless sea,
Some Hermit, from his cell forth-strayed, might pace
In sylvan meditation undisturbed;
As on the pavement of a Gothic church
Walks a lone Monk, when service hath expired,
In peace and silence. But if e'er was heard, –
Heard, though unseen, – a devious traveller,
Retiring or approaching from afar
With speed and echoes loud of trampling hoofs
450 From the hard floor reverberated, then
It was Angelica thundering through the woods
Upon her palfrey, or that gentle maid
Erminia, fugitive as fair as she.
Sometimes methought I saw a pair of knights
Joust underneath the trees, that as in storm
Rocked high above their heads; anon, the din

Of boisterous merriment, and music's roar,
460 With sudden proclamation, burst from haunt
Of Satyrs in some viewless glade, with dance
Rejoicing o'er a female in the midst,   460
A mortal beauty, their unhappy thrall.
The width of those huge forests, unto me
A novel scene, did often in this way
Master my fancy, while I wandered on
With that revered companion. And sometimes –   465
When to a convent in a meadow green,
By a brook-side, we came, a roofless pile,
470 And not by reverential touch of Time
Dismantled, but by violence abrupt –
In spite of those heart-bracing colloquies,   470
In spite of real fervour, and of that
Less genuine and wrought up within myself –
I could not but bewail a wrong so harsh,
And for the Matin-bell to sound no more
Grieved, and the evening taper, and the cross   475
High on the topmost pinnacle, a sign
Admonitory to the traveller,
480 First seen above the woods.
                          And when my friend
Pointed upon occasion to the site   480
Of Romorentin, home of ancient kings,
To the imperial edifice of Blois,
Or to that rural castle, name now slipped
From my remembrance, where a lady lodged,
By the first Francis wooed, and bound to him   485
In chains of mutual passion, from the tower,
As a tradition of the country tells,
Practised to commune with her royal knight
490 By cressets and love-beacons, intercourse
'Twixt her high-seated residence and his   490
Far off at Chambord on the plain beneath;
Even here, though less than with the peaceful house
Religious, 'mid these frequent monuments
Of Kings, their vices and their better deeds,

Of boisterous merriment, and music's roar,
In sudden proclamation, burst from haunt
Of Satyrs in some viewless glade, with dance
460 Rejoicing o'er a female in the midst,
A mortal beauty, their unhappy thrall.
The width of those huge forests, unto me
A novel scene, did often in this way
Master my fancy while I wandered on
With that revered companion. And sometimes –
When to a convent in a meadow green,
By a brook-side, we came, a roofless pile,
And not by reverential touch of Time
Dismantled, but by violence abrupt –
470 In spite of those heart-bracing colloquies,
In spite of real fervour, and of that
Less genuine and wrought up within myself –
I could not but bewail a wrong so harsh,
And for the Matin-bell to sound no more
Grieved, and the twilight taper, and the cross
High on the topmost pinnacle, a sign
(How welcome to the weary traveller's eyes!)
Of hospitality and peaceful rest.
And when the partner of those varied walks
480 Pointed upon occasion to the site
Of Romorentin, home of ancient kings,
To the imperial edifice of Blois,
Or to that rural castle, name now slipped
From my remembrance, where a lady lodged,
By the first Francis wooed, and bound to him
In chains of mutual passion, from the tower,
As a tradition of the country tells,
Practised to commune with her royal knight
By cressets and love-beacons, intercourse
490 'Twixt her high-seated residence and his
Far off at Chambord on the plain beneath;
Even here, though less than with the peaceful house
Religious, 'mid those frequent monuments
Of Kings, their vices and their better deeds,

Imagination, potent to inflame   495
At times with virtuous wrath and noble scorn,
Did also often mitigate the force
Of civic prejudice, the bigotry,
So call it, of a youthful patriot's mind;
And on these spots with many gleams I looked   500
Of chivalrous delight. Yet not the less,
Hatred of absolute rule, where will of one
Is law for all, and of that barren pride
In them who, by immunities unjust,
Betwixt the sovereign and the people stand,   505
His helper and not theirs, laid stronger hold
Daily upon me, mixed with pity too
And love; for where hope is, there love will be
For the abject multitude. And when we chanced
One day to meet a hunger-bitten girl,   510
Who crept along fitting her languid self
Unto a heifer's motion, by a cord
Tied to her arm, and picking thus from the lane
Its sustenance, while the girl with her two hands
Was busy knitting in a heartless mood   515
Of solitude, and at the sight my friend
In agitation said, ''Tis against *that*
Which we are fighting', I with him believed
Devoutly that a spirit was abroad
Which could not be withstood, that poverty   520
At least like this would in a little time
Be found no more, that we should see the earth
Unthwarted in her wish to recompense
The industrious, and the lowly child of toil,
All institutes for ever blotted out   525
That legalized exclusion, empty pomp
Abolished, sensual state and cruel power,
Whether by edict of the one or few;
And finally, as sum and crown of all,
Should see the people having a strong hand   530
In making their own laws; whence better days
To all mankind. But, these things set apart,

Imagination, potent to inflame
At times with virtuous wrath and noble scorn,
Did also often mitigate the force
Of civic prejudice, the bigotry,
So call it, of a youthful patriot's mind;
500 And on these spots with many gleams I looked
Of chivalrous delight. Yet not the less
Hatred of absolute rule, where will of one
Is law for all, and of that barren pride
In them who, by immunities unjust,
Between the sovereign and the people stand,
His helper and not theirs, laid stronger hold
Daily upon me, mixed with pity too
And love; for where hope is, there love will be
For the abject multitude. And when we chanced
510 One day to meet a hunger-bitten girl,
Who crept along fitting her languid gait
Unto a heifer's motion, by a cord
Tied to her arm, and picking thus from the lane
Its sustenance, while the girl with pallid hands
Was busy knitting in a heartless mood
Of solitude, and at the sight my friend
In agitation said, ''Tis against *that*
That we are fighting', I with him believed
That a benignant spirit was abroad
520 Which might not be withstood, that poverty
Abject as this would in a little time
Be found no more, that we should see the earth
Unthwarted in her wish to recompense
The meek, the lowly, patient child of toil,
All institutes for ever blotted out
That legalized exclusion, empty pomp
Abolished, sensual state and cruel power,
Whether by edict of the one or few;
And finally, as sum and crown of all,
530 Should see the people having a strong hand
In framing their own laws; whence better days
To all mankind. But, these things set apart,

Was not the single confidence enough
To animate the mind that ever turned
A thought to human welfare? That henceforth   535
Captivity by mandate without law
Should cease; and open accusation lead
To sentence in the hearing of the world,
540 And open punishment, if not the air
Be free to breathe in, and the heart of man   540
Dread nothing. Having touched this argument
I shall not, as my purpose was, take note
Of other matters which detained us oft
In thought or conversation, public acts,
And public persons, and the emotions wrought
Within our minds by the ever-varying wind   545
Of record and report which day by day
Swept over us; but I will here instead
550 Draw from obscurity a tragic tale
Not in its spirit singular indeed
But haply worth memorial, as I heard
The events related by my Patriot friend
And others who had borne a part therein.

*Love
Story*

Oh, happy time of youthful lovers, (thus
My story may begin). Oh, balmy time,
In which a love-knot, on a lady's brow,   555
Is fairer than the fairest star in Heaven!
To such inheritance of blessedness
560 Young Vaudracour was brought by years that had
A little overstepped his stripling prime.
A town of small repute in the heart of France
Was the youth's birthplace: there he vowed his love
To Julia, a bright maid, from parents sprung
Not mean in their condition; but with rights
Unhonoured of Nobility, and hence
The father of the young man, who had place
Among that order, spurned the very thought
Of such alliance. From their cradles up,
570 With but a step between their several homes

Was not this single confidence enough
To animate the mind that ever turned
A thought to human welfare? That henceforth
Captivity by mandate without law
Should cease; and open accusation lead
To sentence in the hearing of the world,
And open punishment, if not the air
540 Be free to breathe in, and the heart of man
Dread nothing. From this height I shall not stoop
To humbler matter that detained us oft
In thought or conversation, public acts,
And public persons, and emotions wrought
Within the breast, as ever-varying winds
Of record or report swept over us;
But I might here, instead, repeat a tale,
Told by my Patriot friend, of sad events,
That prove to what low depth had struck the roots,
550 How widely spread the boughs, of that old tree
Which, as a deadly mischief, and a foul
And black dishonour, France was weary of.

Oh, happy time of youthful lovers, (thus
My story may begin). Oh, balmy time,
In which a love-knot, on a lady's brow,
Is fairer than the fairest star in Heaven!
So might – and with that prelude *did* begin
The record; and, in faithful verse, was given
The doleful sequel.
                            But our little bark
560 On a strong river boldly hath been launched;
And from the driving current should we turn
To loiter wilfully within a creek,
Howe'er attractive, Fellow-voyager!
Wouldst thou not chide? Yet deem not my pains lost:
For Vaudracour and Julia (so were named
The ill-fated pair) in that plain tale will draw
Tears from the hearts of others, when their own

377

The pair had thriven together year by year,
Friends, playmates, twins in pleasure, after strife
And petty quarrels had grown fond again,
Each other's advocate, each other's help,
Nor ever happy if they were apart:
A basis this for deep and solid love,
And endless constancy, and placid truth;
But whatsoever of such treasures might,
Beneath the outside of their youth, have lain
580 Reserved for mellower years, his present mind
Was under fascination; he beheld
A vision, and he loved the thing he saw.
Arabian fiction never filled the world
With half the wonders that were wrought for him.
Earth lived in one great presence of the spring,
Life turned the meanest of her implements
Before his eyes to price above all gold,
The house she dwelt in was a sainted shrine,
Her chamber-window did surpass in glory
590 The portals of the east, all paradise
Could by the simple opening of a door
Let itself in upon him, pathways, walks,
Swarmed with enchantment till his spirit sank
Beneath the burden, overblessed for life.
This state was theirs, till whether through effect
Of some delirious hour, or that the youth,
Seeing so many bars betwixt himself
And the dear haven where he wished to be
In honourable wedlock with his love
600 Without a certain knowledge of his own,
Was inwardly prepared to turn aside
From law and custom, and entrust himself
To Nature for a happy end of all;
And thus abated of that pure reserve
Congenial to his loyal heart, with which
It would have pleased him to attend the steps
Of maiden so divinely beautiful
I know not, but reluctantly must add

Shall beat no more. Thou, also, there mayst read,
At leisure, how the enamoured youth was driven,
570 By public power abased, to fatal crime,
Nature's rebellion against monstrous law;
How, between heart and heart, oppression thrust
Her mandates, severing whom true love had joined,
Harassing both; until he sank and pressed
The couch his fate had made for him; supine,
Save when the stings of viperous remorse,
Trying their strength, enforced him to start up,
Aghast and prayerless. Into a deep wood
He fled, to shun the haunts of human kind;
580 There dwelt, weakened in spirit more and more;
Nor could the voice of Freedom, which through France
Full speedily resounded, public hope,
Or personal memory of his own worst wrongs,
Rouse him; but, hidden in those gloomy shades,
His days he wasted, – an imbecile mind.

That Julia, yet without the name of wife,
610 Carried about her for a secret grief
The promise of a mother.
                To conceal
The threatened shame the parents of the maid
Found means to hurry her away by night
And unforewarned, that in a distant town
She might remain shrouded in privacy,
Until the babe was born. When morning came
The lover thus bereft, stung with his loss
And all uncertain whither he should turn
Chafed like a wild beast in the toils; at length,
620 Following as his suspicions led, he found,
O joy! sure traces of the fugitives,
Pursued them to the town where they had stopped,
And lastly to the very house itself
Which had been chosen for the maid's retreat.
The sequel may be easily divined,
Walks backwards, forwards, morning, noon and night,
When decency and caution would allow,
And Julia, who, whenever to herself
She happened to be left a moment's space,
630 Was busy at her casement, as a swallow
About its nest, ere long did thus espy
Her lover, thence a stolen interview
By night accomplished, with a ladder's help.

    I pass the raptures of the pair; such theme
Hath by a hundred poets been set forth
In more delightful verse than skill of mine
Could fashion, chiefly by that darling bard
Who told of Juliet and her Romeo,
And of the lark's note heard before its time,
640 And of the streaks that laced the severing clouds
In the unrelenting east. 'Tis mine to tread
The humbler province of plain history,
And, without choice of circumstance, submissively
Relate what I have heard. The lovers came

380

To this resolve, with which they parted, pleased
And confident, that Vaudracour should hie
Back to his father's house, and there employ
Means aptest to obtain a sum of gold,
A final portion, even, if that might be,
650   Which done, together they could then take flight
To some remote and solitary place
Where they might live with no one to behold
Their happiness, or to disturb their love.
Immediately, and with this mission charged
Home to his father's house did he return
And there remained a while without hint given
Of his design; but if a word were dropped
Touching the matter of his passion, still
In hearing of his father, Vaudracour
660   Persisted openly that nothing less
Than death should make him yield up hope to be
A blessèd husband of the maid he loved.

     Incensed at such obduracy and slight
Of exhortations and remonstrances
The father threw out threats that by a mandate
Bearing the private signet of the state
He should be baffled of his mad intent,
And that should cure him. From this time the youth
Conceived a terror, and by night or day
670   Stirred nowhere without arms. Soon afterwards
His parents to their country seat withdrew
Upon some feigned occasion; and the son
Was left with one attendant in the house.
Retiring to his chamber for the night,
While he was entering at the door, attempts
Were made to seize him by three armèd men,
The instruments of ruffian power; the youth
In the first impulse of his rage, laid one
Dead at his feet, and to the second gave
680   A perilous wound, which done, at sight
Of the dead man, he peacefully resigned

His person to the law, was lodged in prison,
And wore the fetters of a criminal.

Through three weeks' space, by means which love devised,
The maid in her seclusion had received
Tidings of Vaudracour, and how he sped
Upon his enterprise. Thereafter came
A silence, half a circle did the moon
Complete, and then a whole, and still the same
690 Silence; a thousand thousand fears and hopes
Stirred in her mind; thoughts waking, thoughts of sleep
Entangled in each other, and at last
Self-slaughter seemed her only resting-place.
So did she fare in her uncertainty.

At length, by interference of a friend,
One who had sway at court, the youth regained
His liberty, on promise to sit down
Quietly in his father's house, nor take
One step to reunite himself with her
700 Of whom his parents disapproved: hard law
To which he gave consent only because
His freedom else could nowise be procured.
Back to his father's house he went, remained
Eight days, and then his resolution failed:
He fled to Julia, and the words with which
He greeted her were these. 'All right is gone,
Gone from me. Thou no longer now art mine,
I thine; a murderer, Julia, cannot love
An innocent woman; I behold thy face,
710 I see thee and my misery is complete.'
She could not give him answer; afterwards
She coupled with his father's name some words
Of vehement indignation; but the youth
Checked her, nor would he hear of this; for thought
Unfilial, or unkind, had never once
Found harbour in his breast. The lovers thus
United once again together lived

For a few days, which were to Vaudracour
Days of dejection, sorrow and remorse
720 For that ill deed of violence which his hand
Had hastily committed: for the youth
Was of a loyal spirit, a conscience nice
And over tender for the trial which
His fate had called him to. The father's mind,
Meanwhile, remained unchanged, and Vaudracour
Learned that a mandate had been newly issued
To arrest him on the spot. Oh pain it was
To part! he could not – and he lingered still
To the last moment of his time, and then,
730 At dead of night with snow upon the ground,
He left the city, and in villages
The most sequestered of the neighbourhood
Lay hidden for the space of several days
Until the horseman bringing back report
That he was nowhere to be found, the search
Was ended. Back returned the ill-fated youth,
And from the house where Julia lodged (to which
He now found open ingress, having gained
The affection of the family, who loved him
740 Both for his own, and for the maiden's sake)
One night retiring, he was seized – But here
A portion of the tale may well be left
In silence, though my memory could add
Much how the youth, and in short space of time,
Was traversed from without, much, too, of thoughts
By which he was employed in solitude
Under privation and restraint, and what
Through dark and shapeless fear of things to come,
And what through strong compunction for the past
750 He suffered breaking down in heart and mind.
Such grace, if grace it were, had been vouchsafed
Or such effect had through the Father's want
Of power, or through his negligence ensued
That Vaudracour was suffered to remain,
Though under guard and without liberty,

In the same city with the unhappy maid
From whom he was divided. So they fared
Objects of general concern, till, moved
With pity for their wrongs, the magistrate,
760 The same who had placed the youth in custody,
By application to the minister
Obtained his liberty upon condition
That to his father's house he should return.

He left his prison almost on the eve
Of Julia's travail; she had likewise been
As from the time indeed, when she had first
Been brought for secrecy to this abode,
Though treated with consoling tenderness,
Herself a prisoner, a dejected one,
770 Filled with a lover's and a woman's fears,
And whensoe'er the mistress of the house
Entered the room for the last time at night
And Julia with a low and plaintive voice
Said 'You are coming then to lock me up',
The housewife when these words, always the same,
Were by her captive languidly pronounced
Could never hear them uttered without tears.

A day or two before her child-bed time
Was Vaudracour restored to her, and soon
780 As he might be permitted to return
Into her chamber after the child's birth
The master of the family begged that all
The household might be summoned, doubting not
But that they might receive impressions then
Friendly to human kindness. Vaudracour
(This heard I from one present at the time)
Held up the new-born infant in his arms
And kissed, and blessed, and covered it with tears,
Uttering a prayer that he might never be
790 As wretched as his father; then he gave
The child to her who bare it, and she too

Repeated the same prayer, took it again
And muttering something faintly afterwards
He gave the infant to the standers-by,
And wept in silence upon Julia's neck.

    Two months did he continue in the house,
And often yielded up himself to plans
Of future happiness. 'You shall return,
Julia,' said he, 'and to your father's house
800 Go with your child, you have been wretched, yet
It is a town where both of us were born,
None will reproach you, for our loves are known;
With ornaments the prettiest you shall dress
Your boy, as soon as he can run about,
And when he thus is at his play my father
Will see him from the window, and the child
Will by his beauty move his grandsire's heart,
So that it shall be softened, and our loves
End happily, as they began.' These gleams
810 Appeared but seldom; oftener he was seen
Propping a pale and melancholy face
Upon the mother's bosom, resting thus
His head upon one breast, while from the other
The babe was drawing in its quiet food.
At other times, when he, in silence, long
And fixedly had looked upon her face,
He would exclaim, 'Julia, how much thine eyes
Have cost me!' During day-time when the child
Lay in its cradle, by its side he sate,
820 Not quitting it an instant. The whole town
In his unmerited misfortunes now
Took part, and if he either at the door
Or window for a moment with his child
Appeared, immediately the street was thronged
While others frequently without reserve
Passed and repassed before the house to steal
A look at him. Oft at this time he wrote
Requesting, since he knew that the consent

Of Julia's parents never could be gained
830   To a clandestine marriage, that his father
Would from the birthright of an eldest son
Exclude him, giving but, when this was done,
A sanction to his nuptials: vain request,
To which no answer was returned. And now
From her own home the mother of his love
Arrived to apprise the daughter of her fixed
And last resolve, that, since all hope to move
The old man's heart proved vain, she must retire
Into a convent, and be there immured.
840   Julia was thunderstricken by these words,
And she insisted on a mother's rights
To take her child along with her, a grant
Impossible, as she at last perceived;
The persons of the house no sooner heard
Of this decision upon Julia's fate
Than everyone was overwhelmed with grief
Nor could they frame a manner soft enough
To impart the tidings to the youth; but great
Was their astonishment when they beheld him
850   Receive the news in calm despondency,
Composed and silent, without outward sign
Of even the least emotion; seeing this
When Julia scattered some upbraiding words
Upon his slackness he thereto returned
No answer, only took the mother's hand
Who loved him scarcely less than her own child,
And kissed it, without seeming to be pressed
By any pain that 'twas the hand of one
Whose errand was to part him from his love
860   For ever. In the city he remained
A season after Julia had retired
And in the convent taken up her home
To the end that he might place his infant babe
With a fit nurse, which done, beneath the roof
Where now his little one was lodged, he passed
The day entire, and scarcely could at length

Tear himself from the cradle to return
Home to his father's house, in which he dwelt
Awhile, and then came back that he might see
870 Whether the babe had gained sufficient strength
To bear removal. He quitted this same town
For the last time, attendant by the side
Of a close chair, a litter or sedan,
In which the child was carried. To a hill,
Which rose at a league's distance from the town,
The family of the house where he had lodged
Attended him, and parted from him there,
Watching below until he disappeared
On the hill top. His eyes he scarcely took,
880 Through all that journey, from the chair in which
The babe was carried; and at every inn
Or place at which they halted or reposed
Laid him upon his knees, nor would permit
The hands of any but himself to dress
The infant or undress. By one of those
Who bore the chair these facts, at his return,
Were told, and in relating them he wept.

This was the manner in which Vaudracour
Departed with his infant; and thus reached
890 His father's house, where to the innocent child
Admittance was denied. The young man spake
No word of indignation or reproof,
But of his father begged, a last request,
That a retreat might be assigned to him,
A house where in the country he might dwell
With such allowance as his wants required
And the more lonely that the mansion was
'Twould be more welcome. To a lodge that stood
Deep in a forest, with leave given, at the age
900 Of four and twenty summers he retired;
And thither took with him his infant babe,
And one domestic for their common needs,
An aged woman. It consoled him here

To attend upon the orphan and perform
The office of a nurse to his young child
Which after a short time by some mistake
Or indiscretion of the father, died.
The tale I follow to its last recess
Of suffering or of peace, I know not which;
910 Theirs be the blame who caused the woe, not mine.

From that time forth he never uttered word
To any living. An inhabitant
Of that same town in which the pair had left
So lively a remembrance of their griefs
By chance of business coming within reach
Of his retirement to the spot repaired
With the intent to visit him: he reached
The house and only found the matron there,
Who told him that his pains were thrown away,
920 For that her master never uttered word
To living soul – not even to her. Behold
While they were speaking, Vaudracour approached;
But, seeing some one there, just as his hand
Was stretched towards the garden-gate, he shrunk,
And like a shadow glided out of view.
Shocked at his savage outside, from the place
The visitor retired.
                          Thus lived the youth
Cut off from all intelligence with man,
And shunning even the light of common day;
930 Nor could the voice of Freedom, which through France *581*
Soon afterwards resounded, public hope,
Or personal memory of his own deep wrongs,
Rouse him; but in those solitary shades
His days he wasted, – an imbecile mind.

X + XI W's agonies of guilt. his
divided loyalties between Engl + Fr, his
gradual disillusion w/ course of Fr.
Rev. brought him to
verge of an emotional breakdown

Book Tenth

RESIDENCE IN FRANCE AND FRENCH
REVOLUTION

"sick, wearied out w/ contrarieties" he
"yielded up moral questions in despair"
at age 29, his recovery was complete

It was a beautiful and silent day
That overspread the countenance of earth,
Then fading, with unusual quietness, 3
When from the Loire I parted, and through scenes
Of vineyard, orchard, meadow-ground and tilth,
Calm waters, gleams of sun, and breathless trees,
Towards the fierce Metropolis turned my steps
Their homeward way to England. From his throne 11
The King had fallen; the congregated host –
10 Dire cloud, upon the front of which was written
The tender mercies of the dismal wind
That bore it – on the plains of Liberty 15
Had burst innocuously. Say more, the swarm
That came elate and jocund, like a band
Of eastern hunters, to enfold in ring
Narrowing itself by moments and reduce
To the last punctual spot of their despair
A race of victims, so they seemed, *themselves*
Had shrunk from sight of their own task, and fled
20 In terror. Desolation and dismay
Remained for them whose fancies had grown rank
With evil expectations; confidence
And perfect triumph to the better cause. 30

and he entered upon the
springtime of his poetic career.

398

Book Tenth

It was a beautiful and silent day
That overspread the countenance of earth,
Then fading with unusual quietness, –
A day as beautiful as e'er was given
To soothe regret, though deepening what it soothed,
When by the gliding Loire I paused, and cast
Upon his rich domains, vineyard and tilth,
Green meadow-ground, and many-coloured woods,
Again, and yet again, a farewell look;
10 Then from the quiet of that scene passed on,
Bound to the fierce Metropolis. From his throne
The King had fallen, and that invading host –
Presumptuous cloud, on whose black front was written
The tender mercies of the dismal wind
That bore it – on the plains of Liberty
Had burst innocuous. Say in bolder words,
They – who had come elate as eastern hunters
Banded beneath the Great Mogul, when he
Erewhile went forth from Agra or Lahore,
20 Rajahs and Omrahs in his train, intent
To drive their prey enclosed within a ring
Wide as a province, but, the signal given,
Before the point of the life-threatening spear
Narrowing itself by moments – they, rash men,
Had seen the anticipated quarry turned
Into avengers, from whose wrath they fled
In terror. Disappointment and dismay
Remained for all whose fancies had run wild
With evil expectations; confidence
30 And perfect triumph for the better cause.

Fr: became a Republic [handwritten marginal note]

The State, as if to stamp the final seal
On her security, and to the world
Show what she was, a high and fearless soul,   *33*
Or rather in a spirit of thanks to those
Who had stirred up her slackening faculties
To a new transition, had assumed with joy
30   The body and the venerable name   *40*
Of a Republic. Lamentable crimes,
'Tis true, had gone before this hour, the work
Of massacre, in which the senseless sword
Was prayed to as a judge; but these were past,
Earth free from them for ever, as was thought, –   *45*
Ephemeral monsters, to be seen but once!
Things that could only show themselves and die.

This was the time in which, inflamed with hope,
To Paris I returned. Again I ranged,
40   More eagerly than I had done before,
Through the wide city, and in progress passed   *50*
The prison where the unhappy monarch lay,
Associate with his children and his wife
In bondage; and the palace, lately stormed
With roar of cannon and a numerous host.
I crossed (a black and empty area then)   *55*
The square of the Carrousel, few weeks back
Heaped up with dead and dying, upon these
And other sights looking, as doth a man
50   Upon a volume whose contents he knows
Are memorable, but from him locked up,   *60*
Being written in a tongue he cannot read,
So that he questions the mute leaves with pain,
And half upbraids their silence. But that night
When on my bed I lay, I was most moved
And felt most deeply in what world I was.
My room was high and lonely, near the roof
Of a large mansion or hotel, a spot

The State, as if to stamp the final seal
On her security, and to the world
Show what she was, a high and fearless soul,
Exulting in defiance, or heart-stung
By sharp resentment, or belike to taunt
With spiteful gratitude the baffled League,
That had stirred up her slackening faculties
To a new transition, when the King was crushed,
Spared not the empty throne, and in proud haste
40   Assumed the body and venerable name
Of a Republic. Lamentable crimes,
'Tis true, had gone before this hour, dire work
Of massacre, in which the senseless sword
Was prayed to as a judge; but these were past,
Earth free from them for ever, as was thought, –
Ephemeral monsters, to be seen but once!
Things that could only show themselves and die.

Cheered with this hope, to Paris I returned,
And ranged, with ardour heretofore unfelt,
50   The spacious city, and in progress passed
The prison where the unhappy Monarch lay,
Associate with his children and his wife
In bondage; and the palace, lately stormed
With roar of cannon by a furious host.
I crossed the square (an empty area then!)
Of the Carrousel, where so late had lain
The dead, upon the dying heaped, and gazed
On this and other spots, as doth a man
Upon a volume whose contents he knows
60   Are memorable, but from him locked up,
Being written in a tongue he cannot read,
So that he questions the mute leaves with pain,
And half upbraids their silence. But that night
I felt most deeply in what world I was,
What ground I trod on, and what air I breathed.
High was my room and lonely, near the roof
Of a large mansion or hotel, a lodge

That would have pleased me in more quiet times,
60   Nor was it wholly without pleasure then.
With unextinguished taper I kept watch,   *70*
Reading at intervals; the fear gone by
Pressed on me almost like a fear to come.
I thought of those September massacres,
Divided from me by a little month,
And felt and touched them, a substantial dread: *75*
The rest was conjured up from tragic fictions,
And mournful calendars of true history,
Remembrances and dim admonishments.
70   The horse is taught his manage, and the wind
Of heaven wheels round and treads in his own steps;
Year follows year, the tide returns again,
Day follows day, all things have second birth;
The earthquake is not satisfied at once;
And in such way I wrought upon myself,   *85*
Until I seemed to hear a voice that cried,
To the whole city, 'Sleep no more.' To this
Add comments of a calmer mind, from which
I could not gather full security,
80   But at the best it seemed a place of fear
Unfit for the repose of night [   ]   *92*
Defenceless as a wood where tigers roam.

    Betimes next morning to the Palace-walk
Of Orleans I repaired and entering there
Was greeted, among divers other notes,
By voices of the hawkers in the crowd
Bawling, 'Denunciation of the crimes   *100*
Of Maximilian Robespierre'; the speech
Which in their hands they carried was the same
90   Which had been recently pronounced, the day
When Robespierre, well knowing for what mark

That would have pleased me in more quiet times;
Nor was it wholly without pleasure then.
70 With unextinguished taper I kept watch,
Reading at intervals; the fear gone by
Pressed on me almost like a fear to come.
I thought of those September massacres,
Divided from me by one little month,
Saw them and touched: the rest was conjured up
From tragic fictions or true history,
Remembrances and dim admonishments.
The horse is taught his manage, and no star
Of wildest course but treads back his own steps;
80 For the spent hurricane the air provides
As fierce a successor; the tide retreats
But to return out of its hiding-place
In the great deep; all things have second birth;
The earthquake is not satisfied at once;
And in this way I wrought upon myself,
Until I seemed to hear a voice that cried,
To the whole city, 'Sleep no more.' The trance
Fled with the voice to which it had given birth;
But vainly comments of a calmer mind
90 Promised soft peace and sweet forgetfulness.
The place, all hushed and silent as it was,
Appeared unfit for the repose of night,
Defenceless as a wood where tigers roam.

    With early morning towards the Palace-walk
Of Orleans eagerly I turned; as yet
The streets were still; not so those long Arcades;
There, 'mid a peal of ill-matched sounds and cries,
That greeted me on entering, I could hear
Shrill voices from the hawkers in the throng,
100 Bawling, 'Denunciation of the Crimes
Of Maximilian Robespierre'; the hand,
Prompt as the voice, held forth a printed speech,
The same that had been recently pronounced,
When Robespierre, not ignorant for what mark

Some words of indirect reproof had been   *105*
Intended, rose in hardihood, and dared
The man who had an ill surmise of him
To bring his charge in openness; whereat,
When a dead pause ensued, and no one stirred,
In silence of all present, from his seat   *110*
Louvet walked singly through the avenue,
And took his station in the Tribune, saying,
100 'I, Robespierre, accuse thee!' 'Tis well known
What was the issue of that charge, and how
Louvet was left alone without support
Of his irresolute friends; but these are things   *120*
Of which I speak, only as they were storm
Or sunshine to my individual mind,
No further. Let me then relate that now –
In some sort seeing with my proper eyes
That Liberty, and Life, and Death would soon   *125*
To the remotest corners of the land
110 Lie in the arbitrement of those who ruled
The capital City; what was struggled for,
And by what combatants victory must be won;
The indecision on their part whose aim   *130*
Seemed best, and the straightforward path of those
Who in attack or in defence alike
Were strong through their impiety – greatly I
Was agitated; yea, I could almost
Have prayed that throughout earth upon all souls,   *135*
By patient exercise of reason made
120 Worthy of liberty, upon every soul
Matured to live in plainness and in truth,
The gift of tongues might fall, and men arrive
From the four quarters of the winds to do   *140*
For France, what without help she could not do,

Some words of indirect reproof had been
Intended, rose in hardihood, and dared
The man who had an ill surmise of him
To bring his charge in openness; whereat,
When a dead pause ensued, and no one stirred,
110   In silence of all present, from his seat
Louvet walked single through the avenue,
And took his station in the Tribune, saying,
'I, Robespierre, accuse thee!' Well is known
The inglorious issue of that charge, and how
He, who had launched the startling thunderbolt,
The one bold man, whose voice the attack had sounded,
Was left without a follower to discharge
His perilous duty, and retire lamenting
That Heaven's best aid is wasted upon men
120   Who to themselves are false.
                                                    But these are things
Of which I speak, only as they were storm
Or sunshine to my individual mind,
No further. Let me then relate that now –
In some sort seeing with my proper eyes
That Liberty, and Life, and Death would soon
To the remotest corners of the land
Lie in the arbitrement of those who ruled
The capital City; what was struggled for,
And by what combatants victory must be won;
130   The indecision on their part whose aim
Seemed best, and the straightforward path of those
Who in attack or in defence were strong
Through their impiety – my inmost soul
Was agitated; yea, I could almost
Have prayed that throughout earth upon all men,
By patient exercise of reason made
Worthy of liberty, all spirits filled
With zeal expanding in Truth's holy light,
The gift of tongues might fall, and power arrive
140   From the four quarters of the winds to do
For France, what without help she could not do,

A work of honour; think not that to this
I added, work of safety: from such thought
And the least fear about the end of things
I was as far as angels are from guilt.   *145*

    Yet did I grieve, nor only grieved, but thought
130 Of opposition and of remedies:
An insignificant stranger and obscure,
Mean as I was, and little graced with power
Of eloquence even in my native speech,   *150*
And all unfit for tumult and intrigue,
Yet would I willingly have taken up
A service at this time for cause so great,
However dangerous. Inly I revolved
How much the destiny of Man had still   *155*
Hung upon single persons; that there was,
140 Transcendent to all local patrimony,
One nature, as there is one sun in heaven;
That objects, even as they are great, thereby
Do come within the reach of humblest eyes;   *160*
That Man was only weak through his mistrust
And want of hope where evidence divine
Proclaimed to him that hope should be most sure;
That, with desires heroic and firm sense,
A spirit thoroughly faithful to itself,
Unquenchable, unsleeping, undismayed,
150 Was as an instinct among men, a stream
That gathered up each petty straggling rill
And vein of water, glad to be rolled on
In safe obedience; that a mind whose rest
Was where it ought to be, in self-restraint,
In circumspection and simplicity,   *175*
Fell rarely in entire discomfiture
Below its aim, or met with, from without,
A treachery that defeated it or foiled.

A work of honour; think not that to this
I added, work of safety: from all doubt
Or trepidation for the end of things
Far was I, far as angels are from guilt.

Yet did I grieve, nor only grieved, but thought
Of opposition and of remedies:
An insignificant stranger and obscure,
And one, moreover, little graced with power
150   Of eloquence even in my native speech,
And all unfit for tumult or intrigue,
Yet would I at this time with willing heart
Have undertaken for a cause so great
Service however dangerous. I revolved,
How much the destiny of Man had still
Hung upon single persons; that there was,
Transcendent to all local patrimony,
One nature, as there is one sun in heaven;
That objects, even as they are great, thereby
160   Do come within the reach of humblest eyes;
That Man is only weak through his mistrust
And want of hope where evidence divine
Proclaims to him that hope should be most sure;
Nor did the inexperience of my youth
Preclude conviction, that a spirit strong
In hope, and trained to noble aspirations,
A spirit thoroughly faithful to itself,
Is for Society's unreasoning herd
A domineering instinct, serves at once
170   For way and guide, a fluent receptacle
That gathers up each petty straggling rill
And vein of water, glad to be rolled on
In safe obedience; that a mind, whose rest
Is where it ought to be, in self-restraint,
In circumspection and simplicity,
Falls rarely in entire discomfiture
Below its aim, or meets with, from without,
A treachery that foils it or defeats;

On the other side, I called to mind those truths   *191*
160 Which are the commonplaces of the schools –
(A theme for boys, too trite even to be felt,)
Yet, with a revelation's liveliness,
In all their comprehensive bearings known   *195*
And visible to philosophers of old,
Men who, to business of the world untrained,
Lived in the shade; and to Harmodius known
And his compeer Aristogiton, known
To Brutus – that tyrannic power is weak,   *200*
Hath neither gratitude, nor faith, nor love,
170 Nor the support of good or evil men
To trust in; that the godhead which is ours
Can never utterly be charmed or stilled;
That nothing hath a natural right to last   *205*
But equity and reason; that all else
Meets foes irreconcilable, and at best
Doth live but by variety of disease.

Well might my wishes be intense, my thoughts
Strong and perturbed, not doubting at that time,   *210*
Creed which ten shameful years have not annulled,
180 But that the virtue of one paramount mind
Would have abashed those impious crests – have quelled
Outrage and bloody power, and, in despite
Of what the People were through ignorance

And, lastly, if the means on human will,
180 Frail human will, dependent should betray
Him who too boldly trusted them, I felt
That 'mid the loud distractions of the world
A sovereign voice subsists within the soul,
Arbiter undisturbed of right and wrong,
Of life and death, in majesty severe
Enjoining, as may best promote the aims
Of truth and justice, either sacrifice,
From whatsoever region of our cares
Or our infirm affections Nature pleads,
190 Earnest and blind, against the stern decree.

On the other side, I called to mind those truths
That are the commonplaces of the schools –
(A theme for boys, too hackneyed for their sires,)
Yet, with a revelation's liveliness,
In all their comprehensive bearings known
And visible to philosophers of old,
Men who, to business of the world untrained,
Lived in the shade; and to Harmodius known
And his compeer Aristogiton, known
200 To Brutus – that tyrannic power is weak,
Hath neither gratitude, nor faith, nor love,
Nor the support of good or evil men
To trust in; that the godhead which is ours
Can never utterly be charmed or stilled;
That nothing hath a natural right to last
But equity and reason; that all else
Meets foes irreconcilable, and at best
Lives only by variety of disease.

Well might my wishes be intense, my thoughts
210 Strong and perturbed, not doubting at that time
But that the virtue of one paramount mind
Would have abashed those impious crests – have quelled
Outrage and bloody power, and, in despite
Of what the People long had been and were

409

And immaturity, and in the teeth   216
Of desperate opposition from without –
Have cleared a passage for just government,
And left a solid birthright to the State,
Redeemed according to example given   220
By ancient lawgivers.
                 In this frame of mind,
190 Reluctantly to England I returned,
Compelled by nothing less than absolute want
Of funds for my support, else, well assured
That I both was and must be of small worth,
No better than an alien in the land,
I doubtless should have made a common cause
With some who perished; haply perished too,   230
A poor mistaken and bewildered offering, –
Should to the breast of Nature have gone back,
With all my resolutions, all my hopes,
200 A Poet only to myself, to men
Useless, and even, belovèd Friend! a soul   235
To thee unknown!
              When to my native land
(After a whole year's absence) I returned
I found the air yet busy with the stir   246
Of a contention which had been raised up
Against the traffickers in Negro blood;
An effort which, though baffled, nevertheless   250

Through ignorance and false teaching, sadder proof
Of immaturity, and in the teeth
Of desperate opposition from without –
Have cleared a passage for just government,
And left a solid birthright to the State,
220 Redeemed, according to example given
By ancient lawgivers.
               In this frame of mind,
Dragged by a chain of harsh necessity,
So seemed it, – now I thankfully acknowledge,
Forced by the gracious providence of Heaven, –
To England I returned, else (though assured
That I both was and must be of small weight,
No better than a landsman on the deck
Of a ship struggling with a hideous storm)
Doubtless, I should have then made common cause
230 With some who perished; haply perished too,
A poor mistaken and bewildered offering, –
Should to the breast of Nature have gone back,
With all my resolutions, all my hopes,
A Poet only to myself, to men
Useless, and even, belovèd Friend! a soul
To thee unknown!
               Twice had the trees let fall
Their leaves, as often Winter had put on
His hoary crown, since I had seen the surge
Beat against Albion's shore, since ear of mine
240 Had caught the accents of my native speech
Upon our native country's sacred ground.
A patriot of the world, how could I glide
Into communion with her sylvan shades,
Erewhile my tuneful haunt? It pleased me more
To abide in the great City, where I found
The general air still busy with the stir
Of that first memorable onset made
By a strong levy of humanity
Upon the traffickers in Negro blood;
250 Effort which, though defeated, had recalled

Had called back old forgotten principles
Dismissed from service, had diffused some truths
210 And more of virtuous feeling through the heart
Of the English people. And no few of those
So numerous (little less in verity
Than a whole nation crying with one voice)
Who had been crossed in this their just intent
And righteous hope, thereby were well prepared
To let that journey sleep awhile, and join
Whatever other caravan appeared
To travel forward towards Liberty
With more success. For me, that strife had ne'er
220 Fastened on my affections, nor did now   255
Its unsuccessful issue much excite
My sorrow, having laid this faith to heart,
That, if France prospered, good men would not long
Pay fruitless worship to humanity,
And this most rotten branch of human shame,   260
Object, as seemed, of a superfluous pains
Would fall together with its parent tree.

Such was my then belief, that there was one,
And only one solicitude for all;
230 And now the strength of Britain was put forth
In league with the confederated host,   265
Not in my single self alone I found,
But in the minds of all ingenuous youth,
Change and subversion from this hour. No shock
Given to my moral nature had I known
Down to that very moment; neither lapse   270
Nor turn of sentiment that might be named
A revolution, save at this one time;
All else was progress on the self-same path
240 On which, with a diversity of pace,
I had been travelling: this a stride at once   275
Into another region. True it is,
'Twas not concealed with what ungracious eyes
Our native rulers from the very first

To notice old forgotten principles,
And through the nation spread a novel heat
Of virtuous feeling. For myself, I own
That this particular strife had wanted power
To rivet my affections; nor did now
Its unsuccessful issue much excite
My sorrow; for I brought with me the faith
That, if France prospered, good men would not long
Pay fruitless worship to humanity,
260   And this most rotten branch of human shame,
Object, so seemed it, of superfluous pains,
Would fall together with its parent tree.
What, then, were my emotions, when in arms
Britain put forth her freeborn strength in league,
Oh, pity and shame! with those confederate Powers!
Not in my single self alone I found,
But in the minds of all ingenuous youth,
Change and subversion from that hour. No shock
Given to my moral nature had I known
270   Down to that very moment; neither lapse
Nor turn of sentiment that might be named
A revolution, save at this one time;
All else was progress on the self-same path
On which, with a diversity of pace,
I had been travelling: this a stride at once
Into another region. As a light

Had looked upon regenerated France,
Nor had I doubted that this day would come.
But in such contemplation I had thought
Of general interests only, beyond this
Had [never] once foretasted the event.
250 Now had I other business for I felt
The ravage of this most unnatural strife
In my own heart; there lay it like a weight
At enmity with all the tenderest springs
Of my enjoyments I, who with the breeze
Had played, a green leaf on the blessèd tree
Of my belovèd country, nor had wished   *280*
For happier fortune than to wither there,
Now from my pleasant station was cut off
And tossed about in whirlwinds. I rejoiced,
260 Yea, afterwards – truth most painful to record! –
Exulted in the triumph of my soul   *285*
When Englishmen by thousands were o'erthrown,
Left without glory on the field, or driven,
Brave hearts! to shameful flight. It was a grief,
Grief call it not, 'twas anything but that,–
A conflict of sensations without name,   *290*
Of which he only who may love the sight
Of a village steeple, as I do, can judge,
When in the congregation bending all
270 To their great Father, prayers were offered up,
Or praises for our country's victories;   *295*
And, 'mid the simple worshippers, perchance,
I only, like an uninvited guest
Whom no one owned, sate silent, shall I add,
Fed on the day of vengeance yet to come?

Oh! much have they to account for, who could tear, *300*
By violence, at one decisive rent,
From the best youth in England their dear pride,
Their joy, in England; this, too, at a time
280 In which worst losses easily might wear
The best of names, when patriotic love   *305*

And pliant harebell, swinging in the breeze
On some grey rock – its birthplace – so had I
Wantoned, fast rooted on the ancient tower
280   Of my belovèd country, wishing not
A happier fortune than to wither there:
Now was I from that pleasant station torn
And tossed about in whirlwind. I rejoiced,
Yea, afterwards – truth most painful to record! –
Exulted, in the triumph of my soul,
When Englishmen by thousands were o'erthrown,
Left without glory on the field, or driven,
Brave hearts! to shameful flight. It was a grief, –
Grief call it not, 'twas anything but that, –
290   A conflict of sensations without name,
Of which *he* only, who may love the sight
Of a village steeple, as I do, can judge,
When, in the congregation bending all
To their great Father, prayers were offered up,
Or praises for our country's victories;
And, 'mid the simple worshippers, perchance
I only, like an uninvited guest
Whom no one owned, sate silent, shall I add,
Fed on the day of vengeance yet to come?

300   Oh! much have they to account for, who could tear,
By violence, at one decisive rent,
From the best youth in England their dear pride,
Their joy, in England; this, too, at a time
In which worst losses easily might wear
The best of names, when patriotic love

Did of itself in modesty give way
Like the Precursor when the Deity
Is come Whose harbinger he is, a time
In which apostasy from ancient faith
Seemed but conversion to a higher creed;   *310*
Withal a season dangerous and wild,
A time in which Experience would have plucked
Flowers out of any hedge to make thereof
290 A chaplet in contempt of his grey locks.

    Ere yet the fleet of Britain had gone forth   *315*
On this unworthy service, whereunto
The unhappy counsel of a few weak men
Had doomed it, I beheld the vessels lie,
A brood of gallant creatures, on the deep
I saw them in their rest, a sojourner
Through a whole month of calm and glassy days   *320*
In that delightful island which protects
Their place of convocation – there I heard,
300 Each evening, walking by the still seashore,
A monitory sound which never failed, –
The sunset cannon. When the orb went down   *325*
In the tranquillity of Nature, came
That voice, ill requiem! seldom heard by me
Without a spirit overcast, a deep
Imagination, thought of woes to come,
And sorrow for mankind, and pain of heart.   *330*

    In France, the men, who, for their desperate ends,
Had plucked up mercy by the roots, were glad
310 Of this new enemy. Tyrants, strong before
In devilish pleas, were ten times stronger now;
And thus, beset with foes on every side,   *335*
The goaded land waxed mad; the crimes of few
Spread into madness of the many; blasts
From hell came sanctified like airs from heaven.
The sternness of the just, the faith of those
Who doubted not that Providence had times   *340*

Did of itself in modesty give way,
Like the Precursor when the Deity
Is come Whose harbinger he was; a time
In which apostasy from ancient faith
310 Seemed but conversion to a higher creed;
Withal a season dangerous and wild,
A time when sage Experience would have snatched
Flowers out of any hedge-row to compose
A chaplet in contempt of his grey locks.

When the proud fleet that bears the red-cross flag
In that unworthy service was prepared
To mingle, I beheld the vessels lie,
A brood of gallant creatures, on the deep
I saw them in their rest, a sojourner
320 Through a whole month of calm and glassy days
In that delightful island which protects
Their place of convocation – there I heard,
Each evening, pacing by the still seashore,
A monitory sound that never failed, –
The sunset cannon. While the orb went down
In the tranquillity of Nature, came
That voice, ill requiem! seldom heard by me
Without a spirit overcast by dark
Imaginations, sense of woes to come,
330 Sorrow for human kind, and pain of heart.

In France, the men, who, for their desperate ends,
Had plucked up mercy by the roots, were glad
Of this new enemy. Tyrants, strong before
In wicked pleas, were strong as demons now;
And thus, on every side beset with foes,
The goaded land waxed mad; the crimes of few
Spread into madness of the many; blasts
From hell came sanctified like airs from heaven.
The sternness of the just, the faith of those
340 Who doubted not that Providence had times

417

Of anger and of vengeance, theirs who throned
The human understanding paramount
320 And made of that their God, the hopes of those
Who were content to barter short-lived pangs
For a paradise of ages, the blind rage   *345*
Of insolent tempers, the light vanity
Of intermeddlers, steady purposes
Of the suspicious, slips of the indiscreet,
And all the accidents of life were pressed
Into one service, busy with one work.   *350*
The Senate was heart-stricken, not a voice
Uplifted, none to oppose or mitigate.   *355*

330   Domestic carnage now filled all the year
With feast-days; the old man from the chimney-nook,
The maiden from the bosom of her love,
The mother from the cradle of her babe,
The warrior from the field – all perished, all –   *360*
Friends, enemies, of all parties, ages, ranks,
Head after head, and never heads enough
For those that bade them fall. They found their joy,
They made it, ever thirsty as a child,
(If light desires of innocent little ones   *365*
340 May with such heinous appetites be matched),
Having a toy, a wind-mill, though the air
Do of itself blow fresh, and make the vane   *370*
Spin in his eyesight, he is not content,
But, with the plaything at arm's length, he sets
His front against the blast, and runs amain,
To make it whirl the faster.
                                        In the depth
Of these enormities, even thinking minds   *375*
Forgot, at seasons, whence they had their being;

Of vengeful retribution, theirs who throned
The human understanding paramount
And made of that their God, the hopes of men
Who were content to barter short-lived pangs
For a paradise of ages, the blind rage
Of insolent tempers, the light vanity
Of intermeddlers, steady purposes
Of the suspicious, slips of the indiscreet,
And all the accidents of life were pressed
350 Into one service, busy with one work.
The Senate stood aghast, her prudence quenched,
Her wisdom stifled, and her justice scared,
Her frenzy only active to extol
Past outrages, and shape the way for new,
Which no one dared to oppose or mitigate.

Domestic carnage now filled the whole year
With feast-days; old men from the chimney-nook,
The maiden from the bosom of her love,
The mother from the cradle of her babe,
360 The warrior from the field – all perished, all –
Friends, enemies, of all parties, ages, ranks,
Head after head, and never heads enough
For those that bade them fall. They found their joy,
They made it, proudly eager as a child,
(If light desires of innocent little ones
May with such heinous appetites be compared),
Pleased in some open field to exercise
A toy that mimics with revolving wings
The motion of a wind-mill; though the air
370 Do of itself blow fresh, and make the vanes
Spin in his eyesight, *that* contents him not,
But, with the plaything at arm's length, he sets
His front against the blast, and runs amain,
That it may whirl the faster.
                                        Amid the depth
Of those enormities, even thinking minds
Forgot, at seasons, whence they had their being;

Forgot that such a sound was ever heard
350 As Liberty upon earth: yet all beneath
Her innocent authority was wrought,
Nor could have been, without her blessèd name.   *380*
The illustrious wife of Roland, in the hour
Of her composure, felt that agony
And gave it vent in her last words. O Friend!
It was a lamentable time for man,
Whether a hope had e'er been his or not;   *385*
A woeful time for them whose hopes did still
Outlast the shock; most woeful for those few,
360 They had the deepest feeling of the grief,
Who still were flattered, and had trust in man.
Meanwhile, the Invaders fared as they deserved: *390*
The Herculean Commonwealth had put forth her arms,
And throttled with an infant godhead's might
The snakes about her cradle; that was well,
And as it should be; yet no cure for those
Whose souls were sick with pain of what would be   *395*
Hereafter brought in charge against mankind.
Most melancholy at that time, O Friend!
370 Were my day-thoughts, – my dreams were miserable;
Through months, through years, long after the last beat
Of those atrocities (I speak bare truth,   *400*
As if to thee alone in private talk)
I scarcely had one night of quiet sleep,
Such ghastly visions had I of despair
And tyranny, and implements of death;
And long orations which in dreams I pleaded   *411*
Before unjust tribunals, – with a voice
Labouring, a brain confounded, and a sense
380 Of treachery and desertion in the place

Forgot that such a sound was ever heard
As Liberty upon earth: yet all beneath
Her innocent authority was wrought,
380 Nor could have been, without her blessèd name.
The illustrious wife of Roland, in the hour
Of her composure, felt that agony,
And gave it vent in her last words. O Friend!
It was a lamentable time for man,
Whether a hope had e'er been his or not;
A woeful time for them whose hopes survived
The shock; most woeful for those few who still
Were flattered, and had trust in human kind:
They had the deepest feeling of the grief.
390 Meanwhile the Invaders fared as they deserved:
The Herculean Commonwealth had put forth her arms,
And throttled with an infant godhead's might
The snakes about her cradle; that was well,
And as it should be; yet no cure for them
Whose souls were sick with pain of what would be
Hereafter brought in charge against mankind.
Most melancholy at that time, O Friend!
Were my day-thoughts, – my nights were miserable;
Through months, through years, long after the last beat
400 Of those atrocities, the hour of sleep
To me came rarely charged with natural gifts,
Such ghastly visions had I of despair
And tyranny, and implements of death;
And innocent victims sinking under fear,
And momentary hope, and worn-out prayer,
Each in his separate cell, or penned in crowds
For sacrifice, and struggling with forced mirth
And levity in dungeons, where the dust
Was laid with tears. Then suddenly the scene
410 Changed, and the unbroken dream entangled me
In long orations, which I strove to plead
Before unjust tribunals, – with a voice
Labouring, a brain confounded, and a sense,
Death-like, of treacherous desertion, felt

The holiest that I knew of, my own soul.   415

    When I began at first, in early youth
To yield myself to Nature, when that strong
And holy passion overcame me first,
Neither the day nor night, evening or morn,
Were free from the oppression. But, Great God!   420
Who send'st Thyself into this breathing world
Through Nature and through every kind of life,
And mak'st man what he is, creature divine,
390 In single or in social eminence,   425
Above all these raised infinite ascents
When reason which enables him to be
Is not sequestered – what a change is here!
How different ritual for this after-worship,
What countenance to promote this second love!   430
That first was service but to things which lie
At rest within the bosom of Thy will.
Therefore to serve was high beatitude;
The tumult was a gladness, and the fear
400 Ennobling, venerable; sleep secure,   435
And waking thoughts more rich than happiest dreams.

    But as the ancient Prophets were enflamed
Nor wanted consolations of their own   440
And majesty of mind, when they denounced
On towns and cities, wallowing in the abyss
Of their offences, punishment to come;
Or saw, like other men, with bodily eyes,
Before them, in some desolated place,   445
The consummation of the wrath of Heaven;
410 So did some portions of that spirit fall
On me, to uphold me through those evil times,
And in their rage and dog-day heat I found
Something to glory in, as just and fit,

In the last place of refuge – my own soul.

When I began in youth's delightful prime
To yield myself to Nature, when that strong
And holy passion overcame me first,
Nor day nor night, evening or morn, was free
420 From its oppression. But, O Power Supreme!
Without Whose care this world would cease to breathe,
Who from the fountain of Thy grace dost fill
The veins that branch through every frame of life,
Making man what he is, creature divine,
In single or in social eminence,
Above the rest raised infinite ascents
When reason that enables him to be
Is not sequestered – what a change is here!
How different ritual for this after-worship,
430 What countenance to promote this second love!
The first was service paid to things which lie
Guarded within the bosom of Thy will.
Therefore to serve was high beatitude;
Tumult was therefore gladness, and the fear
Ennobling, venerable; sleep secure,
And waking thoughts more rich than happiest dreams.

But as the ancient Prophets, borne aloft
In vision, yet constrained by natural laws
With them to take a troubled human heart,
440 Wanted not consolations, nor a creed
Of reconcilement, then when they denounced,
On towns and cities, wallowing in the abyss
Of their offences, punishment to come;
Or saw, like other men, with bodily eyes,
Before them, in some desolated place,
The wrath consummate and the threat fulfilled;
So, with devout humility be it said,
So, did a portion of that spirit fall
On me uplifted from the vantage-ground
450 Of pity and sorrow to a state of being

And in the order of sublimest laws:
And, even if that were not, amid the awe
Of unintelligible chastisement,
I felt a kind of sympathy with power,   455
Motions raised up within me, nevertheless,
Which had relationship to highest things.
420 Wild blasts of music thus did find their way   461
Into the midst of terrible events;
So that worst tempests might be listened to.
Then was the truth received into my heart,
That, under heaviest sorrow earth can bring,   465
Griefs bitterest of ourselves or of our kind,
If from the affliction somewhere do not grow
Honour which could not else have been, a faith,
An elevation and a sanctity,
If new strength be not given or old restored,
430 The blame is ours, not Nature's. When a taunt   470
Was taken up by scoffers in their pride,
Saying, 'Behold the harvest which we reap
From popular government and equality',
I saw that it was neither these nor aught
Of wild belief engrafted on their names   475
By false philosophy that caused the woe,
But that it was a reservoir of guilt
And ignorance filled up from age to age,
That could no longer hold its loathsome charge,
440 But burst and spread in deluge through the land.   480

And as the desert hath green spots, the sea
Small islands in the midst of stormy waves,
So that disastrous period did not want
Such sprinklings of all human excellence,
As were a joy to hear of. Yet (nor less   486
For those bright spots, those fair examples given

That through the time's exceeding fierceness saw
Glimpses of retribution, terrible,
And in the order of sublime behests:
But, even if that were not, amid the awe
Of unintelligible chastisement,
Not only acquiescences of faith
Survived, but daring sympathies with power,
Motions not treacherous or profane, else why
Within the folds of no ungentle breast
460   Their dread vibration to this hour prolonged?
Wild blasts of music thus could find their way
Into the midst of turbulent events;
So that worst tempests might be listened to.
Then was the truth received into my heart,
That, under heaviest sorrow earth can bring,
If from the affliction somewhere do not grow
Honour which could not else have been, a faith,
An elevation and a sanctity,
If new strength be not given nor old restored,
470   The blame is ours, not Nature's. When a taunt
Was taken up by scoffers in their pride,
Saying, 'Behold the harvest that we reap
From popular government and equality',
I clearly saw that neither these nor aught
Of wild belief engrafted on their names
By false philosophy had caused the woe,
But a terrific reservoir of guilt
And ignorance filled up from age to age,
That could no longer hold its loathsome charge,
480   But burst and spread in deluge through the land.

And as the desert hath green spots, the sea
Small islands scattered amid stormy waves,
So *that* disastrous period did not want
Bright sprinklings of all human excellence,
To which the silver wands of saints in Heaven
Might point with rapturous joy. Yet not the less,
For those examples in no age surpassed

425

Of fortitude and energy and love,
And human nature faithful to itself
Under worst trials) was I impelled to think   490
450 Of the glad time when first I traversed France
A youthful pilgrim; above all remembered
That day when through an arch that spanned the street,
A rainbow made of garish ornaments,
Triumphal pomp for liberty confirmed,
We walked, a pair of weary travellers,
Along the town of Arras, place from which
Issued that Robespierre, who afterwards
Wielded the sceptre of the Atheist crew.   502
When the calamity spread far and wide –
460 And this same city, which had even appeared
To outrun the rest in exultation, groaned   505
Under the vengeance of her cruel son,
As Lear reproached the winds – I could almost
Have quarrelled with that blameless spectacle
For being yet an image in my mind
To mock me under such a strange reverse.   510

O Friend! few happier moments have been mine
Through my whole life than that when first I heard
That this foul Tribe of Moloch was o'erthrown,
470 And their chief regent levelled with the dust.
The day was one which haply may deserve
A separate chronicle. Having gone abroad
From a small village where I tarried then,
To the same far-secluded privacy
I was returning. Over the smooth sands
Of Leven's ample estuary lay   515
My journey, and beneath a genial sun,
With distant prospect among gleams of sky
And clouds, and intermingled mountain tops,
480 In one inseparable glory clad,
Creatures of one ethereal substance met   520
In consistory, like a diadem
Or crown of burning seraphs as they sit
426

Of fortitude and energy and love,
And human nature faithful to herself
490 Under worst trials, was I driven to think
Of the glad times when first I traversed France
A youthful pilgrim; above all reviewed
That eventide, when under windows bright
With happy faces and with garlands hung,
And through a rainbow-arch that spanned the street,
Triumphal pomp for liberty confirmed,
I paced, a dear companion at my side,
The town of Arras, whence with promise high
Issued, on delegation to sustain
500 Humanity and right, *that* Robespierre,
He who thereafter, and in how short time!
Wielded the sceptre of the Atheist crew.
When the calamity spread far and wide –
And this same city, that did then appear
To outrun the rest in exultation, groaned
Under the vengeance of her cruel son,
As Lear reproached the winds – I could almost
Have quarrelled with that blameless spectacle
For lingering yet an image in my mind
510 To mock me under such a strange reverse.

O Friend! few happier moments have been mine
Than that which told the downfall of this Tribe
So dreaded, so abhorred. The day deserves
A separate record. Over the smooth sands
Of Leven's ample estuary lay
My journey, and beneath a genial sun,
With distant prospect among gleams of sky
And clouds, and intermingling mountain tops,
In one inseparable glory clad,
520 Creatures of one ethereal substance met
In consistory, like a diadem
Or crown of burning seraphs as they sit

427

In the empyrean. Underneath this show
Lay, as I knew, the nest of pastoral vales
Among whose happy fields I had grown up   *525*
From childhood. On the fulgent spectacle,
Which neither changed nor stirred nor passed away,
I gazed, and with a fancy more alive
490 On this account, that I had chanced to find
That morning, ranging through the churchyard graves
Of Cartmel's rural town, the place in which
An honoured teacher of my youth was laid.   *534*
While we were schoolboys he had died among us,
And was borne hither, as I knew, to rest
With his own family. A plain stone, inscribed
With name, date, office, pointed out the spot,
To which a slip of verses was subjoined,
(By his desire, as afterwards I learnt)
500 A fragment from the elegy of Gray.   *536*
A week, or little less, before his death
He had said to me, 'My head will soon lie low';
And when I saw the turf that covered him,   *540*
After the lapse of full eight years, those words,
With sound of voice and countenance of the Man,
Came back upon me, so that some few tears
Fell from me in my own despite. And now,
Thus travelling smoothly o'er the level sands,   *545*
I thought with pleasure of the verses graven
510 Upon his tombstone, saying to myself:
He loved the Poets, and, if now alive,
Would have loved me, as one not destitute
Of promise, nor belying the kind hope   *550*
Which he had formed, when I, at his command,
Began to spin, at first, my toilsome songs.

      Without me and within, as I advanced,
All that I saw, or felt, or communed with
Was gentleness and peace. Upon a small
And rocky island near, a fragment stood   *555*
520 (Itself like a sea rock) of what had been
428

In the empyrean. Underneath that pomp
Celestial, lay unseen the pastoral vales
Among whose happy fields I had grown up
From childhood. On the fulgent spectacle,
That neither passed away nor changed, I gazed
Enrapt; but brightest things are wont to draw
Sad opposites out of the inner heart,
530   As even their pensive influence drew from mine.
How could it otherwise? for not in vain
That very morning had I turned aside
To seek the ground where, 'mid a throng of graves,
An honoured teacher of my youth was laid,
And on the stone were graven by his desire
Lines from the churchyard elegy of Gray.
This faithful guide, speaking from his death-bed,
Added no farewell to his parting counsel,
But said to me, 'My head will soon lie low';
540   And when I saw the turf that covered him,
After the lapse of full eight years, those words,
With sound of voice and countenance of the Man,
Came back upon me, so that some few tears
Fell from me in my own despite. But now
I thought, still traversing that widespread plain,
With tender pleasure of the verses graven
Upon his tombstone, whispering to myself:
He loved the Poets, and, if now alive,
Would have loved me, as one not destitute
550   Of promise, nor belying the kind hope
That he had formed, when I, at his command,
Began to spin, with toil, my earliest songs.

   As I advanced, all that I saw or felt
Was gentleness and peace. Upon a small
And rocky island near, a fragment stood
(Itself like a sea rock) the low remains
(With shells encrusted, dark with briny weeds)
Of a dilapidated structure, once

A Romish chapel, where in ancient times
Masses were said at the hour which suited those
Who crossed the sands with ebb of morning tide. *561*
Not far from this still ruin all the plain
Was spotted with a variegated crowd
Of coaches, wains, and travellers, horse and foot,
Wading beneath the conduct of their guide *565*
In loose procession through the shallow stream
Of inland water; the great sea meanwhile
530 Was at safe distance, far retired. I paused,
Unwilling to proceed, the scene appeared
So gay and cheerful, when a traveller
Chancing to pass, I carelessly inquired
If any news were stirring; he replied
In the familiar language of the day *572*
That, *Robespierre was dead* – nor was a doubt,
On further question, left within my mind
But that the tidings were substantial truth;
That he and his supporters all were fallen. *575*

540   Great was my glee of spirit, great my joy
In vengeance, and eternal Justice, thus
Made manifest. 'Come now, ye golden times,'
Said I, forth-breathing on those open sands
A hymn of triumph: 'as the morning comes *580*
Out of the bosom of the night, come ye:
Thus far our trust is verified; behold!
They who with clumsy desperation brought
Rivers of Blood, and preached that nothing else
Could cleanse the Augean stable, by the might *585*
550 Of their own helper have been swept away;
Their madness is declared and visible;
Elsewhere will safety now be sought, and earth
March firmly towards righteousness and peace.' –
Then schemes I framed more calmly, when and how *590*
The madding factions might be tranquillized,
And, though through hardships manifold and long,
The mighty renovation would proceed.

A Romish chapel, where the vested priest
560　Said matins at the hour that suited those
Who crossed the sands with ebb of morning tide.
Not far from that still ruin all the plain
Lay spotted with a variegated crowd
Of vehicles and travellers, horse and foot,
Wading beneath the conduct of their guide
In loose procession through the shallow stream
Of inland waters; the great sea meanwhile
Heaved at safe distance, far retired. I paused,
Longing for skill to paint a scene so bright
570　And cheerful, but the foremost of the band
As he approached, no salutation given,
In the familiar language of the day,
Cried, 'Robespierre is dead!' – nor was a doubt,
After strict question, left within my mind
That he and his supporters all were fallen.

　　Great was my transport, deep my gratitude
To everlasting Justice, by this fiat
Made manifest. 'Come now, ye golden times,'
Said I forth-pouring on those open sands
580　A hymn of triumph: 'as the morning comes
From out the bosom of the night, come ye:
Thus far our trust is verified; behold!
They who with clumsy desperation brought
A river of Blood, and preached that nothing else
Could cleanse the Augean stable, by the might
Of their own helper have been swept away;
Their madness stands declared and visible;
Elsewhere will safety now be sought, and earth
March firmly towards righteousness and peace.' –
590　Then schemes I framed more calmly, when and how
The madding factions might be tranquillized,
And how through hardships manifold and long
The glorious renovation would proceed.

Thus interrupted by uneasy bursts
Of exultation, I pursued my way   595
560 Along that very shore which I had skimmed
In former times, when – spurring from the Vale
Of Nightshade, and St Mary's mouldering fane,
And the stone abbot, after circuit made
In wantonness of heart, a joyous crew   600
Of schoolboys hastening to their distant home
Along the margin of the moonlight sea –
We beat with thundering hoofs the level sand.

Thus interrupted by uneasy bursts
Of exultation, I pursued my way
Along that very shore which I had skimmed
In former days, when – spurring from the Vale
Of Nightshade, and St Mary's mouldering fane,
And the stone abbot, after circuit made
600 In wantonness of heart, a joyous band
Of schoolboys hastening to their distant home
Along the margin of the moonlight sea –
We beat with thundering hoofs the level sand.

From this time forth, in France, as is well known,
Authority put on a milder face,
570 Yet every thing was wanting that might give
Courage to those who looked for good by light
Of rational Experience, good I mean   5
At hand, and in the spirit of past aims.
The same belief I, nevertheless, retained;
The language of the Senate, and the acts
And public measures of the Government,
Though both of heartless omen, had not power   10
To daunt me; in the People was my trust
And in the virtues which mine eyes had seen,
580 And to the ultimate repose of things
I looked with unabated confidence.
I knew that wound external could not take
Life from the young Republic; that new foes
Would only follow in the path of shame   15
Their brethren, and her triumphs be in the end
Great, universal, irresistible.
This faith, which was an object in my mind
Of passionate intuition, had effect
Not small in dazzling me; for thus, through zeal,
590 Such victory I confounded in my thoughts
With one far higher and more difficult, –
Triumphs of unambitious peace at home,   20
And noiseless fortitude. Beholding still
Resistance strong as heretofore, I thought
That what was in degree the same was likewise
The same in quality, – that, as the worse
Of the two spirits then at strife remained   25
434

From that time forth, Authority in France
Put on a milder face; Terror had ceased,
Yet every thing was wanting that might give
Courage to them who looked for good by light
Of rational Experience, for the shoots
And hopeful blossoms of a second spring:
Yet, in me, confidence was unimpaired;
The Senate's language, and the public acts
And measures of the Government, though both
10 Weak, and of heartless omen, had not power
To daunt me; in the People was my trust
And in the virtues which mine eyes had seen.
I knew that wound external could not take
Life from the young Republic; that new foes
Would only follow, in the path of shame,
Their brethren, and her triumphs be in the end
Great, universal, irresistible.
This intuition led me to confound
One victory with another, higher far, –
20 Triumphs of unambitious peace at home,
And noiseless fortitude. Beholding still
Resistance strong as heretofore, I thought
That what was in degree the same was likewise
The same in quality, – that, as the worse
Of the two spirits then at strife remained

Untired, the better surely would preserve
The heart that first had roused him, never dreamt
600   That transmigration could be undergone,
A fall of being suffered, and of hope,
By creature that appeared to have received
Entire conviction what a great ascent
Had been accomplished, what high faculties
It had been called to. Youth maintains, I knew,
In all conditions of society,
Communion more direct and intimate
With Nature, and the inner strength she has,   30
And hence, ofttimes, no less, with reason too,
610   Than age or manhood, even. To Nature, then,
Power had reverted: habit, custom, law,
Had left an interregnum's open space
For her to stir about in, uncontrolled.
The warmest judgements and the most untaught
Found in events which every day brought forth
Enough to sanction them, and far, far more
To shake the authority of canons drawn
From ordinary practice. I could see
How Babel-like the employment was of those   35
620   Who, by the recent deluge stupefied,
With their whole souls went culling from the day
Its petty promises, to build a tower
For their own safety; laughed at gravest heads,
Who, watching in their hate of France for signs   40
Of her disasters, if the stream of rumour
Brought with it one green branch, conceited thence
That not a single tree was left alive
In all her forests. How could I believe
That wisdom could, in any shape, come near   45
630   Men clinging to delusions so insane?
And thus, experience proving that no few
Of my opinions had been just, I took
Like credit to myself where less was due,
And thought that other notions were as sound,   50
Yea, could not but be right, because I saw

Untired, the better, surely, would preserve
The heart that first had roused him. Youth maintains,
In all conditions of society,
Communion more direct and intimate
30 With Nature, – hence, ofttimes, with reason too –
Than age or manhood, even. To Nature, then,
Power had reverted: habit, custom, law,
Had left an interregnum's open space
For *her* to move about in, uncontrolled.
Hence could I see how Babel-like their task,
Who, by the recent deluge stupefied,
With their whole souls went culling from the day
Its petty promises, to build a tower
For their own safety; laughed with my compeers
40 At gravest heads, by enmity to France
Distempered, till they found, in every blast
Forced from the street-disturbing newsman's horn,
For her great cause record or prophecy
Of utter ruin. How might we believe
That wisdom could, in any shape, come near
Men clinging to delusions so insane?
And thus, experience proving that no few
Of our opinions had been just, we took
Like credit to ourselves where less was due,
50 And thought that other notions were as sound,
Yea, could not but be right, because we saw

That foolish men opposed them.
                              To a strain
More animated I might here give way,
And tell, since juvenile errors are my theme,
What in those days, through Britain, was performed   55
640 To turn *all* judgements out of their right course;
But this is passion over-near ourselves,
Reality too close and too intense,
And mingled up with something, in my mind,
Of scorn and condemnation personal,   60
That would profane the sanctity of verse.
Our Shepherds, this say merely, at that time
Thirsted to make the guardian crook of law
A tool of murder; they who ruled the State,   65
Though with such awful proof before their eyes
650 That he, who would sow death, reaps death, or worse,
And can reap nothing better, child-like longed
To imitate, not wise enough to avoid,   69
Giants in their impiety alone,
But, in their weapons and their warfare base
As vermin working out of reach, they leagued
Their strength perfidiously, to undermine
Justice, and make an end of Liberty.

    But from these bitter truths I must return
To my own history. It hath been told   75
660 That I was led to take an eager part
In arguments of civil polity,
Abruptly, and indeed before my time:
I had approached, like other youth, the shield
Of human nature from the golden side,   80
And would have fought, even to the death, to attest
The quality of the metal which I saw.
What there is best in individual man,
Of wise in passion, and sublime in power,
What there is strong and pure in household love,
670 Benevolent in small societies,   85
And great in large ones also, when called forth
438

That foolish men opposed them.
                              To a strain
More animated I might here give way,
And tell, since juvenile errors are my theme,
What in those days, through Britain, was performed
To turn *all* judgements out of their right course;
But this is passion over-near ourselves,
Reality too close and too intense,
And intermixed with something, in my mind,
60 Of scorn and condemnation personal,
That would profane the sanctity of verse.
Our Shepherds, this say merely, at that time
Acted, or seemed at least to act, like men
Thirsting to make the guardian crook of law
A tool of murder; they who ruled the State,
Though with such awful proof before their eyes
That he, who would sow death, reaps death, or worse,
And can reap nothing better, child-like longed
To imitate, not wise enough to avoid;
70 Or left (by mere timidity betrayed)
The plain straight road, for one no better chosen
Than if their wish had been to undermine
Justice, and make an end of Liberty.

    But from these bitter truths I must return
To my own history. It hath been told
That I was led to take an eager part
In arguments of civil polity,
Abruptly, and indeed before my time:
I had approached, like other youths, the shield
80 Of human nature from the golden side,
And would have fought, even to the death, to attest
The quality of the metal which I saw.
What there is best in individual man,
Of wise in passion, and sublime in power,
Benevolent in small societies,
And great in large ones, I had oft revolved,

By great occasions, these were things of which
I something knew, yet even these themselves,
Felt deeply, were not thoroughly understood
By reason: nay, far from it; they were yet,
As cause was given me afterwards to learn,
Not proof against the injuries of the day;   *90*
Lodged only at the sanctuary's door,
Not safe within its bosom. Thus prepared,
680   And with such general insight into evil,
And of the bounds which sever it from good,
As books and common intercourse with life   *95*
Must needs have given – to the noviciate mind,
When the world travels in a beaten road,
Guide faithful as is needed – I began
To think with fervour upon management
Of nations, what it is and ought to be,   *100*
And how their worth depended on their laws
And on the constitution of the State.

690   O pleasant exercise of hope and joy!   *105*
For great were the auxiliars which then stood
Upon our side, we who were strong in love!
Bliss was it in that dawn to be alive,
But to be young was very Heaven! O times,
In which the meagre, stale, forbidding ways   *110*
Of custom, law, and statute took at once
The attraction of a country in romance!
When Reason seemed the most to assert her rights
When most intent on making of herself
700   A prime enchanter to assist the work,   *115*
Which then was going forwards in her name!
Not favoured spots alone, but the whole Earth,
The beauty wore of promise – that which sets
(To take an image which was felt, no doubt,
Among the bowers of Paradise itself)   *120*
The budding rose above the rose full blown.
What temper at the prospect did not wake
To happiness unthought of? The inert

Felt deeply, but not thoroughly understood
By reason: nay, far from it; they were yet,
As cause was given me afterwards to learn,
90 Not proof against the injuries of the day;
Lodged only at the sanctuary's door,
Not safe within its bosom. Thus prepared,
And with such general insight into evil,
And of the bounds which sever it from good,
As books and common intercourse with life
Must needs have given – to the inexperienced mind,
When the world travels in a beaten road,
Guide faithful as is needed – I began
To meditate with ardour on the rule
100 And management of nations; what it is
And ought to be; and strove to learn how far
Their power or weakness, wealth or poverty,
Their happiness or misery, depend
Upon their laws, and fashion of the State.

    O pleasant exercise of hope and joy!
For mighty were the auxiliars which then stood
Upon our side, we who were strong in love!
Bliss was it in that dawn to be alive,
But to be young was very Heaven! O times,
110 In which the meagre, stale, forbidding ways
Of custom, law, and statute, took at once
The attraction of a country in romance!
When Reason seemed the most to assert her rights
When most intent on making of herself
A prime enchantress to assist the work,
Which then was going forward in her name!
Not favoured spots alone, but the whole Earth,
The beauty wore of promise – that which sets
(As at some moments might not be unfelt
120 Among the bowers of Paradise itself)
The budding rose above the rose full blown.
What temper at the prospect did not wake
To happiness unthought of? The inert

Were roused, and lively natures rapt away!
710 They who had fed their childhood upon dreams,   125
The play-fellows of fancy, who had made
All powers of swiftness, subtlety, and strength
Their ministers, – used to stir in lordly wise
Among the grandest objects of the sense,
And deal with whatsoever they found there   130
As if they had within some lurking right
To wield it; – they, too, who of gentle mood
Had watched all gentle motions, and to these
Had fitted their own thoughts, schemers more mild,
720 And in the region of their peaceful selves,   135
Did now find helpers to their hearts' desire,
And stuff at hand, plastic as they could wish, –
Were called upon to exercise their skill,
Not in Utopia, – subterraneous fields, –   140
Or some secreted island, Heaven knows where!
But in the very world which is the world
Of all of us, – the place in which, in the end,
We find our happiness, or not at all!

Why should I not confess that Earth was then   145
730 To me what an inheritance, new-fallen,
Seems, when the first time visited, to one
Who thither comes to find in it his home?
He walks about and looks upon the place
With cordial transport, moulds it and remoulds,   150
And is half pleased with things that are amiss,
'Twill be such joy to see them disappear.

An active partisan, I thus convoked
From every object pleasant circumstance
To suit my ends; I moved among mankind   155
740 With genial feelings still predominant;
When erring, erring on the better part,
And in the kinder spirit; placable,
Indulgent ofttimes to the worst desires
As on one side not uninformed that men

Were roused, and lively natures rapt away!
They who had fed their childhood upon dreams,
The play-fellows of fancy, who had made
All powers of swiftness, subtlety, and strength
Their ministers, – who in lordly wise had stirred
Among the grandest objects of the sense,
130 And dealt with whatsoever they found there
As if they had within some lurking right
To wield it; – they, too, who of gentle mood
Had watched all gentle motions, and to these
Had fitted their own thoughts, schemers more mild,
And in the region of their peaceful selves; –
Now was it that *both* found, the meek and lofty
Did both find, helpers to their hearts' desire,
And stuff at hand, plastic as they could wish, –
Were called upon to exercise their skill,
140 Not in Utopia, – subterranean fields, –
Or some secreted island, Heaven knows where!
But in the very world, which is the world
Of all of us, – the place where, in the end,
We find our happiness, or not at all!

       Why should I not confess that Earth was then
To me, what an inheritance, new-fallen,
Seems, when the first time visited, to one
Who thither comes to find in it his home?
He walks about and looks upon the spot
150 With cordial transport, moulds it and remoulds,
And is half pleased with things that are amiss,
'Twill be such joy to see them disappear.

       An active partisan, I thus convoked
From every object pleasant circumstance
To suit my ends; I moved among mankind
With genial feelings still predominant;
When erring, erring on the better part,
And in the kinder spirit; placable,
Indulgent, as not uninformed that men

443

See as it hath been taught them, and that time
Gives rights to error; on the other hand   *161*
That throwing off oppression must be work
As well of License as of Liberty;
And above all – for this was more than all –
750 Not caring if the wind did now and then   *165*
Blow keen upon an eminence that gave
Prospect so large into futurity;
In brief, a child of Nature, as at first,
Diffusing only those affections wider
That from the cradle had grown up with me,   *170*
And losing, in no other way than light
Is lost in light, the weak in the more strong.

   In the main outline, such it might be said
Was my condition, till with open war
760 Britain opposed the liberties of France.   *175*
This threw me first out of the pale of love;
Soured and corrupted, upwards to the source,
My sentiments; was not, as hitherto,
A swallowing up of lesser things in great,
But change of them into their opposites;   *180*
And thus a way was opened for mistakes
And false conclusions of the intellect,
As gross in their degree, and in their kind
Far, far more dangerous. What had been a pride,
770 Was now a shame; my likings and my loves
Ran in new channels, leaving old ones dry;   *185*
And hence a blow which, in maturer age,
Would but have touched the judgement, struck more deep
Into sensations near the heart: meantime,
As from the first, wild theories were afloat,
Unto the subtleties of which, at least,   *190*
I had but lent a careless ear, assured
Of this, that time would soon set all things right,
Prove that the multitude had been oppressed,
780 And would be so no more.
                       But when events

160   See as they have been taught – Antiquity
       Gives rights to error; and aware, no less,
       That throwing off oppression must be work
       As well of License as of Liberty;
       And above all – for this was more than all –
       Not caring if the wind did now and then
       Blow keen upon an eminence that gave
       Prospect so large into futurity;
       In brief, a child of Nature, as at first,
       Diffusing only those affections wider
170   That from the cradle had grown up with me,
       And losing, in no other way than light
       Is lost in light, the weak in the more strong.

          In the main outline, such it might be said
       Was my condition, till with open war
       Britain opposed the liberties of France.
       This threw me first out of the pale of love;
       Soured and corrupted, upwards to the source,
       My sentiments; was not, as hitherto,
       A swallowing up of lesser things in great,
180   But change of them into their contraries;
       And thus a way was opened for mistakes
       And false conclusions, in degree as gross,
       In kind more dangerous. What had been a pride,
       Was now a shame; my likings and my loves
       Ran in new channels, leaving old ones dry;
       And hence a blow that, in maturer age,
       Would but have touched the judgement, struck more deep
       Into sensations near the heart: meantime,
       As from the first, wild theories were afloat,
190   To whose pretensions, sedulously urged,
       I had but lent a careless ear, assured
       That time was ready to set all things right,
       And that the multitude, so long oppressed,
       Would be oppressed no more.
                                        But when events

Brought less encouragement, and unto these   195
The immediate proof of principles no more
Could be entrusted, while the events themselves,
Worn out in greatness, and in novelty,
Less occupied the mind, and sentiments
Could through my understanding's natural growth   200
No longer justify themselves through faith
Of inward consciousness, and hope that laid
Its hand upon its object – evidence
790 Safer, of universal application, such
As could not be impeached, was sought elsewhere.   205

    And now, become oppressors in their turn,
Frenchmen had changed a war of self-defence
For one of conquest, losing sight of all
Which they had struggled for: and mounted up,
Openly in the view of earth and heaven,   210
The scale of liberty. I read her doom,
Vexed inly somewhat, it is true, and sore,
But not dismayed, nor taking to the shame
800 Of a false prophet; but, roused up, I stuck   214
More firmly to old tenets, and, to prove
Their temper, strained them more; and thus, in heat
Of contest, did opinions every day
Grow into consequence, till round my mind   220
They clung, as if they were the life of it.

    This was the time, when, all things tending fast
To depravation, the philosophy
That promised to abstract the hopes of man   225
Out of his feelings, to be fixed thenceforth
810 For ever in a purer element
Found ready welcome. Tempting region that
For Zeal to enter and refresh herself,
Where passions had the privilege to work,   230

Brought less encouragement, and unto these
The immediate proof of principles no more
Could be entrusted, while the events themselves,
Worn out in greatness, stripped of novelty,
Less occupied the mind, and sentiments
200 Could through my understanding's natural growth
No longer keep their ground, by faith maintained
Of inward consciousness, and hope that laid
Her hand upon her object – evidence
Safer, of universal application, such
As could not be impeached, was sought elsewhere.

But now, become oppressors in their turn,
Frenchmen had changed a war of self-defence
For one of conquest, losing sight of all
Which they had struggled for: and mounted up,
210 Openly in the eye of earth and heaven,
The scale of liberty. I read her doom,
With anger vexed, with disappointment sore,
But not dismayed, nor taking to the shame
Of a false prophet. While resentment rose
Striving to hide, what nought could heal, the wounds
Of mortified presumption, I adhered
More firmly to old tenets, and, to prove
Their temper, strained them more; and thus, in heat
Of contest, did opinions every day
220 Grow into consequence, till round my mind
They clung, as if they were its life, nay more,
The very being of the immortal soul.

This was the time, when, all things tending fast
To depravation, speculative schemes –
That promised to abstract the hopes of Man
Out of his feelings, to be fixed thenceforth
For ever in a purer element –
Found ready welcome. Tempting region *that*
For Zeal to enter and refresh herself,
230 Where passions had the privilege to work,

And never hear the sound of their own names.
But, speaking more in charity, the dream
Was flattering to the young ingenuous mind,
Pleased with extremes, and not the least with that
Which makes the human Reason's naked self
The object of its fervour. What delight!   235
820 How glorious! in self-knowledge and self-rule,
To look through all the frailties of the world,
And, with a resolute mastery shaking off
The accidents of nature, time, and place,
That make up the weak being of the past,
Build social freedom on its only basis,
The freedom of the individual mind,   240
Which, to the blind restraints of general laws
Superior, magisterially adopts
One guide, the light of circumstances, flashed
830 Upon an independent intellect.   244

    For howsoe'er unsettled, never once
Had I thought ill of human kind, or been
Indifferent to its welfare, but, inflamed
With thirst of a secure intelligence,
And sick of other passion, I pursued   250
A higher nature; wished that Man should start
Out of the worm-like state in which he is,
And spread abroad the wings of Liberty,
Lord of himself, in undisturbed delight –
840 A noble aspiration! yet I feel   255
The aspiration, but with other thoughts
And happier; for I was perplexed and sought
To accomplish the transition by such means
As did not lie in nature, sacrificed
The exactness of a comprehensive mind
To scrupulous and microscopic views
That furnished out materials for a work
Of false imagination, placed beyond
The limits of experience and of truth.

And never hear the sound of their own names.
But, speaking more in charity, the dream
Flattered the young, pleased with extremes, nor least
With that which makes our Reason's naked self
The object of its fervour. What delight!
How glorious! in self-knowledge and self-rule,
To look through all the frailties of the world,
And, with a resolute mastery shaking off
Infirmities of nature, time, and place,
240   Build social upon personal Liberty,
Which, to the blind restraints of general laws
Superior, magisterially adopts
One guide, the light of circumstances, flashed
Upon an independent intellect.
Thus expectation rose again; thus hope,
From her first ground expelled, grew proud once more.
Oft, as my thoughts were turned to human kind,
I scorned indifference; but, inflamed with thirst
Of a secure intelligence, and sick
250   Of other longing, I pursued what seemed
A more exalted nature; wished that Man
Should start out of his earthy, worm-like state,
And spread abroad the wings of Liberty,
Lord of himself, in undisturbed delight –
A noble aspiration! *yet* I feel
(Sustained by worthier as by wiser thoughts)
The aspiration, nor shall ever cease
To feel it; – but return we to our course.

850   Enough, no doubt, the advocates themselves   *259*
Of ancient Institutions had performed
To bring disgrace upon their very names;
Disgrace, of which, custom and written law,
And sundry moral sentiments as props
And emanations of those institutes,   *265*
Too justly bore a part. A veil had been
Uplifted; why deceive ourselves? 'twas so,
'Twas even so; and sorrow for the man
Who either had not eyes wherewith to see,
860 Or, seeing, hath forgotten! Let this pass,   *270*
Suffice it that a shock had then been given
To old opinions; and the minds of all men
Had felt it; that my mind was both let loose,
Let loose and goaded. After what hath been
Already said of patriotic love,   *274*
And hinted at in other sentiments,
We need not linger long upon this theme.
This only may be said, that from the first
Having two natures in me, joy the one
870 The other melancholy, and withal
A happy man, and therefore bold to look
On painful things, slow, somewhat, too, and stern
In temperament, I took the knife in hand
And stopping not at parts less sensitive,
Endeavoured with my best of skill to probe
The living body of society   *281*
Even to the heart; I pushed without remorse
My speculations forward; yea, set foot
On Nature's holiest places. Time may come
880 When some dramatic story may afford
Shapes livelier to convey to thee, my Friend,
What then I learned, or think I learned, of truth,   *286*
And the errors into which I was betrayed
By present objects, and by reasonings false
From the beginning, inasmuch as drawn
Out of a heart which had been turned aside   *290*
From Nature by external accidents,

Enough, 'tis true – could such a plea excuse
260 Those aberrations – had the clamorous friends
Of ancient Institutions said and done
To bring disgrace upon their very names;
Disgrace, of which, custom and written law,
And sundry moral sentiments as props
Or emanations of those institutes,
Too justly bore a part. A veil had been
Uplifted; why deceive ourselves? in sooth,
'Twas even so; and sorrow for the man
Who either had not eyes wherewith to see,
270 Or, seeing, had forgotten! A strong shock
Was given to old opinions; all men's minds
Had felt its power, and mine was both let loose,
Let loose and goaded. After what hath been
Already said of patriotic love,
Suffice it here to add, that, somewhat stern
In temperament, withal a happy man,
And therefore bold to look on painful things,
Free likewise of the world, and thence more bold,
I summoned my best skill, and toiled, intent
280 To anatomize the frame of social life,
Yea, the whole body of society
Searched to its heart. Share with me, Friend! the wish
That some dramatic tale, endued with shapes
Livelier, and flinging out less guarded words
Than suit the work we fashion, might set forth
What then I learned, or think I learned, of truth,
And the errors into which I fell, betrayed
By present objects, and by reasonings false
From their beginnings, inasmuch as drawn
290 Out of a heart that had been turned aside
From Nature's way by outward accidents,

And which was thus confounded more and more,
Misguiding and misguided. Thus I fared,
890 Dragging all passions, notions, shapes of faith,
Like culprits to the bar; suspiciously   295
Calling the mind to establish in plain day
Her titles and her honours; now believing,
Now disbelieving; endlessly perplexed
With impulse, motive, right and wrong, the ground
Of moral obligation, what the rule   300
And what the sanction; till, demanding *proof*,
And seeking it in every thing, I lost
All feeling of conviction, and, in fine,
900 Sick, wearied out with contrarieties,
Yielded up moral questions in despair,   305
And for my future studies, as the sole
Employment of the inquiring faculty,

And which was thus confounded more and more,
Misguided, and misguiding. So I fared,
Dragging all precepts, judgements, maxims, creeds,
Like culprits to the bar; calling the mind,
Suspiciously, to establish in plain day
Her titles and her honours; now believing,
Now disbelieving; endlessly perplexed
With impulse, motive, right and wrong, the ground
300 Of obligation, what the rule and whence
The sanction; till, demanding formal *proof*,
And seeking it in every thing, I lost
All feeling of conviction, and, in fine,
Sick, wearied out with contrarieties,
Yielded up moral questions in despair.

This was the crisis of that strong disease,
This the soul's last and lowest ebb; I drooped,
Deeming our blessèd reason of least use
Where wanted most: 'The lordly attributes
310 Of will and choice,' I bitterly exclaimed,
'What are they but a mockery of a Being
Who hath in no concerns of his a test
Of good and evil; knows not what to fear
Or hope for, what to covet or to shun;
And who, if those could be discerned, would yet
Be little profited, would see, and ask
Where is the obligation to enforce?
And, to acknowledged law rebellious, still,
As selfish passion urged, would act amiss;
320 The dupe of folly, or the slave of crime.'

Depressed, bewildered thus, I did not walk
With scoffers, seeking light and gay revenge
From indiscriminate laughter, nor sate down
In reconcilement with an utter waste
Of intellect; such sloth I could not brook,
(Too well I loved, in that my spring of life,
Painstaking thoughts, and truth, their dear reward)

Turned towards mathematics, and their clear
And solid evidence – Ah! then it was   *Coleridge*
That thou, most precious Friend! about this time
First known to me, didst lend a living help
To regulate my Soul, and then it was
That the belovèd Woman in whose sight   335
Those days were passed, now speaking in a voice
Of sudden admonition – like a brook
That does but *cross* a lonely road, and now
Seen, heard and felt, and caught at every turn,
Companion never lost through many a league –   340
Maintained for me a saving intercourse
With my true self; for, though impaired and changed
Much, as it seemed, I was no further changed
Than as a clouded, not a waning moon: 344
She, in the midst of all, preserved me still
A Poet, made me seek beneath that name
My office upon earth, and nowhere else;
And, lastly, Nature's self, by human love   350
Assisted, through the weary labyrinth
Conducted me again to open day,
Revived the feelings of my earlier life,
Gave me that strength and knowledge full of peace,
Enlarged, and never more to be disturbed,
Which through the steps of our degeneracy,
All degradation of this age, hath still
Upheld me, and upholds me at this day
In the catastrophe (for so they dream,
And nothing less), when finally, to close
And rivet up the gains of France, a Pope
Is summoned in, to crown an Emperor –   360
This last opprobrium, when we see the dog
Returning to his vomit; when the sun
That rose in splendour, was alive, and moved   365
In exultation among living clouds

910

920

930

454

But turned to abstract science, and there sought
Work for the reasoning faculty enthroned
330 Where the disturbances of space and time –
Whether in matter's various properties
Inherent, or from human will and power
Derived – find no admission. Then it was –
Thanks to the bounteous Giver of all good! –
That the belovèd Sister in whose sight
Those days were passed, now speaking in a voice
Of sudden admonition – like a brook
That did but *cross* a lonely road, and now
Is seen, heard, felt, and caught at every turn,
340 Companion never lost through many a league –
Maintained for me a saving intercourse
342 With my true self; for, though bedimmed and changed
344 Both as a clouded and a waning moon,
She whispered still that brightness would return,
She, in the midst of all, preserved me still
A Poet, made me seek beneath that name,
And that alone, my office upon earth;
And, lastly, as hereafter will be shown,
350 If willing audience fail not, Nature's self,
By all varieties of human love
Assisted, led me back through opening day
To those sweet counsels between head and heart
Whence grew that genuine knowledge, fraught with peace,
Which, through the later sinkings of this cause,
Hath still upheld me, and upholds me now
In the catastrophe (for so they dream,
And nothing less), when, finally to close
And rivet down the gains of France, a Pope
360 Is summoned in, to crown an Emperor –
This last opprobrium, when we see a people,
That once looked up in faith, as if to Heaven
For manna, take a lesson from the dog
Returning to his vomit; when the sun
That rose in splendour, was alive, and moved
In exultation with a living pomp

Hath put his function and his glory off,
940 And, turned into a gewgaw, a machine,
Sets like an Opera phantom.   *370*
                              Thus, O Friend!
Through times of honour, and through times of shame,
Have I descended, tracing faithfully
The workings of a youthful mind, beneath
The breath of great events, its hopes no less
Than universal, and its boundless love –
A story destined for thy ear, who now,   *375*
Among the basest and the lowest fallen
Of all the race of men, dost make abode
950 Where Etna looketh down on Syracuse,
The city of Timoleon! Living God!
How are the mighty prostrated! They first,   *380*
They first of all that breathe should have awaked
When the great voice was heard out of the tombs
Of ancient heroes. If for France I have grieved
Who, in the judgement of no few, hath been
A trifler only, in her proudest day;   *385*
Have been distressed to think of what she once
Promised, now is; a far more sober cause
960 Thine eyes must see of sorrow, in a land
Strewed with the wreck of loftiest years, a land   *388*
Glorious indeed, substantially renowned
Of simple virtue once, and manly praise,
Now without one memorial hope, not even
A hope to be deferred; for that would serve
To cheer the heart in such entire decay.

    But indignation works where hope is not,
And thou, O Friend! wilt be refreshed. There is
One great society alone on earth,
970 The noble Living and the noble Dead: *395*
Thy consolation shall be there, and time
And Nature shall before thee spread in store
Imperishable thoughts, the place itself
Be conscious of thy presence, and the dull

Of clouds – his glory's natural retinue –
Hath dropped all functions by the gods bestowed,
And, turned into a gewgaw, a machine,
370 Sets like an Opera phantom.
                              Thus, O Friend!
Through times of honour and through times of shame
Descending, have I faithfully retraced
The perturbations of a youthful mind
Under a long-lived storm of great events –
A story destined for thy ear, who now,
Among the fallen of nations, dost abide
Where Etna, over hill and valley, casts
His shadow stretching towards Syracuse,
The city of Timoleon! Righteous Heaven!
380 How are the mighty prostrated! They first,
They first of all that breathe should have awaked
When the great voice was heard from out the tombs
Of ancient heroes. If I suffered grief
For ill-requited France, by many deemed
A trifler only in her proudest day;
Have been distressed to think of what she once
Promised, now is; a far more sober cause
Thine eyes must see of sorrow in a land,
Though with the wreck of loftier years bestrewn,
390 To the reanimating influence lost
Of memory, to virtue lost and hope.

    But indignation works where hope is not,
And thou, O Friend! wilt be refreshed. There is
One great society alone on earth:
The noble Living and the noble Dead.

Sirocco air of its degeneracy
Turn as thou mov'st into a healthful breeze
To cherish and invigorate thy frame.

Thine be those motions strong and sanative,
A ladder for thy spirit to reascend
980 To health and joy and pure contentedness;
To me the grief confined, that thou art gone
From this last spot of earth, where Freedom now   400
Stands single in her only sanctuary;
A lonely wanderer art gone, by pain
Compelled and sickness, at this latter day,
This heavy time of change for all mankind.
I feel for thee, must utter what I feel: 405
The sympathies erewhile in part discharged,
Gather afresh, and will have vent again:
990 My own delights do scarcely seem to me
My own delights; the lordly Alps themselves,
Those rosy peaks, from which the Morning looks   410
Abroad on many nations, are not now
Since thy migration and departure, Friend,
The gladsome image in my memory
Which they were used to be; to kindred scenes,
On errand, at a time, how different!
Thou tak'st thy way, carrying a heart more ripe   415
For all divine enjoyment, with the soul
1000 Which Nature gives to Poets, now by thought
Matured, and in the summer of its strength.
Oh! wrap him in your shades, ye giant woods,
On Etna's side; and thou, O flowery vale
Of Enna! is there not some nook of thine,   420
From the first playtime of the infant earth
Kept sacred to restorative delight?

Child of the mountains, among shepherds reared,
Even from my earliest school-day time, I loved
To dream of Sicily; and now a strong
1010 And vital promise wafted from that land

Thine be such converse strong and sanative,
A ladder for thy spirit to reascend
To health and joy and pure contentedness;
To me the grief confined, that thou art gone
400 From this last spot of earth, where Freedom now
Stands single in her only sanctuary;
A lonely wanderer art gone, by pain
Compelled and sickness, at this latter day,
This sorrowful reverse for all mankind.
I feel for thee, must utter what I feel:
The sympathies erewhile in part discharged,
Gather afresh, and will have vent again:
My own delights do scarcely seem to me
My own delights; the lordly Alps themselves,
410 Those rosy peaks, from which the Morning looks
Abroad on many nations, are no more
For me that image of pure gladsomeness
Which they were wont to be. Through kindred scenes,
For purpose, at a time, how different!
Thou tak'st thy way, carrying the heart and soul
That Nature gives to Poets, now by thought
Matured, and in the summer of their strength.
Oh! wrap him in your shades, ye giant woods,
On Etna's side; and thou, O flowery field
420 Of Enna! is there not some nook of thine,
From the first playtime of the infant world
Kept sacred to restorative delight,
When from afar invoked by anxious love?

Child of the mountains, among shepherds reared,
Ere yet familiar with the classic page,
I learnt to dream of Sicily; and lo,
The gloom, that, but a moment past, was deepened
At thy command, at her command gives way;
A pleasant promise, wafted from her shores,
430 Comes o'er my heart: in fancy I behold
Her seas yet smiling, her once happy vales;

Comes o'er my heart; there's not a single name
Of note belonging to that honoured isle,
Philosopher or Bard, Empedocles,
Or Archimedes, deep and tranquil soul!   *435*
That is not like a comfort to my grief:
And, O Theocritus, so far have some
Prevailed among the powers of heaven and earth,
By force of graces which were theirs, that they
Have had, as thou reportest, miracles   *440*
1020 Wrought for them in old time: yea, not unmoved,
When thinking on my own belovèd friend,
I hear thee tell how bees with honey fed
Divine Comates, by his tyrant lord
Within a chest imprisoned impiously;   *445*
How with their honey from the fields they came
And fed him there, alive, from month to month,
Because the goatherd, blessèd man! had lips
Wet with the Muse's nectar.

                  Thus I soothe
The pensive moments by this calm fireside,   *450*
1030 And find a thousand fancied images
That cheer the thoughts of those I love, and mine.
Our prayers have been accepted; thou wilt stand
Not as an exile but a visitant
On Etna's top; by pastoral Arethuse   *465*
Or, if that fountain be in truth no more,
Then, near some other spring, which, by the name,
Thou gratulatest, willingly deceived,

Nor can my tongue give utterance to a name
Of note belonging to that honoured isle,
Philosopher or Bard, Empedocles,
Or Archimedes, pure abstracted soul!
That doth not yield a solace to my grief:
And, O Theocritus, so far have some
Prevailed among the powers of heaven and earth,
By their endowments, good or great, that they
440   Have had, as thou reportest, miracles
Wrought for them in old time: yea, not unmoved,
When thinking on my own belovèd friend,
I hear thee tell how bees with honey fed
Divine Comates, by his impious lord
Within a chest imprisoned; how they came
Laden from blooming grove or flowery field,
And fed him there, alive, month after month,
Because the goatherd, blessèd man! had lips
Wet with the Muse's nectar.

                    Thus I soothe
450   The pensive moments by this calm fireside,
And find a thousand bounteous images
To cheer the thoughts of those I love, and mine.
Our prayers have been accepted; thou wilt stand
On Etna's summit, above earth and sea,
Triumphant, winning from the invaded heavens
Thoughts without bound, magnificent designs,
Worthy of poets who attuned their harps
In wood or echoing cave, for discipline
Of heroes; or, in reverence to the gods,
460   'Mid temples, served by sapient priests, and choirs
Of virgins crowned with roses. Not in vain
Those temples, where they in their ruins yet
Survive for inspiration, shall attract
Thy solitary steps: and on the brink
Thou wilt recline of pastoral Arethuse;
Or, if that fountain be in truth no more,
Then, near some other spring, which, by the name
Thou gratulatest, willingly deceived,

Shalt linger as a gladsome votary,
And not a captive pining for his home.   470

I see thee linger a glad votary,
470 And not a captive pining for his home.

Book Eleventh

IMAGINATION, HOW IMPAIRED AND RESTORED

Long time hath Man's unhappiness and guilt
Detained us, with what dismal sights beset
For the outward view, and inwardly oppressed
With sorrow, disappointment, vexing thoughts,
Confusion of opinion, zeal decayed,   5
And, lastly, utter loss of hope itself
And things to hope for! Not with these began
Our song, and not with these our song must end. –
Ye motions of delight, that through the fields
10 Stir gently, breezes and soft airs that breathe   10
The breath of Paradise, and find your way
To the recesses of the soul; ye brooks
Muttering along the stones, a busy noise
By day, a quiet one in silent night;   20
And you, ye groves, whose ministry it is
To interpose the covert of your shades,   25
Even as a sleep, betwixt the heart of man
And the uneasy world, 'twixt man himself,
Not seldom, and his own unquiet heart:
20 Oh! that I had a music and a voice,
Harmonious as your own, that I might tell   30

Book Twelfth

IMAGINATION AND TASTE,
HOW IMPAIRED AND RESTORED

Long time have human ignorance and guilt
Detained us, on what spectacles of woe
Compelled to look, and inwardly oppressed
With sorrow, disappointment, vexing thoughts,
Confusion of the judgement, zeal decayed,
And, lastly, utter loss of hope itself
And things to hope for! Not with these began
Our song, and not with these our song must end. –
Ye motions of delight, that haunt the sides
10   Of the green hills; ye breezes and soft airs,
Whose subtle intercourse with breathing flowers,
Feelingly watched, might teach Man's haughty race
How without injury to take, to give
Without offence; ye who, as if to show
The wondrous influence of power gently used,
Bend the complying heads of lordly pines,
And, with a touch, shift the stupendous clouds
Through the whole compass of the sky; ye brooks,
Muttering along the stones, a busy noise
20   By day, a quiet sound in silent night;
Ye waves, that out of the great deep steal forth
In a calm hour to kiss the pebbly shore,
Not mute, and then retire, fearing no storm;
And you, ye groves, whose ministry it is
To interpose the covert of your shades,
Even as a sleep, between the heart of man
And outward troubles, between man himself,
Not seldom, and his own uneasy heart:
Oh! that I had a music and a voice
30   Harmonious as your own, that I might tell

What ye have done for me. The morning shines,
Nor heedeth Man's perverseness; Spring returns, –
I saw the Spring return, when I was dead
To deeper hope, yet had I joy for her,
And welcomed her benevolence, rejoiced
In common with the children of her love,
Plants, insects, beasts in field, and birds in bower.   35
So neither were complacency, nor peace,
30 Nor tender yearnings, wanting for my good
Through those distracted times; in Nature still   40
Glorying, I found a counterpoise in her,
Which, when the spirit of evil was at height,
Maintained for me a secret happiness;
Her I resorted to, and loved so much
I seemed to love as much as heretofore;
And yet this passion, fervent as it was,
Had suffered change; how could there fail to be
Some change, if merely hence, that years of life
40 Were going on, and with them loss or gain
Inevitable, sure alternative.

    This history, my Friend! hath chiefly told
Of intellectual power, from stage to stage   45
Advancing, hand in hand with love and joy,
And of imagination teaching truth
Until that natural graciousness of mind   50
Gave way to overpressure of the times
And their disastrous issues. What availed,
When spells forbade the voyager to land,
50 The fragrance which did ever and anon
Give notice of the shore, from arbours breathed   55
Of blessed sentiment and fearless love?
What did such sweet remembrances avail,
Perfidious then, as seemed, what served they then?
My business was upon the barren sea,
My errand was to sail to other coasts.
Shall I avow that I had hope to see,
I mean that future times would surely see,

What ye have done for me. The morning shines,
Nor heedeth Man's perverseness; Spring returns, –
I saw the Spring return, and could rejoice,
In common with the children of her love,
Piping on boughs, or sporting on fresh fields,
Or boldly seeking pleasure nearer heaven
On wings that navigate cerulean skies.
So neither were complacency, nor peace,
Nor tender yearnings, wanting for my good
40 Through these distracted times; in Nature still
Glorying, I found a counterpoise in her,
Which, when the spirit of evil reached its height,
Maintained for me a secret happiness.

   This narrative, my Friend! hath chiefly told
Of intellectual power, fostering love,
Dispensing truth, and, over men and things,
Where reason yet might hesitate, diffusing
Prophetic sympathies of genial faith:
So was I favoured – such my happy lot –
50 Until that natural graciousness of mind
Gave way to overpressure from the times
And their disastrous issues. What availed,
When spells forbade the voyager to land,
That fragrant notice of a pleasant shore
Wafted, at intervals, from many a bower
Of blissful gratitude and fearless love?
Dare I avow that wish was mine to see,
And hope that future times *would* surely see,

The man to come, parted, as by a gulph,
60 From him who had been; that I could no more   60
Trust the elevation which had made me one
With the great family that here and there
Is scattered through the abyss of ages past,
Sage, patriot, lover, hero; for it seemed
That their best virtues were not free from taint   65
Of something false and weak, which could not stand
The open eye of Reason. Then I said,
'Go to the Poets; they will speak to thee
More perfectly of purer creatures; – yet
70 If reason be nobility in man,   70
Can aught be more ignoble than the man
Whom they describe, would fasten if they may
Upon our love by sympathies of truth?'

        Thus strangely did I war against myself;   76
A bigot to a new idolatry
Did like a monk who hath forsworn the world
Zealously labour to cut off my heart
From all the sources of her former strength;   80
And as, by simple waving of a wand,
80 The wizard instantaneously dissolves
Palace or grove, even so did I unsoul
As readily by syllogistic words,
Some charm of logic, ever within reach,
Those mysteries of passion which have made,   85
And shall continue evermore to make,
(In spite of all that Reason hath performed
And shall perform to exalt and to refine)
One brotherhood of all the human race
Through all the habitations of past years
90 And those to come, and hence an emptiness
Fell on the historian's page, and even on that
Of poets, pregnant with more absolute truth.
The works of both withered in my esteem,
Their sentence was, I thought, pronounced; their rights
Seemed mortal, and their empire passed away.

The man to come, parted, as by a gulph,
60 From him who had been; that I could no more
Trust the elevation which had made me one
With the great family that still survives
To illuminate the abyss of ages past,
Sage, warrior, patriot, hero; for it seemed
That their best virtues were not free from taint
Of something false and weak, that could not stand
The open eye of Reason. Then I said,
'Go to the Poets; they will speak to thee
More perfectly of purer creatures; – yet
70 If reason be nobility in man,
Can aught be more ignoble than the man
Whom they delight in, blinded as he is
By prejudice, the miserable slave
Of low ambition or distempered love?'

    In such strange passion, if I may once more
Review the past, I warred against myself –
A bigot to a new idolatry –
Like a cowled monk who hath forsworn the world,
Zealously laboured to cut off my heart
80 From all the sources of her former strength;
And as, by simple waving of a wand,
The wizard instantaneously dissolves
Palace or grove, even so could I unsoul
As readily by syllogistic words
Those mysteries of being which have made,
And shall continue evermore to make,
Of the whole human race one brotherhood.

What then remained in such eclipse? what light
To guide or cheer? The laws of things which lie
Beyond the reach of human will or power;
The life of nature, by the god of love
100 Inspired, celestial presence ever pure;
These left, the soul of youth must needs be rich,
Whatever else be lost, and these were mine,
Not a deaf echo, merely, of the thought,
Bewildered recollections, solitary,
But living sounds. Yet in despite of this,
This feeling, which howe'er impaired or damped,
Yet having been once born can never die.
'Tis true that earth with all her appanage
Of elements and organs, storm and sunshine,
110 With its pure forms and colours, pomp of clouds
Rivers and mountains, objects among which
It might be thought that no dislike or blame,
No sense of weakness or infirmity
Or aught amiss could possibly have come,
Yea, even the visible Universe, was scanned
With something of a kindred spirit, fell
Beneath the domination of a taste   90
Less elevated, which did in my mind
With its more noble influence interfere,
120 Its animation and its deeper sway.

There comes (if need be now to speak of this
After such long detail of our mistakes)
There comes a time when Reason, not the grand
And simple Reason, but that humbler power
Which carries on its no inglorious work
By logic and minute analysis
Is of all idols that which pleases most
The growing mind. A trifler would he be
Who on the obvious benefits should dwell
130 That rise out of this process; but to speak
Of all the narrow estimates of things
Which hence originate were a worthy theme

What wonder, then, if, to a mind so far
Perverted, even the visible Universe
90 Fell under the dominion of a taste
Less spiritual, with microscopic view
Was scanned, as I had scanned the moral world?

For philosophic verse; suffice it here
To hint that danger cannot but attend
Upon a function rather proud to be
The enemy of falsehood, than the friend
Of truth, to sit in judgement than to feel.

O Soul of Nature! excellent and fair!
That didst rejoice with me, with whom I, too,
140 Rejoiced through early youth, before the winds   95
And powerful waters, and in lights and shades
That marched and countermarched about the hills
In glorious apparition, now all eye
And now all ear; but ever with the heart   100
Employed, and the majestic intellect:
O Soul of Nature! that dost overflow
With passion and with life, what feeble men
Walk on this earth! how feeble have I been   105
When thou wert in thy strength! Nor this through stroke
150 Of human suffering, such as justifies
Remissness and inaptitude of mind,
But through presumption; even in pleasure pleased
Unworthily, disliking here, and there   110
Liking, by rules of mimic art transferred
To things above all art; but more, – for this,
Although a strong infection of the age,
Was never much my habit – giving way
To a comparison of scene with scene,   115
Bent overmuch on superficial things,
160 Pampering myself with meagre novelties
Of colour and proportion; to the moods
Of time or season, to the moral power,
The affections and the spirit of the place,   120
Less sensible. Nor only did the love
Of sitting thus in judgement interrupt
My deeper feelings, but another cause,
More subtle and less easily explained,
That almost seems inherent in the creature,   125
Sensuous and intellectual as he is,

O Soul of Nature! excellent and fair!
That didst rejoice with me, with whom I, too,
Rejoiced through early youth, before the winds
And roaring waters, and in lights and shades
That marched and countermarched about the hills
In glorious apparition, Powers on whom
I daily waited, now all eye and now
100　All ear; but never long without the heart
Employed, and man's unfolding intellect:
O Soul of Nature! that, by laws divine
Sustained and governed, still dost overflow
With an impassioned life, what feeble ones
Walk on this earth! how feeble have I been
When thou wert in thy strength! Nor this through stroke
Of human suffering, such as justifies
Remissness and inaptitude of mind,
But through presumption; even in pleasure pleased
110　Unworthily, disliking here, and there
Liking, by rules of mimic art transferred
To things above all art; but more, – for this,
Although a strong infection of the age,
Was never much my habit – giving way
To a comparison of scene with scene,
Bent overmuch on superficial things,
Pampering myself with meagre novelties
Of colour and proportion; to the moods
Of time and season, to the moral power,
120　The affections and the spirit of the place,
Insensible. Nor only did the love
Of sitting thus in judgement interrupt
My deeper feelings, but another cause,
More subtle and less easily explained,
That almost seems inherent in the creature,

170 A twofold frame of body and of mind.
  The state to which I now allude was one
  In which the eye was master of the heart,
  When that which is in every stage of life
  The most despotic of our senses gained
  Such strength in me as often held my mind   *130*
  In absolute dominion. Gladly here,
  Entering upon abstruser argument,
  Would I endeavour to unfold the means
  Which Nature studiously employs to thwart
180 This tyranny, summons all the senses each *135*
  To counteract the other, and themselves,
  And makes them all, and the objects with which all
  Are conversant, subservient in their turn
  To the great ends of Liberty and Power.
  But this is matter for another song;
  Here only let me add that my delights   *140*
  (Such as they were) were sought insatiably,
  Though 'twas a transport of the outward sense,
  Not of the mind, vivid but not profound:
190 Yet was I often greedy in the chase,
  And roamed from hill to hill, from rock to rock,
  Still craving combinations of new forms,
  New pleasure, wider empire for the sight, *145*
  Proud of its own endowments, and rejoiced
  To lay the inner faculties asleep.
  Amid the turns and counterturns, the strife
  And various trials of our complex being,
  As we grow up, such thraldom of that sense *150*
  Seems hard to shun. And yet I knew a maid,
200 Who, young as I was then, conversed with things
  In higher style; from appetites like these
  She, gentle visitant, as well she might,
  Was wholly free, far less did critic rules
  Or barren intermeddling subtleties   *155*
  Perplex her mind; but, wise as women are
  When genial circumstance hath favoured them,
  She welcomed what was given, and craved no more;

A twofold frame of body and of mind.
I speak in recollection of a time
When the bodily eye, in every stage of life
The most despotic of our senses, gained
130   Such strength in *me* as often held my mind
In absolute dominion. Gladly here,
Entering upon abstruser argument,
Could I endeavour to unfold the means
Which Nature studiously employs to thwart
This tyranny, summons all the senses each
To counteract the other, and themselves,
And makes them all, and the objects with which all
Are conversant, subservient in their turn
To the great ends of Liberty and Power.
140   But leave we this: enough that my delights
(Such as they were) were sought insatiably.
Vivid the transport, vivid though not profound;
I roamed from hill to hill, from rock to rock,
Still craving combinations of new forms,
New pleasure, wider empire for the sight,
Proud of her own endowments, and rejoiced
To lay the inner faculties asleep.
Amid the turns and counterturns, the strife
And various trials of our complex being,
150   As we grow up, such thraldom of that sense
Seems hard to shun. And yet I knew a maid,
A young enthusiast, who escaped these bonds;
Her eye was not the mistress of her heart;
Far less did rules prescribed by passive taste,
Or barren intermeddling subtleties,
Perplex her mind; but, wise as women are
When genial circumstance hath favoured them,
She welcomed what was given, and craved no more;

Whatever scene was present to her eyes,
That was the best, to that she was attuned   *160*
210 Through her humility and lowliness,
And through a perfect happiness of soul,
Whose variegated feelings were in this
Sisters, that they were each some new delight: *164*
For she was Nature's inmate. Her the birds
And every flower she met with, could they but
Have known her, would have loved; methought such charm
Of sweetness did her presence breathe around
That all the trees, and all the silent hills,
And every thing she looked on, should have had
220 An intimation how she bore herself   *170*
Towards them and to all creatures. God delights
In such a being; for her common thoughts
Are piety, her life is blessedness.

      Even like this maid, before I was called forth
From the retirement of my native hills,   *175*
I loved whate'er I saw: nor lightly loved,
But fervently, did never dream of aught
More grand, more fair, more exquisitely framed
Than those few nooks to which my happy feet
230 Were limited. I had not at that time   *180*
Lived long enough, nor in the least survived
The first diviner influence of this world,
As it appears to unaccustomed eyes.
I worshipped then among the depths of things,
As my soul bade me; could I then take part   *185*
In aught but admiration, or be pleased
With any thing but humbleness and love?
I felt, and nothing else; I did not judge,
I never thought of judging, with the gift
240 Of all this glory filled and satisfied.   *190*
And afterwards, when through the gorgeous Alps
Roaming, I carried with me the same heart:
In truth, this degradation – howsoe'er
Induced, effect, in whatsoe'er degree,

Whate'er the scene presented to her view,
160   That was the best, to that she was attuned
By her benign simplicity of life,
And through a perfect happiness of soul,
Whose variegated feelings were in this
Sisters, that they were each some new delight.
Birds in the bower, and lambs in the green field,
Could they have known her, would have loved; methought
Her very presence such a sweetness breathed,
That flowers, and trees, and even the silent hills,
And every thing she looked on, should have had
170   An intimation how she bore herself
Towards them and to all creatures. God delights
In such a being; for her common thoughts
Are piety, her life is gratitude.

Even like this maid, before I was called forth
From the retirement of my native hills,
I loved whate'er I saw: nor lightly loved,
But most intensely; never dreamt of aught
More grand, more fair, more exquisitely framed
Than those few nooks to which my happy feet
180   Were limited. I had not at that time
Lived long enough, nor in the least survived
The first diviner influence of this world,
As it appears to unaccustomed eyes.
Worshipping then among the depth of things,
As piety ordained; could I submit
To measured admiration, or to aught
That should preclude humility and love?
I felt, observed, and pondered; did not judge,
Yea, never thought of judging; with the gift
190   Of all this glory filled and satisfied.
And afterwards, when through the gorgeous Alps
Roaming, I carried with me the same heart:
In truth, the degradation – howsoe'er
Induced, effect, in whatsoe'er degree,

Of custom that prepares such wantonness   195
As makes the greatest things give way to least,
Or any other cause which hath been named;
Or lastly, aggravated by the times,
Which with their passionate sounds might often make
250 The milder minstrelsies of rural scenes   200
Inaudible – was transient; I had felt
Too forcibly, too early in my life,
Visitings of imaginative power
For this to last: I shook the habit off
Entirely and for ever, and again   205
In Nature's presence stood, as I stand now,
A sensitive, and a *creative* soul.

     There are in our existence spots of time,
Which with distinct pre-eminence retain
260 A vivifying virtue, whence, depressed   210
By false opinion and contentious thought,
Or aught of heavier or more deadly weight,
In trivial occupations, and the round
Of ordinary intercourse, our minds
Are nourished and invisibly repaired;   215
A virtue, by which pleasure is enhanced,
That penetrates, enables us to mount,
When high, more high, and lifts us up when fallen.
This efficacious spirit chiefly lurks
270 Among those passages of life in which   220
We have had deepest feeling that the mind
Is lord and master, and that outward sense
Is but the obedient servant of her will.
Such moments, worthy of all gratitude,
Are scattered everywhere, taking their date
From our first childhood: in our childhood even   225
Perhaps are most conspicuous. Life with me,
As far as memory can look back, is full
Of this beneficent influence. At a time
280 When scarcely (I was then not six years old)
My hand could hold a bridle, with proud hopes

Of custom that prepares a partial scale
In which the little oft outweighs the great;
Or any other cause that hath been named;
Or lastly, aggravated by the times
And their impassioned sounds, which well might make
200   The milder minstrelsies of rural scenes
Inaudible – was transient; I had known
Too forcibly, too early in my life,
Visitings of imaginative power
For this to last: I shook the habit off
Entirely and for ever, and again
In Nature's presence stood, as now I stand,
A sensitive being, a *creative* soul.

There are in our existence spots of time,
That with distinct pre-eminence retain
210   A renovating virtue, whence, depressed
By false opinion and contentious thought,
Or aught of heavier or more deadly weight,
In trivial occupations, and the round
Of ordinary intercourse, our minds
Are nourished and invisibly repaired;
A virtue, by which pleasure is enhanced,
That penetrates, enables us to mount,
When high, more high, and lifts us up when fallen.
This efficacious spirit chiefly lurks
220   Among those passages of life that give
Profoundest knowledge to what point, and how,
The mind is lord and master – outward sense
The obedient servant of her will. Such moments
Are scattered everywhere, taking their date
From our first childhood. I remember well,
That once, while yet my inexperienced hand
Could scarcely hold a bridle, with proud hopes

I mounted, and we rode towards the hills:
We were a pair of horsemen; honest James
Was with me, my encourager and guide: 230
We had not travelled long, ere some mischance
Disjoined me from my comrade; and, through fear
Dismounting, down the rough and stony moor
I led my horse, and, stumbling on, at length
Came to a bottom, where in former times   235
290 A murderer had been hung in iron chains.
The gibbet-mast was mouldered down, the bones
And iron case were gone; but on the turf,
Hard by, soon after that fell deed was wrought,
Some unknown hand had carved the murderer's name. 240
The monumental writing was engraven
In times long past; and still, from year to year,
By superstition of the neighbourhood,
The grass is cleared away, and to this hour
The letters are all fresh and visible.   245
300 Faltering, and ignorant where I was, at length
I chanced to espy those characters inscribed
On the green sod: forthwith I left the spot
And, reascending the bare common, saw
A naked pool that lay beneath the hills,
The beacon on the summit, and, more near,   250
A girl who bore a pitcher on her head,
And seemed with difficult steps to force her way
Against the blowing wind. It was, in truth,
An ordinary sight; but I should need
310 Colours and words that are unknown to man,   255
To paint the visionary dreariness
Which, while I looked all round for my lost guide,
Did at that time invest the naked pool,
The beacon on the lonely eminence,
The woman and her garments vexed and tossed   260
By the strong wind. When, in a blessèd season
With those two dear ones, to my heart so dear,
When in the blessed time of early love,
Long afterwards, I roamed about

480

I mounted, and we journeyed towards the hills:
An ancient servant of my father's house
230 Was with me, my encourager and guide:
We had not travelled long, ere some mischance
Disjoined me from my comrade; and, through fear
Dismounting, down the rough and stony moor
I led my horse, and, stumbling on, at length
Came to a bottom, where in former times
A murderer had been hung in iron chains.
The gibbet-mast had mouldered down, the bones
And iron case were gone; but on the turf,
Hard by, soon after that fell deed was wrought,
240 Some unknown hand had carved the murderer's name.
The monumental letters were inscribed
In times long past; but still, from year to year,
By superstition of the neighbourhood,
The grass is cleared away, and to that hour
The characters were fresh and visible:
A casual glance had shown them, and I fled,
Faltering and faint, and ignorant of the road:
Then, reascending the bare common, saw
A naked pool that lay beneath the hills,
250 The beacon on the summit, and, more near,
A girl, who bore a pitcher on her head,
And seemed with difficult steps to force her way
Against the blowing wind. It was, in truth,
An ordinary sight; but I should need
Colours and words that are unknown to man,
To paint the visionary dreariness
Which, while I looked all round for my lost guide,
Invested moorland waste, and naked pool,
The beacon crowning the lone eminence,
260 The female and her garments vexed and tossed
By the strong wind. When, in the blessèd hours
Of early love, the loved one at my side,
I roamed, in daily presence of this scene,

320 In daily presence of this very scene,
     Upon the naked pool and dreary crags,
     And on the melancholy beacon, fell   265
     The spirit of pleasure and youth's golden gleam;
     And think ye not with radiance more divine
     From these remembrances, and from the power
     They left behind? So feeling comes in aid
     Of feeling, and diversity of strength   270
     Attends us, if but once we have been strong.
     Oh! mystery of man, from what a depth
330 Proceed thy honours. I am lost, but see
     In simple childhood something of the base
     On which thy greatness stands; but this I feel,   275
     That from thyself it is that thou must give,
     Else never canst receive. The days gone by
     Come back upon me from the dawn almost
     Of life: the hiding-places of my power
     Seem open; I approach, and then they close;   280
     I see by glimpses now; when age comes on,
     May scarcely see at all, and I would give,
340 While yet we may, as far as words can give,
     A substance and a life to what I feel:
     I would enshrine the spirit of the past   285
     For future restoration. – Yet another
     Of these to me affecting incidents
     With which we will conclude: –
                             One Christmas-time,
     The day before the holidays began,
     Feverish, and tired, and restless, I went forth
     Into the fields, impatient for the sight   290
     Of those two horses which should bear us home;
350 My brothers and myself. There was a crag,
     An eminence, which from the meeting-point
     Of two highways ascending, overlooked
     At least a long half-mile of those two roads,
     By each of which the expected steeds might come,
     The choice uncertain. Thither I repaired   296
     Up to the highest summit; 'twas a day

Upon the naked pool and dreary crags,
And on the melancholy beacon, fell
A spirit of pleasure and youth's golden gleam;
And think ye not with radiance more sublime
For these remembrances, and for the power
They had left behind? So feeling comes in aid
270 Of feeling, and diversity of strength
Attends us, if but once we have been strong.
Oh! mystery of man, from what a depth
Proceed thy honours. I am lost, but see
In simple childhood something of the base
On which thy greatness stands; but this I feel,
That from thyself it comes, that thou must give,
Else never canst receive. The days gone by
Return upon me almost from the dawn
Of life: the hiding-places of man's power
280 Open; I would approach them, but they close.
I see by glimpses now; when age comes on,
May scarcely see at all; and I would give,
While yet we may, as far as words can give,
Substance and life to what I feel, enshrining,
Such is my hope, the spirit of the Past
For future restoration. – Yet another
Of these memorials: –

               One Christmas-time,
On the glad eve of its dear holidays,
Feverish, and tired, and restless, I went forth
290 Into the fields, impatient for the sight
Of those led palfreys that should bear us home;
My brothers and myself. There rose a crag,
That, from the meeting-point of two highways
Ascending, overlooked them both, far stretched;
Thither, uncertain on which road to fix
My expectation, thither I repaired,
Scout-like, and gained the summit; 'twas a day

Stormy, and rough, and wild, and on the grass
I sate half-sheltered by a naked wall;
Upon my right hand was a single sheep,   *300*
360 A whistling hawthorn on my left, and there,
With those companions at my side, I watched,
Straining my eyes intensely, as the mist
Gave intermitting prospect of the wood
And plain beneath. Ere I to school returned   *305*
That dreary time, ere I had been ten days
A dweller in my father's house, he died,
And I and my two brothers, orphans then,
Followed his body to the grave. The event,
With all the sorrow which it brought, appeared   *310*
370 A chastisement; and when I called to mind
That day so lately past, when from the crag
I looked in such anxiety of hope;
With trite reflections of morality,
Yet in the deepest passion, I bowed low   *315*
To God, Who thus corrected my desires;
And, afterwards, the wind and sleety rain,
And all the business of the elements,
The single sheep, and the one blasted tree,
And the bleak music of that old stone wall,   *320*
380 The noise of wood and water, and the mist
Which on the line of each of those two roads
Advanced in such indisputable shapes;
All these were spectacles and sounds to which
I often would repair, and thence would drink,   *325*
As at a fountain; and I do not doubt
That in this later time, when storm and rain
Beat on my roof at midnight, or by day,
When I am in the woods, unknown to me
The workings of my spirit thence are brought.   *331*

390   Thou wilt not languish here, O Friend, for whom
I travel in these dim uncertain ways;
Thou wilt assist me as a pilgrim gone
In quest of highest truth. Behold me then
      484

Tempestuous, dark, and wild, and on the grass
I sate half-sheltered by a naked wall;
300 Upon my right hand couched a single sheep,
Upon my left a blasted hawthorn stood;
With those companions at my side, I sate,
Straining my eyes intensely, as the mist
Gave intermitting prospect of the copse
And plain beneath. Ere we to school returned
That dreary time, ere we had been ten days
Sojourners in my father's house, he died,
And I and my three brothers, orphans then,
Followed his body to the grave. The event,
310 With all the sorrow that it brought, appeared
A chastisement; and when I called to mind
That day so lately past, when from the crag
I looked in such anxiety of hope;
With trite reflections of morality,
Yet in the deepest passion, I bowed low
To God, Who thus corrected my desires;
And, afterwards, the wind and sleety rain,
And all the business of the elements,
The single sheep, and the one blasted tree,
320 And the bleak music of that old stone wall,
The noise of wood and water, and the mist
That on the line of each of those two roads
Advanced in such indisputable shapes;
All these were kindred spectacles and sounds
To which I oft repaired, and thence would drink,
As at a fountain; and on winter nights,
Down to this very time, when storm and rain
Beat on my roof, or, haply, at noon-day,
While in a grove I walk, whose lofty trees,
330 Laden with summer's thickest foliage, rock
In a strong wind, some working of the spirit,
Some inward agitations thence are brought,
Whate'er their office, whether to beguile
Thoughts over busy in the course they took,
Or animate an hour of vacant ease.

Once more in Nature's presence, thus restored
Or otherwise, and strengthened once again
(With memory left of what had been escaped)
To habits of devoutest sympathy.

Book Twelfth

From Nature doth emotion come, and moods
Of calmness equally are Nature's gift:
This is her glory; these two attributes
Are sister horns that constitute her strength;   *4*
This twofold influence is the sun and shower
Of all her bounties, both in origin
And end alike benignant. Hence it is,
That Genius, which exists by interchange   *5*
Of peace and excitation, finds in her
His best and purest friend; from her receives
That energy by which he seeks the truth,
Is roused, aspires, grasps, struggles, wishes, craves,
From her that happy stillness of the mind
Which fits him to receive it when unsought.   *10*

Such benefit may souls of humblest frame
Partake of, each in their degree; 'tis mine
To speak of what myself have known and felt;
Sweet task! for words find easy way, inspired
By gratitude and confidence in truth.   *15*
Long time in search of knowledge desperate,
I was benighted heart and mind; but now
On all sides day began to reappear,
And it was proved indeed that not in vain
I had been taught to reverence a Power   *20*
That is the very quality and shape
And image of right reason; that matures
Her processes by steadfast laws; gives birth
To no impatient or fallacious hopes,
No heat of passion or excessive zeal,   *25*

Book Thirteenth

From Nature doth emotion come, and moods
Of calmness equally are Nature's gift:
This is her glory; these two attributes
Are sister horns that constitute her strength.
Hence Genius, born to thrive by interchange
Of peace and excitation, finds in her
His best and purest friend; from her receives
That energy by which he seeks the truth,
From her that happy stillness of the mind
10 Which fits him to receive it when unsought.

    Such benefit the humblest intellects
Partake of, each in their degree; 'tis mine
To speak, what I myself have known and felt;
Smooth task! for words find easy way, inspired
By gratitude, and confidence in truth.
Long time in search of knowledge did I range
The field of human life, in heart and mind
Benighted; but, the dawn beginning now
To re-appear, 'twas proved that not in vain
20 I had been taught to reverence a Power
That is the visible quality and shape
And image of right reason; that matures
Her processes by steadfast laws; gives birth
To no impatient or fallacious hopes,
No heat of passion or excessive zeal,

30 No vain conceits; provokes to no quick turns
Of self-applauding intellect; but lifts
The being into magnanimity;
Holds up before the mind intoxicate
With present objects, and the busy dance   *30*
Of things that pass away, a temperate show
Of objects that endure; and by this course
Disposes her, when over-fondly set
On leaving her incumbrances behind,
To seek in man, and in the frame of life,   *35*
40 Social and individual, what there is
Desirable, affecting, good or fair
Of kindred permanence, the gifts divine
And universal, the pervading grace
That hath been, is, and shall be. Above all   *39*
Did Nature bring again that wiser mood
More deeply re-established in my soul,
Which, seeing little worthy or sublime
In what we blazon with the pompous names
Of power and action, early tutored me
50 To look with feelings of fraternal love   *45*
Upon those unassuming things that hold
A silent station in this beauteous world.

    Thus moderated, thus composed, I found
Once more in Man an object of delight,
Of pure imagination, and of love;   *50*
And, as the horizon of my mind enlarged,
Again I took the intellectual eye
For my instructor, studious more to see
Great truths, than touch and handle little ones.
60 Knowledge was given accordingly; my trust   *55*
Was firmer in the feelings which had stood
The test of such a trial; clearer far
My sense of what was excellent and right;
The promise of the present time retired
Into its true proportion; sanguine schemes,   *60*
Ambitious virtues, pleased me less; I sought

No vain conceits; provokes to no quick turns
Of self-applauding intellect; but trains
To meekness, and exalts by humble faith;
Holds up before the mind intoxicate
30   With present objects, and the busy dance
Of things that pass away, a temperate show
Of objects that endure; and by this course
Disposes her, when over-fondly set
On throwing off incumbrances, to seek
In man, and in the frame of social life,
Whate'er there is desirable and good
Of kindred permanence, unchanged in form
And function, or, through strict vicissitude
Of life and death, revolving. Above all
40   Were re-established now those watchful thoughts
Which, seeing little worthy or sublime
In what the Historian's pen so much delights
To blazon – power and energy detached
From moral purpose – early tutored me
To look with feelings of fraternal love
Upon the unassuming things that hold
A silent station in this beauteous world.

Thus moderated, thus composed, I found
Once more in Man an object of delight,
50   Of pure imagination, and of love;
And, as the horizon of my mind enlarged,
Again I took the intellectual eye
For my instructor, studious more to see
Great truths, than touch and handle little ones.
Knowledge was given accordingly; my trust
Became more firm in feelings that had stood
The test of such a trial; clearer far
My sense of excellence – of right and wrong:
The promise of the present time retired
60   Into its true proportion; sanguine schemes,
Ambitious projects, pleased me less; I sought

For good in the familiar face of life,
And built thereon my hopes of good to come.

    With settling judgements now of what would last
70 And what would disappear; prepared to find   *65*
Ambition, folly, madness, in the men
Who thrust themselves upon this passive world
As Rulers of the world; to see in these,
Even when the public welfare is their aim,
Plans without thought, or bottomed on false thought   *70*
And false philosophy; having brought to test
Of solid life and true result the books
Of modern statists, and thereby perceived
The utter hollowness of what we name
80 'The Wealth of Nations', where alone that wealth
Is lodged, and how increased; and having gained
A more judicious knowledge of what makes   *80*
The dignity of individual man,
Of man, no composition of the thought,
Abstraction, shadow, image, but the man
Of whom we read, the man whom we behold
With our own eyes – I could not but enquire –
Not with less interest than heretofore,   *85*
But greater, though in spirit more subdued –
90 Why is this glorious creature to be found
One only in ten thousand? What one is,
Why may not many be? What bars are thrown
By Nature in the way of such a hope?   *90*
Our animal wants and the necessities
Which they impose, are these the obstacles?
If not, then others vanish into air.
Such meditations bred an anxious wish
To ascertain how much of real worth   *95*
And genuine knowledge, and true power of mind
100 Did at this day exist in those who lived
By bodily labour, labour far exceeding
Their due proportion, under all the weight

For present good in life's familiar face,
And built thereon my hopes of good to come.

With settling judgements now of what would last
And what would disappear; prepared to find
Presumption, folly, madness, in the men
Who thrust themselves upon the passive world
As Rulers of the world; to see in these,
Even when the public welfare is their aim,
70 Plans without thought, or built on theories
Vague and unsound; and having brought the books
Of modern statists to their proper test,
Life, human life, with all its sacred claims
Of sex and age, and heaven-descended rights,
Mortal, or those beyond the reach of death;
And having thus discerned how dire a thing
Is worshipped in that idol proudly named
'The Wealth of Nations', *where* alone that wealth
Is lodged, and how increased; and having gained
80 A more judicious knowledge of the worth
And dignity of individual man,
No composition of the brain, but man
Of whom we read, the man whom we behold
With our own eyes – I could not but enquire –
Not with less interest than heretofore,
But greater, though in spirit more subdued –
Why is this glorious creature to be found
One only in ten thousand? What one is,
Why may not millions be? What bars are thrown
90 By Nature in the way of such a hope?
Our animal appetites and daily wants,
Are these obstructions insurmountable?
If not, then others vanish into air.
'Inspect the basis of the social pile:
Enquire,' said I, 'how much of mental power
And genuine virtue they possess who live
By bodily toil, labour exceeding far
Their due proportion, under all the weight

Of that injustice which upon ourselves
By composition of society
Ourselves entail. To frame such estimate   *100*
I chiefly looked (what need to look beyond?)
Among the natural abodes of men,
Fields with their rural works; recalled to mind
My earliest notices; with these compared
110 The observations of my later youth,   *105*
Continued downwards to that very day.

For time had never been in which the throes
And mighty hopes of Nations and the stir
And tumult of the world to me could yield,
How far soe'er transported and possessed,
Full measure of content; but still I craved   *110*
An intermixture of distinct regards
And truths of individual sympathy
Nearer ourselves. Such often might be gleaned
120 From that great City, else it must have been
A heart-depressing wilderness indeed,   *115*
Full soon to me a wearisome abode;
But much was wanting: therefore did I turn
To you, ye pathways, and ye lonely roads;
Sought you enriched with everything I prized,
With human knidness and with Nature's joy.

Oh! next to one dear state of bliss, vouchsafed   *120*
Alas! to few in this untoward world,
The bliss of walking daily in life's prime
130 Through field or forest with the maid we love,
While yet our hearts are young, while yet we breathe
Nothing but happiness, living in some place   *125*
Deep vale, or any where, the home of both,
From which it would be misery to stir:
Oh! next to such enjoyment of our youth,
In my esteem, next to such dear delight,
Was that of wandering on from day to day   *130*
Where I could meditate in peace, and find

Of that injustice which upon ourselves
100   Ourselves entail.' Such estimate to frame
I chiefly looked (what need to look beyond?)
Among the natural abodes of men,
Fields with their rural works; recalled to mind
My earliest notices; with these compared
The observations made in later youth,
And to that day continued. – For, the time
Had never been when throes of mighty Nations
And the world's tumult unto me could yield,
How far soe'er transported and possessed,
110   Full measure of content; but still I craved
An intermingling of distinct regards
And truths of individual sympathy
Nearer ourselves. Such often might be gleaned
From the great City, else it must have proved
To me a heart-depressing wilderness;
But much was wanting: therefore did I turn
To you, ye pathways, and ye lonely roads;
Sought you enriched with everything I prized,
With human kindnesses and simple joys.

120   Oh ! next to one dear state of bliss, vouchsafed
Alas! to few in this untoward world,
The bliss of walking daily in life's prime
Through field or forest with the maid we love,
While yet our hearts are young, while yet we breathe
Nothing but happiness, in some lone nook,
Deep vale, or any where, the home of both,
From which it would be misery to stir :
Oh! next to such enjoyment of our youth,
In my esteem, next to such dear delight,
130   Was that of wandering on from day to day
Where I could meditate in peace, and cull

The knowledge which I love, and teach the sound
140 Of poet's music to strange fields and groves,   *135*
Converse with men, where if we meet a face
We almost meet a friend, on naked moors
With long long ways before, by cottage bench,   *140*
Or well-spring where the weary traveller rests.

I love a public road: few sights there are
That please me more; such object hath had power
O'er my imagination since the dawn   *145*
Of childhood, when its disappearing line,
Seen daily afar off, on one bare steep
150 Beyond the limits which my feet had trod,
Was like a guide into eternity,   *151*
At least to things unknown and without bound.
Even something of the grandeur which invests
The mariner who sails the roaring sea
Through storm and darkness, early in my mind
Surrounded, too, the wanderers of the earth;   *155*
Grandeur as much, and loveliness far more.
Awed have I been by strolling Bedlamites;
From many other uncouth vagrants (passed
160 In fear) have walked with quicker step; but why
Take note of this? When I began to enquire,   *160*
To watch and question those I met, and held
Familiar talk with them, the lonely roads
Were schools to me in which I daily read
With most delight the passions of mankind,   *164*
There saw into the depth of human souls,
Souls that appear to have no depth at all
To vulgar eyes. And – now convinced at heart

Knowledge that step by step might lead me on
To wisdom; or, as lightsome as a bird
Wafted upon the wind from distant lands,
Sing notes of greeting to strange fields or groves,
Which lacked not voice to welcome me in turn:
And, when that pleasant toil had ceased to please,
Converse with men, where if we meet a face
We almost meet a friend, on naked heaths
140 With long long ways before, by cottage bench,
Or well-spring where the weary traveller rests.

Who doth not love to follow with his eye
The windings of a public way? the sight,
Familiar object as it is, hath wrought
On my imagination since the morn
Of childhood, when a disappearing line,
One daily present to my eyes, that crossed
The naked summit of a far-off hill
Beyond the limits that my feet had trod,
150 Was like an invitation into space
Boundless, or guide into eternity.
Yes, something of the grandeur which invests
The mariner who sails the roaring sea
Through storm and darkness, early in my mind
Surrounded, too, the wanderers of the earth;
Grandeur as much, and loveliness far more.
Awed have I been by strolling Bedlamites;
From many other uncouth vagrants (passed
In fear) have walked with quicker step; but why
160 Take note of this? When I began to enquire,
To watch and question those I met, and speak
Without reserve to them, the lonely roads
Were open schools in which I daily read
With most delight the passions of mankind,
Whether by words, looks, sighs, or tears, revealed;
There saw into the depth of human souls,
Souls that appear to have no depth at all
To careless eyes. And – now convinced at heart

How little that to which alone we give
170 The name of Education, hath to do   *171*
With real feeling and just sense; how vain
A correspondence with the talking world
Proves to the most; and called to make good search
If man's estate, by doom of Nature yoked   *175*
With toil, is therefore yoked with ignorance;
If virtue be indeed so hard to rear,
And intellectual strength so rare a boon –
I prized such walks still more, for there I found
Hope to my hope, and to my pleasure peace   *180*
180 And steadiness, and healing and repose
To every angry passion. There I heard,
From mouths of lowly men and of obscure,
A tale of honour; sounds in unison
With loftiest promises of good and fair.   *185*

There are who think that strong affections, love
Known by whatever name, is falsely deemed
A gift, to use a term which they would use,
Of vulgar nature; that its growth requires
Retirement, leisure, language purified   *190*
190 By manners thoughtful and elaborate;
That whoso feels such passion in excess
Must live within the very light and air
Of elegances that are made by man.
True is it, where oppression worse than death   *195*
Salutes the being at his birth, where grace
Of culture hath been utterly unknown,
And labour in excess and poverty
From day to day pre-occupy the ground
Of the affections, and to Nature's self   *200*
200 Oppose a deeper nature; there, indeed,
Love cannot be; nor does it easily thrive
In cities, where the human heart is sick,
And the eye feeds it not, and cannot feed: *205*
Thus far, no further, is that inference good.

How little those formalities, to which
170 With overweening trust alone we give
The name of Education, have to do
With real feeling and just sense; how vain
A correspondence with the talking world
Proves to the most; and called to make good search
If man's estate, by doom of Nature yoked
With toil, is therefore yoked with ignorance;
If virtue be indeed so hard to rear,
And intellectual strength so rare a boon –
I prized such walks still more, for there I found
180 Hope to my hope, and to my pleasure peace
And steadiness, and healing and repose
To every angry passion. There I heard,
From mouths of men obscure and lowly, truths
Replete with honour; sounds in unison
With loftiest promises of good and fair.

There are who think that strong affection, love
Known by whatever name, is falsely deemed
A gift, to use a term which they would use,
Of vulgar nature; that its growth requires
190 Retirement, leisure, language purified
By manners studied and elaborate;
That whoso feels such passion in its strength
Must live within the very light and air
Of courteous usages refined by art.
True is it, where oppression worse than death
Salutes the being at his birth, where grace
Of culture hath been utterly unknown,
And poverty and labour in excess
From day to day pre-occupy the ground
200 Of the affections, and to Nature's self
Oppose a deeper nature; there, indeed,
Love cannot be; nor does it thrive with ease
Among the close and overcrowded haunts
Of cities, where the human heart is sick,
And the eye feeds it not, and cannot feed.

   – Yes, in those wanderings deeply did I feel
How we mislead each other; above all,
How books mislead us, looking for their fame
To judgements of the wealthy Few, who see
By artificial lights; how they debase   *210*
210 The Many for the pleasure of those Few;
Effeminately level down the truth
To certain general notions, for the sake
Of being understood at once, or else
Through want of better knowledge in the men   *215*
Who frame them; flattering thus our self-conceit
With pictures that ambitiously set forth
The differences, the outside marks by which
Society has parted man from man,
Neglectful of the universal heart.   *220*

220   Here, calling up to mind what then I saw,
A youthful traveller, and see daily now
Before me in my rural neighbourhood,
Here might I pause, and bend in reverence
To Nature, and the power of human minds,   *225*
To men as they are men within themselves.
How oft high service is performed within,
When all the external man is rude in show, –
Not like a temple rich with pomp and gold,
But a mere mountain chapel, such as shields   *230*
230 Its simple worshippers from sun and shower.
Of these, said I, shall be my song; of these,
If future years mature me for the task,
Will I record the praises, making verse
Deal boldly with substantial things; in truth   *235*
And sanctity of passion, speak of these,
That justice may be done, obeisance paid
Where it is due: thus haply shall I teach,
Inspire, through unadulterated ears
Pour rapture, tenderness, and hope, – my theme   *240*
240 No other than the very heart of man,
As found among the best of those who live,

    — Yes, in those wanderings deeply did I feel
How we mislead each other; above all,
How books mislead us, seeking their reward
From judgements of the wealthy Few, who see
210 By artificial lights; how they debase
The Many for the pleasure of those Few;
Effeminately level down the truth
To certain general notions, for the sake
Of being understood at once, or else
Through want of better knowledge in the heads
That framed them; flattering self-conceit with words,
That, while they most ambitiously set forth
Extrinsic differences, the outward marks
Whereby society has parted man
220 From man, neglect the universal heart.

    Here, calling up to mind what then I saw,
A youthful traveller, and see daily now
In the familiar circuit of my home,
Here might I pause, and bend in reverence
To Nature, and the power of human minds,
To men as they are men within themselves.
How oft high service is performed within,
When all the external man is rude in show, –
Not like a temple rich with pomp and gold,
230 But a mere mountain chapel, that protects
Its simple worshippers from sun and shower.
Of these, said I, shall be my song; of these,
If future years mature me for the task,
Will I record the praises, making verse
Deal boldly with substantial things; in truth
And sanctity of passion, speak of these,
That justice may be done, obeisance paid
Where it is due: thus haply shall I teach,
Inspire, through unadulterated ears
240 Pour rapture, tenderness, and hope, – my theme
No other than the very heart of man,
As found among the best of those who live,

Not unexalted by religious hope,
Nor uninformed by books, good books, though few,
In Nature's presence: thence may I select   245
Sorrow, that is not sorrow, but delight;
And miserable love, that is not pain
To hear of, for the glory that redounds
Therefrom to human kind, and what we are.
Be mine to follow with no timid step   250
250   Where knowledge leads me: it shall be my pride
  That I have dared to tread this holy ground,
Speaking no dream, but things oracular;
Matter not lightly to be heard by those
Who to the letter of the outward promise   255
Do read the invisible soul; by men adroit
In speech, and for communion with the world
Accomplished, minds whose faculties are then
Most active when they are most eloquent,
And elevated most when most admired.   260
260   Men may be found of other mould than these,
Who are their own upholders, to themselves
Encouragement, and energy, and will,
Expressing liveliest thoughts in lively words
As native passion dictates. Others, too,   265
There are among the walks of homely life
Still higher, men for contemplation framed,
Shy, and unpractised in the strife of phrase;
Meek men, whose very souls perhaps would sink
Beneath them, summoned to such intercourse: 270
270   Theirs is the language of the heavens, the power,
The thought, the image, and the silent joy:
Words are but under-agents in their souls;
When they are grasping with their greatest strength,
They do not breathe among them: this I speak   275
In gratitude to God, Who feeds our hearts
For His own service; knoweth, loveth us,
When we are unregarded by the world.

    Also about this time did I receive

Not unexalted by religious faith,
Nor uninformed by books, good books, though few,
In Nature's presence: thence may I select
Sorrow, that is not sorrow, but delight;
And miserable love, that is not pain
To hear of, for the glory that redounds
Therefrom to human kind, and what we are.
250 Be mine to follow with no timid step
Where knowledge leads me: it shall be my pride
That I have dared to tread this holy ground,
Speaking no dream, but things oracular;
Matter not lightly to be heard by those
Who to the letter of the outward promise
Do read the invisible soul; by men adroit
In speech, and for communion with the world
Accomplished; minds whose faculties are then
Most active when they are most eloquent,
260 And elevated most when most admired.
Men may be found of other mould than these,
Who are their own upholders, to themselves
Encouragement, and energy, and will,
Expressing liveliest thoughts in lively words
As native passion dictates. Others, too,
There are among the walks of homely life
Still higher, men for contemplation framed,
Shy, and unpractised in the strife of phrase;
Meek men, whose very souls perhaps would sink
270 Beneath them, summoned to such intercourse:
Theirs is the language of the heavens, the power,
The thought, the image, and the silent joy:
Words are but under-agents in their souls;
When they are grasping with their greatest strength,
They do not breathe among them: this I speak
In gratitude to God, Who feeds our hearts
For His own service; knoweth, loveth us,
When we are unregarded by the world.

    Also about this time did I receive

Convictions still more strong than heretofore,   *280*
280   Not only that the inner frame is good,
And graciously composed, but that, no less,
Nature through all conditions hath a power
To consecrate, if we have eyes to see,   *285*
The outside of her creatures, and to breathe
Grandeur upon the very humblest face
Of human life. I felt that the array
Of outward circumstance, and visible form,
Is to the pleasure of the human mind
What passion makes it; that meanwhile the forms   *290*
290   Of Nature have a passion in themselves,
That intermingles with those works of man
To which she summons him; although the works
Be mean, have nothing lofty of their own;
And that the Genius of the Poet hence   *295*
May boldly take his way among mankind
Wherever Nature leads; that he hath stood
By Nature's side among the men of old,
And so shall stand for ever. Dearest Friend!
Forgive me if I say that I, who long
300   Had harboured reverentially a thought
That Poets, even as Prophets, each with each   *301*
Connected in a mighty scheme of truth,
Have each for his peculiar dower, a sense
By which he is enabled to perceive
Something unseen before; forgive me, Friend,   *305*
If I, the meanest of this band, had hope
That unto me had also been vouchsafed
An influx, that in some sort I possessed
A privilege, and that a work of mine,
310   Proceeding from the depth of untaught things,   *310*
Enduring and creative, might become
A power like one of Nature's. To such mood,
Once above all, a traveller at that time
Upon the Plain of Sarum was I raised;
There on the pastoral downs without a track   *315*
To guide me, or along the bare white roads

280　Convictions still more strong than heretofore,
　　Not only that the inner frame is good,
　　And graciously composed, but that, no less,
　　Nature for all conditions wants not power
　　To consecrate, if we have eyes to see,
　　The outside of her creatures, and to breathe
　　Grandeur upon the very humblest face
　　Of human life. I felt that the array
　　Of act and circumstance, and visible form,
　　Is mainly to the pleasure of the mind
290　What passion makes them; that meanwhile the forms
　　Of Nature have a passion in themselves,
　　That intermingles with those works of man
　　To which she summons him; although the works
　　Be mean, have nothing lofty of their own;
　　And that the Genius of the Poet hence
　　May boldly take his way among mankind
　　Wherever Nature leads; that he hath stood
　　By Nature's side among the men of old,
　　And so shall stand for ever. Dearest Friend!
300　If thou partake the animating faith
　　That Poets, even as Prophets, each with each
　　Connected in a mighty scheme of truth,
　　Have each his own peculiar faculty,
　　Heaven's gift, a sense that fits him to perceive
　　Objects unseen before, thou wilt not blame
　　The humblest of this band who dares to hope
　　That unto him hath also been vouchsafed
　　An insight that in some sort he possesses,
　　A privilege whereby a work of his,
310　Proceeding from a source of untaught things,
　　Creative and enduring, may become
　　A power like one of Nature's. To a hope
　　Not less ambitious once among the wilds
　　Of Sarum's Plain, my youthful spirit was raised;
　　There, as I ranged at will the pastoral downs
　　Trackless and smooth, or paced the bare white roads

Lengthening in solitude their dreary line,
While through those vestiges of ancient times
I ranged, and by the solitude o'ercome,
320 I had a reverie and saw the past,
Saw multitudes of men, and, here and there,   *321*
A single Briton in his wolf-skin vest,
With shield and stone-axe, stride across the wold;
The voice of spears was heard, the rattling spear
Shaken by arms of mighty bone, in strength,   *325*
Long mouldered, of barbaric majesty.
I called upon the Darkness – and it took,
A midnight darkness seemed to come and take
All objects from my sight; and lo! again
330 The Desert visible by dismal flames;   *330*
It is the sacrificial altar, fed
With living men – how deep the groans! the voice
Of those in the gigantic wicker thrills
Throughout the region far and near, pervades
The monumental hillocks, and the pomp
Is for both worlds, the living and the dead.   *335*
At other moments (for through that wide waste
Three summer days I roamed) when 'twas my chance
To have before me on the downy Plain
340 Lines, circles, mounts, a mystery of shapes
Such as in many quarters yet survive,
With intricate profusion figuring o'er
The untilled ground, the work, as some divine,
Of infant science, imitative forms
By which the Druids covertly expressed
Their knowledge of the heavens, and imaged forth   *341*
The constellations; I was gently charmed,
Albeit with an antiquarian's dream,
I saw the bearded teachers, with white wands   *345*
350 Uplifted, pointing to the starry sky,
Alternately, and plain below, while breath
Of music seemed to guide them, and the waste
Was cheered with stillness and a pleasant sound.

Lengthening in solitude their dreary line,
Time with his retinue of ages fled
Backwards, nor checked his flight until I saw
320   Our dim ancestral Past in vision clear;
Saw multitudes of men, and, here and there,
A single Briton clothed in wolf-skin vest,
With shield and stone-axe, stride across the wold;
The voice of spears was heard, the rattling spear
Shaken by arms of mighty bone, in strength,
Long mouldered, of barbaric majesty.
I called on Darkness – but before the word
Was uttered, midnight darkness seemed to take
All objects from my sight; and lo! again
330   The Desert visible by dismal flames;
It is the sacrificial altar, fed
With living men – how deep the groans! the voice
Of those that crowd the giant wicker thrills
The monumental hillocks, and the pomp
Is for both worlds, the living and the dead.
At other moments (for through that wide waste
Three summer days I roamed) where'er the Plain
Was figured o'er with circles, lines, or mounds,
That yet survive, a work, as some divine,
340   Shaped by the Druids, so to represent
Their knowledge of the heavens, and image forth
The constellations; gently was I charmed
Into a waking dream, a reverie
That, with believing eyes, where'er I turned,
Beheld long-bearded teachers, with white wands
Uplifted, pointing to the starry sky,
Alternately, and plain below, while breath
Of music swayed their motions, and the waste
Rejoiced with them and me in those sweet sounds.

        This for the past, and things that may be viewed   *350*
Or fancied in the obscurities of time.
Nor is it, Friend, unknown to thee, at least
Thyself delighted, who for my delight
Hast said, perusing some imperfect verse
Which in that lonesome journey was composed,
360 That also I must then have exercised   *355*
Upon the vulgar forms of present things,
And actual world of our familiar days,
A higher power; have caught from them a tone,
An image, and a character, by books
Not hitherto reflected. Call we this   *360*
But a persuasion taken up by thee
In friendship; yet the Mind is to herself
Witness and judge; and I remember well
That in life's every-day appearances
370 I seemed about this period to have sight
Of a new world – a world, too, that was fit   *370*
To be transmitted, and made visible
To other eyes; as having for its base
That whence our dignity originates,
That which both gives it being and maintains
A balance, an ennobling interchange   *375*
Of action from within and from without;
The excellence, pure spirit, and best power
Both of the object seen, and eye that sees.

350   This for the past, and things that may be viewed
        Or fancied in the obscurity of years
        From monumental hints: and thou, O Friend!
        Pleased with some unpremeditated strains
        That served those wanderings to beguile, hast said
        That then and there my mind had exercised
        Upon the vulgar forms of present things,
        The actual world of our familiar days,
        Yet higher power; had caught from them a tone,
        An image, and a character, by books
360   Not hitherto reflected. Call we this
        A partial judgement – and yet why? for *then*
        We were as strangers; and I may not speak
        Thus wrongfully of verse, however rude,
        Which on thy young imagination, trained
        In the great City, broke like light from far.
        Moreover, each man's Mind is to herself
        Witness and judge; and I remember well
        That in life's every-day appearances
        I seemed about this time to gain clear sight
370   Of a new world – a world, too, that was fit
        To be transmitted, and to other eyes
        Made visible; as ruled by those fixed laws
        Whence spiritual dignity originates,
        Which do both give it being and maintain
        A balance, an ennobling interchange
        Of action from without and from within;
        The excellence, pure function, and best power
        Both of the object seen, and eye that sees.

Book Thirteenth

CONCLUSION

In one of these excursions, travelling then
Through Wales on foot, and with a youthful friend,
I left Bethgelert's huts at couching-time,
And westward took my way, to see the sun   5
Rise from the top of Snowdon. Having reached
The cottage at the mountain's foot, we there
Roused up the shepherd who by ancient right
Of office is the stranger's usual guide;
And after short refreshment sallied forth.   10

10   It was a summer's night, a close warm night,
Wan, dull and glaring, with a dripping mist
Low-hung and thick that covered all the sky,
Half threatening storm and rain; but on we went
Unchecked, being full of heart and having faith
In our tried pilot. Little could we see
Hemmed round on every side with fog and damp,
And, after ordinary travellers' chat   16
With our conductor, silently we sank
Each into commerce with his private thoughts:
20   Thus did we breast the ascent, and by myself
Was nothing either seen or heard the while   20
Which took me from my musings, save that once
The shepherd's cur did to his own great joy
Unearth a hedgehog in the mountain crags
Round which he made a barking turbulent.
This small adventure, for even such it seemed   25
In that wild place and at the dead of night,
Being over and forgotten, on we wound
In silence as before. With forehead bent

Book Fourteenth

CONCLUSION

In one of those excursions (may they ne'er
Fade from remembrance!) through the Northern tracts
Of Cambria ranging with a youthful friend,
I left Bethgelert's huts at couching-time,
And westward took my way, to see the sun
Rise from the top of Snowdon. To the door
Of a rude cottage at the mountain's base
We came, and roused the shepherd who attends
The adventurous stranger's steps, a trusty guide;
10   Then, cheered by short refreshment, sallied forth.

It was a close, warm, breezeless summer night,
Wan, dull, and glaring, with a dripping fog
Low-hung and thick that covered all the sky;
But, undiscouraged, we began to climb
The mountain-side. The mist soon girt us round,
And, after ordinary travellers' talk
With our conductor, pensively we sank
Each into commerce with his private thoughts:
Thus did we breast the ascent, and by myself
20   Was nothing either seen or heard that checked
Those musings or diverted, save that once
The shepherd's lurcher, who, among the crags,
Had to his joy unearthed a hedgehog, teased
His coiled-up prey with barkings turbulent.
This small adventure, for even such it seemed
In that wild place and at the dead of night,
Being over and forgotten, on we wound
In silence as before. With forehead bent

30 Earthward, as if in opposition set
    Against an enemy, I panted up   30
    With eager pace, and no less eager thoughts.
    Thus might we wear perhaps an hour away,
    Ascending at loose distance each from each,
    And I, as chanced, the foremost of the band;
    When at my feet the ground appeared to brighten,   35
    And with a step or two seemed brighter still;
    Nor had I time to ask the cause of this,
    For instantly a light upon the turf
40 Fell like a flash: I looked about, and lo!
    The Moon stood naked in the heavens, at height   40
    Immense above my head, and on the shore
    I found myself of a huge sea of mist,
    Which, meek and silent, rested at my feet.
    A hundred hills their dusky backs upheaved
    All over this still ocean; and beyond,
    Far, far beyond, the vapours shot themselves,
    In headlands, tongues, and promontory shapes,   45
    Into the sea, the real sea, that seemed
50 To dwindle, and give up its majesty,
    Usurped upon as far as sight could reach.
    Meanwhile, the Moon looked down upon this show
    In single glory, and we stood, the mist
    Touching our very feet; and from the shore
    At distance not the third part of a mile
    Was a blue chasm; a fracture in the vapour,
    A deep and gloomy breathing-place through which
    Mounted the roar of waters, torrents, streams
    Innumerable, roaring with one voice!   60
60 The universal spectacle throughout
    Was shaped for admiration and delight,
    Grand in itself alone, but in that breach
    Through which the homeless voice of waters rose,
    That dark deep thoroughfare, had Nature lodged
    The soul, the imagination of the whole.

    A meditation rose in me that night

Earthward, as if in opposition set
30 Against an enemy, I panted up
With eager pace, and no less eager thoughts.
Thus might we wear a midnight hour away,
Ascending at loose distance each from each,
And I, as chanced, the foremost of the band;
When at my feet the ground appeared to brighten,
And with a step or two seemed brighter still;
Nor was time given to ask or learn the cause,
For instantly a light upon the turf
Fell like a flash, and lo! as I looked up,
40 The Moon hung naked in a firmament
Of azure without cloud, and at my feet
Rested a silent sea of hoary mist.
A hundred hills their dusky backs upheaved
All over this still ocean; and beyond,
Far, far beyond, the solid vapours stretched,
In headlands, tongues, and promontory shapes,
Into the main Atlantic, that appeared
To dwindle, and give up his majesty,
Usurped upon far as the sight could reach.
50 Not so the ethereal vault; encroachment none
Was there, nor loss; only the inferior stars
Had disappeared, or shed a fainter light
In the clear presence of the full-orbed Moon,
Who, from her sovereign elevation, gazed
Upon the billowy ocean, as it lay
All meek and silent, save that through a rift –
Not distant from the shore whereon we stood,
A fixed, abysmal, gloomy, breathing-place –
Mounted the roar of waters, torrents, streams
60 Innumerable, roaring with one voice!
Heard over earth and sea, and, in that hour,
For so it seemed, felt by the starry heavens.

When into air had partially dissolved
That vision, given to spirits of the night
And three chance human wanderers, in calm thought

Upon the lonely mountain when the scene
Had passed away, and it appeared to me
The perfect image of a mighty mind,   70
70 Of one that feeds upon infinity,
That is exalted by an underpresence,
The sense of God, or whatsoe'er is dim
Or vast in its own being, above all
One function of such mind had Nature there
Exhibited by putting forth, and that
With circumstance most awful and sublime,   80
That domination which she oftentimes
Exerts upon the outward face of things,
So moulds them, and endues, abstracts, combines,
80 Or by abrupt and unhabitual influence
Doth make one object so impress itself
Upon all others, and pervade them so
That even the grossest minds must see and hear   85
And cannot choose but feel. The power, which these
Acknowledge when thus moved, which Nature thus
Thrusts forth upon the senses, is the express
Resemblance, in the fullness of its strength
Made visible, a genuine counterpart
And brother of the glorious faculty
90 Which higher minds bear with them as their own.   90
That is the very spirit in which they deal
With all the objects of the universe:
They from their native selves can send abroad
Like transformation; for themselves create
A like existence; and, whene'er it is   95
Created for them, catch it by an instinct;
Them the enduring and the transient both   100
Serve to exalt; they build up greatest things
From least suggestions; ever on the watch,
100 Willing to work and to be wrought upon,

Reflected, it appeared to me the type
Of a majestic intellect, its acts
And its possessions, what it has and craves,
What in itself it is, and would become.
There I beheld the emblem of a mind
That feeds upon infinity, that broods
Over the dark abyss, intent to hear
Its voices issuing forth to silent light
In one continuous stream; a mind sustained
By recognitions of transcendent power,
In sense conducting to ideal form,
In soul of more than mortal privilege.
One function, above all, of such a mind
Had Nature shadowed there, by putting forth,
'Mid circumstances awful and sublime,
That mutual domination which she loves
To exert upon the face of outward things,
So moulded, joined, abstracted, so endowed
With interchangeable supremacy,
That men, least sensitive, see, hear, perceive,
And cannot choose but feel. The power, which all
Acknowledge when thus moved, which Nature thus
To bodily sense exhibits, is the express
Resemblance of that glorious faculty
That higher minds bear with them as their own.
This is the very spirit in which they deal
With the whole compass of the universe:
They from their native selves can send abroad
Kindred mutations; for themselves create
A like existence; and, whene'er it dawns
Created for them, catch it, or are caught
By its inevitable mastery,
Like angels stopped upon the wing by sound
Of harmony from Heaven's remotest spheres.
Them the enduring and the transient both
Serve to exalt; they build up greatest things
From least suggestions; ever on the watch,
Willing to work and to be wrought upon,

They need not extraordinary calls
To rouse them; in a world of life they live,   *105*
By sensible impressions not enthralled,
But quickened, roused, and made thereby more fit
To hold communion with the invisible world.
Such minds are truly from the Deity,
For they are Powers; and hence the highest bliss
That can be known is theirs – the consciousness
Of Whom they are, habitually infused   *115*
110 Through every image and through every thought,
And all impressions; hence religion, faith,
And endless occupation for the Soul,
Whether discursive or intuitive;   *120*
Hence sovereignty within and peace at will,
Emotion which best foresight need not fear,
Most worthy then of trust when most intense.
Hence cheerfulness in every act of life,
Hence truth in moral judgements and delight
That fails not in the external universe.

120   Oh! who is he that hath his whole life long   *130*
Preserved, enlarged, this freedom in himself?
For this alone is genuine liberty:
Witness, ye solitudes! where I received

They need not extraordinary calls
To rouse them; in a world of life they live,
By sensible impressions not enthralled,
But by their quickening impulse made more prompt
To hold fit converse with the spiritual world,
And with the generations of mankind
110 Spread over time, past, present, and to come,
Age after age, till Time shall be no more.
Such minds are truly from the Deity,
For they are Powers; and hence the highest bliss
That flesh can know is theirs – the consciousness
Of Whom they are, habitually infused
Through every image and through every thought,
And all affections by communion raised
From earth to heaven, from human to divine;
Hence endless occupation for the Soul,
120 Whether discursive or intuitive;
Hence cheerfulness for acts of daily life,
Emotions which best foresight need not fear,
Most worthy then of trust when most intense.
Hence, amid ills that vex and wrongs that crush
Our hearts – if here the words of Holy Writ
May with fit reverence be applied – that peace
Which passeth understanding, that repose
In moral judgements which from this pure source
Must come, or will by man be sought in vain.

130   Oh! who is he that hath his whole life long
Preserved, enlarged, this freedom in himself?
For this alone is genuine liberty:
Where is the favoured being who hath held
That course unchecked, unerring, and untired,
In one perpetual progress smooth and bright? –
A humbler destiny have we retraced,
And told of lapse and hesitating choice,
And backward wanderings along thorny ways:
Yet – compassed round by mountain solitudes,
140 Within whose solemn temple I received

My earliest visitations, careless then   *141*
Of what was given me; and where now I roam,
A meditative, oft a suffering man,   *143*
And yet, I trust, with undiminished powers,
Witness, whatever falls my better mind,
Revolving with the accidents of life,
130 May have sustained, that, howsoe'er misled,
I never, in the quest of right and wrong,   *150*
Did tamper with myself from private aims;
Nor was in any of my hopes the dupe
Of selfish passions; nor did wilfully
Yield ever to mean cares and low pursuits,
But rather did with jealousy shrink back   *155*
From every combination that might aid
The tendency, too potent in itself,
Of habit to enslave the mind, I mean
140 Oppress it by the laws of vulgar sense,
And substitute a universe of death,   *160*
The falsest of all worlds, in place of that
Which is divine and true. To fear and love,
To love as first and chief, for there fear ends,
Be this ascribed; to early intercourse,
In presence of sublime and lovely forms,   *165*
With the adverse principles of pain and joy –
Evil as one is rashly named by those
Who know not what they say. From love, for here
150 Do we begin and end, all grandeur comes,
All truth and beauty, from pervading love;
That gone, we are as dust. – Behold the fields   *170*
In balmy spring-time full of rising flowers
And happy creatures; see that pair, the lamb
And the lamb's mother, and their tender ways
Shall touch thee to the heart; in some green bower
Rest, and be not alone, but have thou there
The One who is thy choice of all the world: *178*
There linger, lulled and lost, and rapt away,
160 Be happy to thy fill; thou call'st this love
And so it is, but there is higher love   *175*

My earliest visitations, careless then
Of what was given me; and which now I range,
A meditative, oft a suffering man –
Do I declare – in accents which, from truth
Deriving cheerful confidence, shall blend
Their modulation with these vocal streams –
That, whatsoever falls my better mind,
Revolving with the accidents of life,
May have sustained, that, howsoe'er misled,
150　Never did I, in quest of right and wrong,
Tamper with conscience from a private aim;
Nor was in any public hope the dupe
Of selfish passions; nor did ever yield
Wilfully to mean cares or low pursuits,
But shrunk with apprehensive jealousy
From every combination which might aid
The tendency, too potent in itself,
Of use and custom to bow down the soul
Under a growing weight of vulgar sense,
160　And substitute a universe of death
For that which moves with light and life informed,
Actual, divine, and true. To fear and love,
To love as prime and chief, for there fear ends,
Be this ascribed; to early intercourse,
In presence of sublime or beautiful forms,
With the adverse principles of pain and joy –
Evil as one is rashly named by men
Who know not what they speak. By love subsists
All lasting grandeur, by pervading love;
170　That gone, we are as dust. – Behold the fields
In balmy spring-time full of rising flowers
And joyous creatures; see that pair, the lamb
And the lamb's mother, and their tender ways
Shall touch thee to the heart; thou callest this love,
And not inaptly so, for love it is,
Far as it carries thee. In some green bower
Rest, and be not alone, but have thou there
The One who is thy choice of all the world:

Than this, a love that comes into the heart
With awe and a diffusive sentiment;
Thy love is human merely; this proceeds
More from the brooding soul, and is divine.

This Love more intellectual cannot be
Without Imagination, which, in truth,
Is but another name for absolute strength   190
And clearest insight, amplitude of mind,
170 And Reason in her most exalted mood.
This faculty hath been the moving soul
Of our long labour: we have traced the stream
From darkness, and the very place of birth
In its blind cavern, whence is faintly heard   195
The sound of waters; followed it to light
And open day; accompanied its course
Among the ways of Nature, afterwards
Lost sight of it bewildered and engulphed:
Then given it greeting as it rose once more   200
180 With strength, reflecting in its solemn breast
The works of man and face of human life;
And lastly, from its progress have we drawn
The feeling of life endless, the great thought
By which we live, Infinity and God.   205

Imagination having been our theme,
So also hath that intellectual Love,
For they are each in each, and cannot stand
Dividually. – Here must thou be, O Man!
Strength to thyself; no Helper hast thou here;   210
190 Here keepest thou thy individual state:
No other can divide with thee this work:
No secondary hand can intervene
To fashion this ability; 'tis thine,

There linger, listening, gazing, with delight
180 Impassioned, but delight how pitiable!
Unless this love by a still higher love
Be hallowed, love that breathes not without awe;
Love that adores, but on the knees of prayer,
By heaven inspired; that frees from chains the soul,
Bearing, in union with the purest, best,
Of earth-born passions, on the wings of praise
A mutual tribute to the Almighty's Throne.

This spiritual Love acts not nor can exist
Without Imagination, which, in truth,
190 Is but another name for absolute power
And clearest insight, amplitude of mind,
And Reason in her most exalted mood.
This faculty hath been the feeding source
Of our long labour: we have traced the stream
From the blind cavern whence is faintly heard
Its natal murmur; followed it to light
And open day; accompanied its course
Among the ways of Nature, for a time
Lost sight of it bewildered and engulphed:
200 Then given it greeting as it rose once more
In strength, reflecting from its placid breast
The works of man and face of human life;
And lastly, from its progress have we drawn
Faith in life endless, the sustaining thought
Of human Being, Eternity, and God.

Imagination having been our theme,
So also hath that intellectual Love,
For they are each in each, and cannot stand
Dividually. – Here must thou be, O Man!
210 Power to thyself; no Helper hast thou here;
Here keepest thou in singleness thy state:
No other can divide with thee this work:
No secondary hand can intervene
To fashion this ability; 'tis thine,

The prime and vital principle is thine   215
In the recesses of thy nature, far
From any reach of outward fellowship,
Else 'tis not thine at all. But joy to him,
Oh, joy to him who here hath sown, hath laid
Here the foundations of his future years!   220
200 For all that friendship, all that love can do,
All that a darling countenance can look
Or dear voice utter, to complete the man,
Perfect him, made imperfect in himself,
All shall be his: and he whose soul hath risen   225
Up to the height of feeling intellect
Shall want no humbler tenderness; his heart
Be tender as a nursing mother's heart;
Of female softness shall his life be full,
Of little loves and delicate desires,   230
210 Mild interests and gentlest sympathies.

     Child of my Parents! Sister of my Soul!
Elsewhere have strains of gratitude been breathed
To thee for all the early tenderness
Which I from thee imbibed: and true it is   235
That later seasons owed to thee no less;
For, spite of thy sweet influence and the touch
Of other kindred hands that opened out
The springs of tender thought in infancy,
And spite of all which singly I had watched   240
220 Of elegance, and each minuter charm
In nature and in life, still to the last,
Even to the very going-out of youth,
The period which our story now hath reached,
I too exclusively esteemed that love,
And sought that beauty, which, as Milton sings,   245
Hath terror in it. Thou didst soften down
This over-sternness; but for thee, sweet Friend!
My soul, too reckless of mild grace, had been
Far longer what by Nature it was framed,
230 Longer retained its countenance severe,   250

The prime and vital principle is thine
In the recesses of thy nature, far
From any reach of outward fellowship,
Else is not thine at all. But joy to him,
Oh, joy to him who here hath sown, hath laid
220 Here, the foundation of his future years!
For all that friendship, all that love can do,
All that a darling countenance can look
Or dear voice utter, to complete the man,
Perfect him, made imperfect in himself,
All shall be his: and he whose soul hath risen
Up to the height of feeling intellect
Shall want no humbler tenderness; his heart
Be tender as a nursing mother's heart;
Of female softness shall his life be full,
230 Of humble cares and delicate desires,
Mild interests and gentlest sympathies.

    Child of my parents! Sister of my soul!
Thanks in sincerest verse have been elsewhere
Poured out for all the early tenderness
Which I from thee imbibed: and 'tis most true
That later seasons owed to thee no less;
For, spite of thy sweet influence and the touch
Of kindred hands that opened out the springs
Of genial thought in childhood, and in spite
240 Of all that unassisted I had marked
In life or nature of those charms minute
That win their way into the heart by stealth,
Still to the very going-out of youth,
I too exclusively esteemed *that* love,
And sought *that* beauty, which, as Milton sings,
Hath terror in it. Thou didst soften down
This over-sternness; but for thee, dear Friend!
My soul, too reckless of mild grace, had stood
In her original self too confident,
250 Retained too long a countenance severe;

A rock with torrents roaring, with the clouds
Familiar, and a favourite of the stars:
But thou didst plant its crevices with flowers,
Hang it with shrubs that twinkle in the breeze,
And teach the little birds to build their nests   255
And warble in its chambers. At a time
When Nature, destined to remain so long
Foremost in my affections, had fallen back
Into a second place, well pleased to be
240   A handmaid to a nobler than herself,   260
When every day brought with it some new sense
Of exquisite regard for common things,
And all the earth was budding with these gifts
Of more refined humanity, thy breath,
Dear Sister! was a kind of gentler spring   265
That went before my steps.

              With such a theme,   275
Coleridge! with this my argument, of thee
Shall I be silent? O most loving Soul!
Placed on this earth to love and understand,
250   And from thy presence shed the light of love,
Shall I be mute, ere thou be spoken of?   280
Thy gentle spirit to my heart of hearts
Did also find its way; and thus the life
Of all things and the mighty unity
In all which we behold, and feel, and are,

A rock with torrents roaring, with the clouds
Familiar, and a favourite of the stars:
But thou didst plant its crevices with flowers,
Hang it with shrubs that twinkle in the breeze,
And teach the little birds to build their nests
And warble in its chambers. At a time
When Nature, destined to remain so long
Foremost in my affections, had fallen back
Into a second place, pleased to become
260 A handmaid to a nobler than herself,
When every day brought with it some new sense
Of exquisite regard for common things,
And all the earth was budding with these gifts
Of more refined humanity, thy breath,
Dear Sister! was a kind of gentler spring
That went before my steps. Thereafter came
One whom with thee friendship had early paired;
She came, no more a phantom to adorn
A moment, but an inmate of the heart,
270 And yet a spirit, there for me enshrined
To penetrate the lofty and the low;
Even as one essence of pervading light
Shines in the brightest of ten thousand stars,
And the meek worm that feeds her lonely lamp
Couched in the dewy grass.
       With such a theme,
Coleridge! with this my argument, of thee
Shall I be silent? O capacious Soul!
Placed on this earth to love and understand,
And from thy presence shed the light of love,
280 Shall I be mute, ere thou be spoken of?
Thy kindred influence to my heart of hearts
Did also find its way. Thus fear relaxed
Her overweening grasp; thus thoughts and things
In the self-haunting spirit learned to take
More rational proportions; mystery,
The incumbent mystery of sense and soul,
Of life and death, time and eternity,

Admitted more habitually a mild   288
Interposition, closelier gathering thoughts
Of man and his concerns, such as become   290
A human creature, be he who he may,
260 Poet, or destined to an humbler name;
And so the deep enthusiastic joy,
The rapture of the hallelujah sent
From all that breathes and is, was chastened, stemmed
And balanced by a reason which indeed   296
Is reason, duty and pathetic truth;
And God and Man divided, as they ought,
Between them the great system of the world
Where Man is sphered, and which God animates.

And now, O Friend! this history is brought
270 To its appointed close: the discipline
And consummation of the Poet's mind,
In everything that stood most prominent,   305
Have faithfully been pictured; we have reached
The time (which was our object from the first)
When we may, not presumptuously, I hope,
Suppose my powers so far confirmed, and such
My knowledge, as to make me capable   310
Of building up a Work that should endure.
Yet much hath been omitted, as need was;
280 Of books how much! and even of the other wealth
Which is collected among woods and fields,
Far more: for Nature's secondary grace,   315
That outward illustration which is hers,
Hath hitherto been barely touched upon,
The charm more superficial, and yet sweet,
Which from her works finds way, contemplated
As they hold forth a genuine counterpart
And softening mirror of the moral world.

Yes, having tracked the main essential Power,
290 Imagination, up her way sublime,
In turn might Fancy also be pursued

Admitted more habitually a mild
Interposition – a serene delight
290   In closelier gathering cares, such as become
A human creature, howsoe'er endowed,
Poet, or destined for a humbler name;
And so the deep enthusiastic joy,
The rapture of the hallelujah sent
From all that breathes and is, was chastened, stemmed
And balanced by pathetic truth, by trust
In hopeful reason, leaning on the stay
Of Providence; and in reverence for duty,
Here, if need be, struggling with storms, and there
300   Strewing in peace life's humblest ground with herbs,
At every season green, sweet at all hours.

And now, O Friend! this history is brought
To its appointed close: the discipline
And consummation of a Poet's mind,
In everything that stood most prominent,
Have faithfully been pictured; we have reached
The time (our guiding object from the first)
When we may, not presumptuously, I hope,
Suppose my powers so far confirmed, and such
310   My knowledge, as to make me capable
Of building up a Work that shall endure.
Yet much hath been omitted, as need was;
Of books how much! and even of the other wealth
That is collected among woods and fields,
Far more: for Nature's secondary grace
Hath hitherto been barely touched upon,
The charm more superficial that attends
Her works, as they present to Fancy's choice
Apt illustrations of the moral world,
320   Caught at a glance, or traced with curious pains.

Finally, and above all, O Friend! (I speak
With due regret) how much is overlooked
In human nature and her subtle ways,

Through all her transmigrations, till she too
Was purified, had learned to ply her craft
By judgement steadied. Then might we return
And in the rivers and the groves behold
Another face, might hear them from all sides
Calling upon the more instructed mind
To link their images with subtle skill
Sometimes, and by elaborate research,
300 With forms and definite appearances
Of human life, presenting them sometimes
To the involuntary sympathy
Of our internal being, satisfied
And soothed with a conception of delight
Where meditation cannot come, which thought
Could never heighten. Above all how much
Still nearer to ourselves we overlook
In human nature and that marvellous world
As studied first in my own heart, and then   *324*
310 In life among the passions of mankind
And qualities commixed and modified
By the infinite varieties and shades
Of individual character. Herein
It was for me (this justice bids me say)
No useless preparation to have been
The pupil of a public school, and forced,
In hardy independence, to stand up
Among conflicting passions, and the shock
Of various tempers; to endure and note   *335*
320 What was not understood though known to be;
Among the mysteries of love and hate,
Honour and shame, looking to right and left,
Unchecked by innocence too delicate,
And moral notions too intolerant,   *340*
Sympathies too contracted. Hence, when called
To take a station among men, the step
Was easier, the transition more secure,
More profitable also; for, the mind
Learns from such timely exercise to keep   *345*

As studied first in our own hearts, and then
In life among the passions of mankind,
Varying their composition and their hue,
Where'er we move, under the diverse shapes
That individual character presents
To an attentive eye. For progress meet,
330 Along this intricate and difficult path,
Whate'er was wanting, something had I gained,
As one of many schoolfellows compelled,
In hardy independence, to stand up
Amid conflicting interests, and the shock
Of various tempers; to endure and note
What was not understood, though known to be;
Among the mysteries of love and hate,
Honour and shame, looking to right and left,
Unchecked by innocence too delicate,
340 And moral notions too intolerant,
Sympathies too contracted. Hence, when called
To take a station among men, the step
Was easier, the transition more secure,
More profitable also; for, the mind
Learns from such timely exercise to keep

330 In wholesome separation the two natures,
     The one that feels, the other that observes.

        Let one word more of personal circumstance,
     Not needless, as it seems, be added here.
     Since I withdrew unwillingly from France,
     The story hath demanded less regard
     To time and place; and where I lived, and how,
     Hath been no longer scrupulously marked.
     Three years, until a permanent abode
     Received me with that Sister of my heart
340 Who ought by rights the dearest to have been
     Conspicuous through this biographic verse,
     Star seldom utterly concealed from view,
     I led an undomestic wanderer's life;
     In London chiefly was my home, and thence
     Excursively, as personal friendships, chance
     Or inclination led, or slender means
     Gave leave, I roamed about from place to place,
     Tarrying in pleasant nooks, wherever found,
     Through England or through Wales. A Youth (he bore
350 The name of Calvert – it shall live, if words   *355*
     Of mine can give it life,) without respect
     To prejudice or custom, having hope
     That I had some endowments by which good
     Might be promoted, in his last decay
     From his own family withdrawing part
     Of no redundant patrimony, did
     By a bequest sufficient for my needs
     Enable me to pause for choice, and walk   *360*
     At large and unrestrained, nor damped too soon
360 By mortal cares. Himself no Poet, yet
     Far less a common spirit of the world,
     He deemed that my pursuits and labours lay
     Apart from all that leads to wealth, or even   *365*
     Perhaps to necessary maintenance,
     Without some hazard to the finer sense;
     He cleared a passage for me, and the stream

In wholesome separation the two natures,
The one that feels, the other that observes.

Yet one word more of personal concern –
Since I withdrew unwillingly from France,
350   I led an undomestic wanderer's life,
In London chiefly harboured, whence I roamed,
Tarrying at will in many a pleasant spot
Of rural England's cultivated vales
Or Cambrian solitudes. A youth – (he bore
The name of Calvert – it shall live, if words
Of mine can give it life,) in firm belief
That by endowments not from me withheld
Good might be furthered – in his last decay
358a Withdrawing, and from kindred whom he loved,
358b A part of no redundant patrimony
By a bequest sufficient for my needs
360   Enabled me to pause for choice, and walk
At large and unrestrained, nor damped too soon
By mortal cares. Himself no Poet, yet
Far less a common follower of the world,
He deemed that my pursuits and labours lay
Apart from all that leads to wealth, or even
A necessary maintenance insures,
Without some hazard to the finer sense;
He cleared a passage for me, and the stream

Flowed in the bent of Nature.

              Having now
Told what best merits mention, further pains   *370*
Our present labour seems not to require,
And I have other tasks. Call back to mind
The mood in which this poem was begun,
O Friend! The termination of my course
Is nearer now, much nearer; yet even then,   *375*
In that distraction and intense desire,
I said unto the life which I had lived,
Where art thou? Hear I not a voice from thee
Which 'tis reproach to hear? Anon I rose
As if on wings, and saw beneath me stretched   *380*
Vast prospect of the world which I had been
And was; and hence this Song, which like a lark
I have protracted, in the unwearied heavens
Singing, and often with more plaintive voice
Attempered to the sorrows of the earth,   *385*
Yet centring all in love, and in the end
All gratulant, if rightly understood.

    Whether to me shall be allotted life,
And, with life, power to accomplish aught of worth,
Sufficient to excuse me in men's sight
For having given this record of myself,   *391*
Is all uncertain: but, belovèd Friend!
When, looking back, thou seest, in clearer view
Than any sweetest sight of yesterday,
That summer when on Quantock's grassy hills   *395*
Far ranging, and among the sylvan combs,
Thou in delicious words, with happy heart,
Didst speak the vision of that Ancient Man,
The bright-eyed Mariner, and rueful woes   *400*
Didst utter of the Lady Christabel;
And I, associate with such labour, walked
Murmuring of him who, joyous hap, was found,

Flowed in the bent of Nature.
                                        Having now
370 Told what best merits mention, further pains
Our present purpose seems not to require,
And I have other tasks. Recall to mind
The mood in which this labour was begun,
O Friend! The termination of my course
Is nearer now, much nearer; yet even then,
In that distraction and intense desire,
I said unto the life which I had lived,
Where art thou? Hear I not a voice from thee
Which 'tis reproach to hear? Anon I rose
380 As if on wings, and saw beneath me stretched
Vast prospect of the world which I had been
And was; and hence this Song, which like a lark
I have protracted, in the unwearied heavens
Singing, and often with more plaintive voice
To earth attempered and her deep-drawn sighs,
Yet centring all in love, and in the end
All gratulant, if rightly understood.

    Whether to me shall be allotted life,
    And, with life, power to accomplish aught of worth,
390 That will be deemed no insufficient plea
For having given this story of myself,
Is all uncertain: but, belovèd Friend!
When, looking back, thou seest, in clearer view
Than any liveliest sight of yesterday,
That summer, under whose indulgent skies,
Upon smooth Quantock's airy ridge we roved
Unchecked, or loitered 'mid her sylvan combs,
Thou in bewitching words, with happy heart,
Didst chant the vision of that Ancient Man,
400 The bright-eyed Mariner, and rueful woes
Didst utter of the Lady Christabel;
And I, associate with such labour, steeped
In soft forgetfulness the livelong hours,
Murmuring of him who, joyous hap, was found,

After the perils of his moonlight ride,   *405*
Near the loud waterfall; or her who sate
In misery near the miserable Thorn;
When thou dost to that summer turn thy thoughts,
And hast before thee all which then we were,
To thee, in memory of that happiness,   *410*
It will be known, by thee at least, my Friend!
Felt, that the history of a Poet's mind
Is labour not unworthy of regard:

410   To thee the work shall justify itself.

    The last and later portions of this gift   *415*
Which I for thee design, have been prepared
In times which have from those wherein we first
Together wantoned in wild Poesy,
Differed thus far, that they have been, my Friend!
Times of much sorrow, of a private grief
Keen and enduring, which the frame of mind   *420*
That in this meditative history
Hath been described, more deeply makes me feel;

420   Yet likewise hath enabled me to bear
More firmly; and a comfort now, a hope,
One of the dearest which this life can give,
Is mine; that thou art near, and wilt be soon   *425*
Restored to us in renovated health;
When, after the first mingling of our tears,
'Mong other consolations, we may find
Some pleasure from this offering of my love.

    Oh! yet a few short years of useful life,   *430*
And all will be complete, thy race be run,

430   Thy monument of glory will be raised;
Then, though (too weak to tread the ways of truth)
This age fall back to old idolatry,
Though men return to servitude as fast   *435*
As the tide ebbs, to ignominy and shame
By nations sink together, we shall still
Find solace in the knowledge which we have,

After the perils of his moonlight ride,
Near the loud waterfall; or her who sate
In misery near the miserable Thorn;
When thou dost to that summer turn thy thoughts,
And hast before thee all which then we were,
410 To thee, in memory of that happiness,
It will be known, by thee at least, my Friend!
Felt, that the history of a Poet's mind
Is labour not unworthy of regard:
To thee the work shall justify itself.

    The last and later portions of this gift
Have been prepared, not with the buoyant spirits
That were our daily portion when we first
Together wantoned in wild Poesy,
But, under pressure of a private grief,
420 Keen and enduring, which the mind and heart,
That in this meditative history
Have been laid open, needs must make me feel
More deeply, yet enable me to bear
More firmly; and a comfort now hath risen
From hope that thou art near, and wilt be soon
Restored to us in renovated health;
When, after the first mingling of our tears,
'Mong other consolations, we may draw
Some pleasure from this offering of my love.

430 Oh! yet a few short years of useful life,
And all will be complete, thy race be run,
Thy monument of glory will be raised;
Then, though (too weak to tread the ways of truth)
This age fall back to old idolatry,
Though men return to servitude as fast
As the tide ebbs, to ignominy and shame
By nations sink together, we shall still
Find solace – knowing what we have learnt to know,

Blest with true happiness if we may be
United helpers forward of a day   *440*
Of firmer trust, joint labourers in a work
440   (Should Providence such grace to us vouchsafe)
Of their redemption, surely yet to come.
Prophets of Nature, we to them will speak
A lasting inspiration, sanctified   *445*
By reason and by truth: what we have loved,
Others will love, and we may teach them how;
Instruct them how the mind of man becomes
A thousand times more beautiful than the earth
On which he dwells, above this frame of things   *450*
(Which, 'mid all revolutions in the hopes
450   And fears of men, doth still remain unchanged)
In beauty exalted, as it is itself
Of substance and of fabric more divine.

Rich in true happiness if allowed to be
440 Faithful alike in forwarding a day
Of firmer trust, joint labourers in the work
(Should Providence such grace to us vouchsafe)
Of their deliverance, surely yet to come.
Prophets of Nature, we to them will speak
A lasting inspiration, sanctified
By reason, blest by faith: what we have loved,
Others will love, and we will teach them how;
Instruct them how the mind of man becomes
A thousand times more beautiful than the earth
450 On which he dwells, above this frame of things
(Which, 'mid all revolutions in the hopes
And fears of men, doth still remain unchanged)
In beauty exalted, as it is itself
Of quality and fabric more divine.

Notes

Italic line numbers refer to the 1850 text. *F.Q. Faerie Queene*;
P.L. Paradise Lost; *P.R. Paradise Regained*

BOOK I

1–141
1–131 The primary reference of these lines is to the settlement
at Grasmere at the end of 1799, and the city of line 7 is
London, though he had not in 1799 been 'long immured'
there, and there may be a conflation with the settlement at
Racedown in October 1795, before which he had spent six
months in London. The 'pleasant loitering journey' has been
shown by John Finch to be one from Ullswater to Grasmere,
18–19 November 1799, after parting from Coleridge. The
Preamble (lines 1–54) was therefore composed on 18 Novem-
ber. The earlier idea that Wordsworth wrote the Preamble in
1795 is stylistically impossible; moreover, a fragmentary draft
of lines 43–7 appears in the JJ MS of 1798–9.

7 *vast city* Miltonic: *Areopagitica* (Columbia edn, IV 340), of
London.

15 *The earth is all before me* Milton, *P.L.* XII 646, 'The world
was all before them'. Adam and Eve have just been driven out
of Paradise at the very end of the poem.

46 *redundant* overflowing.

55 *Friend* Coleridge.

104 *Aeolian* The aeolian harp, played on by the wind (and
named after Aeolus, god of the winds), is a favourite romantic
image for poetic inspiration (see also III 137–8): see Cole-
ridge's *The Eolian Harp* (1795), and M. H. Abrams, *The
Mirror and the Lamp* (1953), pp. 51–2, and his article, *The
Correspondent Breeze: A Romantic Metaphor* (1937), revised
and reprinted in *English Romantic Poets: Modern Essays in
Criticism*, M. H. Abrams (ed.) (1960).

102–3 *shed|Mild influence* Milton, *P.L.* VII 374–5, 'the Pleiades...
shedding sweet influence'.

131 *floating loose about* Milton, *Samson Agonistes* 675, 'wand'ring
loose about'.

539

151–2   *dove|Sits brooding*   Milton, *P.L.* I 21, of the divine spirit, 'Dove-like sat'st brooding'.

180   *Milton*   He had once projected an epic on King Arthur.

175   *dire enchantments*   Milton, *Il Penseroso* 119, 'enchantments drear'. Wordsworth uses 'dire' in a similar supernatural context in a passage originally written in 1798 of *The Excursion* I 182, 'dire faces, figures dire'.

181–4   *More . . . tales*   Reminiscent of Spenser, who is more explicitly echoed at line *185*: *F.Q.* I Prol. 1, 'Fierce warres and faithfull loves'.

186–8   *Mithridates . . . Odin*   From Gibbon, *Decline and Fall*, ch. 10; though he does not identify the two. Wordsworth also read of Mithridates (131–63 BC), King of Pontus, in Plutarch's *Lives*.

190   *Sertorius*   Roman general (*c.* 112–72 BC), the subject of one of Plutarch's *Lives*. Proscribed by the dictator Sulla, he held Spain for some years, but was then murdered. His followers were said to have fled to the Fortunate Isles (the Canaries). The story referred to in lines 195–8 is told in a Spanish work of 1594 by Alonso de Espinosa.

205   *one Frenchman*   'Dominique de Gourgues, a French gentleman who went in 1568 to Florida to avenge the massacre of the French by the Spaniards there' (1850 note, from Hakluyt's *Navigations*).

211   *Gustavus*   Gustavus I of Sweden (1496–1560), who freed his country from Danish rule.

213   *Wallace*   William Wallace (*c.* 1272–1305), Scottish general and patriot, executed by the English in London.

237   *cherishes*   cheers; postdates *OED*'s last example (1734) of this obsolete sense.

233   *immortal verse*   Milton, *L'Allegro* 137.

234   *Orphean lyre*   Milton, *P.L.* III 17; Orpheus was a legendary singer of early Greece.

248   *lock my functions up*   Pope, *Imitations of Horace* Ep. I i 40, 'lock up all the functions of my soul'.

255   *vacant*   carefree, leisurely.

270   *false steward*   As in the Biblical parable, Matthew xxv 14–30.

271   *Was it for this* With this, begins the portion first drafted in Germany, 1798–9.

275   *holms* flat ground by river (rather than river islands).

278   '*sweet Birthplace*' Coleridge, *Frost at Midnight* 28.

298   *groundsel* a kind of weed; Wordsworth uses the spelling 'grunsel', corresponding to an older pronunciation.

308   *belovèd Vale* Esthwaite.

311   *Nine summers* The 1850 text is more accurate. Wordsworth entered Hawkshead school at Whitsuntide 1779, after his ninth birthday (7 April).

326   *cultured* cultivated. Shenstone, *Elegy* XXV v 2 has 'cultured vales'.

376   *Patterdale* On Ullswater. The precise 'craggy ridge' (line 398) seems to have been Stybarrow Crag, about one and a quarter miles from the inn, and the 'huge cliff' Black Crag.

388   *Though bent on speed* Milton, *P.L.* XII 2.

392–3   *glittering . . . track* Perhaps influenced by Coleridge, *Ancient Mariner* 274, 'tracks of shining white' (with 'light' as rhyme-word).

425–6   *But . . . men* One of the few places in *The Prelude* where a doubt about punctuation affects the sense. Early MSS have no punctuation after 'forms', 'live' or 'men', which has been thought to give colour to Garrod's proposal to read 'forms that do not live, |Like living men moved'. This is destructive of the Wordsworthian feeling – they *do* live, though not like living men – and fortunately, as Havens points out, the commas after 'forms' and 'men' are present in Dorothy's transcription in a letter to Coleridge (*Early Letters*, no. 105), and in MS. v.

460–61   *All . . . ice* Erasmus Darwin, *The Economy of Vegetation* (1791), 'Hang o'er the sliding steel, and hiss along the ice'.

450   *reflex* reflection (a rare usage; no later examples recorded).

485–6   *earth . . . visible . . . diurnal* The same three words occur close together in Milton, *P.L.* VII 22–3, 'Within the visible diurnal sphere; |Standing on earth'.

497   *characters* distinguishing marks.

538   *With . . . o'er* Milton, *P.L.* VIII 83, 'With centric and eccentric scribbled o'er'. The first mock-heroic use of Milton in *The Prelude*.

543   *Loo*   Spelt 'Lu' in MSS. A round card-game.

549   *plebeian cards*   Pope, *Rape of the Lock* III 54, 'One plebeian card'.

558   *Vulcan*   God of fire and metal work, thrown from Heaven by Jupiter, *Iliad* I 590–94.

570   *Bothnic*   northern Baltic.

571–2   *sedulous ... Nature*   Milton, *P.L.* IX 27, 'Not sedulous by Nature'.

578   *Those ... sense*   Wordsworth seems to be recalling, and reversing, *Measure for Measure*, I iv 59, 'The wanton strings and motions of the sense'. W. Empson, *The Structure of Complex Words* (1951), pp. 296–7, quotes both lines but does not link them.

615–16a   *fancying ... cheered*   The last line of this final version seems to have been a further afterthought, for the MS has a full stop after 'survive' (and none after 'cheered'). For the printer's difficulties in this passage, see de Selincourt.

BOOK II

20   *And needs*   It is hard to believe that Wordsworth ever intended this, though it persists until MS D. The sense requires either 'Nor needs', as in 1850, or 'And needs no'.

39   *Assembly-room*   The Town Hall, built in 1790.

44   *Dame*   Her name given in a rejected, and almost illegible, MS revision may be 'Rowe'.

59–65   Wordsworth gives an account of the islands in Windermere in his *Guide to the Lakes* (edited by de Selincourt, 1906, p. 170).

82   *Sabine*   frugal. The Sabines were traditionally sturdy and simple in Latin literature, and Dryden's *Georgics* II 777, has 'frugal Sabines'.

83   *weekly stipend*   threepence to sixpence.

101–2   *where ... worshipped*   Various Lake District stone circles were associated with the Druids: see also XII 345.

108   *structure*   Furness Abbey.

144   Repeated X 567.

147   *inn* The White Lion, Bowness.

151   *blood-red wine* As in the ballad of Sir Patrick Spens.

152   *or ere* before.

174   *Minstrel* Robert Greenwood, afterwards Senior Fellow of Trinity College, Cambridge.

197   *dream away* In a moon context, this perhaps echoes *A Midsummer Night's Dream* I i 8, 'Four nights will quickly dream away the time'.

219   *succedaneum* substitute.

232   *Hard task* Perhaps echoing Milton, *P.L.* V 564, on the 'sad task and hard' of depicting the war in Heaven; if so, one of Wordsworth's implied claims (see especially, III 182) for epic, or more than epic, status for his poem.

314   '*best society*' Milton, *P.L.* IX 249.

321–41   *for ... pursue* One of the earliest parts of *The Prelude*, written, in much the present form, for *The Pedlar*, early in 1798.

349   *hours of school* From 6 a.m. in summer and 7 a.m. in winter.

352   *Friend* The Reverend John Fleming, of Rayrigg, Windermere (1850 note). He died in 1835.

341–2   *thrush ... sate* See Textual Notes. Probably, as de Selincourt suggests, the 1850 editor disliked the word 'reveillé'.

381   *plastic* shaping: a Coleridgean word.

393   *did converse* Wordsworth must have meant 'I' to be the subject of this, but his revision left it either with no subject or with the inappropriate 'power'.

416–34   *From ... undisturbed* Another early passage, adapted from *The Pedlar*.

421–6   The repeated 'all' recalls the *Benedicite* in the Prayer Book.

453–6   *selfishness ... minds* In a letter to Wordsworth, *c.* 10 September 1799, Coleridge wrote of 'those, who, in consequence of the complete failure of the French Revolution, have thrown up all hopes of the amelioration of mankind, and are sinking into an almost epicurean selfishness, disguising the same under the soft titles of domestic attachment and contempt for visionary *philosophes*'. He urged Wordsworth to write a poem in blank verse addressed to such persons.

459   *more than Roman*   Perhaps because not to despair of human nature goes deeper than not to despair of the republic, for which the general Gaius Terentius Varro was commended after his defeat by Hannibal at Cannae in 216 BC.

466–7   *reared|In the great city*   Coleridge's own words in *Frost at Midnight* 51–2.

BOOK III

55   *pealing organ*   Milton, *Il Penseroso* 161 (but also stock poetic diction).

63   *recusants*   resisters of authority.

65–6   *Examinations . . . balance*   Wordsworth plays on the derivation of 'examination' from Latin *examen*, balance.

182   *heroic argument*   Milton, *P.L.* IX 13 ff., describes his 'argument' (= theme) as 'not less but more heroic' than those of traditional epics.

191   *heartless*   dejected.

201   *Uphold . . . steps*   Milton, *Samson Agonistes* 666, 'And fainting spirits uphold'.

274   *Dictators at the plough*   Cincinnatus was ploughing when summoned to become Roman dictator in 458 BC.

276   *Trompington*   Now spelt 'Trumpington'; the scene of Chaucer's *Reeve's Tale*.

281–2   *Spenser . . . pace*   Wordsworth echoes various phrases in Milton, *P.L.* IV 606–7, 'The moon/Rising in clouded majesty', VIII 164–6, 'With inoffensive pace . . . On her soft axle . . . And bears thee soft'.

286   *Darkness . . . behind*   Milton, *P.L.* VII 27, 'In darkness, and with dangers compassed round'.

291   *A boy, no better*   Perhaps echoing the opening line of Spenser, *Shepheards Calendar*, 'A Shepeheards boye (no better doe him call)', which Wordsworth also seems to recall in *The Excursion* VII 851–2, 'A Peasant-youth, so call him, for he asked/No higher name'.

291–2   *rosy cheeks|Angelical*   Milton's fair complexion caused him to be known as 'the Lady of Christ's'.

295   *class-fellow*   Edward Joseph Birkett.

297   *Time out of mind*   Wordsworth hints, rightly, that the tradition is very doubtful.

312   *Cassandra*   Daughter of Priam of Troy; the most notable thing about her was that her prophecies were not believed, but here 'wearisome' seems to convey the only point of analogy.

340   *floating island*   Perhaps suggested by the island on Derwentwater, described by Wordsworth in his *Guide to the Lakes*, p. 38; but also recalling the wandering islands of Spenser, *F.Q.* II xii 12.

345   *vistos*   A common eighteenth-century variant of 'vistas'. Whether the alteration in MS E to 'vistas' was deliberate may be doubted.

388   *bodied forth*   *A Midsummer Night's Dream* V i 14–15, 'as imagination bodies forth|The forms of things unknown'. No example in *OED* before Shakespeare.

427   *Science*   Learning.

452–4   *the pelican ... himself*   From William Bartram's *Travels through North and South Carolina* (1794), p. 48, 'Behold, on yon decayed, defoliated cypress tree, the solitary wood pelican, dejectedly perched upon its utmost elevated spire; ... like an ancient venerable sage ...'.

486–7   *An obolus ... to a poor scholar*   Alludes to the legend of the Byzantine general, Belisarius, fallen from power, asking 'give an obol to Belisarius'.

489   *Bucer, Erasmus, ... Melancthon*   Scholars, the first and third Protestant; their dates, respectively, 1491–1551, c. 1466–1536, 1497–1560.

546–9   *Even ... beholds*   There is a general resemblance to Thomson, *Castle of Indolence*, I 30.

592–4   *Of colours ... hues*   Several echoes of Spenser, *F.Q.* III xi 28: 'arras', 'Woven with gold and silke', 'lurked', 'Like a discolourd Snake'.

BOOK IV

7   *Ferryman* T. W. Thompson in *Wordsworth's Hawkshead* (1970) identifies him as George Robinson.

11   *Valley* Hawkshead.

14   *Charon* He ferried the dead across the rivers of the underworld in Greek mythology.

17   *old Dame* Ann Tyson, who died in 1796, aged 83.

75   *regret?* No MS has a question-mark at this point, but the sense demands either that (proposed by Moore Smith and read by Nowell Smith), or 'nor' for 'and' in line 69 (Knight).

104–8   A rewording of lines 18–24 of a very early poem (*c.* 1786), *The Dog – An Idyllium*.

148   *weariness* All MSS before B² have 'weakness', an obvious slip.

199   *some . . . cheek* Milton, *Lycidas* 65, 'the homely slighted shepherd's trade'; not a very pointed echo, and probably unintentional.

237   *Seven* the Pleiades, or Seven Sisters.

274   *feast . . . revelry* Milton, *L'Allegro* 127, 'pomp and feast and revelry'.

282   *To Nature and to books* Just about the time of composing this, Wordsworth urged the undergraduate De Quincey in a letter to 'love Nature and Books' (6 March 1804).

283   *shipped* This word puzzled Havens, who conjectured 'slipped'; but the metaphorical use of the synonymous 'embarked' is common.

318   *promiscuous rout* miscellaneous assembly. Both words are Miltonic in this sense: *P.L.* I 380, 'promiscuous crowd', and 'rout' frequently.

335   *Grain-tinctured* 'drenched in the crimson of the sky at dawn' (de Selincourt, who notes the Miltonic original, 'sky-tinctured grain', *P.L.* V 285).

338   *melody of birds* Milton, *P.L.* VIII 528.

378   *strenuous idleness* Young, *Night Thoughts* I 150. Horace, *Epistles* I xi 28, 'strenua . . . inertia'. Wordsworth quotes the Latin in a letter of 17 June 1791.

383   *lapse* flow (Miltonic).

434   *specious cowardice* Wordsworth must mean that what assumed the guise of reluctance to intrude on pain was really cowardice.

BOOK V

25   '*weep to have*' Shakespeare, *Sonnet* 64 14.

55–139   It used to be believed that the version, first introduced into the 1839 revision, according to which W. himself dreamed this dream, was the more biographically accurate. But it is now agreed that it probably does belong to the 'friend' of line 49, and that the dream is based on that of Descartes in 1619, recorded in Baillet's *Life* (1691). Miss Darbishire thought that the friend was Coleridge, but this seems an impossible mystification in a poem addressed to Coleridge. Possibly, as Mrs Smyser suggested, it is Beaupuy.

178   *slender* weak. Recorded with similar application in *OED* before Wordsworth only in Cowper, *Task* VI 78, 'slender notes' (of the redbreast).

201   *Whether . . . verse* Milton, *P.L.* V 150, 'In prose or numerous verse'; 'numerous' = rhythmical.

205–7   *that . . . England* Milton.

235   *bye-spots* lonely spots; a Cumberland word.

245   *prelibation* offering of first fruits.

246–7   *brood . . . feathered* Milton, *P.L.* VII 418–20, 'Their brood . . . feathered soon and fledge'.

256   *Early* March 1778.

262   *others'* A and B both clearly have 'other's', and no MS has an unambiguous 'others'': D is unclear and E has no apostrophe; but normal usage demands the 1850 reading.

268   *for* MSS up to C have 'from', no doubt caught, as de Selincourt suggests, from the previous line.

271   *virtual* powerful.

307   *notices* observations.

340   *deep experiments* *Henry IV Part I* III i 49. Wordsworth seems still to have this scene in mind at line 346, 'old grandame earth', echoing Shakespeare's line 32, 'the old beldam earth'.

367   *Sabra* The King of Egypt's daughter, married by St George in the folk play.

371–2 *Who ... futurity* The irony is underlined by the allusion to Milton, *P.L.* X 282 ff., describing the highway driven over Chaos by Sin and Death.

389–413 In the original version, written in Germany in 1798–9, Wordsworth is the boy. In a later note he mentioned a William Raincock as pre-eminent in this art, though without identifying him as the boy of this passage. The early death of lines 414–15 seems to be purely imaginary in this context, though no doubt some of his schoolfellows did die in childhood.

390   *Winander* Windermere.

450–81 T. W. Thompson, *Wordsworth's Hawkeshead* (1970), identifies the drowned man as 'James Jackson School-Master of Sawrey'.

425   *erewhile* IV 14.

534–5 *I ... come* In contrast to the speculations of the Immortality Ode about pre-existence.

584   *heretofore* II 352.

589   *conning* learning by heart.

598   *inordinate* unordered; rather than the modern sense of 'excessive'.

596   *viewless winds* Measure for Measure III i 122.

606–13 These lines survive, unerased and unrevised, in MS E.

BOOK VI

6   *Granta* The name of the Cam above Cambridge: hence Cambridge.

27–8   *devoured ... perused* Bacon, *Essays*, 'Of Studies', 'Some books are to be tasted, others to be swallowed, and some few to be chewed and digested.'

29–30 *detached ... cares* He had decided not to read for honours.

61   *Four ... week* 7 April 1804.

101   *Foot-bound* Not in *OED*; perhaps suggested by 'root-bound' in Milton, *Comus* 660–61, 'as Daphne was/Root-bound, that fled Apollo'.

127–34   Coleridge also discusses this drawback of a classical education in *Biographia Literaria*, ch. 1.

160–74   From John Newton's *Authentic Narrative* (1764). Dorothy had copied out the passage in a notebook of 1798–9.

200   *Bard* James Thomson, *The Castle of Indolence* (1748). 'Good-natured lounging' (line 202) is from I 15.

209   *Dovedale* In Derbyshire.

193   *spiry rocks* John Dyer, *The Fleece* (1757) I 658.

212–13   *seemed . . . noon* Milton, *P.L.* V 310–11, on the archangel Raphael.

216   *Now* In fact July–August 1787, though, as de Selincourt notes, events of 1788 and 1789 are run together with those of 1787.

219   *Emont* Now spelt Eamont, the outlet of Ullswater.

220   *that . . . castle* Brougham Castle, a mile and a half east of Penrith.

223   *Sidney* Sir Philip Sidney (1554–86) cannot have visited the Countess of Pembroke at Brougham Castle, as stated in James Clarke's *Survey of the Lakes* (1787, 1789), which confused Mary Herbert, Sidney's sister, wife of the second Earl of Pembroke, with Anne Clifford (1590–1676), the 'great Countess of Pembroke', wife of the fourth Earl of Pembroke.

226   *dome* building.

233   *Another maid* Mary Hutchinson (1770–1859), Wordsworth's wife.

242   *Border Beacon* Penrith Beacon, just above Penrith; the scene also of XI 279–323.

249   *Far . . . health* He had sailed for Malta on 9 April 1804.

260   *Etesian* N.W. winds blowing in Mediterranean for about forty days in summer. T. Parnell, *Health: An Eclogue* 11, refers to 'mild Etesian air'.

276   *liveried schoolboy* At Christ's Hospital.

281–2   *shut . . . stream* Echoing Coleridge's own *Sonnet to the River Otter* (*Poems*, 1797).

286–8   *scarcely . . . guided* He came up to Jesus College in October 1791.

302–5   Wordsworth uses a similar figure in writing to Sir George Beaumont, 17 October 1805.

309   *schoolmen*   medieval (scholastic) philosophers.

339   *fellow student*   Robert Jones, whose home was in Denbighshire.

353   *standing . . . hours*   Shakespeare, *Sonnet* 16 5, 'Now stand you on the top of happy hours'.

356   *eve*   13 July 1790.

403–4   *angels . . . Abraham*   Genesis xviii 2 ff.

425–6   *riotous . . . inmates*   An error of Wordsworth's: the expulsion was not till May 1792; and the troups were on a 'domiciliary visit'.

439   *streams . . . Death*   The 'Guiers vif' and 'Guiers mort', called 'the mystic streams of Life and Death' in *Descriptive Sketches* 73, which unite to form the Guiers below the Grande Chartreuse.

480   *Vallombre*   One of the valleys of the Chartreuse, as Wordsworth records in a note to *Descriptive Sketches* 78.

509–10   *compassed . . . danger*   Milton, *P.L.* VII 27, 'with dangers compassed round'.

526   *the eye . . . song*   *Much Ado About Nothing* IV i 231, 'the eye and prospect of his soul'.

527   *here*   i.e., at the moment of composition of the preceding lines.

561   From *Descriptive Sketches* (1793) 130 (which has 'Thy' for 'The'); lines 563–4 closely follow lines 249–50 of the same poem.

572   *Of . . . end*   Milton, *P.L.* V 165, 'Him first, him last, him midst, and without end'.

587   *Locarno's Lake*   Lake Maggiore.

601–2   *I told/Your praises*   In *Descriptive Sketches* 80–119.

630   *Gravedona*   On the west shore of the north end of Lake Como.

713   *woods.*   This strengthening of punctuation, made by Nowell Smith, ought to have followed 1850's raising of commas after 'birds', etc., to semi-colons. 1805 made it clear that 'The cry . . . ' is in apposition to 'These', line *723*.

645   *darkness visible*   The later revision is perhaps due to a desire to remove an irrelevant echo of Milton, *P.L.* I 63, where 'visible' qualifies 'darkness'.

737   *mean*   I agree with de Selincourt in suspecting an error of
        transcription in D, but 'mere' could be a genuine revision.

691   *Brabant armies*   The forces of the 'États belgiques unis',
        established in January 1790, and now preparing to oppose the
        Emperor Leopold.

BOOK VII

1   *Five years*   The later alteration to 'six' is hard to explain,
        since the interval between the composition of the 'preamble'
        (November 1799) and the date of these lines (autumn 1804)
        was rather less than five years. But a number of 1850 alter-
        ations change accurate to inaccurate statements (see X 190,
        XI 367).

3   *the City's walls*   Whatever the reference in these lines, the
        1850 note, 'The city of Goslar in Lower Saxony', is certainly
        wrong: Wordsworth means London.

11   *for years*   1801–3: the interval between the 'first' and
        'second' versions, see Introduction, p. 19.

16   *departure*   In April 1804; he had decided to go in November
        1803.

57–9   *Returned . . . students*   He went back to Cambridge in
        November 1790, and took his degree on 21 January 1791.

73   *first beheld*   Perhaps in the summer, or the Christmas,
        vacation, 1788.

85   *Alcairo, Babylon*   Milton, *P.L.* I 717–18, 'Not Babylon |Nor
        great Alcairo'.

86   *pilgrim friars*   Wordsworth could have read about a 'towne
        hauing walles of silver, and bulwarks or towers of golde' at
        the end of Richard Hakluyt's translation of the Itinerarium of
        William de Rubruquis, a thirteenth-century Franciscan,
        Navigations (1598), p. 117.

95   *cripple*   Philip Braithwaite. Identified by T. W. Thompson
        in *Wordsworth's Hawkshead* (1970).

117   *Articulate music*   The lines, 'Turn again, Whittington, Lord
        Mayor of London.'

123   *Vauxhall and Ranelagh*   Fashionable pleasure-gardens on the
        south side of the Thames.

131	*Giants* Gog and Magog, wooden figures made in 1708.
132	*Bedlam . . . maniacs* The hospital for lunatics in Moorfields, with statues carved by Caius Gabriel Cibber about 1680 – the 'Cibber's brazen, brainless brothers' of Pope's *Dunciad* I 32.
135	*Monument* Recording the Fire of London.
182	*Boyle* Robert Boyle (1627–91), the chemist.
186	*sequestered nook* Milton, *Comus* 499.
190	*raree-show* peep-show.
219	*travelling cripple* Samuel Horsey, 'King of the Beggars', described also by Charles Lamb in his essay, 'A Complaint of the Decay of Beggars in the Metropolis'.
288	*Half-rural* As Islington then was.
306	'*Hid . . . cave*' Milton, *Samson Agonistes* 89.
288	'*forms and pressures of the time*' *Hamlet* III ii 27.
312	*Thespian* Thespis was the founder of Greek tragedy, sixth century BC.
321	*Maid of Buttermere* Mary, born 1772, daughter of the inn-keeper of the Fish, bigamously married in 1802 to an adventurer, John Hope (really Hatfield), who was later hanged for forgery. The Sadler's Wells melodrama on the story was produced in 1803.
322	'*a bold bad Man*' Spenser, *F.Q.* I i 37.
328	*When . . . saw* November 1799.
341–2	*For . . . mountains* Milton, *Lycidas* 23, 'For we were nursed upon the selfsame hill'.
345	*Coker's stream* The Cocker flows from Buttermere to Cockermouth.
386	*as she is* as she is when; the 1850 comma after 'is' gives an unfortunate suggestion that this is how woman, as such, really is.
397–8	*those . . . furnace* Shadrach, Meshach and Abed-nego in Daniel iii 27.
401	*argument* Identical in meaning with the 'theme' of the earlier text: a Miltonic usage (see I 182).
406	*Siddons* Sarah Siddons (1755–1831), then acting at Drury Lane.
440	*lustres* chandeliers.
460	*Prate . . . whereabout* *Macbeth* II i 58.

506   *suburbs of the mind* *Julius Caesar* II i 285–6, 'the suburbs|Of your good pleasure'.

525–8   *One . . . of* *Henry V* IV iii 51–5; 'the fifth Harry' is from *Henry IV Part II* IV v 131.

529–42   This seems to refer principally to William Pitt (1759–1806).

532   *Aurora* dawn.

538   *He . . . horn* Milton, *Lycidas* 28, 'What time the gray-fly winds her sultry horn'.

512–43   The praise of Burke is perhaps the most striking single example of insertion in later revision of sympathies alien to the earlier Wordsworth. The answer to the rhetorical question of lines *540–43* would seem to be 'Yes'.

533   *Aeolian cave* Aeolus, the god of the winds, which he kept chained in a cave.

550   *lead . . . maze* Milton, *L'Allegro* 142, 'The melting voice through mazes running'.

559   *The Death of Abel* By Solomon Gessner, published in German in 1758 and translated 1761. *Doctor Young* Edward Young (1683–1765), author of *Night Thoughts* (1742–5).

560   *Ossian* The supposed author of Gaelic poems 'translated' by James Macpherson (1736–96) in 1760–63.

649–51   *Fair . . . Bartholomew* Held on the five days beginning 3 September (the New Style equivalent of the old festival of 24 August), in Smithfield, the site of the martyrdoms in Queen Mary's reign. Wordsworth visited it with Lamb in 1802.

660   *dream* The revision to 'phantasma' shows that Wordsworth was thinking of *Julius Caesar* II 1 65, 'Like a phantasma or a hideous dream', with 'motion' (line 661) in the preceding line.

687   *All . . . things* Milton, *P.L.* II 625, 'Perverse, all monstrous, all prodigious things'; part of the description of Hell as 'a universe of death'.

688   *Promethean* Ironically for 'inventive'. Prometheus introduced the arts to mankind.

724   *prospect . . . soul* See note on VI 526.

BOOK VIII

33 *raree-show* peep-show.

48–52 1850 notes that four lines are from '*Malvern Hills* – by one of Mr Wordsworth's oldest friends, Mr Joseph Cottle.' Cottle (1770–1853) published *Lyrical Ballads* and his own *Malvern Hills* in the same year (1798).

75 *complacency* desire to please others.

86 *Redounding* eddying.

103–4 *the spectacle | Is common* Wordsworth may be thinking of the description of a similar scene in James Clarke's *Survey of the Lakes* (2nd edn 1789), pp. 72–3.

119–43 Based on Milton's claims for the superiority of Paradise to the other lovely scenes of history and legend, *P.L.* IV 205–87, IX 439–41.

123 *Gehol's . . . gardens* Wordsworth follows the description by Lord Macartney, quoted by John Barrow, *Travels in China* (1804).

128 *boon Nature's* Milton, *P.L.* IV 242, 'Nature boon' (= bountiful).

129–34 *Scene . . . groves* Milton, *P.L.* IX 115–18, 'sweet interchange|Of hill and valley . . . shores with forest crowned| Rocks, dens, and caves'.

135 *obsequious* in obedience to the will of the landscape gardener. Wordsworth may have in mind the 'obsequious darkness' of Milton, *P.L.* VI 10, where alternation of light and dark is described.

129 *Saturn* The father of Jupiter, who reigned in the Golden Age (Virgil, *Eclogues* IV 6).

   Latian Belonging to Latium, the area surrounding Rome.

187–8 *As Shakespeare . . . Ganymede As You Like It.*

189–90 *Or . . . King The Winter's Tale.*

191 *Spenser Shepheardes Calendar, May*; the 'posts' and 'kirkpillars' (line 199) are from lines 11–12.

221 *my household Dame* Ann Tyson.

223 *A shepherd* In an earlier draft called 'Michael'; so originally intended to find a place in *Michael*, composed October–December 1800.

229–44   *Dove Crag* Above Ambleside, between the Rydal Valley and Dovedale. Deepdale runs parallel to Dovedale, to the north, with Brotherswater between. Fairfield is to the north-west. Between it and Dove Crag is Hart Crag, not, on modern maps, Arthur's Seat (Stone Arthur is a lower hill to the south-west, just above Grasmere). St Sunday's Pike (or Crag) is to the north-east, between Deepdale and Grisedale. Seat Sandal (line 237) is due west of Fairfield, with Grisedale Tarn between. Helvellyn is more than two miles due north, with Striding Edge to the east. Russet Cove (properly 'Ruthwaite', pronounced 'Ruthet') is to the south again, a little further east, on the way back to Grisedale Tarn.

314   *Galesus* Galaesus, a river in Calabria, mentioned by Virgil, *Georgics*, IV 126 and Horace, *Odes*, II vi 10.

315   *Adria's* The Adriatic Sea.

316–19   *snow-white herd . . . Clitumnus* Virgil, *Georgics* II 146, 'albi, Clitumne, greges'. Clitumnus, like Galaesus, was a river in Calabria.

321   *Lucretilis* A hill overlooking Horace's Sabine farm (*Odes*, I 17; Wordsworth follows the Latin identification of Faunus in the same ode with Pan).

349   *Goslar* Wordsworth was there from 6 October 1798 to about 23 February 1799. He noted in his *Lines Written in Germany* that the Franconian emperors had kept their court there.

353   *Hercynian forest* The ancient name for mountain ranges, including the Harz, in central Germany.

366–7   *the spring|Looks out* Thomson, *Seasons*, *Winter* 16, 'Looked out the joyous Spring'.

246   *portending* stretching out: see Textual Notes.

401   *In size . . . fog* Thomson, *Seasons*, *Autumn* 727–9, 'The Shepherd stalks gigantic . . . sits the general fog'.

408   *Above all height* Milton, *P.L.* III 58, of God the Father.

420–22   *Corin . . . Phyllis* Common names in pastoral poetry.

422   *coronal* Not found elsewhere in the sense Wordsworth must mean, a circle of dancers; normally, a circlet or garland.

483   *three-and-twenty* The revision to 'two-and-twenty' shows that Wordsworth wanted to place the change before the

summer of 1792; no doubt during the winter of 1791–2 when he was in the company both of Beaupuy and of Annette Vallon.

507   ''*Mid...boats*' Montrose, 'My dear and only love' ('The tossing seas, the...').

511   *first* supreme.

459   *Thurston-mere* Coniston Lake.

466   *high eastern hill* Hamlet I i 167.

468–72   *Dear native Region...one memorial gleam* Wordsworth echoes his poem on leaving school, written at the age of seventeen.

680–81   *flowers...mantle* Milton, *Lycidas*, 104–6, 'His mantle hairy...Inwrought with figures dim...Like to that sanguine flower'.

713   *Antiparos* A Cycladic island, in the Aegean Sea.

714   *Yordas* Near Ingleton, Yorkshire.

716–17   *sees, or thinks|He sees* Milton, *P.L.* I 783–4, 'sees,|Or dreams he sees'. But perhaps from Milton's source, Virgil, *Aeneid* VI 454, which has 'thinks' (*putat*), not 'dreams'.

763   *punctual* confined to one point in space; see X 17.

771   *popular* in which the people ruled (i.e. republican).

620   *their* The noun, 'events', to which this originally belonged has disappeared in revision.

819–23   *when...fraught* Milton, *P.L.* XI 203 ('Why in the east') –7 (with 'yon ... draws ... And slow descends' for 'the ... drew ... Descending slow'). 1805 enclosed lines 822–3 only in inverted commas; 1850 gave a reference to 'XI 204'.

680   '*busy hum*' Milton, *L'Allegro* 118.

BOOK IX

13   *argument* theme (as in III 182). Like Milton in *P.L.* IX, Wordsworth is turning to a more tragic subject.

31   *A year* In fact, three and a half months; the 'scarcely ... a year' of line *28* is still an overstatement.

39   *city* Orleans, which he reached on 6 December 1791. He moved to Blois early in 1792. Wordsworth does not distinguish the two, here or at lines 80 ff.

43   *field of Mars* The site of the Federation fête, 14 July 1790.

44   *suburbs of St Antony*   Faubourg St Antoine, a working-class district in the east.

45   *Mont Martyr*   Montmartre, in the north.

45–6   *Dome|Of Geneviève*   The Pantheon, in the south.

47   *National Synod*   The National Assembly met in the *salle de manège*, Rue de Rivoli.

        Jacobins   The Jacobin Club, near Rue St Honoré.

50–51   *Palace . . . Of Orleans*   Palais Royal.

56   *hubbub wild*   Milton, *P.L.* II 951.

77   *Le Brun*   Charles Le Brun (1619–90); the *Magdalene* was in the Carmelite convent, Rue d'Enfer.

178   *Carra, Gorsas*   Girondist deputies. Carlyle describes Wordsworth as claiming, in 1840, to have been present at Gorsas's execution, 7 October 1793. There is no other evidence of a visit at this time, but it is not contradicted by known facts and recent scholars tend to accept it.

293   *one*   Michel Arnaud Beaupuy (1755–96). He achieved the rank of general, and was killed at the battle of the Elz, 19 November 1796, not as, Wordsworth thought (line 430), in the Vendée, where he was dangerously wounded, but recovered.

369–70   *as pure . . . good*   Apparently means, 'as pure as individual life is in the wise and good man'.

385   *scattered tribes*   The most obvious example is the rise of Islam.

414–23   *Such . . . Philosophers*   Wordsworth draws on Plutarch's *Life of Dion*. Dion succeeded in deposing his nephew, Dionysius the Younger of Syracuse, in 357 BC.

425   *Beaupuis*   Wordsworth never corrected the spelling.

441   *High . . . over-arched*   Milton, *P.L.* IX 1106–7, 'a pillared shade,|High over-arched': the 'shade' of line *434* strengthens the echo.

443   *In . . . undisturbed*   Perhaps echoing *A Midsummer Night's Dream* II i 164, 'In maiden meditation, fancy-free'.

453   *Angelica*   In Ariosto's *Orlando Furioso*: her flight opens the poem.

455   *Erminia*   In Tasso's *Gerusalemme Liberata* Canto VII.

461–3   *Of Satyrs . . . thrall*   Spenser, *F.Q.* III 10 43–4, of Hellenore;

rather than I 6 13, of Una, who is not 'unhappy' among the satyrs.

482   *Romorentin* Properly, 'Romorantin', twenty-five miles from Blois.

484   *rural castle* Probably Beauregard, four-and-a-half miles from Blois.

485   *lady* Anne de Pisseleu d'Heilly.

516   *heartless* See note on III 191.

540–41   *if not . . . in* De Selincourt, in suggesting that 'not' was a slip for 'but', missed the point. The meaning is, 'if it is too much to hope for that punishment should be completely abolished'.

555–934   The story of Vaudracour and Julia, separately published in 1820, but omitted from the final text of *The Prelude*, is paralleled in Helen Maria Williams's *Letters Written in France . . .* (1790). The name of Vaudracour may come from Lieutenant de Vaudrecourt, an officer in 1791 of Beaupuy's battalion. Though the story bears no close resemblance to that of Wordsworth and Annette Vallon, that episode, completely ignored in *The Prelude*, helps to account for its inclusion.

637–41   *chiefly . . . east Romeo and Juliet* III v 8, 'Do lace the severing clouds in yonder east'. Wordsworth recalls the same play in line 556 of the 1805 text, 'Two of the fairest stars in all the heaven' (II ii 15).

BOOK X

4   *from . . . parted* He left Orleans about the end of October.

9   *The King had fallen* He was deposed on 9 August 1792.

13   *burst innocuously* They were defeated at Valmy on 20 September.

17   *punctual spot* Milton, *P.L.* VIII 23 ('punctual' as in VIII 763).

18–19   *Great Mogul . . . Agra or Lahore* Milton, *P.L.* XI 391, 'To Agra and Lahore of Great Mogul'.

20   *Omrahs* Grandees of the Great Mogul's court.

22   *the signal given* Milton, *P.L.* I 776.

33   *massacre* The September massacres (line 64).

42	*prison* The Temple, in the north-east of Paris.
44	*Palace* The Tuileries, stormed on 10 August.
70	*The horse ... manage* *As You Like It* I i 13–16, 'His horses ... are taught their manage'.
77	*'Sleep no more'* *Macbeth* II ii 35.
83	*next morning* 30 October.
107	*proper* own.
148	*thoroughly* 1850 has the metrically easier 'throughly', but, like all the MSS in both passages, retains 'thoroughly', at XI 87.
166–7	*Harmodius ... And .. Aristogiton* In 514 BC, they attempted to overthrow the Athenian tyrants, the sons of Pisistratus, and killed the younger, Hipparchus, but were themselves killed.
168	*Brutus* The assassin of Julius Caesar, rather than his ancestor who expelled the Tarquins from Rome.
190	*to England I returned* Late in November or early in December. The 1805 version of line 203 is more accurate than the 1850, which can only be defended on the ground that *part* of two winters was spent out of England.
207	*though baffled* A bill to abolish the slave trade passed the Commons in 1792 but was postponed by the Lords, and subsequently rejected by them in 1793.
230	*now* France declared war on Britain on 1 February 1793; Britain on France on 11 February.
269–70	*bending ... Father* Coleridge, *Ancient Mariner* 607, 'While each to his great Father bends'.
280	*worst losses* The loss of patriotism and ancient faith described in the following lines.
289	*island* The Isle of Wight, where Wordsworth spent July 1793.
310–11	*Tyrants ... devilish pleas* Milton, *P.L.* IV 393–4, 'with necessity,|The tyrant's plea, excused his devilish deeds'.
314–15	*blasts ... heaven* *Hamlet* I iv 41, 'Bring with thee airs from heaven or blasts from hell'.
318–20	*throned ... God* An allusion to the establishment in Notre Dame of the worship of the Goddess of Reason on 10 November 1793.
353–5	*wife of Roland ... last words* Madame Roland, a Girondist,

executed 8 November 1793. The 'last words' were 'Liberty, what crimes are committed in thy name!'

363–5   *The Herculean . . . cradle*   Hercules throttled two snakes, while still an infant in his cradle.

378   *unjust tribunals*   Milton, *Samson Agonistes* 695.

387   *this breathing world*   *Richard III* I i 21. A rather unfortunate echo, which Wordsworth perhaps removed for that reason.

410–11   *So . . . me*   2 Kings ii 9, 'Elisha said, I pray thee, let a double portion of thy spirit be upon me'.

455   *We walked*   16 July 1790.

458   *Atheist crew*   A Miltonic phrase (*P.L.* VI 370) utterly inapplicable to Robespierre, an ardent deist.

469   *Moloch*   The 'horrid King besmeared with blood' of Milton *P.L.* I 392.

473   *village*   Rampside in Low Furness.

481   *ethereal substance*   Milton, *P.L.* VI 330.

482   *In consistory*   Milton, *P.R.* I 42, 'A gloomy consistory'.

483   *burning seraphs*   Milton, *At a Solemn Music* 10, 'bright seraphim in burning row'.

493   *honoured teacher*   William Taylor (1754–86). The lines from Gray's *Elegy* were the last four, somewhat misquoted on the tombstone.

519   *rocky island*   Chapel Island.

536   Robespierre was executed on 28 July 1794. Wordsworth must have heard the news in the second half of August.

549   *cleanse . . . stable*   One of the labours of Hercules was the cleansing of the stables of King Augeas, after thirty years' neglect, which he did by diverting the rivers Alpheus and Peneus.

567   Repeats II 144. 1850 ends Book X at this point, probably in accordance with W.'s original intention (see above, p. 21).

577   *heartless*   discouraging.

600   *transmigration*   of the spirit of the Republic's enemies into the Republic itself.

626   *one green branch*   A confusing application of the story of the dove in the Deluge (Genesis viii 11), which was argument for, not against, the survival of living trees. Wordsworth, in re-

moving the reference, must have decided he had attributed too 'insane' a 'delusion' to his opponents.

653   *Giants* The giants of Greek mythology who made war on the gods.

663-4   *shield . . . side* The shield of the medieval fable, gold on one side and silver on the other, over whose real colour two knights, approaching from opposite sides, fought.

724   *subterraneous fields* The one Utopia so located seems to be the *Nicolai Klimii Iter Subterraneum* (1741) of Ludvig Holberg, translated into English in 1742.

775   *wild theories* Godwin's *Enquiry Concerning Political Justice* (1793) is often cited, but how far it can be called 'wild', and how far Wordsworth was ever a Godwinian, is very uncertain.

792   *now* Apparently, as early as the latter months of 1794.

795-7   *mounted up . . .The scale of liberty* Milton, *P.L.* IV 996-1014, where the 'mounted scale' of Satan portends his defeat. (The image is originally Homeric.)

829-30   *the light . . . intellect* Wordsworth quotes his own unpublished play, *The Borderers* 1494-6, where the words are spoken by the villian. Parallels in Godwin, not very convincing, have been cited by those who hold that *The Borderers* represents Wordsworth's anti-Godwinian reaction.

880   *some dramatic story* Wordsworth may have in mind something like *The Excursion*, but more 'dramatic' and 'lively' than that work turned out to be; certainly the 'errors' of the Solitary there are similar to those he here attributes to himself.

900   *wearied . . . contrarieties* S. Daniel, *Civil Wars* VI 36, 'Weary the soul with contrarieties'.

906   *about this time* Wordsworth first met Coleridge in August or September 1795. Wordsworth was a 'very dear friend' in a Coleridge letter of 13 May 1796.

909   *belovèd Woman* Dorothy Wordsworth.

917/XI 343   *Much . . . changed* De Selincourt writes of this line being 'restored' in 1850, but fails to make clear that MS E gives no authority for the restoration; Wordsworth's final intentions were as printed here.

933-4   *Pope . . . Emperor* Pius VII crowned Napoleon (or rather,

561

Napoleon crowned himself in the Pope's presence) on 2 December 1804.

935–6   *dog . . . vomit*   2 Peter ii 22; Wordsworth balances this by an Old Testament reference (Exodus xvi 15) in XI *362–3*.

951   *Timoleon*   He drove Dionysius the Younger out of Syracuse, 343 BC. Wordsworth read about him in Plutarch's *Lives*.

952   *How . . . prostrated*   2 Samuel i 25, 'How are the mighty fallen'.

965–6   *A hope . . . decay*   The situation is even worse than that embodied in the proverb (Proverbs xiii 12), 'Hope deferred maketh the heart sick'.

986   *This . . . change*   Milton, *Lycidas*, 37 'But O the heavy change now thou art gone'.

1003–4   *flowery . . . Enna*   Milton, *P.L.* IV 268–9, 'that fair field|Of Enna, where Proserpin, gathering flowers . . .'.

1013   *Empedocles*   c. 493–c. 433 BC. Alleged to have thrown himself into Etna. He wrote in verse, and Wordsworth's 'Philosopher or Bard' might reflect the controversy whether he should be reckoned a poet or a philosopher writing in verse. (Aristotle, *Poetics*, ch. 1, 1447 b 17–20, took the latter view.)

1014   *Archimedes*   Mathematician, c. 287–212 BC.

1016   *Theocritus*   Pastoral poet, c. 310–250 BC.

1022–8   *how . . . nectar*   Theocritus, *Idyll* VII 78–83.

XI *458*   *wood or echoing cave*   Milton, *P.L.* IV 681, 'echoing hill or thicket'.

1034   *Arethuse*   A spring at Syracuse in Sicily, famous in pastoral poetry.

BOOK XI

23–4   *Spring . . . return*   Milton, *P.L.* III 41–2, 'Seasons return; but not to me returns|Day'.

108   *appanage*   endowment.

199   *a maid*   Mary Hutchinson, later Wordsworth's wife.

279–316   The site is Cowdrake Quarry near Penrith Beacon. The murderer was Thomas Nicholson, and the victim Thomas Parker (1766). There is some uncertainty just what initials were cut.

323   Repeated from VI 245.

345   *Christmas-time* 1783. The scene appears to have been above the road from Cockermouth to Skelwith.

366   *he died* 30 December.

367   *two brothers* Shown to be more accurate than the 'three brothers' of 1850 by a letter of Dorothy Wordsworth (28 December 1807). Christopher was not present.

382   *indisputable shapes* Perhaps echoing the 'questionable shape' of *Hamlet* I iv 43; but that does not really explain a puzzling epithet.

384–5   *repair . . . fountain* Milton, *P.L.* VII 364–5, 'Hither, as to their fountain, other stars|Repairing'.

BOOK XII

78   *statists* politicians, or political theorists. Wordsworth elsewhere used the word in a derogatory sense in *A Poet's Epitaph* 1–2 (first in the 1837 revision; earlier 'Statesman'), 'Art thou a Statist in the van/Of public conflicts trained and bred?'

80/XIII 78 *'The Wealth of Nations'* Not in quotation marks, as the title of Adam Smith's book (1776), in the early MSS, but Wordsworth must from the start have meant the phrase to recall that.

149   *one bare steep* The road over Hay Hill from Cockermouth to Isel.

158   *Bedlamites* madmen.

228   *temple . . . gold* Milton, *P.L.* I 372, 'gay religions full of pomp and gold'.

313   *at that time* About August 1793.

345   *Druids* Eighteenth-century fantasies about the Druids and monuments such as Stonehenge are described by A. L. Owen in *The Famous Druids* (1962).

358   *some imperfect verse* The poem eventually published in 1842 as *Guilt and Sorrow* (part of it in *Lyrical Ballads*, 1798, as *The Female Vagrant*); it was read by Coleridge in March 1796, and he may have heard Wordsworth read a version of it in September 1795.

BOOK XIII

1   *one . . . excursions* Summer 1791. The reference of 'these'
(or, in 1850, 'those') is not clear, and seems to be the remnant
of an intention to place this episode elsewhere.

2   *youthful friend* Robert Jones (see VI 339).

3   *Bethgelert* In MSS A and B, spelt Bethkelet.

11   *glaring* Here and in *An Evening Walk* (1793) 54, 'Breath'd
a pale steam around the glaring hill', the normal sense is in-
appropriate. It seems to be a variant of the word given as
glaurie in the *English Dialect Dictionary* and the *Scottish
National Dictionary*, with the glosses, 'of the weather: dull,
rainy' (EDD) and 'of the weather: sticky, clammy' (SND).
The second seems the more appropriate: both dictionaries
quote Carlyle, 'clammy, glarry days'; *glairie* in this sense
was recognized by a present-day native of Grasmere. The
use of the verb seems to be influenced by this sense in *The
Excursion* I 2–3, 'Southward the landscape indistinctly glared|
Through a pale steam', first drafted in 1798, and dependent
on the *Evening Walk* lines.

45   *hills . . . upheaved* Milton, *P.L.* VII 285–6, 'the mountains
huge appear|Emergent, and their broad bare backs upheave'.

XIV 71–2 *broods . . . abyss* Milton, *P.L.* I 21.

101–2   *extraordinary . . . rouse* Milton, *Samson Agonistes* 1382–3,
'Some rousing motions in me which dispose|To something
extraordinary my thoughts'.

113   *discursive or intuitive* Milton, *P.L.* V 488.

XIV 126–7 *peace . . . understanding* Philippians iv 7, 'The peace of
God, which passeth all understanding'.

141   *a universe of death* Milton, *P.L.* II 622.

188   *Dividually* Recorded only once before Wordsworth, who
probably formed it after the adjective in Milton, *P.L.* XII 85,
'dividual being', which he echoes in *The Excursion* VI 386.

208–9   *softness . . . delicate desires* *Much Ado About Nothing* I i 305,
'soft and delicate desires'.

212   *Elsewhere* Especially in *The Sparrow's Nest* (1801; published 1807). The 1850 version of 209 (*230*) echoes line 18 of that poem, 'And humble cares, and delicate fears'.

225   *Milton* P.L. IX 490–91, 'though terror be in love,|And beauty'.

XIV 268   *no more a phantom* Alluding to the poem on his wife, written in 1804, beginning 'She was a phantom of delight'.

338   *Three years* A little less; February 1793 to September 1795. Wordsworth always exaggerated the time he lived in London (see IX 31), and, in spite of line 344, only a little over a year, in all, was spent there. The 'permanent abode' of line 338 continues to blur the distinction between Racedown and Grasmere (see I 1–141).

350   *Calvert* Raisley Calvert, who died in January 1795, leaving Wordsworth £900.

356   *redundant* excessively large.

393   *Quantock's grassy hills* Above Alfoxden, where Wordsworth lived from July 1797 to June 1798. The 'summer' must be that of 1798, though *The Ancient Mariner* and *Christabel* were written late in 1797.

400   *him* The idiot boy in the poem of that name.

416   *private grief* The death of his brother John, by shipwreck, on 5 February 1805.

BOOK III

120   Upholder, [D]   Upholder
125   I had ascended [E²]   that I was mounting [E]
126–9   truth.| . . . subdued, [D]   truth – | . . . subdued [E has a dash, to indicate a new paragraph, at the beginning of 127, which 1850 transfers to the end of 126, thus failing to introduce a new paragraph]
140–41   influence: . . . passion, [D²]   influence . . . passion; [E influence, . . . passion,]
191   himself? (W. M. Rossetti, 1870)   himself, [E² failed to adjust the punctuation to a revised text]
269   nobler [D]   noble
271   precincts, [D]   precincts
279–80   Chaucer; . . . shade [D Chaucer,]   Chaucer . . . shade;
358–9   mountains; . . . captivity, [D]   mountains, . . . captivity;
394–5   endure. . . . day [D]   endure . . . day
522   resembled [C]   resembles
604   guile; [D]   guile [which de Selincourt regards as 'obviously an improvement', though, he believes, accidental; but it is neat rather than Wordsworthian]

BOOK IV

51   froward [D]   famous
84   regret? [Moore Smith, 1896]   regret;
148   wear [C]   wear,
172   love, [E]   love
289   daily yearnings [E]   yearnings
339   rendezvous my . . . time, [D]   rendezvous! My . . . time
392   measure [E]   measure,
434   ghastly [D]   ghostly

BOOK V

12   work [D²]   Verse
169–71   unpraised. . . . infancy, . . . childhood, even [B]   unpraised, . . . infancy; . . . childhood even,

194   pleasure, sown [D]   pleasure sown,
499   Fictions . . . ladies, [C]   Fictions, . . . ladies
517–18   powers, . . . vassalage; [D]   powers; . . . vassalage
530   Faculties; [D Faculties, –]   Faculties
599–600   changes there, . . . home. [D]   changes, – there, . . . home,
606–13   [E] omitted 1850

BOOK VI

31   more [E]   now
65   admire [E]   achieve
199   she [E]   her
603   harbours, . . . old. [D]   harbours; . . . old,
662   privacy, [D]   privacy.
713   woods. The [Nowell Smith, 1908]   woods; the [when the earlier commas after 'birds', 'light' and 'clouds' were strengthened to semi-colons, this further change became necessary to clarify the construction]
737   mean [E]   mere

BOOK VII

38   shining [E]   shining,
58   Yet [E]   Yet,
118   nor [E]   not
161–2   title-page . . . toe; . . . saints, [D]   title-page, . . . toe, . . . saints; [E toe; . . . saints]
196   down [E]   down; [E lacks punctuation also after 'merit', 1850 made the wrong choice]
258   stone, [E]   stone
260   Add [D]   And
264   degree [E]   degree,
309   Not . . . time [E]   We since that time not unfamiliarly
351   infantine, [D]   infantine
361   women; . . . caressed, [D]   women, . . . caressed;
386   is [E]   is,
497   Salisburys [D and 1850 Errata]   Salsburys
675   those [C, also A and B, *pace* de S.]   these

720 receiving, [D] receiving
737 acquisitions first, [C] acquisitions, first [no comma in either
   place in D or E]
747 Indian. On . . . sands [E] Indian, on . . . sands:

BOOK VIII

31 year [C] year,
42 with, [E²] with
45 and [E] and,
96 landscape [E] landscape,
183 invisible [E] Invisible
246 portending [E, *pace* de Selincourt, who records it only from A²
   and C] protending [an unnecessary 'correction': see *OED* for
   the currency of both forms]
307 whencesoever [C] wheresoever
433 grave? [W. M. Rossetti, 1870] grave,
468 Region [E²] Regions [no doubt editorially altered to agree
   with the early poem alluded to]
500 eclipsed [C] eclipse
670 hearts [B] hearts;

BOOK IX

61 are [E] is
144 eat [E] eaten
176 Gorsas [C, also 1850 Notes] Gorcas
230 lay open [E] open lay
248 rather come [E] come rather
275 merely, [D] merely
366 could [E] would
403 benediction [E] benediction,
554 My . . . may [E] The . . . might [no doubt altered to agree
   with 557]

BOOK X

167 thoroughly [E] throughly
299 come? [C] come.
304 wear [E] wean
318 deep [B] deep;
364 it, proudly [E] it proudly, [E's comma after 'it' is in pencil, and seems to be deleted in pencil, but the sense requires it]
365 light [B] like
407 forced [E] fond
421 care [D] call
571 given, [D] given

BOOK XI

11–12 trust . . . seen. [D²] trust: . . . seen,
103 depend [E²] depends
107 we [E] us
115 enchantress [C Enchanter] enchantress – [in altering 'Enchanter' to 'Enchantress', D², perhaps accidentally, added the dash]
209 and [E] now
292 confounded . . . more, [B] confounded, . . . more
331 matter's various [Garrod] matters various, [E² has 'matters', but also lacks the comma after 'various']
344 Both . . . moon, [E²] Much, as it seemed, I was no further changed|Than as a clouded and [E not] a waning moon: [I supply the comma, absent in E², at the end of 344]
359 rivet down [E] seal up all
389 Here in E²; after 391 in 1850
449 Muse's [B] Muses'

BOOK XII

111 Liking, [B Liking] Liking;
244–5 that . . . were [E 'that' altered to 'this', which is again deleted; 'were' unaltered] this . . . are

302 sate [E²] watched
305–6 returned . . . time, [E] returned, – . . . time, –
320 of [E²] from

BOOK XIII

176 is [E] be
279 Also [B] Also,

BOOK XIV

187–7 Bearing . . . A mutual [E²] Lifted . . . Bearing a [by conflation with D]
242–3 stealth, Still . . . youth, [B, substantially] stealth, (Still . . . youth) [brackets first in D, round XIII 222–3 of the 1805 text]
273–4 Shines . . . And [E] Shines, . . . And,
358 a–b [E] omitted in 1850
391 this [E] the
451 revolutions [E] revolution

Also in Penguins

William Wordsworth

EDITED BY GRAHAM MCMASTER

Graham McMaster is Lecturer in English at the
University in Lublin, Poland

Part One   Contemporaneous Criticism

Introduction. William Wordsworth, Francis Wrangham, Charles Lamb,
Henry Crabbe Robinson, Samuel Taylor Coleridge, John Wilson,
Critical Review, Francis Jeffrey, James Montgomery, Robert Southey,
William Hazlitt, Dorothy Wordsworth, Benjamin Robert Haydon,
Josiah Conder, Lord Byron, Percy Bysshe Shelley.

Part Two   The Developing Debate

Introduction. John Ruskin, Robert Browning, Walter Bagehot,
A. H. Clough, Walter Pater, Leslie Stephen, Matthew Arnold,
John Ruskin, A. C. Swinburne, Gerard Manley Hopkins,
A. C. Bradley.

Part Three   Modern Views

Introduction. Helen Gardner, A. N. Whitehead, F. R. Leavis,
James Smith, J. S. Lyon, Donald Davie, W. W. Robson, David Ferry,
John Jones, Jonathan Bishop, Robert Mayo, Geoffrey H. Hartman,
F. W. Bateson, D. G. James, Jonathan Wordsworth, Christopher Ricks.

Penguin Critical Anthologies